Great Web Typography

Great Web Typography

Wendy Peck

WILEY

Wiley Publishing, Inc.

Great Web Typography

Published by
Wiley Publishing, Inc.
909 Third Avenue
New York, NY 10022
www.wiley.com

Copyright © 2003 by Wiley Publishing, Inc., Indianapolis, Indiana

Library of Congress Control Number: 2002111062

ISBN: 0-7645-3700-8

Manufactured in the United States of America

10 9 8 7 6 5 4 3 2 1

1K/SY/QR/QT/IN

Published by Wiley Publishing, Inc., Indianapolis, Indiana
Published simultaneously in Canada

Wiley Publishing, Inc. is a trademark of Wiley Publishing, Inc.

About the Author

Wendy Peck has been a graphic designer since 1989, when her first glance at a desktop publishing program instigated an instant jump over the fence from fashion design. Her print work included brochures, catalogues, newsletters, magazines, and even the occasional video production. Originally she learned Web design to enhance her print business services. However, she was captivated by the immediacy of the Web, and the flexibility, and now only does print work as an added service for her best Web clients. Wendy is an active Web designer, with clients across the U.S. and Canada, and has written three previous books for Hungry Minds (now John Wiley and Sons). She also writes a regular graphics column for WebReference.com (ProductionGraphics.com).

Wendy lives in the heart of the Canadian Shield, in Northwestern Ontario, where she is getting used to total freedom now that her three kids have flown the nest pursuing higher education. Always an expert at entertaining herself, she has discovered that an empty nest is . . . well, rather peaceful.

Credits

Acquisitions Editor
Michael Roney

Project Editor
Kenyon Brown

Technical Editor
Kyle Bowen

Copy Editor
Paula Lowell

Editorial Manager
Rev Mengle

Vice President and Executive Group Publisher
Richard Swadley

Vice President and Executive Publisher
Bob Ipsen

Executive Editorial Director
Mary Bednarek

Project Coordinator
Dale White

Graphics and Production Specialists
Beth Brooks
Gabriele McCann
Kristin McMullan
Heather Pope
Mary Virgin
Erin Zeltner

Quality Control Technicians
Laura Albert
Tyler Connoley
Angel Perez
Charles Spencer

Proofreading and Indexing
Sossity R. Smith
Sharon Hilgenberg

For Val: Your belief in me more oft' than not exceeds my own.

Foreword

The simple fact that this book exists is a testament to how much the Web has changed in the last few years. When I created HomeSite in 1994, Web typography was a limited proposition. If you knew how to make something bold and change the font face, then you were an expert in Web typography.

Many people — including myself — simply fell into Web authoring without any formal design training. Despite a brief stint as a cartoonist (it's a long story, but let's just say that my early attempts at Web design evoked more belly laughs than my cartoons ever did), I was clueless about basic design, let alone typography. Luckily, the Web was primitive enough that it didn't matter, because you had little control over anything. Truth is, you were better off without a background in design, because the more you knew, the more frustrating the limitations would be.

But that was then.

These days, designers have far more control, and they can finally apply their skills to creating Web sites. Thanks to cascading style sheets, designers can specify margins, padding, letter spacing, and fonts in ways that used to be impossible. The result is a Web in which typography is far more important than it used to be.

Which, of course, leaves people like me fumbling around for help. So it's about time that someone had the foresight to write this book. I could've used it a long time ago, and I'm betting you'll be as glad as I am to have it on your shelf (or, as the case may be, dog-eared and battered in front of your monitor). Before reading this book I thought typography was simply about fonts, but now I see it's really about structuring type in a way that improves legibility and draws attention to areas of importance. It's about how the correct use of spacing and design elements can help you get your point across. In my case that means selling more software, so you can bet that I'll apply what I've read the next time I redesign the TopStyle site.

But this book isn't just for the design-impaired — it's also for experts making the transition to the Web from other media. Even if you dream about kerning, you'll find plenty of new information here. Web design may have come a long way since the early days, but there are still enough restrictions to make skilled designers flog their browsers in despair. Even if, unlike me, you know all there is to know about typography, you'll find Web design far less frustrating after reading this book.

Nick Bradbury
Creator of HomeSite and TopStyle
www.bradsoft.com/topstyle/

Preface

Welcome to the world of text. It takes many skills to place a page on the Web, but technical skill, or design talent alone will not convey a message to your visitors. Text does. This book looks at every aspect of creating text for the Web, from working with a small selection of fonts, to controlling text with CSS and creating text as an image. There's even a section dedicated to Macromedia Flash text.

Why devote an entire publication to text on the Web? It's a big subject, and most information about text is designed with print production in mind. The Web presents very different challenges than a printed page. Knowing how to create a perfectly optimized graphic text image does not help when you need to create a menu with CSS-controlled text. Catching a visitor's attention with a headline calls for different skills than presenting hard information in an accessible way, especially considering a Web reader's short attention span. Many designers struggle with text because they have not found a complete source for text information. This book solves that problem.

I worked for many years as a commercial graphic artist producing print material before moving to Web design. In the print world, type is everything. More than half of your professional skill is measured by how well you work with text. Unfortunately, in Web development, the focus more often goes to page layout, and how a page performs on various browsers. That is, of course, vitally important, but that focus often leaves text presentation as a distant, "if we get to it" concern. The result is often inaccessible information, often on beautiful, highly stable pages. But because no attention has been directed to how easily a page is read and the information absorbed, site goals are not met. This book not only addresses the techniques for controlling text on the Web, but also how

text is presented from a full-page perspective. This book brings the fierce attention paid to text in the print world to the Web format.

When you present a balanced page, with relevant information that can be read in seconds, your visitors are compelled to delve deeper into your site. They stick around. They come back for more. They tell their friends about your site. They link to your site. The search engines find your site. There is no compromise to be considered when you create pages with great text. Great text improves the appearance, download speed, search engine relevance, accessibility . . . the list goes on. And all it costs is a little learning time. This book is appropriate for Web designers at any level. A beginner can use the techniques shown in this book, and veteran designers can benefit from the new information presented. You'll find tips and hints, checklists, and interviews that provide an inside glimpse at how highly successful designers work. If you are moving from the print world to the Web, you can use this book as a dictionary to translate what you know about type into Web-appropriate methods. You don't have to be an artist to appreciate the information presented in this book. Perhaps you're a developer, concentrating on dynamic pages. You may not care that you present the prettiest pages, but you should care that visitors can read your carefully crafted return results.

Text is fun. After you understand the basic principles of page design and text layout, and add a few simple techniques to your toolbox, you will find that designing with text is fun. Nothing can compare to the satisfaction of creating great pages with highly accessible text. With a few tools, form and function marry perfectly. That's art!

Acknowledgments

Writing a book is a major project that tends to overwhelm your life. I am always most grateful that the people in my life understand and stand back while I write — except to be on call when I need them as I so often do. My kids, Shawnda, Danille, and Brian, always bear the brunt of my inattention, and return the best support any parent could desire. You guys really are the best! My friends, Val, Marion, Elsie, Tanis, Linda, Jeff, and Andy accept that some days I can visit, the next I don't exist. That's a tough one, and you all do it so well. My Mom, Isabel MacLean, taught me to speak and write correctly, forcing into me the most valuable skills I possess. My sisters, Debbie and Heather, are always there, never intruding, always available. There is a repeating theme of support without demand through the people in my life. That is the very reason I can do what I do, and still have so much human support and connection — my true wealth.

The people at John Wiley and Sons turn my ideas and words into books. Michael Roney, my Acquisitions Editor, is the one who originally gave me the opportunity to bring my teaching experience to print. Project Editor, Kenyon Brown kept all the pieces in the right places, and all the people doing what they do best. My Technical Editor, Kyle Bowen caught the little slips that can sneak in when my focus was on the words, and Copy Editor, Paula Lowell, caught all the little slips in words that crept in when I was focused on the techniques. Rev Mengle kept the process going in the background as Editorial Manager. Thanks to all for a great project.

Contents at a Glance

Contents

Chapter 12
Putting It All Together   233

PART IV
Typography for Flash   259

Chapter 13
Creating Basic Type in Flash   261

Chapter 14
Perfecting Type in Flash   277

Appendix A
Where To From Here?   289

Getting Started with Web Typography

HTML? CSS? IMAGE?

font

<h1

Let me breathe

NO! NO! NO!

ALL CAPS Never!

Chapter 1

Defining Web Type Issues

You most likely bought this book because you're confused about Web type. You're in good company with that feeling, as many people find that the first steps into Web publishing are like walking through a minefield. Veer in one direction, and you're likely to step on another problem. How do you know which of the information you find about type is accurate, right for you, or completely outdated and categorically wrong?

By the end of this book, you will see that the rules and restrictions surrounding Web type do make sense, and after you understand why Web type works as it does, you will wonder what seemed so hard. But you have a lot of exploring to do to get from your initial confusion to total clarity. To begin the journey, you should start with a Web type overview to ensure that you understand the basic concepts.

Understanding How Web Type Works

Imagine that you're working on a document in a word processor, and you discover that all the fonts you once had to work with had disappeared, and only six or seven of the most basic fonts remained. Suddenly, you also must guess at what your paper size will be. Welcome to Web type. Those are real variables you must accept when you set your sights on publishing to the Web (1.1).

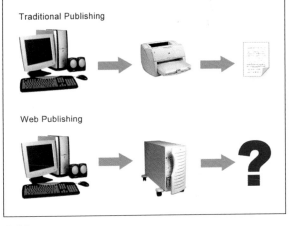

● 1.1

When you work on your home or office computer, you're working with a closed system. The fonts you use work with your monitor and your printer or printers. Even if a commercial printer will print your work, you can identify what fonts or other parameters the output device can deliver. Although you can print to varied paper sizes, you set the paper size you desire.

In contrast, when you output to the Web, you're working with an open system in that the final destination equipment is completely unknown to you, unknown not because you have failed to do your homework, but unknown because no possible way exists for you to know. Your work will be displayed on individual computers that can be located anywhere in the world. Some visitors will view your work on the latest and greatest monitors, while others will have antiquated equipment. You have no way to know whether visitors have a Mac or a PC, what resolution they are using for their monitors, which browser they are using, or which fonts they have installed on their machines.

The unknown final destination of your content when publishing to the Web is the reason a book like this is necessary. Typography books for printed work can help you understand the basics of good typography in general, but methods and solutions are based on control that you do not have when designing for the Web. Learning to work with type that may or may not appear as it does on your screen is an interesting challenge. That is the best way to look at type issues.

Many designers have tried to "cheat" the restrictions that using type on the Web demands, through methods like forcing font downloads and producing text as an image instead of as HTML text. Trends and excitement have rippled through the professional design world as yet another new way to solve the type "problem" appears. Intrusive methods like using JavaScript to set visitor window size provide more control for the designer, but tend to leave visitors confused and often angry. However, as the Web reaches the first level of maturity, most serious designers have learned to work within the natural bounds of HTML text and browser display, and use their design skills to create great-looking pages with the tools at hand.

[WARNING]

You can create text in a graphic program, place it on the page as an image, and maintain total control of the appearance. Doing so is an excellent solution for decorative text (see Part III, "Graphic Type for the Web," of this book). However, the graphic method to create text should not be used for content text. Graphic text takes longer to display, is harder to edit, and offers no opportunity for the visitor to customize text size. I firmly believe that HTML text should be used for *all* content text.

Looking at Basic Web Type Variables

Before I talk about type creation specifics or designing with type, it is important that you have a quick overview of some problems that designers face when working with content text for Web pages. Throughout this book, I show you many tricks and tips to help you create professional-quality type. For now, you start with the most basic, but critical variables that affect your text design.

[NOTE]

Type for Web pages created with Macromedia Flash has no similarity to type created for HTML pages. Part IV, "Typography for Flash," of this book is dedicated to using type for Flash pages.

Selecting Fonts

All fonts fall into one of two categories: serif and sans serif. Serif fonts have little feet, called serifs, on the characters. Sans-serif fonts do not (1.2). Note that each of the characters in the serif fonts have tiny horizontal elements, while the sans-serif fonts do not (Palatino and Avant Garde should not be used for Web content type).

Designing for the Web leaves you with precious few content text font choices. Your page sends a message to the visitor's computer to display the words and images that are set out in the HTML commands on the page. However, the font that displays must be installed on the visitor's computer, and therein lies the problem. Although most computers have dozens, if not hundreds of fonts installed, your page must call for the fonts that are available on *every* computer — a very short list. In fact, there is even a generic font command for this short list in case a visitor arrives without the most common fonts on board.

Web fonts are specified as a first, second, or third choice, along with the always-works choice of a

Serif Fonts	Sans-Serif Fonts
Times New Roman	Arial
Palatino	Avant Garde
Georgia	Verdana

● 1.2

generic font of the desired type. Consider the following HTML text code:

```
<font face="Verdana, Arial,
    Helvetica, sans-serif">Sans-serif
    display text.</font>
```

The preceding code requests that the text be displayed with Verdana font. The visitor's computer will check to see whether that font is available. If it's not, the computer then searches for Arial, then Helvetica, and if it still doesn't find the font, then the system sans-serif default font will display. So this one sentence could appear in any of the forms (1.3).

[N O T E]

I added the font names for easy identification. The font names in parentheses are not included in the code shown earlier. The default sans-serif font differs on every computer.

So, what are your choices? Although the list of acceptable fonts for the Web is short, you do have a few choices (1.4). The default font is shown in the

Sans-serif display text. (Verdana)

Sans-serif display text. (Arial)

Sans-serif display text. (Helvetica)

Sans-serif display text. (Sans-serif)

● 1.3

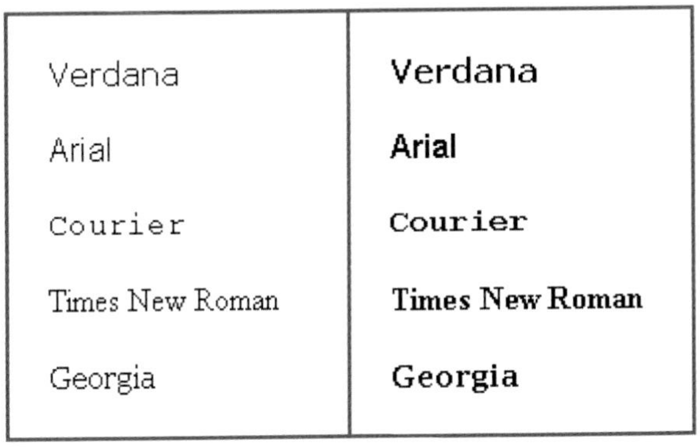

Verdana	**Verdana**
Arial	**Arial**
Courier	**Courier**
Times New Roman	**Times New Roman**
Georgia	**Georgia**

● 1.4

left column, with the bold for each style in the right column.

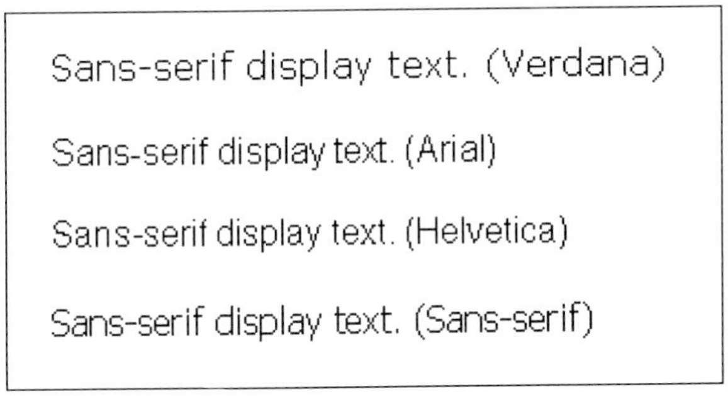

[W A R N I N G]

You can specify an italic attribute for any font, but italic fonts for content text are a very bad idea on the Web. At the low resolution offered by monitors, italic fonts display with highly jagged edges, and are very hard to read. Occasionally, italic fonts can be used for emphasis for a few words, but never for full paragraphs.

When designing for print, it is generally accepted that serif fonts are easier to read in heavy text passages. The standard for pages with heavy text content is to use serif fonts for body text and sans-serif text for headlines. The horizontal lines on the characters have been proven to help guide a reader's eye along the line. Of course, this formula is not always used, and adjusting other attributes, like line spacing, can add legibility to sans-serif fonts, but that serif fonts are easier to read is a long-accepted standard.

However, when you publish to the Web, you can usually assume that your content will be viewed on a monitor only. Because the resolution of a monitor is much more coarse than the ink on a printed page, the very attribute that makes serif fonts easier to read in print, the tiny vertical elements, delivers the opposite effect on a screen. The clean lines of sans-serif fonts are usually easier to read on a monitor, and have become the accepted standard for Web pages (1.5).

Understanding Flexible Page Size

After you understand that you must work within a small range of fonts for your Web pages, you must accept another fact of Web type. You cannot know what monitor resolution the visitor will be using to view your pages. This is the equivalent of not

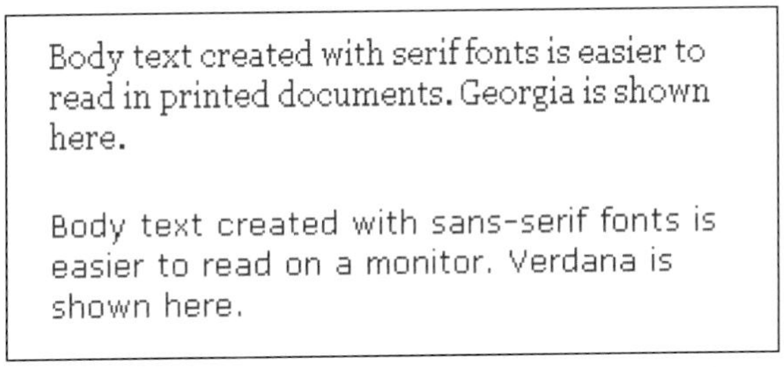

Body text created with serif fonts is easier to read in printed documents. Georgia is shown here.

Body text created with sans-serif fonts is easier to read on a monitor. Verdana is shown here.

● 1.5

knowing your page size when preparing a printed page. Even today, with many years of Web design under my belt, I find this factor is the most difficult when dealing with Web type.

You can see the effect of different monitor resolutions in action in the Strategy page from my Web site (`http://wpeck.com/strategy.html`). When a monitor is set to 800 px by 600 px (1.6), the look is quite different from the same page viewed with monitor resolution set to 1024 px by 768 px (1.7). Note how the wider resolution allows many more words per line, and shows much more content on the entry screen. The font size is much smaller with the higher resolution, and paragraph lengths vary considerably.

It is important to remember that your pages will be seen at varied widths. The examples of my site (1.6, 1.7) are shown with the browser window expanded to full size. Not all visitors to your site will use a full-screen display for their browsers, so there is an infinite number of possible display sizes for your pages. You learn some tricks to help equalize resolution differences in Part II, "Controlling Web Type with Cascading Style Sheets (CSS)," of this book. For now, put page width on your list of important things to consider when you work with text for the Web.

Type and Browsers

You can do little work for the Web before you realize that every browser in common use displays a page in a slightly different way. Web standards are finally starting to take effect, making newer browsers much more consistent in the way that they display content. However, many Web users still use older versions of browsers, and you must be aware of how your pages display on older browsers. In this book, you will find out how to make sure the type on your pages displays well for all visitors.

Content text is one of the few areas of Web design where the browser used by your visitors makes little difference, however. Fonts display reasonably consistently no matter what browser is in use, dependent only on installed fonts, as you learned earlier. Page sizes are also consistent. A visitor using an older version of Netscape with a Mac computer and the monitor set to 800 px by 600 px sees the same type of arrangement as another visitor with the latest Microsoft Explorer version on a PC computer with the display set to 800 px by 600 px (assuming that the page-layout control is cross-browser consistent).

Using my site again as an example, notice that the view in Netscape 4.5 (1.8) varies little from the same page in Internet Explorer 6 (1.9). Although several years separate the competing browser versions, there is no discernable difference in the text display.

Having said that, I have to quickly jump in and qualify what I just said. HTML type does display consistently. However, read on for an introduction to CSS (Cascading Style Sheet) text control. CSS-controlled text is not at all consistent across all browsers.

HTML Versus CSS Type Control

HTML text attributes are controlled by the font tag `<font>`. Among other choices, you can specify bold

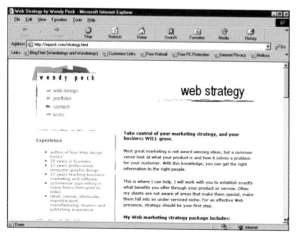

● 1.6

● 1.7

<b>, italic <i>, font size <font size>, and color <font color>. As an example, the following code creates the text shown in 1.10.

```
<font color="#CCCCCC" size="4"
    face="Verdana, Arial, Helvetica,
    sans-serif"><b>
Sooner or later, all good things must
    come to an end.</b></font>
```

Specifying font attributes with the font tag works. However, the font tag is becoming increasingly rare because controlling text with CSS is a much better solution. I could pretend to be objective on this subject, offering the benefits of using the font tag, presenting the same for CSS, and helping to guide you to your own conclusion. Unfortunately, I would be hard pressed to find many positive things to say for the font tag, and would have just as much trouble trying to find the drawbacks to using CSS font control.

I am going to skip that whole process and come out strongly with my opinion. Learn and use CSS font control! Part II, "Controlling Web Type with Cascading Style Sheets (CSS)," of this book is devoted to controlling text with CSS, so I won't go into detail on the methods right now. However, I want to introduce the CSS concept and explain why I feel so strongly about CSS as the only sensible way to work with text for Web design.

To create the same text effect as in the previous example (1.10), you can use a CSS-defined style to write the code as follows:

```
<span class="quote">Sooner or later,
    all good things must come to an
    end</span>
```

There is no difference in the final result between the CSS-controlled text and the HTML controlled text (1.11). The top sentence is controlled by the font tag. The lower sentence is controlled by the CSS style as just described.

Although there is no difference in the final appearance of the text, you can easily see that the CSS-defined style uses far less code, which is reason enough to consider CSS font control. However, controlling fonts with CSS also saves a great deal of time for the designer, and provides consistency throughout your site. You don't have to remember what color you used, what font size, or what style. You simply

● 1.8

● 1.9

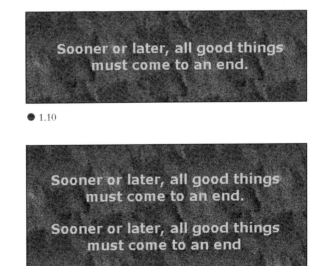

● 1.10

●1.11

apply the same style to the text on every page, and consistency is guaranteed.

When you prepare a site with a linked CSS file controlling your text, you can change all the text on your site at any time by making changes in one spot. Imagine the difference between changing one line of code in a file, and changing 1,000 individual font tags on a site. CSS font control also offers decorative options, like background color and borders that are not available with the font tag.

Professional designers are using CSS to control their fonts. Within a few years, the font tag will be rare. I do occasionally use the bold tag for specific content text emphasis, but that is the only time I use the font tag. If you create just one site with CSS font control, I guarantee that you won't go back to using the font tag to control your text.

Creating Graphic Type for the Web

Early in this chapter, I gave you a warning that you should not use graphic text to overcome the challenges that creating type for the Web presents. Newcomers to Web design are often tempted to take the easy way out, creating pages in graphics programs like Adobe Photoshop or Macromedia Fireworks. I'll admit that controlling text is much easier in a graphic program than in an HTML page. I'll also admit that a page created from a graphic program does not require anywhere near the knowledge to deliver a page that can be viewed in any browser. So, what's the big problem? Why not just take the easy way?

Using Graphic Text Unwisely

File size is a major reason to abstain from large images, when the same information can be delivered with HTML text. Even if every visitor could be expected to have a high-speed connection, and only about half do, large files demand a lot of bandwidth. Bandwidth can be expensive, especially if your site becomes popular.

You also lose flexibility on your page by using large graphics. Sure, creating the page is easier in a graphics program, but what if you want your page to fill the screen no matter what monitor resolution a visitor is using? Solid graphics do not stretch the way a table or layer can. Look at the same page

(http://anglobuilding.com/building.html) at different resolutions (1.12 and 1.13), but with a flexible layout. Note how the content fills the page in both cases. With a fixed layout, which I created as an example, the content does not move (1.14). At a lower resolution, the page in this example is the same as the flexible version (1.12). But at the higher resolution, a portion of the page at the right is empty. Which look do you prefer?

Finally, when you create your page mainly with HTML text, making changes is much easier. You gain the time you save in the original creation, because you can make changes directly on the HTML page. If you have created the page with a large graphic, or with graphic text, you must return to the graphic

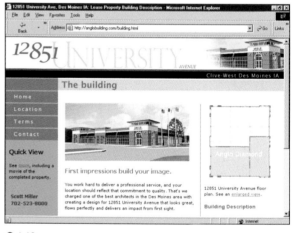

 1.12

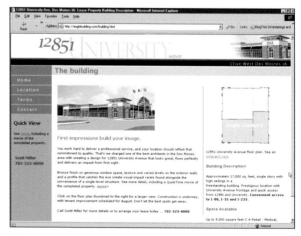

1.13

program, then export the file again, then place the file in your page — not an efficient way to make changes to a page.

[WARNING]

Using images to present text also robs you of a valuable tool to catch the attention of the search engines. Search engines seek relevant text on pages as a measure for inclusion in their listings. If your content is not text, but graphic images, the search engines will pass on by. (This explanation is a gross simplification of how search engines work. See Part II, "Controlling Web Type with Cascading Style Sheets (CSS)," of this book for a more detailed look at search engine optimization.)

Using Graphic Text Wisely

Although I hate to see graphic text misused, it has a place on the Web, especially if it's well done. (Part III, "Graphic Type for the Web," of this book leads you through all the steps to create very effective graphic text.) Menu items lend themselves well to using an image containing text, as do headlines on some sites. If you are creating a look that depends on a font, by all means create graphic headlines and menu items.

At times, graphic use adds more than enough benefit to the mood of a page to warrant extra file size and a little more work (1.15). The two columns of text shown in the figure are identical, except that the left side has the headline and end decoration created

with a novelty font. The lively colors in the right column don't deliver the same fun mood that the funky font delivers. The font actually delivers part of the message that is missed when the headline is plain.

Note also that the headline in the right column is rough. HTML text does not offer anti-aliasing, or blending between the edge pixels and the background. You should create large headlines, even when using fonts that are available for Web use, from graphics files to prevent this rough appearance. The ending character has to be a smaller size to fit on the line of text, as well. You have a lot more design options when working with graphics.

[NOTE]

All the methods that are used to create this text, or discussed in this section, are covered in depth in Part III, "Graphic Type for the Web," of this book.

Sometimes you must fit many menu items into a small space. Special fonts, often called pixel fonts, have been developed to create smooth, legible text at small sizes for the Web. Tenacity, designed to be used at 10 pixels, works very well for menus (1.16). This font is part of a series developed by Joe Gillespie for this purpose. (See `http://wpdfd.com/pixelfonts.htm` for more information about this special family of fonts.) I cover creating menus using these fonts in Part III, "Graphic Type for the Web," of this book.

● 1.14

● 1.15

home | scores | people | events | contest | live action | contact

● 1.16

Although I avoid using graphic text whenever possible, I still do plenty of text work in my graphics programs. I always ask myself whether I can accomplish the same effect without using a graphic file. If the answer is a clear no, then I create as small an image file as possible. If the answer is yes, or even almost, I usually lean to creating the effect using HTML text, especially when working for clients. I prefer to leave as much easy editing capability in their hands, and for that purpose, HTML text wins hands down.

[T I P]

Don't worry yet if you're still uncertain when to use images and when to use text. As you work through the sections on CSS and graphic text, your new knowledge will make the choice quite clear in most cases.

Movies and Text

Not all Web sites feature pages created with HTML commands. Macromedia Flash, which is often associated only with moving pictures on the Web, is also a full-featured program that offers advanced scripting tools to create a fully functional site completely in Flash format. Similar programs are Adobe LiveMotion and Corel Rave, although Flash is by far the industry leader. Macromedia Shockwave can also be included in this category. Movies are created with the software mentioned previously and embedded in an HTML page, which often contains nothing but the movie placement. The movie controls the site.

[N O T E]

Any page with a movie requires a plug-in to work. The Flash player has been included with popular browsers for many years, so you can safely assume that nearly all visitors to a site have the ability to view most Flash movies (new features in Flash, like dynamic data demand a current Flash player). Popular movie software can produce movies that will play in the Flash player.

Movie-creation software is also used hand-in-hand with HTML content. The Radius Product Development site (www.radiuspd.com) is an excellent example of both Flash-only pages and HTML pages that are enhanced with Flash (1.17, 1.18). The menu system is Flash. The entry page (1.17) is almost entirely Flash. Its News page (www.radiuspd.com/news.html) has decorative Flash elements in the left column, as well as a Flash menu (1.18). The rest of the page is constructed using HTML and CSS font control.

Designers love working with movies, as many of the variables I discussed at the beginning of this chapter do not exist for Flash sites. As long as the visitor has the correct player for the movie on a page, you can absolutely control the final appearance. You can use any font installed on your computer, and the Flash movie embeds the font the visitor requires to view the page as it was designed. Columns and text length can be absolute, or flexible as desired. The Radius entry page works well at a higher resolution

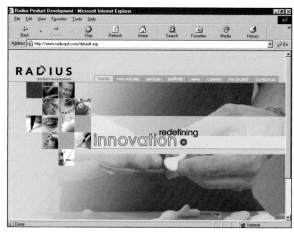

 1.17

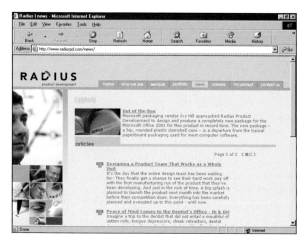

 1.18

(1.19). Note how the components of the page have simply increased proportionately to fill the page. (Photos do not usually resize with good results. This page works because the photo is shaded back, and other elements on the page distract from the quality loss. If you look closely, however, you can see some jagged edges in the background photo.) The scripting capabilities in some movie programs have advanced so far that you can also incorporate dynamically generated content into a Flash movie.

Why isn't the entire Web built with movies, if it is such a great answer to all the great Web design dilemmas? Although the Flash player has penetrated nearly the complete market, *nearly* is an important word for many designers. Without a Flash player, a Flash-only site is useless. Although file size can be controlled, not a lot of attention has been paid to optimizing Flash movie sites, and many of them require a long download before visitors can view the site. With viewers often ready to leave a page in as little as eight seconds, long downloads can cause far too many lost visitors.

Designing for Flash is also a completely different skill from designing with HTML. That is why I include a separate part in this book for working with text in Flash (see Part IV, "Typography for Flash"). There is little crossover between the two ways to include content on a page. Although most professional designers have at least a limited ability to create Flash movies, the number of expert Flash designers is much lower than those who work with other methods.

At one time, it seemed that the Web was heading for movie-type pages as the norm. I don't think this situation will come to pass, with standards pushing ahead for HTML and CSS. In my opinion, movies will remain an important component of Web design, but will not replace HTML as the main method to display pages. However, movies are a valuable tool that can offer capabilities that are not possible in other ways. Creating movies is also fun — plenty of fun — reason enough to make it part of your Web design skill set.

Ten Steps to Professional Web Type

This list may seem a little premature. However, I wanted to bring it to you right up-front, because this list can form a checklist for you as you proceed through the book. Those of you with Web design experience may already have the skills to start creating better pages instantly, simply by adopting the practices listed here.

[T I P]

Make a copy of this list and post it close to your computer so you have a constant reminder to keep your text quality at its best.

1. **Do not use too many fonts on one page (1.20).**
   Even with the small number of fonts available to designers on the Web, I still see many pages with too many different fonts and font styles on

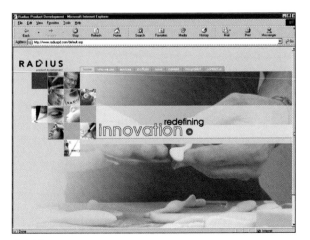

● 1.19

● 1.20

a page. As a general rule, all but those who are experts at working with fonts should use no more than two font families per page. Arial and Arial Narrow (which requires graphic text) are in the same font family. Use boldface type sparingly, and never use italic type in content type.

2. **Do not use centered, right, or full-justified text on a Web page (1.21).**
   Centered paragraphs are very difficult to read, and add an instant amateur touch to your work. A few exceptions exist, of course, like poetry, and perhaps quotes, but left-justified type is the standard because it's the easiest to read. You may right-justify short passages of text for artistic effect, but be aware that by doing so you reduce legibility. Justified type may be acceptable in print, but you can't create the same effect on a Web page. When preparing type for a printed page, your computer can adjust the spacing between characters and words to create a straight right margin. HTML text can only adjust spacing between words, and unsightly gaps appear between words to create the solid right margin. Those gaps stop the reader's eye, and interfere seriously with the legibility of the text.

3. **Give your text room to breathe (1.22).**
   I can tell instantly that a designer has had no typography training when I see text jammed against a margin, or very large type with no line spacing. Our readers are able to absorb our message only because they can follow the text across a line, and easily jump to the next line at the right time. Without spaces to direct a reader's eye, the message will be lost. A page with crowded text even feels uncomfortable. I get the same feeling looking at a page with no breathing space as I do in a room that's too crowded. Both situations can make me decide to leave. I'm not talking about busy pages here. This problem is one of text without space.

4. **Do not use bold type for paragraph text (1.23).**
   Bold type is designed for emphasis, not reading. A full page in bold text is very difficult to read, which is ironic, because I'm sure most bold text is used as an attempt at making the text easier to read. You will learn many ways to make text more legible, but stop using bold text for content this instant. I can't think of one case I have seen where using passages of text with a bold-face font improved the legibility of a page.

5. **Never, never, never use all capitalized text (1.24).**
   Reading text that's created with all capital letters is almost impossible. Yet, many designers place their most important messages in caps, no doubt thinking that the reader will pay attention. They do notice it, but reading it feels much like trying to break code, because not

● 1.21

 1.22

enough definition exists between characters for the brain to translate the lines into a message. I do use all caps for headlines, especially in CSS menus with subcategories. This can be an effective way to make a heading stand out, but it is also the best way to make body text impossible to read.

6. Use plenty of headlines and subheads (1.25).
The Web is an instant gratification medium. Visitors usually want information fast, and in bite-sized chunks. Using many headings, both headlines and subheadings, helps divide the page visually, as well as leads your visitor

quickly through the most important information on your page. Headings are a perfect way to add color to your page as well. This principle is also important in print. You can find excellent examples of text that is divided with headlines in top-level brochures and product information packages.

7. Divide your page into columns (1.26).
The majority of Web users now visit sites with a monitor display resolution of 800 px wide and higher. That is simply too much space for one column of text. Dividing your page into two or three columns provides your visitor

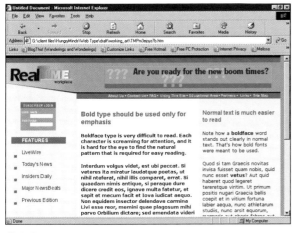

● 1.23

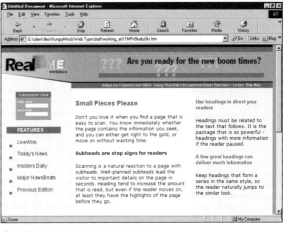

● 1.25

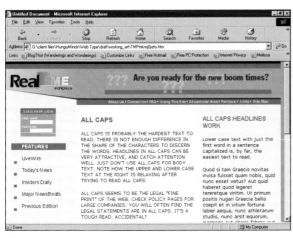

● 1.24

● 1.26

with shorter, easier-to-read, line length; prevents long, one-line paragraphs; and allows a much more interesting layout for presenting the small pieces of information that are so effective on the Web.

8. **Don't use huge text (1.27).**
Many new designers have a tendency to use fonts that are too large, believing that it is easier to read. In fact, the opposite is true. If you increase the font size, especially without adjusting the line spacing, you actually reduce

● 1.27

legibility. I have also seen too much super-jumbo headline text. I suppose the idea is that the reader will not miss the message. In reality, it is like trying to get someone's attention with a baseball bat. Most people respond better to a tap on the shoulder than a large bat.

This tip carries a special warning for designers working on a Mac, but PC designers should listen, too. Text displays in different ways on a Mac and PC computer, regardless of the browser that is in use. The same font appears smaller on a Mac than it does on a PC. PC designers pay close attention to this if you tend to work with small type. Mac owners should make sure to see their work on a PC before deciding on text size. Either testing your pages yourself on the opposite platform, or at the very least, having someone send you a screen shot of your pages from the other platform is always a good idea.

9. **Do not use underlined text for anything but a link (1.28).**
In print, using underlined text is never okay. This common error is a hangover from the days of the typewriter when few ways to highlight text existed. That is history, and underlining is bad typography. On the Web, it's close to a crime. The universal symbol for a

link is underlined text (and I do recommend capitalizing on this instant message and advise using underlined links). When you underline text for emphasis, not only are you breaking the rules for good typography, but you're frustrating your visitors. Clicking underlined text is supposed to deliver a reward.

10. **For graphic text, learn correct typography (1.29).** You can't create content text on the Web with traditional typography adjustments like character kerning, or adjusting the amount of space

between characters. However, when you create text in a graphics program, use the typography tools you have available. Part III, "Graphic Type for the Web," of this book takes you through the typography methods you require for Web design. Nothing says "professional" faster than a beautifully crafted section of text. The art of typography is beautiful, but it also dramatically improves the legibility of text and provides endless opportunities for decorative text effects.

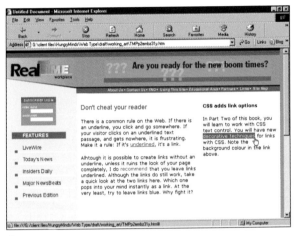

● 1.28

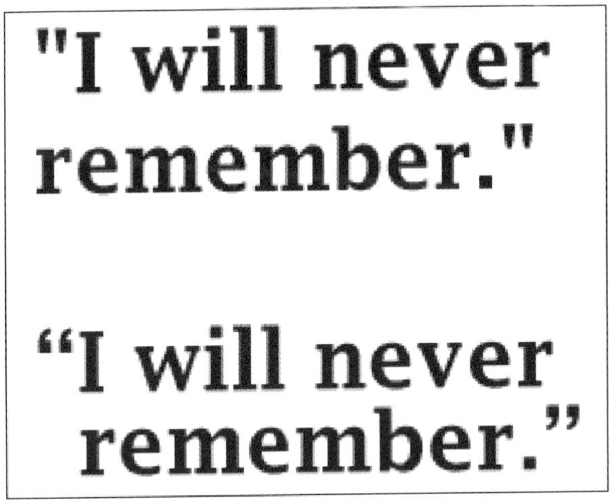

● 1.29

<h1>

font

LEGIBILITY

balance   balance

Novelty?
Be Careful!

CONTRAST

Chapter 2

Design Principles for Web Type

Legendary restaurants offer great food, in the perfect atmosphere, at the right price. If any of these ingredients are missing, it might be a worthwhile place, but never truly great. Web pages follow the same pattern. Deliver great content, with the perfect atmosphere, without the high cost of frustration or confusion for visitors, and you have a truly great site. It's really quite simple.

WENDY PECK

This book is about type. Type can be beautiful. With no help from other elements, type can provide the entire look and feel for a site. No doubt, it is a powerful design element. However, first and foremost you must remember that type has a special role to play. It delivers a message, with its beauty, color, and presence at times, but the message is always the important factor in type. I take a hard-line stance on type. If it cannot be read at a glance, it is a design element, not type. In this chapter, you learn how to use type as a design element for your page, without sacrificing legibility. If you take the time to understand design principles, and how text can contribute to well-balanced pages, your readers will find information quickly in a comfortable setting.

Legibility Is the First Principle

Many things can affect the legibility of type: Font choice, size, color, white space . . . the list goes on. A font that you use successfully on one site in a dark green may be impossible to read on another site, simply because you require a slightly smaller font size in red. There are few hard, fast rules to help guide you with your text choices, but you should start by looking at what can affect legibility.

Choosing a Font

The font you use is the most important element of type legibility. As in most Web type discussions, I must separate the type you create with a graphics program from the type used for content text. Type created in a graphics program offers far more choices, and with that choice, far more chances to produce illegible type. As you learned in Chapter 1, "Defining Web Type Issues," you have few font choices for content text on a Web page. However, it is possible to reduce legibility even with few fonts.

Text Created in a Graphics Program

Type created in a graphics program can be created with any font installed on the designer's system. Designers have been self-confessed fontaholics since the beginning of computer graphics. At one time, we were reined in by the cost and availability of fonts. However, graphics programs began to include hundreds of fonts, providing designers with low-cost access to many novelty fonts. The Web has multiplied access to fonts by many times. This access is a good thing, right? Yes and no.

When we were putting out serious money for fonts, we were very careful with our choices, and usually invested in classic font faces. Novelty fonts were usually out of the question for most designers, as we just could not justify the cost. In my early days as a print designer, classic fonts (2.1) were the objects of my desire. As I built my print business in the late 1980s, some of my profits were always put back into purchasing more classic fonts.

There is almost nothing you can do to classic fonts that will make them illegible. Not so with many of

the fonts that are available today. Consider the novelty fonts here (2.2). I would not use any of these fonts for a word. They may have some use as decorative initial caps, or as graphic elements, but discerning the word that is featured is simply too hard for a reader, and a single word is the easiest test for legibility.

Watching font legibility does not mean that you're restricted to classic fonts if you want to create great text. Many font designers have managed to add excitement and novelty to their fonts, but have maintained the qualities that allow our eyes to read the

● 2.1

● 2.2

Behind the Scenes

Production Graphics: Choosing a Font I Would Never Choose

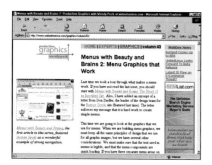

I write a graphics column at WebReference.com (http:// productiongraphics.com). The body text for this column is Times Roman, a highly unusual choice for me.

I am not a Times fan, even in my former role as a print designer. However, for this application, Times Roman was the best solution to several outside factors in my font choice. This choice is classic Web design compromise.

My column is part of a larger network, and there are restrictions to what I can do for text control. I was asked to keep text control through CSS to a minimum, depending on the master CSS file (for the parent site) where possible. I wasn't able to use a fixed font size. WebReference.com receives incredibly high traffic, and it is important not to override default values for a general audience.

So, I could not use a fixed font size. At default settings, the sans-serif choices

for Web fonts have far too tight a line spacing, but I could not adjust line height and stay within the goals of the parent site for unified CSS text control.

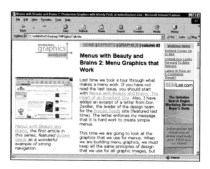

Believe me, I tried every variation of flexible fonts available, and only Times text was legible under the restrictions I faced. My judgement call was that Times

text at a glance. Highly stylized fonts exist that communicate effectively (2.3). When you're choosing a novelty font, test it for all the words you will feature. What works for one word may be illegible with a different combination of characters.

● 2.3

A font being legible is not enough reason to use a novelty font. Your font choice creates a mood for your page. That your look and feel of the page matches the intended message is still important. If you pay a visit to corporate pages and the largest commercial companies on the Web, you rarely see novelty fonts in use. Even on high-quality art sites, where novelty fonts are almost always present, the novelty font rarely serves as more than a small decorative element. As you learn more about typography techniques in Part III, "Graphic Type for the Web," I hope that you will use more and more classic fonts in your work, especially for essential elements like menus. Unless you're trying to put across a particular message, like fun, irreverence, or satire, great typography with classic fonts is still an excellent choice for most font work.

Sprinkling novelty fonts throughout a page with both classic text as images and content text provides Roman, though not as good for character shape, was better than Arial or Verdana for line spacing. Line spacing was more important than character shape for this column.

Why not just use a font tag?

The `<font size="2">` tag would have made my pages look just as I wanted with a sans-serif font. The font would be adjustable, and be legible for everyone. However, there were compelling reasons not to place a constant extra tag through my pages.

First, and this is a big one, the font tag would add a lot of code. WebReference.com as a whole promotes cleaner code and fast downloads.

Probably not a single bit of code exists that can bloat the size of a page faster than a font tag. Even without the WebReference.com protocol, Andy King, optimization guru, and author of *Speed Up Your Site — Web Site Optimization* (New Riders 2003), was my editor at the time. I would still be working trying to get Andy to approve a font tag in every page of every article (and would be no closer to approval, I'm sure).

Finally, WebReference.com is a very large operation with many different tutorial areas. It is also part of a huge family through INT Media group, our parent company, which also owns and operates internet.com. Although all the experts are responsible for their own sites, site-wide changes often occur. Most times, the changes do not affect individual areas, but sometimes they do. I have no interest in changing anything in 500+ pages to bring my area into line after a global change. By using CSS, I know that situation will not happen. If changes are needed, I can change my linked CSS file, and the entire site will change as soon as I upload.

So, using the font tag to control text size was not an option, and my only choice was Times Roman for my site. I do not, however, want to go into history as a fan of Times Roman for Web use. I have never, and likely will never, use it on a site I do for a client (unless, of course, my client faces the same restrictions I faced in this specific example).

a good balance between art and function on a page. The entry page for NapaStyle.com, a large, kitchen supply site is a perfect example (2.4).

The designer balances font use well, enhancing a lighthearted look and feel by using a casual font for headlines. Note that the left menu, although created with images, features a classic, easy-to-read font. The menu at the top of the page is CSS-controlled text.

The headline fonts are very legible. Glance quickly at the titles, and you will have no trouble understanding the words. Note that she has left plenty of space around the titles, enhancing legibility considerably. This same font may have been hard to read as a menu item, where the free space would be reduced, and the font would have had to be used at a smaller size. You must take extra care with novelty fonts to make sure that legibility remains.

Web Content Text

The fonts available for content text are generally quite legible. The sections that follow reveal a few pitfalls for working with content text, but when choosing fonts for content text, the main consideration is mood.

Serif fonts like Times or Georgia tend to provide a sedate, more scholarly look and feel to a page. Arial and Verdana are similar. Verdana, with its rounded characters, provides a more "friendly" tone for the body text on a page. Arial's characters are a bit tighter together than Verdana's, and I find it is a great choice for headlines and subheads. Any of the content text fonts make an acceptable body text, with Arial and Verdana usually preferred because sans-serif fonts are easier to read on a monitor. Be sure to read the tale (Production Graphics: Choosing a Font I Would Never Choose) of how I came to choose Times Roman for the content text on the text-heavy, graphics column site.

Selecting Type Color

How can you take a fully legible font and make it illegible? It's easy when you choose the wrong color for a font. I have seen Web pages with fonts in bright greens on white, red on bright blue, light gray on medium gray. In some cases, when I desperately wanted the information (the only reason I would remain on a page that was hard to read), I have had to select the text with the mouse in order to read it.

Contrast is what makes text legible. Your eyes separate the color of the character from the color of the background. Anything that interferes with the contrast reduces legibility. Black type on a white background is the best for contrast — no ifs, ands, or buts about it. Notice how legibility suffers as the contrast is reduced (2.5, 2.6). In the first example the left column shows increasingly lighter shades of gray text. In the right column, the effect is magnified. Reversed type, or light text on a dark background, is harder to read even with full black/white contrast. In the second sample, the left column features black type with colored background. The right column features a black background with colored text.

Does this mean you must only use black text on a white background? No. Many combinations of type with reduced contrast work very well on Web pages.

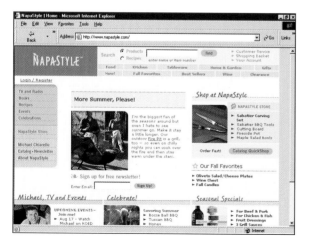
● 2.4

● 2.5

On the Glass Loon site shown (2.7 and 2.8), you can see where I have deliberately used fonts with low contrast. This site features handcrafted art, much of it very colorful. The menu items shown on the entry page (2.9) are white, with a medium blue as a rollover color. On the gray background, there is little contrast. However, the menu and the rollover still stand out.

The body text for this site is on a white background, but is a medium gray (Hex #666666). This low contrast combination (2.8) was deliberate. I wanted the text to have a supporting role to the art images. It is still quite legible, because I have used a clean font and have provided plenty of white space in the page layout. The look and feel for this entire site is quite subdued, with only the art allowed to grab attention. The effect must fit the purpose on every page. This color choice would not be good for an information site.

[WARNING]

Do not gamble with more than one effect that can reduce legibility. For example, if you are using a low-contrast color for text, do not use a very small font. I am careful with color on my column site, the one with Times Roman body text, because the contrast is very important with the serif font. You must take every step away from easy-reading type very seriously.

Picking a Font Size

There is probably no more complicated subject in Web type than size for HTML text. In Chapter 3, "Working with HTML Text ," I go into great detail about specifying size for HTML and CSS type. I don't want to slide by the legibility focus without adding font size to the equation (2.9).

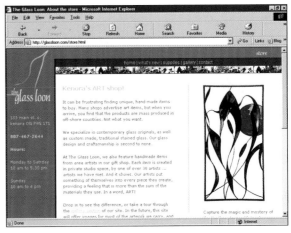

● 2.8

Contrast is a very important attribute for text legibility.	Contrast is a very important attribute for text legibility.
Contrast is a very important attribute for text legibility.	Contrast is a very important attribute for text legibility.
Contrast is a very important attribute for text legibility.	Contrast is a very important attribute for text legibility.
Contrast is a very important attribute for text legibility.	Contrast is a very important attribute for text legibility.

● 2.9

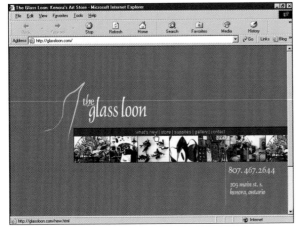

Contrast is a very important attribute for text legibility.	Contrast is a very important attribute for text legibility.
Contrast is a very important attribute for text legibility.	Contrast is a very important attribute for text legibility.
Contrast is a very important attribute for text legibility.	Contrast is a very important attribute for text legibility.
Contrast is a very important attribute for text legibility.	Contrast is a very important attribute for text legibility.

● 2.6

● 2.7

I've talked about using too large a font without enough line spacing. I would like to bring the opposite problem to your attention now: small type. Throughout this book, I show you how to use very small type for menus and other detail areas, but I don't want you take any of the discussion about small type as a way to present content on the Web.

Although not as common today as it was in the early days of Web pages moving from utilitarian to much more artistic, you will still see beautiful pages with very tiny type. Often, these pages feature a dark background with light text. That's two legibility problems, and the result is very hard to read. As type size is reduced to very small sizes, reading it is nearly impossible.

[R E M I N D E R]

Be sure to address the issues presented in the Ten Steps to Professional Type list at the end of Chapter 1, "Defining Web Type Issues," when you are designing easy-to-read pages.

Balancing Text Areas on a Page

Have you ever been to a Web site where something bothers you? You may not be able to identify why you're not comfortable, but something makes you want to move on. Often, balance is the problem. Most people understand that if they hang a picture on the wall, another is needed to balance it unless it is centered (usually a boring arrangement). Web pages must be balanced in exactly the same way.

Identifying Balance in a Page

Balance doesn't depend on symmetrical design (2.10). The collection of objects in the top example is balanced. Although the shapes and colors are different, the size, intensity of color, and placement of the objects creates a balance. However, note how the lower collection of objects does not have the same balance. The intensity of the color in the rectangle has been reduced.

Type also has weight, and it must be balanced with the rest of the page. Solid type areas have about as much visual weight as a light gray area. However, the

line spacing, number of paragraphs, and boldface type can change the visual weight and affect page balance. Columns of type can be balanced, even though one column is much more open and shorter than another (2.11). The colored bullets and line help to even out the differing amounts of text.

However balance can be lost, even when the length of the columns is more closely matched (2.12). The large amount of bold text, plus the colored elements, makes the right column considerably "heavier" than the left. If you focus on this example, you may find your head tipping to the left to compensate for the lack of balance.

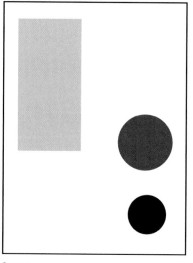

● 2.10

Weighing Your Pages

Each element on a page has weight. Images and graphic elements generally have more weight than type. Graphic objects with solid color areas have more weight than varied tonal objects like photographs. Large type has more weight than small type, and boldface text has more weight than normal type. Black type has more weight than colored type. Most balance issues make sense when examined individually, but are harder to spot over an entire page.

To complicate the balance issue further, when you have worked for a long time on a page, you tend to lose your perspective for the balance. Luckily, you can do several tricks to test for balance. All the following suggestions have one thing in common: You're trying to disrupt your view of individual elements in order to see the "big picture." Compare the clear example (2.14) to the blurred example (2.13). Note how the weight of the black text is more apparent when the detail is reduced.

- **Step back from your monitor.** I am fortunate that my office is just off an open area, and I can get back nearly 30 feet from my monitor. At a distance, the screen loses all detail, but you're still able to identify the structure of the page. Pages that seem fine up close can be obviously out of balance when you stand back. Move as far away from the screen as you can, and pay attention to how you feel as you view the page. If your eyes move smoothly around the screen without being dragged constantly to one area, your page is likely balanced. A page that is out of balance pulls your eyes to the heavy area as if they were attached with elastic.
- **Sneak up on your monitor.** Sometimes leaving your computer and returning to just take a quick glance at the monitor reveals balance problems that are not obvious when you view the page in the normal way. With a very quick glance, you should be able to take in the whole screen. If one area is grabbing too much attention, a quick glance will leave only that area in your mind.

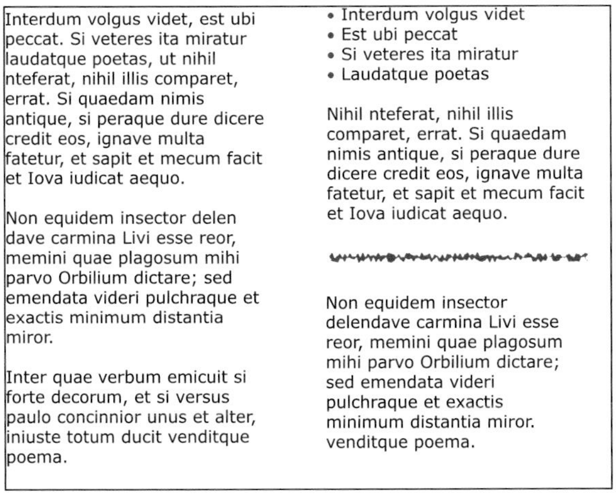

● 2.11

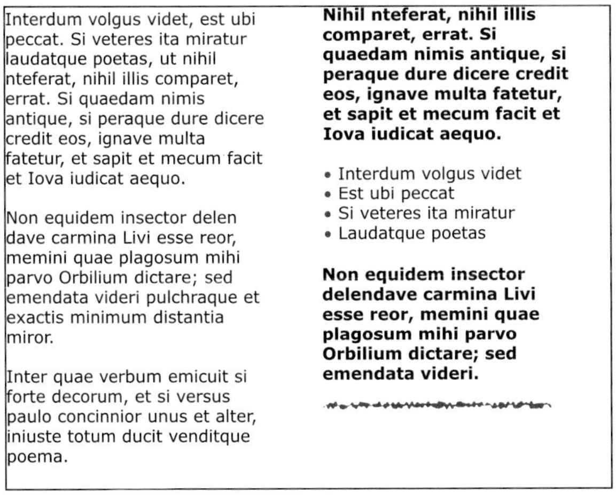

● 2.12

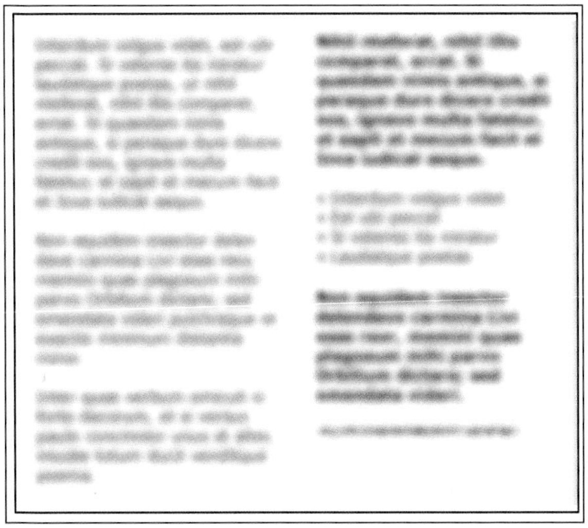

● 2.13

- **Squint.** If you can't move far from your screen and still have a view, for a quick test, try squinting your eyes until you can no longer see the detail on the page. (Some people can get the same effect by crossing their eyes, but I have not had much luck with that testing route.) Practice on the examples in 2.13 and 2.14. This test works in print as well as on a monitor.
- **Use a mirror.** A small hand mirror is a handy balance test tool. Viewing a page as a mirror image removes all the preconceptions you have of the page. Your mind has a harder time instantly assigning importance to an element, using logic to override what your eye sees, as it takes too long to place everything when the image is reversed.

Although an element on a page may be vital to the function of the site, like a menu, or a product shot, the page must still be balanced. Your eyes understand this, and want balance, but your brain is trying to make sure that the important things stand out. You can have balance as well as clear directions for visitors to find areas of your page. Refer to the example with the bulleted list (2.13). Although the columns of text are balanced, note how your eye gently goes to the bulleted list. If this page were out of balance, your eye might be dragged elsewhere. In other cases, improper balance may lead the eye to the right place, but too aggressively, making it hard for the visitor to see any other information on the page.

The Broward Avian and Exotic Animal Hospital site at `www.exoticanimalcare.com/`, (2.14), is a great example of a page that directs visitor attention to important areas, has strong design elements, yet is perfectly balanced.

[N O T E]

The Broward site was designed by Christine Kilger. You will find out more about her work later in this chapter.

Working with Images and Text

Talking about artistic applications of text is never a complete subject without looking at how text and images interact. Anyone who cares enough about

---

Behind the Scenes

Christine Kilger: Creating Great Pages with Type, Balance, and Mood

Christine Kilger created one of my all-time favorite sites. Her business site, BellaDonna Design (`www.belladonnadesign.com`) could win an award for the world's smallest, effective site. I've been following Christine's work for quite a while now, and am happy to bring her design wisdom to you as the first interview in this book. Christine lives in south Florida, with her husband and four bunnies. Originally, from southern California, she has also lived and worked in the Bay area, Connecticut, and New York City. Although she has worked in some of the best known design cities, I think you will recognize a common-sense wisdom and love for the work she does that is at the heart of her success as a designer.

Q: How did you come to be a Web designer?

A: I started out doing some print design back in 1995 and then in early 1997 I started to teach myself HTML for a personal Web site I wanted to do and just really loved it. I love the immediacy of it, being able to work in full color, not having to deal with pre-press and printers. I like that a site is always editable and evolving. I love being able to publish something to the world. I can't imagine working in any other medium.

Q: Your site, Belladonna Design, is one of my all-time favorite sites for its beauty, and stark simplicity. How did you decide on this format?

the look of a page to read a book on typography almost certainly will also be using images to help with the look and feel for his or her site. I'm not going to dive deeply into the topic of images in this book, because this is a type book. (I cover type as an image thoroughly in Part III, "Graphic Type for the Web.") My only concern is to introduce you to the idea of combining your type and images wisely.

● 2.14

You can combine images and text in many ways on the Web. You can use tables or layers to isolate images from text in page layout. You can also insert images as inline images, with text wrapping around the image, or use them as backgrounds for pages or portions of pages. No matter which method you choose to include your images, you must first determine what you need to accomplish with your text and images.

Choosing the Star of Your Page

Images can have an extremely important supporting role for text. Or, text can have an extremely important supporting role for images. One or the other is true, and understanding which is true for each situation is important, because that definition determines how your text and images will work together. If you fail to determine which element is the star, and which is the supporting element, your pages won't deliver your message in the most efficient way.

The Broward site entry page (2.14) places a heavy emphasis on the images, perfect for delivering the message about the product, as well as invoking a positive emotion for pet owners. In contrast, see how the

A: I decided on the format for my portfolio site by visiting and reviewing other portfolio sites, printing them out, and noting things I liked (and disliked) about each site. As I examined these sites it was clear to me that I enjoyed portfolio sites that were clean, simple, and easy to navigate.

Simplicity helps keep the focus on the work. I also liked having a variety of small thumbnails to choose from, which could launch a more detailed view of the design. I really liked it when the designer or firm would add an annotation that explained the design inspiration or process a bit. While I enjoy portfolio sites contain a page with personal details about the designer, I felt more comfortable creating an ephemera page where I listed my favorite design and development tools as well as books that I felt were really excellent resources.

Q: Can you tell us a little about how you choose which fonts you use?

A: Good typography is often the one thing that can distinguish a professional-looking

Web site from an amateur-looking one. My criteria in choosing fonts for the Web is to choose fonts that: 1) excel in legibility on the Web and 2) create the appropriate image and mood for the design. A typeface and the style it conveys (romantic, modern, funky) can really be as powerful in your design as actual graphic images are. However typefaces that are clearly a particular style (usually display faces) can become dated quickly — like trendy clothes — so you don't always need to pick fonts that are so easy to pigeonhole.

Sometimes I use a more conservative or standard typeface like Arial or Times Roman or Myriad and then apply techniques such as modifying the tracking,

continued

images have taken a supporting role on an interior page (2.15). The same images are used, providing consistency in the look and feel for the site, but there is no doubt that the text message has taken over as the star.

You can decide whether images or text will be the star element page by page. A retail site often features pages where text information provides the background about the company and detailed information about a line of products. On the same site, the product pages may bring the image of products as the main communicator, with text used as a supporting element to draw visitor attention to the detail shown in the image. Type and images take turns being the star in this case.

A Mexican restaurant site designed by Kelly Brown of 2 Girls Design (`http://2girlsdesign.com`) is another example of trading star status. On the entry page of the Mexico Viejo site (2.16), images are front and center. I count the creative background color that implies the Mexican flag as an image. However, when the topic changes to the menu (2.17), although the design elements are still present, there is no doubt that the designer wants the visitor to read the text. Making a clear decision regarding what element is providing the message on a page is the first step toward working well with both images and text.

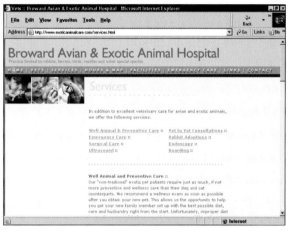

● 2.15

(continued)

altering the kerning, adjusting the transparency, or changing the size of certain letters to create typographical effects without having to rely on a typeface that may become dated. One key thing to remember is that you don't have to use a font "as is".

Q: Why do you use CSS for your font control, and has it made a difference to your page design?

A: I use CSS because it makes Web sites easier to maintain, and the type looks consistent across both Mac and PC platforms if you use pixels as your measurement. I use external style sheets so that updating the typography on a site is really easy. It also makes the HTML code smaller

because there are fewer font tags. CSS also allows one to adjust leading (linespacing), which I love to do.

Q: Your sites feel very comfortable. Do you have any tricks to share on how you balance a page?

A: I think the choice of warm colors and curved lines and texture in my designs are one reason my sites have a friendly or comfortable feel.

As far as balance goes, once I have an idea of the content I usually start with a few very rough thumbnails of possible layouts. Even in the thumbnails you will notice some layouts just balance better than others. I then start designing some specs in Photoshop. One graphical technique that can be particularly helpful in

balancing a page is the use of gradients. Gradients are very powerful elements that, even when used subtly, can really tie and anchor together elements that might otherwise feel like they are floating or unrelated. They also can give a depth and sophistication to a design that can make it appear more finished and complex.

Q: Your sites often include many images, and you often place them in unusual ways, creating energetic pages. How do you decide what to do with images to create a great look without overwhelming the text content?

A: Working in Photoshop (or any image editor) to do layouts rather than in an HTML editor like Dreamweaver helps me to view the page as a whole rather than in rectangular parts. I view the images as an integrated part of the whole page.

Placing Images

You can incorporate images with your text on a Web page in four ways. No rules exist to stop you from using one, two, or even four methods on any one page. The important thing is to choose the best method for each image placement.

● 2.16

Using Background Images

You can use page, table, or CSS-style backgrounds to place an image behind the text on your page. This method is the only way in Web design that allows text to run over an image, unless you create an image that incorporates the text (see Part III, "Graphic Type

● 2.17

Think of integrating text and images on a page like you would when putting together an outfit to wear: every piece of clothing and accessory should complement and coordinate with the other elements of your outfit. To keep this harmony from getting boring or making the page look static I often utilize techniques such as breaking images out of the grid or layer them over other elements. I may also change opacity levels or add a motion blur to add interest to a static photograph.

Q: The Broward Avian and Exotic Animal Hospital site (`www. exoticanimalcare.com/`) is an excellent example of a beautiful site, clearly delivering an appropriate mood, yet the information is easy to read. Can you tell us a little about how you came up with the design and layout for this

site? Did you have any special problems to overcome?

A: I knew that I wanted the site to be earthy and natural and yet professional since it's a site of an excellent exotic animal veterinarian. The tone on tone, natural background colors contrast with both the color of the exotic animal photos and the clean, bold type. The grid design helps keep a professional tone.

One important element in keeping type easily readable – and inviting – is to keep line widths to around 400-500 pixels. Chunking paragraphs (breaking them into shorter sections) also helps. The hardest part was deciding on what images to use because there were so many great images of animals to choose from. Then it came to me: It's all about the relationship between people and their pets. Once I had

that theme or concept in mind, picking photos became much easier. The Flash animation and photos were chosen to illustrate the close relationship that people have with their animal companions. This theme also led me to the use the quotes that are on the main page. These quotes change randomly at each visit and they are used both as a reinforcement of the theme and as a graphical element, which helps to balance the page.

Q: Do you have a favorite CSS or graphic text trick or tip you would like to share?

A: Sometimes I like to anchor the very bottom or top of a word, logo, or graphic text to a thin rule or to the edge of an image. Other times, if I am using text over an image, I will have some of the type descenders break out of the image rectangle.

for the Web"), a method I usually do not recommend. Dick Lehman's pottery site is an excellent example of a subtle background image behind text (2.18).

[WARNING]

Be careful when you use this method, because many images can seriously interfere with the legibility of your text. If you place text over a background image, the text must be the star. In the Lehman site, the background provides a visual image of the product, but it truly fades to the background, allowing the text to do the majority of the work in the message.

Michael Demopoulos of RDVO (see Chapter 14, "Perfecting Type in Flash," for an interview with Michael) has a creative way to use background image placement for creating clear graphic images on a photo-type background. When exporting a text headline with a photo-type background, choosing the correct format is hard. The background image calls for a JPG format, yet text quality is much better with GIF format.

Try Michael's method:

1. **Export your text with a transparent background in GIF format.**

2. **Export the background without the text as a JPG image.**

3. **In your document, place the text GIF file in a separate cell in a table.**

4. **Set the background of that cell to the JPG background that you saved without the text. The result is crisp text on a smooth background (2.19). I cover creating graphic text in detail in Part III, "Graphic Type for the Web."**

Separating Images and Text

The most common combination of text and images on the Web is to place them separately. Designers place images in a separate table cell or layer, with text placed in its own area. This method is easy and logical, and provides a certain amount of automatic organization to the page.

However, be careful that your pages do not become too static. Placing images in a tidy row is certainly the easiest way to organize the page, but you lose interest. The National Public Radio (NPR) site (http://npr.org) illustrates how a tiny change

can break the static look that many images in a row can have. On NPR's entry page (2.20), the designers face quite a challenge, because the headlines with images change frequently. In that setting, there is no way to apply fancy artwork to add excitement to the layout. However, the designers have managed to create a much more interesting page, simply by placing the headlines across the top of the image instead of aligned to the left edge of the text. Often the tiny things are what make a page great.

Always try to break a line of images. You can place them alternately at the left or the right of text or vary the image size and orientation. Look for opportunities to break a pure lineal presentation of any information, but keep the goal for the page in mind. The NPR designers stayed true to the nature of the page — still the most important factor when creating a Web page.

Wrapping Text Around Images

Adding an image doesn't require that you have a separate area. You can place an image within text, and by using the align attribute with your image tag, force

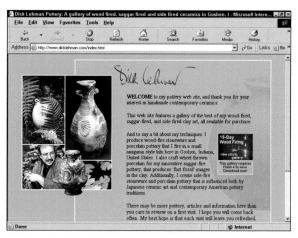

● 2.18

● 2.19

the text around the image. I only recommend using `align="left"` or `align="right"` when using the wrap image command. Although you can center the image within text, there is no correct situation to break text in the middle of a line to place an image.

When placing images within text, the default settings provide no space around the image. To add a little breathing room for your image, you also want to add a horizontal space to the image `hspace="value in pixels"` and perhaps space at the top and bottom with `vspace="value in pixels"`.

The NPR Noah Adams biography page at `www.npr.org/about/people/bios/nadams.html` (2.21), provides an excellent example of this method for placing an image. In this case, the image has been aligned left, and the text wraps around the image to the right. Vertical and horizontal space of 5 pixels has been added to hold the image away from the text.

Placing Inline Images

Finally, you can place a tiny image in a line of text. Because the line spacing between the line containing the image and the line above must accommodate the height of the image, this method only has value for very small images. However, even with that restriction, it is a valuable technique. I often use small images to help create the look and feel for a page and to direct visitors to important information. The images are always tiny, adding little to download time, especially when they are used repeatedly throughout a site.

Many pages feature images at the end of paragraphs providing a link to more information. Bullets are another common use of this inline technique, because you have much more control over the placement of a bullet as an image than using an image in a list style through CSS (see Chapter 7, "Designing with CSS Content Text"). At times, you may want to create a list without using the list style. Simply placing an image in the desired location on a line of text creates a customized list (2.22).

With that basic overview of working with images and text, I now move on to more design issues. Don't panic, though. I return to graphics in a big way in Part III, "Graphic Type for the Web," including tutorials for creating text effects with images.

Understanding the Power of Color and Contrast

When looking at the basic design issues that affect a page, you can't ignore color and contrast. In fact,

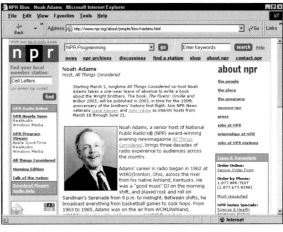

● 2.21

● 2.22

● 2.20

color and contrast are the tools you use to create many of the effects that I have already discussed. For example, your page requires balance, as you learned earlier in this chapter, but color and contrast are the major tools used to create that balance. I start the discussion with color and move to contrast, although one affects the other so strongly that they are barely separate topics.

Understanding Web Page Color

Many factors affect the colors used on a Web page. You may choose a color because you like it, or because it creates a great backdrop for images on the site. You may want to create a certain mood, or, for professional designers, may need to match corporate identities, or at least a logo. Rarely are all colors used on a page determined at the outset, however. Usually, you have at least accent colors to choose, and that can be quite a task. However, you need to address a few issues before you get to choose colors.

Web-Safe Color

Many years ago, as the Web as we know it was just getting rolling, monitors were several generations behind what is in common use today. Many were set to display only 256 colors at best. Considering that limitation, Web design was restricted to using only the colors that would display well on every monitor, much like our font restriction. A Web-safe palette was created, and most designers stuck like glue to this less-than-exciting selection of colors. The cost for using other colors could be a dithered mess where the designer wanted solid color — a high price to pay for pretty color. Dreamweaver MX features a Web-safe palette as a default value (2.23).

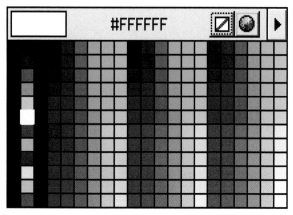

Today, most monitors display more than 256 colors and many designers are moving away from Web-safe color restrictions, because dithering of the colors chosen is highly unlikely to happen. Lynda Weinman (http://lynda.com), the undisputed color guru for years in this industry, has advised that designers no longer need to hold tight to Web-safe color. I agree — with the following reservations. When possible, I still use Web-safe color.

I have not done scientifically valid research on this issue, but my experience has been that I get more consistent results with color across various computers when using the Web-safe palette. Dithering is not a problem, but color shifting can be. Technically, the color-shifting problem should be no better with Web-safe color than with any color. My, perhaps twisted, thought is that if color shifts when you use a Web-safe color, the visitors see the same shift as they do on most sites. In other words, all sites probably look less than perfect. By using a non–Web-safe color, your site may be the only one that looks bad. And some shifts are dramatic, especially in the beige, tan, and taupe color families. Many will shift to pink or violet. If you have used an earth-tone palette, and all of a sudden your page goes pink . . . I think you get the message.

Lately, I use Web-safe color for large solid areas whenever possible, and if I can't get the look I need with the limited palette, I use a JPG image as a background for large color blocks. I use the non–Web-safe match to that color for small areas like text headlines. I suspect that I am being a little paranoid with this method, but there seems to be less color shifting with a JPG background than with the equivalent HTML color. Note the language here, though. Seems to be, suspect, and so on. I'm not trying to pass on an absolute fact, but sharing my experiences.

Mac Versus PC Gamut

The subject of Mac versus PC isn't new to most professional designers, as Mac use is much higher in the design world than in the home computer market. However, a difference exists between the color that is displayed on a Mac computer and on a PC computer. That difference is important to you as a designer, even though for most pages, the variation is not a big problem. However, you should be aware of this variation, especially for situations where you work with low-contrast effects.

● 2.23

You can see a clear difference between the Windows display (2.24) and Mac display (2.25). When you work with light colors and low-contrast pages, make sure you test on both Mac and PC machines. Many graphics programs, like Photoshop, provide the normal display for both programs. If you create your site proofs in a program that displays the gamut for the opposite platform from the one you use, then testing each display as you work through your design is a good idea.

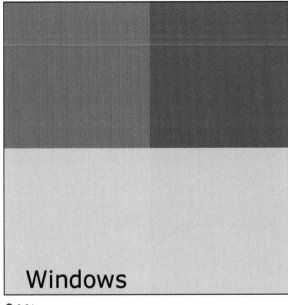

● 2.24

● 2.25

Finding Color Resources

Color and contrast is a huge, well-researched subject. Because this book is about text, not design, I can only cover the most important concepts of this subject. However, I urge you to research both color and contrast in any form you can find. A great deal of psychology is associated with color, a subject I cannot even touch here. Adjusting contrast between colors has as much effect as changing tone or shade. If you're not familiar with the color wheel and how it works, I advise that you start with that research. A good site for basic color information is Color Matters (www.colormatters.com/colortheory.html). For a rich supply of color information as it relates to the Web, don't miss Shirley Kaiser's Web information portal, Web Site Tips (www.websitetips.com/color/).

If you're not one of the lucky ones who was born with innate color sense (and some are) don't fret. Color can be intuitive, but more than enough tutorials exist on working with color to create tangible tools for those without in-born skill. Suzanne Stephens has a terrific series of articles about working with color on the site Web Page Design for Designers (http://wpdfd.com). If you find that you need to see all colors in order to understand how they relate, it is hard to beat Visibone's series of printed color products (www.visibone.com/). You can also find color tutorials and tools on Visibone's site.

Finally, you can find tools to help with color, like Color Schemer (www.colorschemer.com/). This tool works on the desktop and allows you to compare colors and color schemes, and to make adjustments easily (2.26). There is also a very good color tutorial on the Color Schemer site.

● 2.26

Selecting Color

After the technical aspects of color selection are out of the way, you're still left with a blank canvas that you must fill with color. You use color to divide your page, direct the reader around the page, and please the eye. Your choice of color is very important to your goals.

Let me start by making a strong case for white. Yes, it is on almost every page on the Web. Yes, most pages have more white areas than any other color. Yes, you are a designer and want to create something "different." But white is a standard on the Web for the same reason it is a standard in print. It works! There is no better background for text than white. Period. Not all the text on all my sites is on white, but where it counts, you can bet those words are sitting on a white background. I am more likely to use colored text on white than black text on any background color for content areas.

With that out of the way, we can talk color. A page contains many non–content-text areas. Menus can, and usually do go on a colored background to help them stand out from the content. Content in the right or left columns on a page are usually short pieces, and can be placed on colored backgrounds. The header or title areas on pages are a great place to incorporate color and create the mood for the page.

When choosing page color, consider the mood you want to convey. Is your site fun and funky? Bright color may be in order. Is your site putting across a very somber message? Perhaps dark or muted colors are in order. One site I did (that is no longer active) required a fun mood (2.27). A muted color scheme presents the opposite feeling with totally different colors (2.28). Color sets the mood more than almost any other element on a page.

One of the first decisions I make is the color of my text. If it is going to be black, I try to incorporate at least a tiny amount of black into the page design. Often it is no more than a thin line in the menu area, but I do like to tie the black text into the design elements. Small design features can make all the difference (2.29). Note how adding two small black lines in the lower version of this simple mockup makes the text an integral part of the design. With no black accents, it seemed to be an add-on.

If I choose a dark color for text, like gray, brown, or blue, that color will always be extracted from the design of the page. I admit I am pretty fussy with what colors and backgrounds create acceptable text, but keep in mind that your text is a design element and you should integrate the color with the rest of your page.

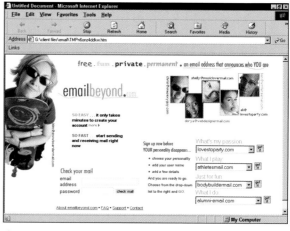

● 2.27

● 2.28

creates a darker appearance. I often choose a slightly darker color for my content text to create a visual match. Don't do this for headline text, because the difference in color will show. Keep careful track of the colors you use for design elements and text.

You have many other considerations when choosing colors for a site. The Glass Loon site (2.30) features changing art work, which may contain any color of the rainbow. Creating a neutral backdrop for the art was important. The interior pages feature the same color scheme, with a white background for the content text. There is nothing in the page design to interfere or clash with any art that may come in. Do you have elements with strong color that will appear on your pages? Make sure that your site color choice allows for content image color.

I've just scratched the surface of color for Web pages, but I do hope that you follow up on my

research suggestions. The more you learn about color, how to use it, and how people react to color, the stronger your design will be.

Working with Contrast

I can't cover all the key areas of design in one small section of a book. Volumes would be necessary to cover all aspects of contrast in design. However, I can give you a peek into how contrast works in design, and you can keep your eyes open for the effects in your pages. After you become aware of the issues, you will start to correct contrast problems automatically.

[T I P]

The best information about design, contrast and balance can be found in the fine-art section of your local bookstore or library. You'll find entire books dedicated to the subject, and painting and drawing books often devote many chapters to balance in design. The principles that combine to deliver a great painting or drawing are relevant to creating a page for the Web.

Using Contrast for Balance

One of the most valuable roles that contrast plays is to help balance the weight of your page. A strong contrast weighs more than a weak contrast. You can use this weight to your advantage. In a simple colored

● 2.29

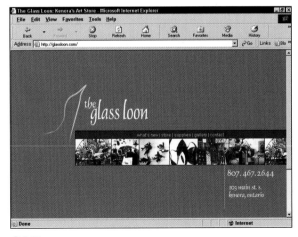

● 2.30

cube (2.31), the contrast between the colors on the right side of the cube attracts your attention. If you really look at this example closely, you can "feel" that the right side also has more weight. That feeling is accomplished completely through contrast. The squares of color are all the same size and from the same color family. Only the sharp contrast between the black and the white is playing the trick of weight on your eyes.

You can use this attribute to obtain or correct balance on your pages. If you need to add weight to an area, try increasing contrast. A high-contrast line in a light area often adds enough weight to bring the page into balance. Or, if one area is too heavy, reducing the contrast in one or more areas can have the same effect. Before you add extra elements to a page, check to see whether you can create the effect you require by adjusting contrast (2.32). I adjusted the contrast so that both the left and the right columns have approximately the same contrast. Note how both sides now feel like the same weight. The black square in the upper right still grabs your attention, but the columns are balanced.

Using Contrast to Catch Attention

Although a page must be balanced overall, you naturally want to attract attention to specific areas of your pages. You work to place content so your visitors can find it, but you also want to direct their behavior to some extent, especially if you are promoting a product, and almost all sites fall into this category.

● 2.31

[N O T E]

A product doesn't necessarily mean a bottle or box containing hard merchandise that visitors can order. A product can also mean getting visitors to write to a politician, participate in a poll for research, or to add a link to your site.

You can use contrast to draw your visitor's attention to a portion of the page you want them to see. In order to keep the concept clear, I have prepared another set of simplistic samples. (Getting caught up in color, shape, or other attributes is too easy with more realistic examples.) Take a quick look at a simple example (2.33, 2.34). Note how the word *special* stands out much better in the second example (2.34). Nothing has been changed but the contrast between

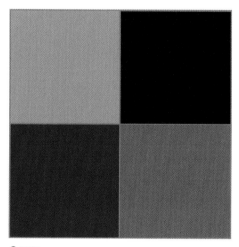

● 2.32

Indignor quicquam reprehendi, non quia crasse compositum illepedeve putetur, sed quia nuper, nec veniam antiquis, sed honorem et praemia posci. Recte necne crocum floresque perambulet Attae fabula si dubitem, clament periisse pudorem cuncti paene patres, ea cum reprehendere coner, quae gravis Aesopus, quae doctus Roscius egit; vel quia nil rectum, nisi quod placuit sibi, ducunt, vel quia turpe putant parere minoribus, et quae imberbes didicere senes.

Indignor quicquam reprehendi, non quia crasse compositum illepedeve putetur, sed quia nuper, nec veniam antiquis, sed honorem et praemia posci. Recte necne crocum floresque perambulet Attae fabula si dubitem, clament periisse pudorem cuncti paene patres,

Special!

Attae fabula si dubitem, clament periisse pudorem cuncti paene patres, ea cum reprehendere coner, quae gravis Aesopus, quae doctus Roscius egit; vel quia nil rectum, nisi quod placuit sibi, ducunt, vel quia turpe putant parere minoribus, et quae imberbes didicere senes.

● 2.33

the background color and the text color. All of a sudden that one word grabs first attention. Keep the power of contrast in mind.

Using Contrast to Hide Information in Plain View

You can use contrast to take attention away from information that you want available in an accessable area, but do not want it to attract attention away from the rest of the page. Contact information is often treated in this way. I often place the address and phone number on every page, usually in the left column. However, I do reduce the contrast by using a shaded background, or light-colored text, or both.

Kate Kline May is a photographer, and her shots are the most important element of her site at `www.kateklinemay.com/` (2.35). The site designer,

Tricia McGillis, lets the images have star status, yet manages to keep the housekeeping menu right in front of the visitor by using a low contrast text and background combination. The category links, featured in each of the pictures, have a higher contrast so that visitors can see that the images are also links. At first glance you think you're looking at images only. But very quickly, the navigation method settles into your eye, without distracting your attention from the real message — the quality of the photographs.

Contrast is a valuable tool when creating a site, or even when adding new information to an existing site. When your page balance is off, check to see whether a contrast adjustment fixes the problem. When you want to attract attention, again, increase your contrast. Finally, if you want to fade information into the background without moving it to an inaccessible place on your page, reduce the contrast. Understanding contrast gives you great design power.

Creating Accessible Pages

Accessibility has become a common word in the professional Web design world. It is still a little mysterious for those who don't work with it every day. I feature this short introduction to the subject because type has so much to do with whether a site is accessible, and because I talk about it throughout the book. Also, if you follow the recommendations I make throughout this book, your sites will be, at most, just a few short steps away from being fully accessible to those who don't have the same viewing, listening, or typing capability that most of your visitors possess.

From a short-sighted view, accessibility may only be of concern for those who distribute information or products for a market that includes people with physical impairment. But that is not true. Often those with communication impairment use the Internet more than the average person. Your site may be many times more valuable to a person with visual impairment. By making your site accessible, you include everyone, no matter how they use the Internet. Doing so just makes sense. Even the most sophisticated testing has yet to truly predict exactly what is important on the Web — it's just too new. For all

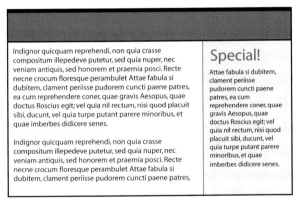

● 2.34

● 2.35

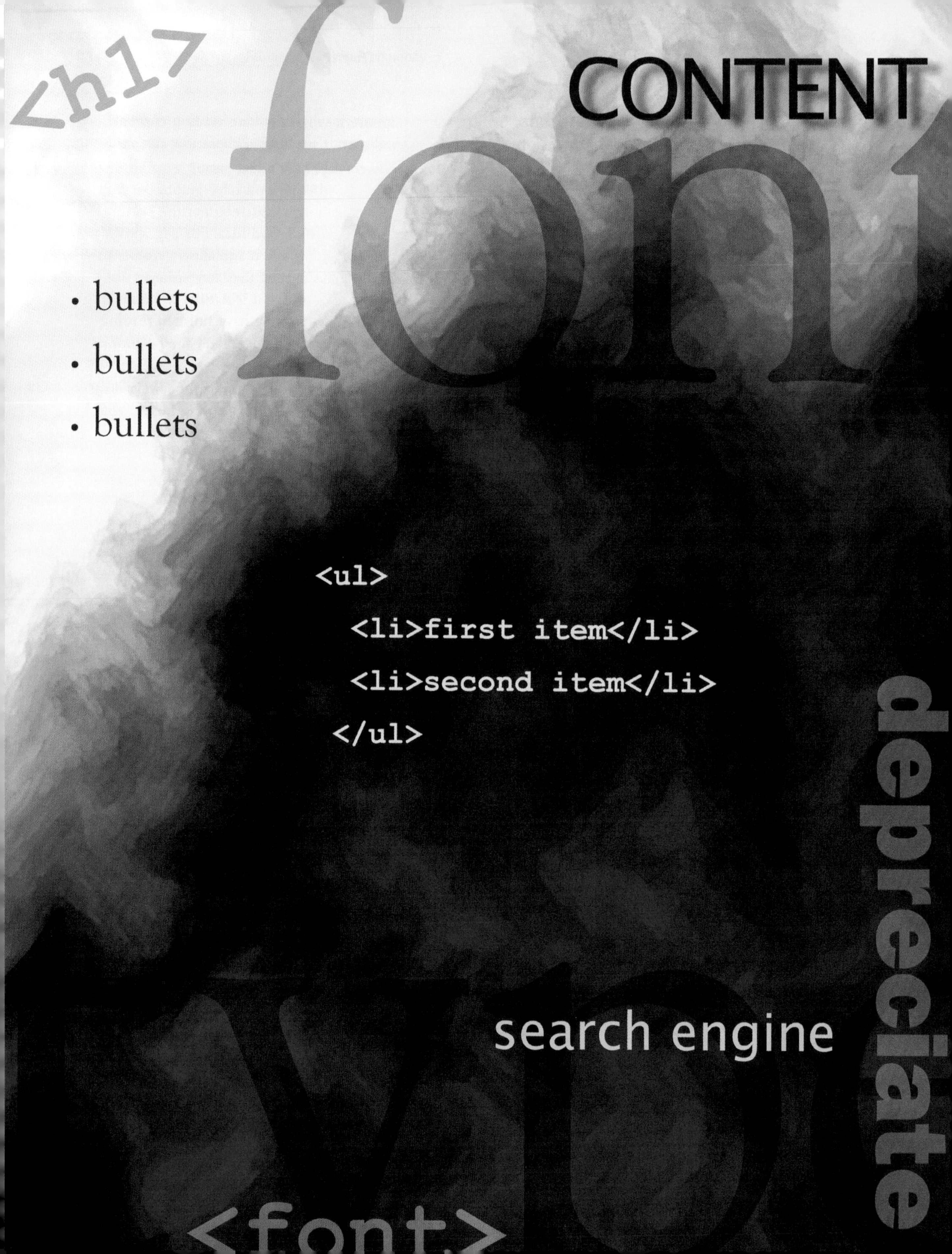
<h1>
CONTENT
font
• bullets
• bullets
• bullets
<ul>
<li>first item</li>
<li>second item</li>
</ul>
depreciate
search engine
<font>

Chapter 3

Working with HTML Text

Don't ask why you should use CSS for text control. Try to come up with one reason why not. That's your answer.

WENDY PECK

You have probably already guessed that I am a CSS text control fan. If you've looked at the Table of Contents, you can see that I include a lot in this book about CSS. So, why are you reading an HTML text chapter? Because CSS controls HTML text. You must learn about HTML text before you can hope to understand how CSS works to create the effects you desire.

Creating HTML Text

I am guessing that most of you have already created a few Web pages, so you probably have some knowledge of how HTML text works. We'll start at the beginning, though, as it is easy to miss important points as you work through the initial stages of Web development.

I also stretch this topic a little to include some important, text-related subjects. I provide a peek into optimizing your pages for search engine placement, and take the opportunity to do a little campaigning for keeping Web pages as small as possible. Although questionable as direct "type" topics, these issues involve text, and affect the overall quality of your pages. Through the technique sections of the book, I refer to file size and search engine "friendliness," so this chapter sets the stage with an overview of topics to come later in the book.

Working with the <font> Tag

This is the one place where I discuss the method, and then advise that you never use what you learn here. The text attributes that are controlled with the <font> tag are better handled with CSS. However, you must understand how the <font> tag works, even if you never use it.

[N O T E]

The <font> tag has been depreciated with HTML 4. Although the tag still works in browsers supporting HTML 4, support for the <font> tag will eventually disappear. It's best to avoid depreciated tags.

that code to a few short characters and accomplish the same results. That's as far as I am going to go with text control tags in HTML for now. I want to take a look at the <p> and <h*> tags.

Starting a section of text with the <p> tag and ending with </p> creates a paragraph unit, with a predefined space inserted between paragraphs. The following code produces paragraphs that are separate units (3.5). (I have controlled the display with a table, but I only show the code for the text in the following examples.)

```
<p><font size="2" face="Arial,
    Helvetica, sans-serif">You can
    create separate paragraphs with
    the paragraph tag. The tag will
    automatically insert a space
    following each paragraph.
    </font></p>
```

```
<p><font size="2" face="Arial,
    Helvetica, sans-serif">You can
    create separate paragraphs with
    the paragraph tag. The tag will
    automatically insert a space
    following each paragraph.
    </font></p>
```

The headline tags are critical, as search engine spiders pay special attention to these tags. I don't think I have ever used the default values for the <h1> and <h2> tags (3.6), but you already know how to adjust font and size.

```
<h1>H1 is the level 1 headline
    tag</h1>
    <p><font size="2" face="Arial,
    Helvetica, sans-serif">You can
    create separate
```

● 3.5

● 3.6

dS. *(continued)*

"bail out" of their pages to go elsewhere to find a more responsive site. Just a few K can make a big difference in bail out rates. Where that threshold is depends on a number of factors, including feedback, perceived complexity, and user experience (and is the subject of an entire chapter in my book). Users also experience "cumulative frustration" that can happen across multiple pages.

Q: What is the best way to work with type from an optimization standpoint?

A: Use as little as possible. Seriously, the more you substitute text for graphics the better speed- and usability-wise. In terms of speed, one font face is as good as another (assuming they are both not downloaded), but for optimizing legibility and comprehension that's another matter.

Q: While acknowledging that Search Engine Optimization is an entire field

of study, are there any simple tips you can pass on for working with text that makes pages more attractive to search engines?

A: Yes. In key areas avoid "stop" words like "a," "the," "an," and so on that search engines ignore anyway. Avoid graphic text; search engines can't read or index it. Use CSS text instead, and always use descriptive "ALT" text for functional graphics. Carefully craft your <title> tag to put your top one or two terms up

```
    paragraphs with the paragraph
tag. The tag will automatically
insert a space
    following each paragraph.
</font></p>
    <h2>H2 is the level 2 headline
tag</h2>
    <p><font size="2" face="Arial,
Helvetica, sans-serif">You can
create separate paragraphs with
the paragraph tag. The tag will
automatically insert a space
following each paragraph.</font>
</p>
```

The last font tag I want to discuss in this lightning-fast tutorial are the tags to create a list of items using HTML. The list tags, `<ul>` to start the list and `<li>` for each list item, automatically indent the list and place a bullet with each new paragraph (3.7). The code for this effect follows:

```
<p><font size="2" face="Arial,
    Helvetica, sans-serif">Items in a
    list can be automatically
    formatted with the list
    tags.</font></p>

<ul>
    <li><font size="2" face="Arial,
    Helvetica, sans-serif">first
    item</font></li>
    <li><font size="2" face="Arial,
    Helvetica, sans-
    serif">seconditem</font></li>
```

```
    <li><font size="2" face="Arial,
    Helvetica, sans-serif">third
    item</font></li>
    <li><font size="2" face="Arial,
    Helvetica, sans-
    serif">fourthitem</font></li>
</ul>
```

The bulleted text is a great way to present information, but it's an awful lot of code for a few words. With CSS, the code is cut many times, and you have more options. You learn how to accomplish all the effects shown in this section with CSS in Part II, "Controlling Web Type with Cascading Style Sheets (CSS)," but I wanted to make sure that you understood how the tags for text work in HTML, so that you can convert the effects to CSS.

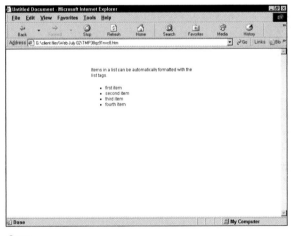

 3.7

This may be the first time you have considered the tags that run HTML. With visual editors like Macromedia's Dreamweaver and Adobe's GoLive, your never seeing a tag is entirely possible. Please don't consider that you have had a full HTML text tutorial. I just gave you enough to move ahead with CSS.

Working Without the <font> Tag

Now that I have gone over the basics of controlling HTML text, it's time to show you a much better way to control your text. Starting in the next chapter, "What Is CSS?," you learn how to control all your text with CSS. Before I take you to the methods, however, I want to introduce you to CSS text control, and convince you there is no other way to work.

HTML text control methods get the job done. After you know the code, manipulating your text to the exact appearance you desire is easy. However, although the method is easy, it is also cumbersome. Every time you want to change a font attribute, you must add the code. Even if I were not concerned with file size (the font tag can balloon your page size very quickly), I would not want to be back to the days when I had to apply font attributes to every piece of text on my pages.

Take a look at the code that follows and compare it to the code that creates the look in the previous example (3.7). Compare that list to the list that is controlled by the code shown here (3.8).

```
<p>Items in a list can be
    automatically formatted with the
    list tags.</p>

<ul>
    <li>first item</li>
    <li>second item</li>
    <li>third item</li>
    <li>fourth item</li>
</ul>
```

CSS controls the fonts. The CSS code that creates this effect is shown here:

```
p {
    font-family: Arial,Helvetica,sans-
        serif;font-size: 12px;
}
```

```
ul {
    font-family: Arial,Helvetica,sans-
        serif;
    font-size: 12px;
}
```

[WARNING]

If you're new to CSS, don't try to make any great sense of CSS code just yet. I am simply showing you where we are headed in Part II, "Controlling Web Type with Cascading Style Sheets (CSS)." I will lead you step-by-step through creating a CSS file and applying it to your pages in Chapter 4, "What Is CSS?."

I think, for me, the number one reason that I jumped early on the CSS text control bandwagon, and that is still my main delight with CSS text control, is consistency. I usually use a linked file for CSS control, simply telling each page to refer to that file for the font control information. Think of what that means! Whether I am creating my first or my fiftieth page on a site, I know there is no way my fonts can be different on any page. One file controls the text appearance.

The other related benefit to the same feature is that you can change your page appearance at any time by changing the CSS style sheet. I use fixed font size (this issue comes up in a big way in Chapter 5, "Creating Cascading Style Sheets") but the day may come when I will want to change everything I've done to variable size fonts. When a method that works for my needs arrives, I make that change on every site in less than a day, with testing time included.

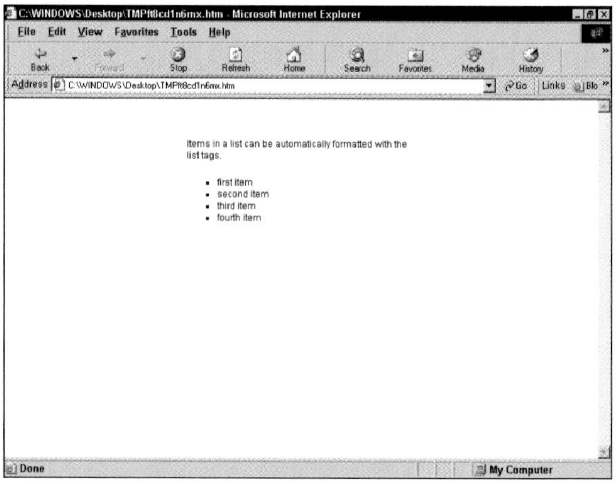

● 3.8

Eric Meyer, CSS guru and author of several CSS books (you meet Eric in Chapter 4, "What Is CSS?"), has a dynamic example of CSS versatility on his personal site. Figures 3.9 and 3.10 show two versions of the same page. The effect is worth a trip to his site (www.meyerweb.com/eric/css/). You can toggle the look of the page among several choices simply by clicking the menu at the right of the page (3.9, 3.10). Simple JavaScript changes the style sheet when you click the selection, but nothing on the page changes. This feature is a wonderful example of the design power that CSS places in your hands. Make sure you visit.

If you are accustomed to using HTML text control, CSS can seem a little overwhelming for a little while. Part II, "Controlling Web Type with Cascading Style Sheets (CSS)," takes you step by step through everything you need to know about controlling your text

with CSS. After you grasp the concept of CSS, you will soon be saying, "What <font> tag?"

[WARNING]

From this point forward, because this chapter is an introduction to concepts, and I take you through what you need to do to implement techniques, I will assume you're using CSS control for your text. I see no point in teaching you more about methods I don't recommend that you use.

Designing with Lists

Lists are a designer's friend. One of the problems that developers face on the Web is short visitor attention span. Andy King's book, *Speed Up Your Site: Web Site Optimization*, devotes an entire chapter to the psychology of Web surfing. (See the interview with Andy earlier in this chapter.) Amazing studies have been done on how people absorb information on the Web, and the news is that this crowd is not a patient crew. If you're serious about keeping your visitors, you should pay attention to the reality of visitor patience.

One of the best ways to deliver information quickly is by using lists. Lists not only remove the need for correct sentence structure, and therefore, many words, but the physical presentation of a list format is also much easier to absorb with a quick glance.

Compare the following two examples (3.11). The top example is a paragraph presentation of information. The lower example presents the same information in

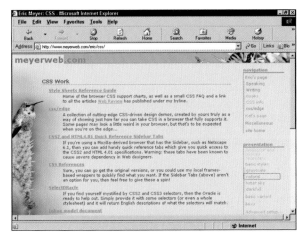

● 3.9

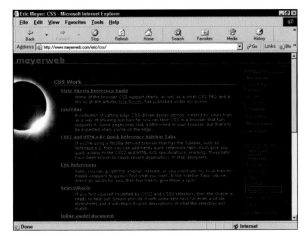

● 3.10

Weekend Pass

A Weekend Pass includes entry to the Art Show, Art Through Music and Backstage. In addition, you will be entitled to discounts at all food and entertainment venues, and are automatically entered in door prize draws for over $5,000 in merchandise and gift certificates.

Weekend Pass includes:

- Art Show entry
- Art Through Music
- Backstage
- Food and entertainment venue discounts
- Door prizes of $5,000 in merchandise and gift certificates

● 3.11

a list format. Which is easier to absorb if you were the visitor to this site? Not only can the list presentation be read more quickly, but readers are also more likely to see every point.

[NOTE]

The green bullets featured in this list are created by a tiny image, placed with CSS control on the `<ul>` tag. Not only is CSS easier to use, but it provides more options as well. You learn to place images like this in Chapter 7, "Designing with CSS Content Text," of this book.

Lists on the Web are controlled by the `<ul>` tag, formatted with CSS control. When you have the CSS in place, all you have to do is place your list between `<ul>` and `</ul>` tags, with each new entry placed between `<li>` and `</li>` tags. Your lists automatically indent, and entries of more than one line wrap to the indented position. See the last line of text in the previous list (3.11) for an example of how the text aligns in a list.

I also use lists for CSS-controlled menus when there are many items in the list and I need to separate content in a large menu (3.12). Note the background color change as the mouse passes over the link — another CSS gem.

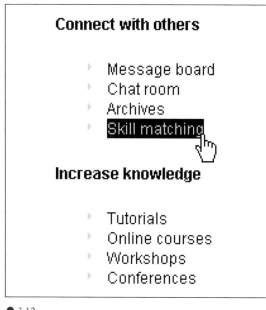

● 3.12

Starting now, place lists firmly in your toolbox as a problem solver. Chapter 7, "Designing with CSS Content Text," takes you through creating and controlling lists and list attributes, but creating the code is not the most important aspect of using this effectively. Creating a list is shockingly simple. The harder part is to fix them in your mind as one of the best ways to present information on the Web.

[NOTE]

In addition to teaching you how to create and control lists, I also provide a way to present information using tables, rather than the list tag to create the list look. Lists are great, but they are limited in formatting options. Most designers look for more control. Chapter 7, "Designing with CSS Content Text," also covers manual list creation using CSS control — especially valuable for menus.

Content Text and Search Optimization

Search Engine Optimization (SEO) involves creating the best environment on your Web pages to achieve a listing, preferably high, with the major search engines, like Google or Yahoo!. I do not pretend to be an SEO expert. People exist who specialize in this field, and I will not insult their highly researched work by pretending to be their equal on this topic.

The goal of this book is not to teach you how to optimize your content for search engines. However, this book is on text, and I can introduce you to the concept of optimizing your text content so that search engines can find you. Achieving high listings in the major engines will not follow automatically by adopting these simple points, but you can be sure the search engines will have a hard time finding you if you ignore these basic points.

Using the Right Keywords

Keywords, placed in the header of your document, are important. You establish the words that your potential visitors will type into a search engine, and include them in your keyword list. However, because so many people were abusing keyword listings, search engine developers have been placing less and less emphasis on determining listings through keywords. In fact, keywords can be dangerous. Try to plant too many similar words to enhance the importance of a subject to the search engines, and you may find your site blacklisted by the search engines.

When you place keywords, make them highly relevant to content you have on your pages, and watch that you're not placing duplicates. Many experts recommend using keyword phrases, rather than single words, to help your listings. Suppose you breed West Highland Terrier dogs. Including "dog" as a keyword is most likely a waste of time. Far too much competition exists, and even if a miracle happened, and you reached a high placement for the word "dog," most of the visitors to your site would have no interest in your product. However, if you use the phrase "West Highland Terrier breeder," you are more likely to achieve a listing, and visitors who search that phrase will be excellent potential customers for your product.

A sample of keywords that would be appropriate to a bakery in my hometown appear in the following code. I'm not in the bakery business, and have never had a bakery client, so I have no doubt missed some words that may be appropriate for this business, but the listing gives you an idea of the syntax used for keywords. You enter keywords in the Keywords screen in Dreamweaver MX (3.13).

```
<meta name="keywords"
    content="Kenora, lunch, European
    pastries, donuts, doughnuts,
    catering, homemade soup, bread,
    sandwiches, vegetarian menu,
    smoke-free dining, specialty
    coffee, cappuccino, cookies,
    dainties, main street">
```

Seeding Your Pages with Relevant Content

Putting content that is relevant to your product on your pages sounds like common sense, right? Sure it is, but unless you actually focus on the words that your potential visitors will type into a search, you can miss this point easily. As a communicator, this requirement is one that makes my heart soar. Most Web designers want a great search engine placement for their personal or business site. Including long-winded, irrelevant content on pages is the kiss of death for search engine placement.

The first content on your pages is the most important. This content just happens to help your visitors get a quick idea of what you offer, so go for your hook with gusto. In the first couple of paragraphs, make sure that you use clear and concise language to describe exactly what visitors can find on that page. Your important content words should match the keywords you have placed, and the page title (see the next section). If you don't have great writing skills, consider hiring a Web-wise copy writer, or trading design services with a writer.

Getting the perfect content in a few words at the beginning of every page is not easy, but the rewards can be high. Your visitors will understand your site purpose immediately, and the search engines will consider your page a valuable listing to return to those searching for what you offer. With no downside to creating great content early in your pages, you have no excuse for not following this tip.

I have used a blue background to mark keywords seeded through the content (3.14). Note the descriptive title on the graphic that appears when the mouse

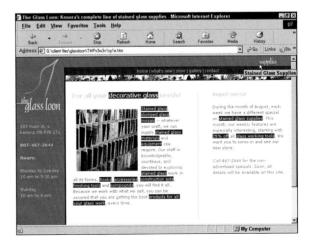

3.13

3.14

passes over the graphic page title. This feature is known as the "alt" attribute of the <image> tag, and can also help with search engine placement. I cover the <image> tag in Chapter 10, "Customizing Graphic Text for the Web," of this book.

Developing Useful Page Titles

Page titles, placed in the head of your HTML documents, are important to search engines. Perhaps more important, page titles form the title line of a returned listing, and should entice potential visitors to click through. What good is a high listing, if visitors don't actually visit your site?

Page titles should contain as many relevant keywords for that page as is reasonable to create a title that describes the page. Don't just seed your title with all of your keywords. Search engines can identify that technique, and can reject or even blacklist your page for trying to use the page title as a second keyword listing. Create a meaningful title, incorporating your keywords in the early words where possible. Page titles also create the explanatory text when visitors bookmark a page — yet one more reason to create page titles with meaning.

The following code creates a page title. You place this code between the <head> and </head> tags

of the HTML document. You enter the page title in the Title field of the Dreamweaver MX main toolbar (3.15).

```
<title>The Glass Loon: Kenora's
    complete line of stained glass
    supplies</title>
```

Creating a Page Description

A thoughtful page description can add great value to your site. A visitor cannot see a <meta> tag description on your page, but they will see it in a search engine return. Search engine descriptions for your listing come from your <meta> tag description.

The code for a sample description follows:

```
<meta name="description"
    content="Kenora's premier coffee
    shop, conveniently located on
    Second Street, just one block
    from the Kenora Shopper's Mall.">
```

Don't miss this easy way to attract visitors with your search engine listing.

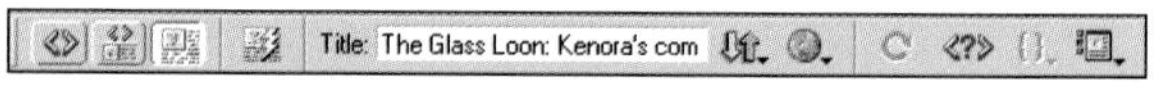

● 3.15

Treating Each Page Separately

You may be tempted to copy and paste keywords, page descriptions, and titles from one page to another. After all, keywords should apply across a site, right? No way! First, you lose the opportunity to have individual pages attract high listings for different searches. You can never be quite sure what your potential visitors will use as a search string, and adding the number of possibilities to catch them through different pages should not be ignored. After you have a visitor land on any page in your site, if your navigation is good, he will work his way through your site, assuming your content is right for him.

Treat each page as a separate entity, and start fresh for all attributes that affect search engine placement. This technique takes a little extra time in the development

stage, but it pays off with the search engines and the quality of visitors you attract. As a side benefit, assigning keywords, watching early content vigilantly, and creating great page titles helps to unify your pages and creates a much more valuable resource for your visitors.

For the Glass Loon site, the content keywords (highlighted in blue), page title, and "alt" text on interior pages (3.16) are completely different from the example for the entry page (3.14), as this page features a different aspect of the business.

Don't Stop Here with SEO

The information contained in this book is only designed to whet your appetite for search engine optimization wisdom. The best site in the world is a waste if nobody ever finds it. Keep up to date on new developments with search engines, and continually check your pages to see whether your titles, keywords, and early content still reflect what you want to communicate. You can start your research with the following links. Each of these links contains basic information to help you optimize your pages:

- `www.submit-it.com/subopt.htm`
- `www.rankwrite.com/`
- `http://searchenginewatch.com/`
- `www.searchengines.com/search_engines_101.html`
- `http://websitetips.com/search/`

 3.16

Controlling Web Type with
Cascading Style Sheets (CSS)

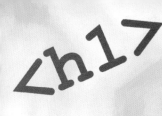

IMPORT

font

content
——————
layout

HTML? CSS?

link/embed

font

Chapter 4

What Is CSS?

Wow! This is what I have been waiting for!

ERIC MEYER (THE FIRST TIME HE SAW A CSS DEMONSTRATION IN 1996)

One thing separates CSS from HTML in a big way. With HTML, the code controlling the text is embedded into the text. Code and content are woven into a whole. CSS is the opposite. With CSS, you create your layout, and the control that is applied to text within that layout is completely independent of the content. This feature is the one that gives CSS its power.

CSS is not difficult when you understand the basics. This chapter takes you through the concepts for CSS controlled text, as well as methods to include CSS control in HTML pages and basic syntax. Spend some quality time with the basics if you are new to controlling your text with CSS. The time you spend now will be repaid many times as you delve deeper into CSS in the next few chapters, and in your work.

[N O T E]

The idea of separating content and layout goes much further with CSS positioning, but I focus completely on text control with CSS in this book. In controlled situations, you can complete the entire layout of a page using CSS, but we have not yet reached the place where all browsers react in a predictable way to CSS-controlled layout. Even if the Web were a safe place for full CSS positioning, that topic would be outside the scope of this book.

Separating Content from Page Layout

I'm going to risk repetition from the previous chapter, "Working with HTML Text," and give another simple example of the fundamental difference between CSS and HTML text control. It is essential that you understand the basic concept of CSS before moving to the techniques.

Take a look at a paragraph with a title (4.1). The text is dark blue, and the font size has been adjusted from the default for both the headline and paragraph styles.

Don't miss the excitement

The grounds are prepared, the vendors are onsite. Tomorrow morning, Victory park will fill with thousands of people, as the best in Bluegrass music begins to fill the air.

● 4.1

This first example of code shows the HTML control for the text shown in 4.1. Note how the appearance of the text is controlled by code that is directly associated with the text.

```
<h1><strong><font color="#000066"
    size="3" face="Arial, Helvetica,
    sans-serif">Don't miss the
    excitement
    </font></strong></h1><p><font
    color="#000066" size="2"
    face="Arial, Helvetica, sans-
    serif">The grounds are prepared,
    the vendors are onsite. Tomorrow
    morning, Victory park will fill
    with thousands of people, as the
    best in Bluegrass music begins to
    fill the air. </font></p>
```

The next sample of code creates the same final result, but this time CSS controls the text appearance. The first set of code creates the text content. Note that no appearance commands are embedded in this code.

```
<h1>Don't miss the excitement</h1>

<p>The grounds are prepared, the
    vendors are onsite. Tomorrow
    morning, Victory park will fill
    with thousands of people, as the
    best in Bluegrass music begins to
    fill the air.</font></p>
```

The appearance of the previous content is controlled by the following CSS code to create the final look (4.1). You can place this code in the head of your document, or more commonly, in a separate file.

```
p {
    font-family: Arial, Helvetica,
    sans-serif;
    font-size: 12px;
    color: #000066;
}

h1 {
    font-family: Arial, Helvetica,
    sans-serif; font-size: 14px;
    font-weight: bold;
    color: #000066;
}
```

The separation of the formatting from the content is the biggest benefit with CSS control. Suppose you wanted to change the body text color of the previous example (4.2). The sample here is tiny, of course, but assume that you have a multiple page site to change.

To change the paragraph text color with the HTML-controlled text, you would have to remove the color reference from every <font> tag. For the CSS-controlled text, no matter how many pages the site contains, a change to the CSS file would make

Don't miss the excitement

The grounds are prepared, the vendors are onsite. Tomorrow morning, Victory park will fill with thousands of people, as the best in Bluegrass music begins to fill the air.

● 4.2

Behind the Scenes

**Meat, Potatoes, and Dessert CSS:
An Interview with Eric Meyer**

Eric Meyer accidentally encountered a CSS in 1996, when it was in its infancy. Although he was one of the first to focus his energy on CSS, his success cannot be relegated to an early start. When Eric talks about CSS, it is clear that he is still quite fascinated by it, and after many years, still believes in the technology. Eric works from a home office in Cleveland, Ohio, although he is a full-time Netscape employee. His business cards list his title as Standards Evangelist, though he has a more mundane title with Human Relations. Eric works with a team of people devoted to "finding standards-based solutions for multiple browsers."

His books include *Eric Meyer on CSS, Cascading Style Sheets: The Definitive Guide, Cascading Style Sheets 2.0 Programmer's Reference,* and *CSS Pocket Reference.*

Q: When and why did you first become interested in CSS? What motivated you to delve so deeply into CSS that you have become known as one of the world authorities on it?

A: I first discovered CSS in 1996, at the 5th IWWW conference, where I was presenting a paper on something completely unrelated to Web design or layout. CSS1

the changes on every page (assuming you're using a linked CSS file — see the next section). Because the text control is not an integrated part of the page, you can edit content and formatting separately.

To continue with the example, the HTML code would be as follows. The default color for HTML text is black, so removing the color attribute from the font tag creates black text. You would have to make this change in every case that the `color="#000066"` occurs with the `<p>` tag.

```
<h1><strong><font color="#000066"
    size="3" face="Arial, Helvetica,
    sans-serif">Don't miss the
    excitement
    </font></strong></h1><p><font
    size="2" face="Arial, Helvetica,
    sans-serif">The grounds are
    prepared, the vendors are onsite.
    Tomorrow morning, Victory park
    will fill with thousands of
    people, as the best in Bluegrass
    music begins to fill the air.
    </font></p>
```

In comparison, to change the text color with the CSS-controlled sample, the change is made away from the content, in the CSS specifications. Your content on the page doesn't change, and your CSS code is as follows:

```
p {
    font-family: Arial, Helvetica,
    sans-serif;
    font-size: 12px;
}
```

Removing the color specification for the `<p>` tag changes every instance of the text.

You should be getting a pretty good idea of how CSS control differs from HTML text control by now. It's time to roll up your sleeves and learn the techniques you require to use CSS.

Measuring the Difference Between CSS and HTML Control

Seeing the difference that using CSS control can make to a page can be hard. I have designed a visual representation of changing a font attribute with HTML or CSS control (4.3, 4.4). The first example represents a document constructed with HTML text control (4.3). The white squares represent content. The orange

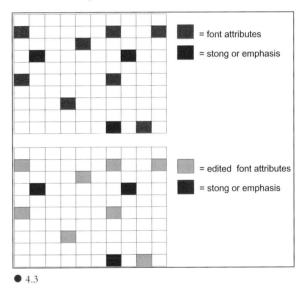

= font attributes

= stong or emphasis

= edited font attributes

= stong or emphasis

● 4.3

Eric Meyer
on CSS

Mastering the Language
of Web Design

was not even finalized at that time, but there was a short demonstration of CSS as part of the W3C track. After watching for just a few minutes, I remember thinking, "Wow! This is exactly what I've been waiting for." As soon as I got back home, I tore through the CSS1 specification and started trying to use it. Sadly my initial attempts at using CSS fell flat, so I created a test suite, arrogantly believing that the faults must lie with the browser, not my authoring. I shared the tests with the CSS Working Group, and then with Netscape and Microsoft, and used it to publish a small chart of CSS1 support in Macintosh Web browsers. That led to published articles and the Browser Style Compatibility Chart at WebReview.com, which in turn led to writing books and conference presentations of my own.

Q: Can we look forward to reliable standards for CSS across the industry in the foreseeable future?

A: That depends on what parts of CSS you are talking about. For type control, we are pretty much there. There are still some issues around font sizing, especially with

continued

squares represent embedded `<font>` tag entries. I have separated the `<strong>` (commonly known as bold) and `<em>` (commonly known as italic) tags, as they are applied in the same way no matter which font control you use. The lower example shows the `<font>` tag with a different color, indicating that a change to one of the attributes has taken place. Every tag has been selected and changed.

The next example illustrates the much simpler font attribute editing available with CSS control (4.4). The `<strong>` and `<em>` (emphasis) tags are the only tags embedded in the white content squares. To make a change in a font attribute, only one orange square is selected and changed. Not only is the time to make the change shorter, your chance for error is significantly reduced. In the CSS example, font attributes changes are accomplished away from document content. Most troubleshooting time is spent repairing code errors that occur when making changes within a document.

Adding CSS Styles to Web Pages

I've hammered at you with the concept of CSS to this point. Now you start to learn how to incorporate CSS control into your pages. I'll keep my explanations as simple as possible. Terminology for CSS can be overwhelming, and for text control purposes, covering every possible way CSS can be used is not necessary. I've used CSS text control since 1997, and concentrate on the CSS features that I use over and over. I would advise that you follow the CSS information in the order it is presented, as I take you through the easiest concepts first, and then onto more complex techniques. Understanding what a

class style is all about is hard when you don't have a firm grasp of defining an HTML style.

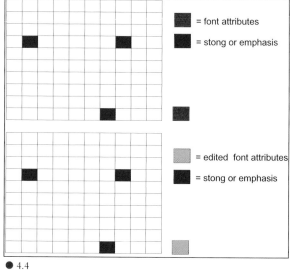

= font attributes

= stong or emphasis

= edited font attributes

= stong or emphasis

● 4.4

(continued)

relative font sizing and nested tables, which can create what I call the "incredible shrinking text." But we are really reaching consistency in that area. For positioning, it's not the same. If you are designing in a controlled environment, like an intranet site, go for it. But for the general Web, we are not there yet for positioning.

Q: Are there any CSS text properties that you recommend avoiding because of browser compatibility?

A: Small caps do not work consistently in browsers. It's still legible, but designers who use small caps are usually not the ones who want their text appearance to be unpredictable. Also, though it is not a property, designers should avoid using points to specify text size. Fixed-size fonts should always be set to pixel values.

The other text-styling property that deserves some caution is line-height. Type designers usually assume that a property called line-height must set the exact height of lines, which is certainly

understandable. However, in CSS line-height actually sets the minimum height of a line. Content like images or even superscripts can force a line to be taller than the value of line-height. This isn't a major problem, but it does lead to some angst, and there are proposals to address the issue in CSS3.

Q: Do you care to enter the raging pixel versus relative debate for CSS text control?

Placing CSS into a Document

You can add CSS control to your document in several ways. You can place CSS commands within the document, or in a separate file, depending on what you require for each page. I find that a simple linked file meets the need for most sites, but complex sites may be better served by importing the CSS control from various files. Requiring an embedded CSS style on a few pages in a site is not that unusual. Rarely, you may want to apply an inline style, meaning that you place the CSS style right within the code. I step you through each method to include CSS into a document, and list the benefits for each method.

Creating a Linked File

All CSS commands for a site can be contained in a simple text file, with your choice of filename, usually followed by a `.css` extension. CSS files are often edited in Windows Notepad, one of the simplest text editors in use today (4.5). This style sheet, `webnew.css`, is an actual file in use on one of my sites, but don't worry about what goes into the file just yet. You'll spend plenty of time learning what to put into a CSS file, but right now you're only concerned with connecting it to your document.

[N O T E]

You can create a CSS file in a text file, or an HTML editor like Dreamweaver MX, or you can use a dedicated CSS creation program like Bradbury's TopStyle. How you create the file does not matter. The linking concept and syntax is the same.

To tell the document to look to the file you created, you place a line of code between the `<head>` and `</head>` tags of the document with the path to the file and the filename. The browser reads this line of code and retrieves the CSS information contained in the file and applies it to the content for the entire page. Each page requires a link to the file. The code to place `webnew.css`, the file featured in the previous example (4.5), follows:

```
<link rel="stylesheet"
    href="/webnew.css">
```

This line of code tells the browser that there is a link to a CSS style sheet, in the same directory, with the name `webnew.css`. Yes, it is as simple as it looks. Any CSS styles contained in `webnew.css` will now be applied to the page containing the link to the file. (I've included an illustration of the

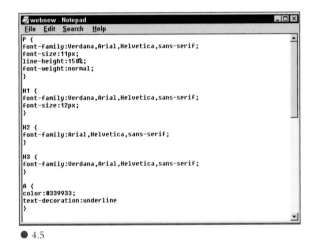

● 4.5

A: Sure! While it is great to have visitors control their text size by using relative font sizing, pixel fonts provide a more reliable, cross-browser experience. On the other hand, pixel fonts are not resizable in Explorer for Windows, which means that if the text is too small for users to read, they can't easily change it. As you can tell, I remain conflicted on this issue. On my personal site, I address this problem by sizing every style relatively, but setting my body text to 11 pixels. As an advanced

solution, you can allow visitors to choose a different style sheet, one that changes the basic body text size.

The best solution is that all browsers provide the option for visitors to adjust the type size, even when fixed-font sizes have been specified. That capability exists in most browsers now. Unfortunately, Internet Explorer for Windows does not provide the option to adjust pixel-sized text.

Q: Do you see common CSS errors when you are surfing the Web?

A: Most of the common errors I see could be caught by running the pages through a CSS validator (see links in the "When You Want More Than I Have Room to Give" sidebar later in this chapter). I run my CSS through a validator because it's easy to get lazy, but it's just as easy to miss a semicolon or make some other simple typographical error. Some browsers will

(continues)

process (4.6). The link to the CSS file in the document tells the browser to check the CSS file for formatting information. The information contained in the CSS file is sent to the browser, with the effects scattered through the page as required. The light green boxes represent where the attributes may be applied, but the CSS file remains independent of the HTML document.

[WARNING]

Don't try to make linking a CSS file, or placing CSS information into a document, harder than they are. These are the most common mistakes I have seen with beginners. After they get over the mystique around adding CSS to a document and realize that CSS concept really is very easy, they grasp the techniques immediately.

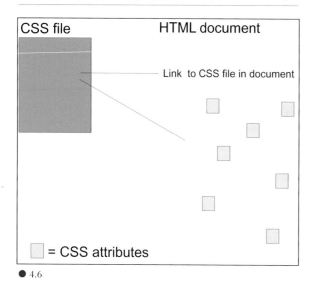

● 4.6

Creating a separate file is the most common method designers use to work with CSS styles. As much as I can in my work, I use only one CSS file per site, and place all my CSS formatting in that file. The sites I work on are usually mid-sized at best, and often have a unified appearance throughout. If you have a very large site, with varying requirements for a number of pages, or for different sections, the methods that follow can help you customize CSS control for your site.

Embedding CSS Styles in the Document

You can place CSS styles directly in the head of your HTML document. I don't recommend this method of including CSS commands, unless your site contains only one or two pages, or you want to include special styles for one page. Styles embedded into a document override styles in a linked CSS file. Although embedding your styles works every bit as well as a linked file for formatting your text, changes must be made on each individual page, rather than in one file as with a linked file. You lose the most powerful tool that CSS offers. However, in some cases you will want individual page control, so you should make sure you understand how to embed your CSS and how embedded styles format your page.

You list embedded styles between the `<head>` and `<head>` tags. You must let the HTML document know that CSS follows by specifying the style type as shown in the following statement:

```
<style type="text/css"></style>
```

You add comment tags to the statement to prevent the CSS information from being read by pre-CSS

(continued)

accept these errors and display correctly, which can make it tough to pick them up. The validator is there to make sure the CSS is right. A few common errors are: using an = (equal sign) for a : (colon) to separate properties and values, or leaving the units off a value, like 100 instead of 100px; leaving a space between values and units like 100 px instead of 100px; omitting the # (octothorpe) in HEX numbers; or using inconsistent cases for class and ID names, like having a rule that uses

`.MenuRed` and thinking it will apply to `class="menured"` in the text.

Q: Do you have any pet peeves with how CSS is used on Web sites?

A: I have two, although they are related. Some people believe that CSS will provide total control, and they work hard to take any control away from the reader. It's wiser to consider that CSS provides a very strong suggestion to a browser. If the reader can, and chooses to change that, why should anyone be upset?

The secondary pet peeve is people who create hugely complicated style sheets with tables inside tables, inside tables. Sometimes I wish I could, just once, gather all the Web developers in the world in one place, and try to explain what CSS is for.

Q: Do you EVER use the `<font>` tag?

A: Not since 1996. I never liked it and as soon as I had a better option with CSS, I never went back. I do use `<strong>` and `<em>`, because those are more structural in nature, but never the `<font>` tag.

(very, very old) browsers, which will just offer the statement in text on the screen. Although the chance of many visitors having browsers of that vintage is small, the solution is so simple that you should include it. The CSS statement now looks like the following: the area between the comment tags (<!-- and -->) is where your CSS styles are placed.

```
<style type="text/css">
   <!--
   -->
</style>
```

Finally, place your styles. In the following example, the <p> tag is defined in an embedded style.

```
<style type="text/css">
   <!--

p {
    font-family: Verdana, Arial,
     Helvetica, sans-serif;
    font-size: 11px;
}

   -->
</style>
```

In this example, only the <p> tag is defined, but you can include any number of CSS styles in an embedded style sheet. You may want to have the link colors changed on one page, or perhaps change the font size for one page to allow better layout for tabular data. In those cases, embedding the desired styles for one page will do the job.

In this illustration (4.7) you can see how the CSS styles are passed to the HTML document. Compare

this illustration to the previous illustration (4.6) to see how the information is passed to the HTML document in a different way.

Adding Inline CSS

You can also place CSS styles exactly where the style will be applied, in the HTML code. You need no information in the head of the document. Simply place the style within the tag to be affected, as shown in the following example:

```
<P style="font-size: 12px> The text
   you wish to affect. </P>
```

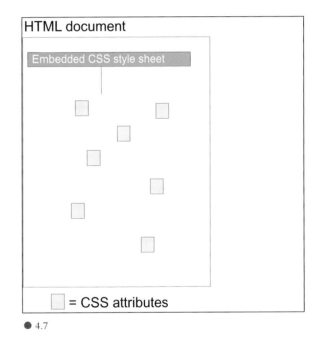

● 4.7

Occasionally, I will use an inline style for a single occurrence. CSS is just too compelling not to use it for formatting instead of relying on HTML-based hacks.

Q: In the experimental section of your site, I love the last line of the introductory paragraph: "It's a rejection of what's practical in favor of what's possible." Would you like to tell us a little about the exploration you are doing with this site (www.meyerweb.com/eric/css/edge/)?

A: The "complex spiral" demonstration was actually the beginning of css/edge. I was

in the thinking box (my stand-up shower) thinking of something to do with CSS; I can't remember what it was any longer. In one of those bolt-from-the-blue flashes you hear about, the idea for the complex spiral layout came to me almost exactly as it appears on the Web today, and I needed a place to try it, thinking there was no *way* it could actually work. Imagine my surprise when it did! That was when I decided I would create a place to try cool stuff, pushing the edge of CSS as hard as I could. I spend a lot of time teaching the basics, and that's certainly necessary, but I also want to move people out of a

mindset about limits. There's a tendency to think, "Well, we've figured out everything Web design can do, and there are things that just aren't possible." Rather than just learning to live within the limits, I'd like to see people taking the limits and going beyond them. So I started devising ways to flow text along curves, create translucent background effects, make elements appear and disappear without JavaScript, and more. That's the kind of thing I'm talking about, and it's what really interests me these days. Even after six years of working with CSS, it still has

continued

The text for the paragraph in this example will be only 12 pixels. Using an inline style is similar to using the `<font>` tag, except that you can apply attributes to text that are not available when using HTML. To edit the style, you must edit the actual code for that one attribute. You can't use an inline style on a different page, or even in a different location on the page, without entering the style again. With other methods, you lose both the editing ease and automatic consistency of CSS. All the cautions that come with the `<font>` tag, as I list in Chapter 3, "Working with HTML Text," apply to using inline styles for CSS. There is almost always a better way.

Check the illustration for a visual example of inline styles and how they work in a document (4.8). Note that the attributes are not coming from anywhere. Styles are placed every time they are used, and their role stops with the individual occurrence.

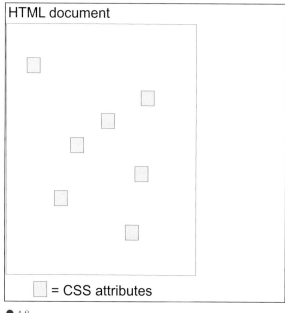

● 4.8

Importing CSS Style Sheets

I've left this method to the end of the list, partially because it can be very confusing if listed immediately following the linked file method. Also, support for imported CSS styles was the last method to be accepted by browsers, though if you're designing for version 4 and above browsers, as most designers do today, the method works well.

The basic idea behind imported styles is to allow flexibility with CSS styles on a site. You can combine many style sheets in one site, and import the appropriate sheet into each page. I strongly recommend that you have one main style sheet controlling the basic appearance of your text for each site. It is important that your visitors don't feel that they have somehow left your site. Changing all the parameters for text can leave that impression.

However, you may need different menu colors for each section in a site. Or, you may want your headline colors to change. You can handle all of these changes through a series of style sheets.

Just as an example, suppose you have all your basic text attributes defined in a file called `main.css`. You have three sections with a different color palette for menus, so you set up your menu attributes in three files: `blue.css`, `green.css`, and `orange.css`. In this case, you would import `main.css` into every page, and include `blue.css` for your blue menu sections, `green.css` for the green menu sections, and `orange.css` for the orange menu sections.

You can see a visual rendering of this process in this illustration (4.9). `main.css`, which is shown in brown, provides the basic formatting for the text on the three different pages shown. An additional CSS file is then imported into the matching document, controlling attributes that have been specified with that particular page, or section in mind. On each of the samples, I have placed one attribute of the second file color over one that was imported from `main.css`. Attributes that are specified from the first file imported will be overwritten if the second file imported contains a new definition for that attribute.

Implementing imported files requires a special reference, with comments, as required for embedded styles, which I talked about earlier in this chapter. For the blue page shown in the figure (4.9), the style sheets are imported with the following statement:

```
<style type="text/css">
   <!--
   @import url("/main.css");
   @import url("/blue.css");
   -->
</style>
```

Order is important. In this case, I want `blue.css` to override any attributes of `main.css` when both files specify the same attribute. Because `blue.css` is placed after `main.css`, it rules.

Determining Final Attributes

When specifying CSS style sheets in a document, a definite pecking order exists. Linked files lose out to imported files. Embedded files override imported styles. Finally, an inline style wins out over all else. I've prepared an illustration to show how the battle shakes out when four different types of CSS <p> styles are specified (4.10). An inline style always overrides other CSS. Victory is not total, however. HTML-specified styles beat out any CSS-specified style.

To simplify, I've placed the pecking order in list form, from the back of the line to the leader: linked, imported, embedded, inline, and HTML. In no way does that mean that HTML is more important. In fact, from a practical standpoint for working in CSS, the order of value in design is the exact opposite to this list. Some would argue that imported styles are the most versatile, but I am still happiest when I can control all the text on my site with one file.

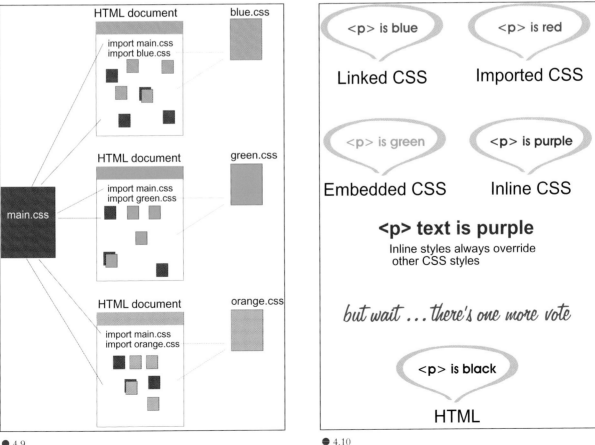

● 4.9

● 4.10

Introducing CSS Terminology

You now know how to get CSS style sheets into your documents, but I haven't touched on what goes into your style sheet. You should understand several points well before you move to creating a working style sheet. You may be tempted to jump in and just cut and paste code to create your sheets, but time spent understanding what CSS terms mean and how inheritance works will come back to you many times. I'll take you through the CSS that you need for great text on your pages. If you want more, see the sidebar "When You Want More Than I Have Room to Give."

On the positive side of ignoring much of what CSS has to offer, you can easily master all the text techniques that you need to create dynamic, professional pages. I'm confident that if you read Part II, "Controlling Web Type with Cascading Style Sheets (CSS)," of this book and practice what you have learned on a few pages, you will be very comfortable working with CSS.

With the explanations out of the way, I'll move into the heart of CSS text control.

Each CSS style is made up of three basic parts. In this section, I'll work step-by-step through the terminology for the following code (4.11). I've included labels for each of the three terms in this style.

Meeting the Key CSS Players

First, you must specify a *selector*, which makes sense, because you must tell the browser which element you want to affect. Any HTML element can be a selector. For example, if you want to define the type style for the entire document through the <body> tag, the selector is body.

Next, you must specify a *property*. The property describes the attribute you want to specify for the selector. In this example, I am working with the font-size property (4.11).

Finally, to complete this style, you must specify a *value* for the property. For text that is 11 pixels, the value is 11px.

[WARNING]

There should be *no* space between the value and the unit for that value. For example, `11px` is correct syntax for a CSS value. `11 px` is incorrect.

When You Want More Than I Have Room to Give

Hundreds of CSS specifications exist. In fact, one of the first blocks to learning CSS is facing a long list of terminology and rules, not understanding which are critical to working with CSS, and which you will likely never use. In this book, I concentrate on the CSS terms and methods you need to create exciting text on your pages, as well as great menus, plus I give you the tools to create pages with your own style. Many of the more obscure and advanced CSS terminology and methods do not come into my discussions.

You can easily become hooked on CSS, however, and I encourage you to use the work you do in this book as a solid start, and then delve deeper into the subject. To start your research, take a look at the many great Web sites with a wealth of information about CSS.

You can find a complete listing of CSS terminology, as well as a browser compatibility chart, and more at WebReview (www.webreview.com/style/). Eric Meyer, the name you see most often in the WebReview CSS pages, is featured in an interview earlier in this chapter. Also, the W3C site has many CSS tools, including listings of all terminology, a CSS FAQ page, and a CSS validator (www.w3.org/Style/CSS/). The CSShark site (www.mako4css.com/) provides terrific explanations in easy-to-understand language. WebReference.com takes a slightly different, common-sense approach, combining CSS and HTML in Stephanos Piperoglou's column, HTML with Style (http://webreference.com/html/).

Understanding Syntax

I admit that it took me a while to get used to CSS syntax and formatting. However, after I started to use it regularly, I understood why the code is presented as it is. So that you can focus on the code, I prepared an illustration of the code you saw in the previous sample (4.11), but with the selector, property, and value in a lighter color (4.12). Labeling text is in the same color as the related item.

Every style starts by naming the selector, followed by a { (opening or left brace, commonly known as a curly bracket). Conventional formatting places only the selector and the left brace on the first line.

WARNING

Although CSS will work if you don't follow standard formatting (syntax must be followed exactly, of course), I strongly recommend that you follow convention when creating CSS styles. After you have several defined styles in your style sheet, editing with the standard format is much easier.

On the next line, the property is stated, with a colon (:) separating the property and value. The final syntax is the semicolon (;), which signifies the end of a property declaration, and separates one property from the next.

[TIP]

Placing a semicolon (;) separator at the end of your property declarations, as well as between them, is good practice, as follows. The separators are marked in red.

```
body {
    font-size: 11px;
    font-family: Verdana, Arial,
    Helvetica, sans-serif;
    color: #333333;
}
```

Although the final separator is not necessary, it does no harm. Adding properties at another time is not unusual, and placing the separator guarantees that it will not be omitted when you edit the file.

Working with Inheritance in CSS

You now have the terminology and syntax that creates CSS styles. In the previous section, you learned how one CSS style sheet can override another. Inheritance is the final piece to the CSS puzzle. Elements in CSS can pass on attributes to other styles. This relationship is referred to as parent and child elements, and can add to consistency and save you time when creating style sheets.

Refer to the end of the previous section to view the style I presented to demonstrate the separators between properties. This style sets the overall text style for the document to be 11 px Verdana, and a dark gray color.

Text with the <p> tag applied will have the same attributes as defined in the <body> style. The <p> tag is a child of the <body> tag. Carry it one step further, and understand that the <strong> tag also inherits the attributes that I defined for the body tag. The <strong> tag is a child of the <p> tag. The <p> tag passes on the attributes it inherits from the <body> tag to the <strong> tag (4.13).

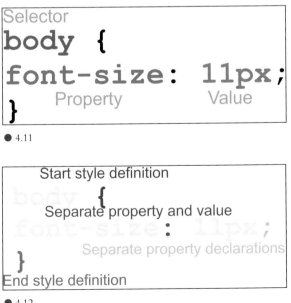

● 4.11

● 4.12

● 4.13

The CSS code that is described in the previous illustration (4.13) is shown here. The text appears red and bold when previewed (4.14).

```
body {
    font-family: Verdana, Arial,
    Helvetica, sans-serif; font-size:
    11px;
}

p {
    color: #000066;
}

strong {
    color: #FF0000;
}
```

[N O T E]

You can place the CSS styles shown here in a separate file, or embed them in the document as explained earlier in this chapter. There is no difference in the way the styles are defined no matter how you add the CSS to the document.

The following code creates the text shown in the previous sample (4.14). This clean, simple example shows how the content is separated from the formatting, one of the greatest benefits of CSS.

Text with no formatting will be black (default).

```
<p>When a paragraph style is added,
    the text is the same, but is now
    blue.</p>

<p>The strong tag applies bold to the
    text, and <strong>changes to
    red</strong>.
</p>
```

To illustrate the power of inheritance, I changed the font specification for the <body> tag to Georgia as shown in the code that follows. No other changes were made to any style (4.15). Changing the font for the <body> tag changed the font for the child tags (<p> and <strong>) automatically.

```
body {
    font-family: Georgia, "Times New
    Roman", Times, serif;
    font-size: 12px;
}
```

Accessibility and Browser Issues with CSS

With any Web development technique, you must consider how the method affects accessibility, and how the most common browsers will react to your pages if you include that technique. CSS is a good news story on both fronts. Display is quite consistent across popular browsers. Accessibility not only meets

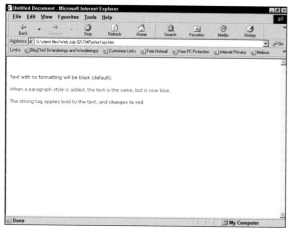

● 4.14

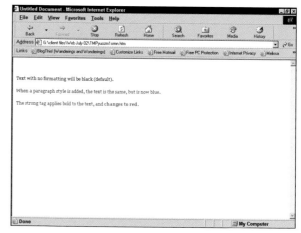

● 4.15

accessibility standards, it is the very method that allows much access through non-standard devices.

Keeping Up with Browser Standards

At one time, browser issues were a high priority for controlling text with CSS. One of the first CSS sites I created nearly made me certifiably insane. The site was an art-based site, and I decided to stretch my text design, and apply extra line spacing for the text. It looked great. Unfortunately, my images also were flying all over the page when I tested the work in one of the version 3 browsers. I pulled out a fair amount of hair trying to fix this problem.

Luckily, a woman on a design list heard my plea for help, and had experienced the same problem. Specifying line height in a linked file sent the images on the page helter-skelter across the page (I'm not talking just out of place a little — this was a jumble) in one version 3 browser. I confess that I didn't even look to CSS text control.

To correct the problem, I simply created an embedded style for the line height, and all was fine. That was CSS in the early days. It's a testament to how great a tool it is that so many designers stuck with it.

Today, most browsers in common use handle the CSS used for text control reliably. The most notable exception is Netscape version 4 browsers, which will not display a change on mouseover when the hover style is applied (you work with hover a lot in the next

chapter, "Creating Cascading Style Sheets"). This problem is not considered fatal, however, because the links still work, and the cursor does change to indicate a link. In almost all cases, when an effect doesn't work in CSS text control, your visitor can still use the site without problems.

The following examples show a page from my site, with fonts fully controlled with CSS, in Internet Explorer 6 (4.16), Netscape 4.5 (4.17), and Opera 5 (4.18). Almost no difference exists between these examples.

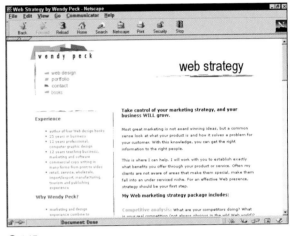

 4.17

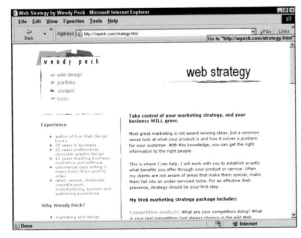

4.16

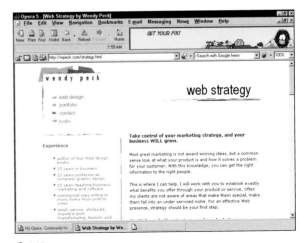

 4.18

Working with CSS to Reach Accessibility Goals

Picture someone surfing the Web using a special device because they have a vision impairment. One of the variety of reading software programs available reads the content to provide information to the visitor. The reading device depends on well-designed pages to discern the content that the user requires. Now that you're more familiar with the way that CSS works, think of a page with text controlled by CSS, and one that is controlled with HTML. There is simply no contest when it comes to how easily you can separate content from layout.

Accessibility standards call for CSS-controlled text. You don't have to do anything special with CSS to meet standards, with the exception of providing variable font size. That's one of the beautiful things about CSS. It works like a charm to save the designer work, and meets the needs of visitors at the same time.

Many people have some visual impairment — not enough to require a reading aid, but enough that much of the text on the Web is too hard to read. The ability to adjust text size is important to these visitors. Look at a page from my Web site displayed in Netscape 6 with default values (4.19), and the same page, but with text size set to 130% (4.20).

[N O T E]

Fixed versus variable font size is a raging debate. You hear more about this issue in the interview with Eric Meyer earlier in this chapter, and I cover it at length in the next chapter, "Creating Cascading Style Sheets." Some of you may have noticed that my examples so far feature fixed font size. I use it, but that doesn't mean I like it. Hold that thought until I have the opportunity explain.

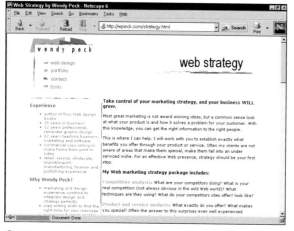

● 4.19

● 4.20

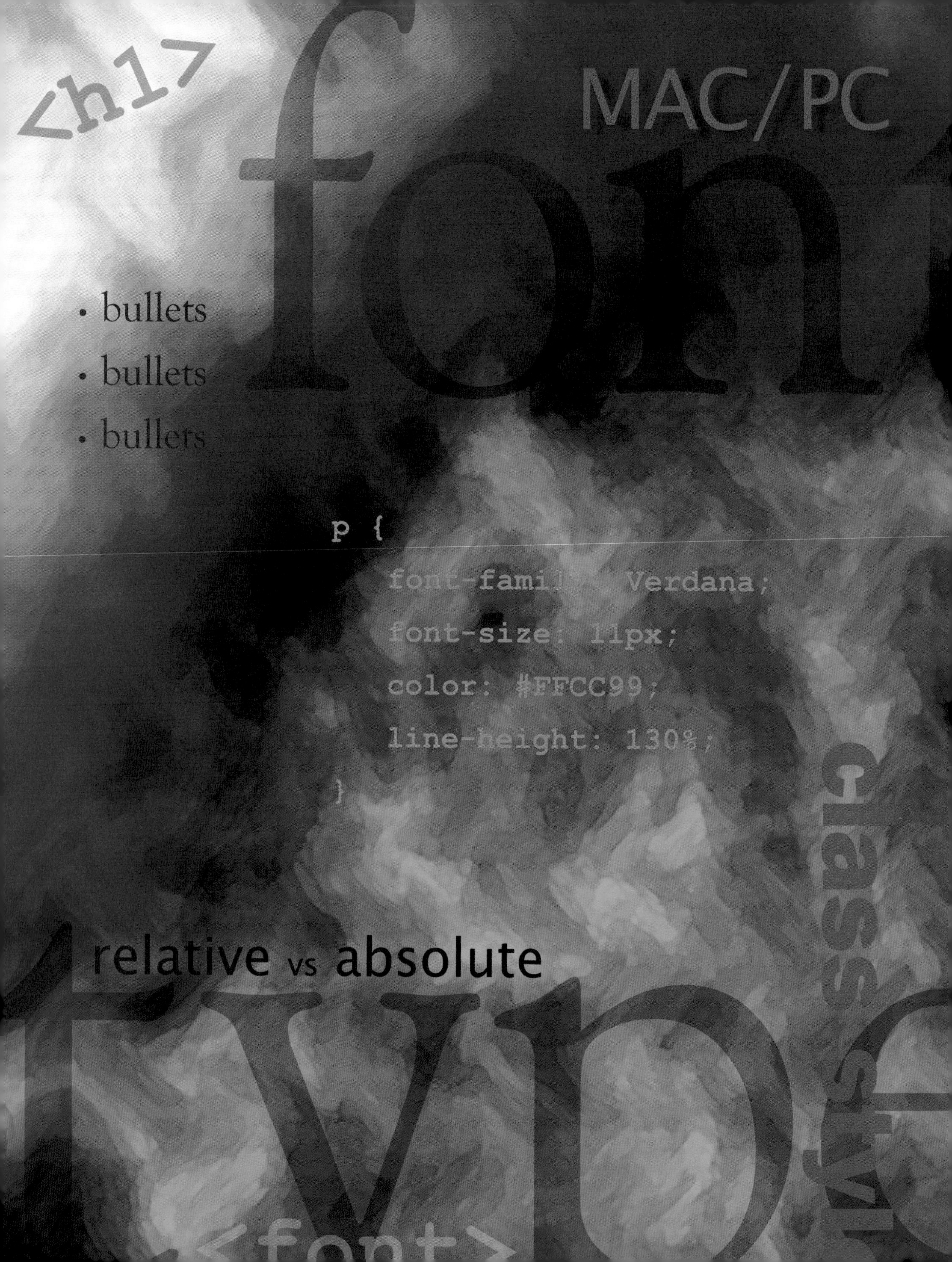
<h1>
MAC/PC
font
• bullets
• bullets
• bullets
p {
font-family: Verdana;
font-size: 11px;
color: #FFCC99;
line-height: 130%;
}
class
relative vs absolute
type
<font>

Chapter 5

Creating Cascading Style Sheets

I want to design a site that works for my clients and their visitors. I don't ever want to design for the sake of the design.

TRICIA MCGILLIS, MCGILLIS.COM

I think I'm pretty typical as a designer. The first thing I establish when I'm creating a site is how the fonts will look. Will I use Arial for headlines and Verdana for content text? Is the text black? What about the headlines? Black? Colored? What size? Subheadings get attention at this point as well.

You touched on the basic concepts and syntax of CSS in Chapter 4, "What Is CSS?." In this chapter, you roll up your sleeves and start producing CSS style sheets. You'll learn to control standard font specifications, and start to explore customized styles. I've also included exercises to introduce CSS production in Dreamweaver and TopStyle.

Selecting Font Properties

Designers often start with graphic representation of a page to establish the look and feel. However, you can have many false starts if you don't consider your text colors before a pixel of design is placed. Headlines usually look great wearing one of the main page colors. Subheads almost cry out for color treatment, making their point with color instead of size, and unifying the page appearance. However, unless you are testing how your page colors look as headlines, you may end up with a gorgeous design, but one that has no colors available for headlines or links.

Take a look at an interior page on IBM.com (5.1). Three colors of blue are used on this page, but note that only one is used as a text color. Blue is tough for text. All but dark blue tends to fade into the background. The blue text in the IBM page repeats the

color at the top right of the page, actually a blue-green. The added green, plus using a darker shade helps to define the characters. Note how much lighter the text color seems to be than the solid color in the heading. I've done a mockup of the IBM.com page shown earlier (5.2), but using the light blue found in the upper menu at the left as the link color. The text is barely visible.

● 5.1

IBM helps the United States Tennis Association (USTA) deliver the whole Grand Slam experience online. The official US Open Web site usopen.org is designed, built and hosted by IBM. The site can simultaneously provide huge numbers of fans with up-to-the-second match statistics, live radio and interviews. Using a combination of e-business infrastructure and an IBM e-business on demand solution, the USTA can scale up its technology to 50 times normal capacity to handle the massive demand for information during two critical weeks of the year and scale it down when the tournament has ended. In e-business, winning means delivering a tremendous overall experience, no matter where you are.

● 5.2

Notice the white text in the IBM.com page, as well. The lighter blues are used through the page, but with a reverse type/background setup. You can often include a color that is too light to be used as text by reversing the text and background colors.

I like what NPR has done on its page (5.3). The designer uses the blue from the logo to form headlines, which are also links. This setup is excellent for visitor recognition of news-type links. The color and underline style leave no doubt there is a link, yet the color ties in with the logo to present a consistent and unified page. Again note how much lighter the text appears to be than the solid color of the logo.

On this page, red is used only for rare highlights, and never for text. Red is a very loud color in text, and it would overwhelm the blue headline links. The gray and white text treatment is easy to read and again unifies the color flow of the page. As an example, and

proof positive that the NPR designer knows how to design a page, see what happens when I changed the left menu link color to red (5.4). The elegant side menu that once shared the stage perfectly with the news briefs now yells and screams for attention. Early text design is critical to the success of a page.

Selecting Font Size

Probably no CSS topic has had more discussion than font sizing. The first section of this topic addresses the controversy and explains the issues around the battle. With that out of the way, as much as it can be at this time, I show you some font/size samples, before you move on to specifying several font styles on a style sheet.

Absolute or Relative Font Sizing?

Okay, folks. I enticed Eric Meyer into commenting on this topic in Chapter 4, "What Is CSS?," perhaps hoping I could just say, "Whatever Eric says is fine with me." Then if the debate blew my way, I could

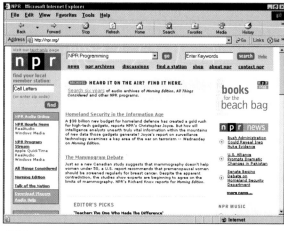
● 5.3

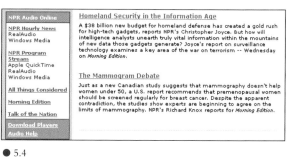
● 5.4

Behind the Scenes

Iromie Weeramantry for IBM.com: Pioneering Spirit and a Commitment to a Usable Web

IBM has taken a leadership role in the corporate Web world for many years. The commitment to accessibility and usability is evident in their site design, but also in the content the site offers for developers. The IBM.com site contains articles for Web developers and business owners to help make inclusive Web development choices. It's no accident that CSS plays a big role in IBM's goals. Iromie Weeramantry, who has worked for IBM since 1997, and is currently the Information Architecture Director for the

IBM.com site, takes us for a peek behind the scenes of this industry leader.

Q: What is your position with IBM? What is/has been your involvement with IBM.com?

A: I am currently Information Architecture Director for IBM.com Site Strategy and Standards and have also served in the capacity of Senior Creative Director for IBM.com. I lead a team of information architects and visual designers in developing the overall user experience strategy just blame him. However, that is not really my style, and because I agree with Eric, naturally, will toss my hat (on this issue, head may be a more fitting analogy) into the ring.

Why so much fuss? What the heck is the fuss? Let me describe the scene for you. Think back to dances when you were twelve or thirteen. All the boys on one side, and all the girls on the other. In this case, you have all the flexible-font people on one side, and all the fixed-font people on the other. The center of the floor is empty, because there is really no compromise position. The good news is that the center of the floor is no longer completely empty, thanks mainly to advancements in browser technology, and work by people like Eric Meyer.

Fixed fonts are specified in pixels, and set an absolute value for the browser to display text. Variable size fonts are specified in ems or percentages, or, for extreme relative evangelists, have no specified size.

Both sides have valid arguments. Relative fonts are the most inclusive. Nobody disputes that fact. If you specify no font sizing, or use relative, or flexible font sizing, the visitor has complete control of how the fonts display — assuming they know how to adjust the font size on their browser, that is, which is by no means 100 percent of the browsing population. The whole argument is based on choice so that legibility is as good as it can be.

The trouble is that default and relative sizing is at best unpredictable and certainly not exactly the same on every browser, and at worst, detrimental to the legibility of text. In Chapter 2, "Design Principles for Web Type," I discuss how line spacing and character size work together for legibility. Relative fonts can offer the worst to the large numbers of surfers who have no clue how to adjust font size in a browser. From a pure, inclusive argument, there is no doubt that visitors have more choice with relative sizing.

On the other side, you have fixed, well-behaved, controllable fonts. You can control the line spacing easily, and present a really pretty page that is the same for everyone. Hmmm. So, what's the downside? It's exactly what the upside is for relative fonts. Internet Explorer, any version, for the PC does not allow any resizing of absolute or fixed size fonts. There is no effect to resizing text size with a fixed font size in Internet Explorer. The first example (5.5) shows a page from my site at default text size, and the menu to adjust font size. Even when I select Largest for the text size (5.6), there is no difference between the pages.

● 5.5

pursued on IBM.com. We are responsible for navigation and visual design standards that are implemented on a worldwide basis. We act as consultants for internal IBM groups and guide the activities of several interactive agency partners.

In my five years at IBM, I have witnessed the centralization of Web functions across the company and the ensuing benefits: development of a single set of standards and consistent "look and feel," consolidation of content and functions on our Web pages and streamlining of Web-related production processes globally. All of the above have helped strengthen our digital brand and unify over two million Web pages.

Q: What led you to working on the IBM Web team?

A: A friend of mine persuaded me to interview at IBM, although I had reservations about working for such a large corporation. After the initial interview, however, I was captivated. This was 1997 and IBM was buzzing with excitement about the potential of the Web. I had been pursuing a career in design — advertising, editorial, multi-media that had evolved into Web design and art direction by 1995 and was working happily as Design Director for an interactive agency. IBM offered a new kind of challenge — on a larger scale than any previous endeavors. I started out as a Creative Director for the North America Internet Programs, then joined IBM.com eight months later.

Q: IBM has blazed a trail in corporate Web presence and goals rather than following existing practice. What is behind this attitude?

continued

The rest of the current browser crop allows text scaling, even for pixel-sized fonts. Internet Explorer for the Mac does have resizing, as does Netscape and Opera. Unfortunately, that one exception is a pretty big one. Even with conservative estimates, Internet Explorer for Windows is used by more than 80 percent of the market.

What's the answer? I don't have it. In the previous chapter, "What Is CSS?," I admitted that, while I use fixed fonts, I don't like the choice much. However, I dislike the other choice more. There is a movement now towards stopping the fight over which is best, and putting pressure on Microsoft to add adjusting fixed font size to the next version of Internet Explorer. That one move would instantly solve the problem.

I won't tell you what to do. Follow this issue, and maybe do a little lobbying yourself. Currently, most working designers are using fixed font size. It's our job to create a page that is legible and attractive, as well as consistent for visitors. Fixed size fonts is the only text control that guarantees these criteria now.

Selecting Font Face and Size

You don't have a lot of font choice in Web design. However, you must understand the strengths and weaknesses of the common Web-available fonts if you want to create great pages. I have already come down strongly in favor of sans-serif fonts for Web content. The clean lines of these fonts are easier on monitor-weary eyes. However, as in most things on the Web, you must consider many variables.

Headlines

I use Arial for headlines most of the time. It packs more tightly on the line, and displays as a unit better than Verdana for headlines. Compare Arial and Verdana in headlines (5.7).

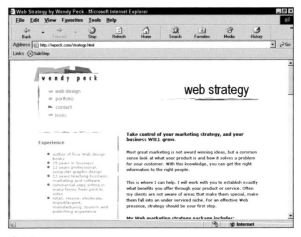

● 5.6

● 5.7

(continued)

A: Many factors contributed to this pioneering attitude including a great deal of vision on the part of both our early Web practitioners and our executives. We were always aware of our responsibility as a technology leader to lead the way in terms of corporate Web functionality and design and to reach our different audiences across the world. We had to address the challenges of scale including the need to embrace complexity while never losing sight of usability. And overall — IBM has a strong commitment to the Web as both a communications and sales channel.

Q: How large is the IBM design team? How does the team communicate and share work to achieve a unified result?

A: Approximately 40 people are involved in developing global user experience strategy, information architecture, and design, including a few extended team members in Europe, Asia, and Latin America. Together we communicate with Web counterparts in various worldwide divisions who promote our standards throughout their organizations. In addition, IBM.com account managers assist divisions with Web strategy issues and standards compliance issues.

At the heart of our unified presentation is an extensive set of IBM.com standards that cover visual design, navigation strategy, usability, accessibility, globalization, technical, writing, and other standards. New IBM sites are not deployed unless they adhere to these standards.

Q: IBM is a great resource for Web developers who are interested in creating visitor-centered sites. What drives this leadership role towards a useable Web?

A: The breadth of our offerings and the need to satisfy a range of worldwide users including people with a variety of

You can also use serif fonts, like Georgia and Times, quite successfully for headline text. Courier can add an artsy touch to headlines, and is easy to read at large sizes (5.8).

Comic Sans (5.9) is the only novelty font that is available on most computers.

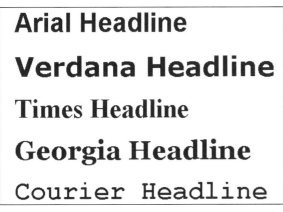

● 5.8

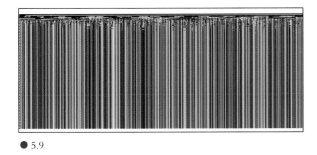

● 5.9

Mac and PC Type Size

Type displays at a different size on the Mac and PC platforms. Mac type displays at 72 ppi (pixels per inch) and PC computers display text at 96 ppi, which creates a difference in the way that visitors see type on the screen. Designers working on one platform should always test their pages on the opposite platform to ensure that their text can be easily read. Overall, text appears smaller on a Mac computer monitor.

Mac Designers: Default HTML type sizing creates the biggest problem for pages designed on a Mac and viewed on a PC. Default values for text look great on a Mac. However, the resulting text is difficult to read on a PC. The characters are large and line spacing is not sufficient to allow easy reading — a heads-up for Mac designers who have yet to see their work on a PC, especially those using default, or relative font sizing. Pixel sizing is the same on either platform. Also, don't forget that Internet Explorer users with a PC cannot resize their text.

PC Designers: Be very careful with small text. Because the Mac display for text is a little coarser, what will display on a PC monitor may completely break up on a Mac monitor. I'm not talking about being too small to read. I'm talking about pieces of the characters missing completely. Don't use any type size smaller than 9 point, or a percentage value less than 85% or you will be delivering incomplete characters to your Mac viewers.

---

disabilities drives us to create usable accessible Web pages.

Q: The IBM site uses CSS text for nearly every word on the site. Why?

A: Separating a document's content from its appearance affords many advantages in a large site such as ours. The benefits include precise control over layout, typography, and color, the ability to update the appearance and formatting of an unlimited number of pages by changing just one document, ease of maintenance, more efficient code, smaller pages, and lowered

production costs. Above all, it allows us to easily deploy standards and templates on a global basis thereby reinforcing the IBM.com digital brand identity.

As part of our standards, we require the use of a "template generator," developed by the IBM.com Corporate Webmaster Team, which creates our basic page design (universal masthead and customized left navigation bar) and places the appropriate IBM.com CSS in the HEAD section of the XHTML document.

Q: When did IBM move to CSS menus? Why?

A: Our first implementation of CSS took place on May 20th 2000 when we launched our v10 site redesign. CSS allowed us to have full control of all aspects of design. By applying a default font we guaranteed that all IBM.com pages would automatically use Arial in the content space. This eliminated the need to use `<font>` tags or CSS class references for our default font. This level of control was critical for IBM to achieve its "OneIBM" look and feel.

continued

[W A R N I N G]

Comic sans is available on most computers, and some Web designers do use it. I strongly recommend that you pass on this option, however. First, a page that looks good with Comic Sans is probably not going to look good with a different font, and not every computer has this font, or a defined substitute available. Second, although it has an attractive light feeling at first glance, over an entire site, it is hard to read, and does impart an amateur feeling to the pages.

Body Text

Verdana is my common choice for body text. This font was designed specifically for viewing on a monitor, and is more rounded, with fewer diagonal lines than Arial. Diagonal lines are often jagged on a monitor, because the resolution is just not fine enough to create a smooth diagonal line. Compare these two fonts to see the difference between them (5.10).

On the other hand, Arial at times fits the mood for the page more closely, especially if information is offered in small sections. A block of body text in Arial has more weight than the same block in Verdana, and if your page has strong design elements, you may find that Arial is a better choice. You can see how much more compact Arial is than Verdana (5.10).

The two serif fonts both have serious legibility problems. I put the labels for the fonts in Figure 5.10 in reverse type to show especially how cluttered the serif fonts can be. Also note the bold and italic samples in the text, as well as a link. I think if you compare all

the fonts in this way, it becomes immediately apparent that the serif fonts are weaker for legibility.

That's not to say you shouldn't use serif fonts. In Chapter 2, "Design Principles for Web Type," I explain why I used a serif font for my site on WebReference.com. *The New York Times* uses serif fonts successfully, maintaining the look of a traditional newspaper, while sneaking in sans-serif fonts for small text for legibility (5.11). The text is presented in short bursts on this page, and the underlined headlines give instant direction for how to see more on the story.

● 5.10

[dS.]   *(continued)*

Q: Has the use of CSS menus provided more flexibility for site features and additions?

A: Definitely, CSS allows for a more expandable design system in several ways:

Globalizing: Using external CSS's allows greater flexibility for supporting language-specific requirements. For example, if we need to increase the font sizes or change a specific style that affects only the IBM.com Japan Web site, we can make

these changes to our CSS's and affect all pages referencing them.

Adding new styles: When new style classes are added to our external CSS's they are automatically available to be used on the live site. There is no need to worry about the actual CSS coding. Only the class name and usage is required by Web developers.

Q: You use a 12-pixel font as the base font for the site. Why did you decide to go this route?

A: In order to support the various browsers, there are 4 CSS's, which are downloaded depending on which browser is used. The default stylesheet uses pixels since this allows our pages to render exactly the same way across the different browser platforms. One problem in using pixels is that on some browsers, font control is disabled. To work around this issue we have added additional stylesheets that are browser specific.

Next is an example of the font base that is applied depending on specific browser or system:

Web Fonts and Antialiasing

Web fonts don't have any antialiasing. Antialiasing blends edge pixels with the background color to trick the eye into seeing a smoother line. At content text sizing, the lack of antialiasing is a good thing. For headlines, your text can become noticeably jagged with large font sizes. The top example in the following figure (5.12) is an Arial headline in HTML text controlled by CSS. The lower example is the same size headline, but prepared in a graphic program that allows antialiasing, and imported as a GIF file.

Using <h> Styles

Every Web designer recognizes <h1> or <h2>. Almost everyone knows that these HTML styles are intended to be headlines. But not as many realize how significant these styles can be, and why using

them correctly is so important. The default appearance for <h1> and <h2> is as follows (5.13):

<h1> is known officially as a Level One Header. That sounds a little more impressive than "the big headline," right? Unfortunately, many designers treat the <h> family as if its role was to provide pre-set headline styles for design convenience. In fact, they should define the structure of your page.

<h1> headings should contain the most important heading for that page. I state this emphatically, not because I was raised to believe that the world is a better place with solid rules, but because of the search engines. Search engines give a higher mark to relevant words that they find enclosed in the <h1> tag than in an <h2> tag, which gets more attention than an <h3> tag, and so on. The poor <p> tag is definitely the "poor cousin" when it comes to respect from the search engine spiders.

● 5.11

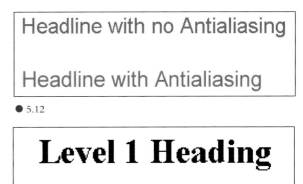

● 5.12

● 5.13

Font Base/ Browser

Percentage (%) / Internet Explorer on Windows

Points (pt) / Netscape 4.x on Windows

Pixels (px) / Netscape 6+, Opera, Internet Explorer with JavaScript disabled, Internet Explorer on Mac

Q: The IBM logo is perfect for optimizing on the Web with its horizontal color pattern. Was this accidental, or is this a special Web-perfect version of the corporate mark?

A: The current 8-bar, blue IBM logo was designed in 1972 by Paul Rand. It is a credit to the enduring quality of Rand's design that it remains the single enduring symbol in all expression of our brand, worldwide. Rand created a number of variations of the logo, including a variety of colors, artwork optimized for use in the negative (i.e., reversed out of a color/image background) and a 12-bar version for use in high-resolution print reproduction (i.e., engraved materials).

In the early 90s, IBM reduced the number of artwork variations used in order to achieve a single, bold presentation of our

brand identity. So today, only the blue 8-bar version is used. Also in the early 90s, special artwork of the IBM logo was optimized for use in low resolution or on-screen environments. To retain the highest level of reproduction quality of our trademark, we established a pixels-per-bar ratio. A limited number of IBM logo sizes were developed for use on-screen (1,2, 3 . . . pixels per bar). The 2-pixel version is most often used online, including in the IBM.com masthead. IBM.com works closely with IBM Corporate Identity & Design on all matters having to do with the display of the IBM logo.

Before you make plans to include every important keyword in an <h1> tag, slow down. The spider knows. Your visitors also must be able to make sense of your page structure; otherwise, what's the point in getting them there? Design your page with great structure, usually one headline, and maybe a few <h2> tags. Don't use more than three or four <h> tag styles, unless you are designing pages that call for an exceptional number of information categories (legal documents come to mind). This book has only three heading levels, and if you flip through, you will see that I don't use the smallest heading often. Take a look at a page from one of my sites (5.14). The headlines in the first content column are all <h1> headings. These listings tend to be about topics with great keywords. The headlines in the right column are <h2> headings. They identify the less important topics on each page.

With CSS, you choose the attributes each of the <h> styles will have. The same text and formatting as was shown with the default HTML values (5.13), is shown with styles set by CSS (5.15). Making the <h1> tag

more prominent than an <h2> tag makes sense because your visitors can figure out your page, but you don't feed the search engine spiders. The <h1> definition is what they seek. Search engines don't reward good looks or easy reading on a page — a fact that was no doubt evident from your first search.

Enhancing Type with CSS Control

To this point, I have been talking about text control that you could do with HTML controls. By now, if I've done my job, you should know that CSS is a better way to work, even if CSS only offered exactly what HTML control offers. However, that is not the case. CSS text control offers many decorative options that HTML just cannot match. Many of the techniques that follow are much more than just pretty additions. CSS type attributes provide you with powerful tools to enhance legibility and page organization.

Selecting Line Height

I have often mentioned the relationship between line spacing and legibility in this book. Font size is important, but the spacing between lines often has more effect on how easily your readers can absorb your message than the actual font face or font size (5.16). The font attributes in each example is identical, with the exception of the line spacing. Note how much easier the second and third samples are to read.

● 5.14

● 5.15

Verdana 11 px	You can read text much more easily if there is adequate line spacing. Your eye follows along the line of text, without the next line trying to take away the attention. Your page will also have a more relaxing feeling if there is space between lines. If you require an artistic look, using exaggerated line spacing can be very attractive.
Verdana 11 px 16 px line-space	You can read text much more easily if there is adequate line spacing. Your eye follows along the line of text, without the next line trying to take away the attention. Your page will also have a more relaxing feeling if there is space between lines. If you require an artistic look, using exaggerated line spacing can be very attractive.
Verdana 11 px 25 px line-space	You can read text much more easily if there is adequate line spacing. Your eye follows along the line of text, without the next line trying to take away the attention. Your page will also have a more relaxing feeling if there is space between lines. If you require an artistic look, using exaggerated line spacing can be very attractive.

● 5.16

Increasing line height helps with legibility, but it also reduces the number of lines of text that appear on the opening screen for your page. Just because a style looks great with 25-pixel spacing doesn't mean that it's appropriate for every setting. Keep your site purpose in mind, and if you have pages with lots of information, make sure that your line spacing, as well as the number of lines that fit on the page, fit. When your page contains three screens of information, increasing line spacing could add another screen full of information. Less scrolling is always better for the visitor, as long as the text is quite legible. Extra line spacing is critical for small and reversed type (5.17). Notice how much more legible the type is in the second sample, although only the line spacing has been changed.

[WARNING]

If you insist on using very tiny text, please at least increase the line spacing as a courtesy to your readers. Many of the most visually attractive sites use very small type, possibly because it is perceived to be more artistic. I have to admit that many of those sites are stunning, and larger text would not look quite as good, but always remember that the content is the reason for the site. Simply increasing line spacing helps visitors read the content more easily.

Setting the line height is easy. You simply add it as an attribute of the font, and set it as a value in pixels, or as a percentage of the line height. The code that follows shows a <p> tag with line height set to 130%.

```
p {
    font-family: Verdana, Arial,
     Helvetica, sans-serif;
    font-size: 11px;
```

● 5.17

```
    color: #FFCC99;
    line-height: 130%;
}
```

Underlining Text for Links

If this were a book about type for print, my strong exclamation would be, "Never use underlined text!" Underlined text is a hangover from typewriter days, and has no place in modern type presentation.

However, the Web is different. Underlining on a Web page is a universal symbol indicating that the underlined text provides a link. I believe that all content text links should be underlined. I don't care how many pages are out there with CSS-controlled links that are not underlined, I still believe you are harming the usability of your page if you don't use underlined text for your links.

Look quickly at the following two paragraphs (5.18) before you continue reading. These paragraphs are excerpts from a Web page.

● 5.18

How many links do you see on a fast glance? I'm confident that you will see three, and they will all be in the left column. That's because so many links are blue and underlined on the Web, that a visitor's brain sees the link and registers it without having to actually think about it.

[NOTE]

My strong beliefs about underlined links are for content text only. In the next chapter, "CSS Menus," I talk about CSS-controlled text menus, and recommend that you do not underline text in a menu. Links in a well-designed menu are obviously links, so you don't need to provide the visual underlining clue that is required in content text.

Using CSS, you can style a link to have any appearance, any color, and with backgrounds. You can have a background on link text, or a background on linked text when the mouse passes over (5.19).

[N O T E]

I discuss how to create backgrounds a little later in this section.

Although background styling for text links does stand out, it also seriously interrupts reading flow. Compare the text in the previous example (5.19), to the same text , but using underline styling for the text link, and adding a background for the mouseover styling on the link (5.20). The reading flow is not interrupted, yet the visitor knows there is a link. The background for mouseover does provide an excellent confirmation of the link.

[W A R N I N G]

The mouseover effect will not show in Netscape 4 version browsers. However, it does degrade well, as the link works, and visitors see the hand icon to indicate a link. Generally, CSS decorative style support is weak in Netscape version 4 browsers. If an effect is critical to the function of your page, make sure that you carefully test your pages in a Netscape 4 browser.

If you are interested in the beach and night life, we have it.

Enjoy solitude and nature? South Beach is perfect for you, and is where the artists are usually found.

● 5.19

If you are interested in the beach and night life, we have it.

Enjoy solitude and nature? South Beach is perfect for you, and is where the artists are usually found.

● 5.20

Using an underline style for links is quite simply the best way to provide your visitor with a map through your site. The method to create an underlined link is as easy as it can be. Just do nothing. The HTML default for linked text is underlining. However, as you will likely want to remove the underline in some cases, for menus, or on your mouseover styling, the following code shows an example of a link with and without underlining.

An underlined link with a specified color:

```
a:link {
    color: #0000FF;
}
```

The same style with underline removed:

```
a:link {
    color: #0000FF;
    text-decoration: none;
}
```

Using the Correct Order for Link Specification

The order in which you place the styles required for links in CSS does count. Remember from Chapter 4, "What Is CSS?," that CSS stands for Cascading Style Sheets, and the cascade in the title refers to which instructions the browser will observe. That cascade is important for links.

First, you specify your link attributes (a:link). All styles that follow inherit properties from the link, and you make only the changes that you require for the subsequent states. This link is blue and displays the HTML default underline style.

```
a:link {
    color: #0000FF;
}
```

The visited state (a:visited), or how the link appears when the visitor has already been to that link, comes next. You want this style to be placed at this point so that the mouseover attributes that you add next apply to both unvisited and visited links. In this case, a link that has been visited displays purple text.

```
a:visited {
    color: #660066;
}
```

Next in line to be added is the mouseover style (a:hover). This style, because it is placed in the style sheet after the link and visited styles, overrides any common attributes of those styles. That's what you want. In the following code, when the mouse passes over a link, the text changes color and shows a gray background and no underline.

```
a:hover {
    color: #FF0000;
    background-color: #CCCCCC;
    text-decoration: none;
}
```

Finally, you can specify an active link color (a:active). The text changes to the specified attributes when a visitor is actively clicking the link. For this example, the text color changes to a light gray, and the text background reverts to white.

```
a:active {
    color: #999999;
    background-color: #FFFFFF;
}
```

Make a note of the following code. As you move on to creating text menus with CSS, this basic pattern is critical. The combined code required to specify the links from this example is as follows:

```
a:link {
    color: #0000FF;
}

a:visited {
    color: #660066;
}

a:hover {
    color: #FF0000;
    background-color: #CCCCCC;
    text-decoration: none;
}

a:active {
    color: #999999;
    background-color: #FFFFFF;
}
```

Adding Bold or Italics to CSS Type

You can add bold and italics to your type with CSS in two ways. You can add the attributes to the actual styles, or you can add a <strong> tag for bold or an <em> tag for italics (emphasis) to individual words or phrases. Let the number of times the enhancement is required be your guide. If you need to add impact once or twice on a single page, using HTML tags is most often the most efficient way to add an attribute, especially because you can define the attributes that are used for the <strong> or <em> tags with CSS. However, if you're using a bold or italic style for repeated elements, like headlines or captions, creating a style and adding the attribute to the style is best.

[NOTE]

You learn how to create class styles in the next chapter, "CSS Menus." You can apply class styles to selected portions of an HTML block style. Don't worry if this sounds a little confusing. It all becomes clear in the next chapter. I just wanted to give you a heads-up if you were scratching your head wondering how you could apply a style to a selection of text.

Using the <strong> and <em> Tags with CSS

Adding the <strong> and <em> tags to your page is the same whether or not you use CSS. Place the tag at the beginning of the text you want to affect, and use a closing tag of </strong> or </em>. Unless you specify values for these tags with CSS, default values will display (5.21). The code that follows represents only the affected text.

```
<strong>bold</strong>
<em>italic</em>
```

Text that is placed between a <strong> and </strong> tag will appear as **bold** with default values. Text that is placed between an <em> and </em> tag displays as *italic* for the default value.

● 5.21

The previous code and effects sample should be familiar to anyone who has worked with HTML at all. However, with CSS, you get to decide how the text affected by the <strong> or <em> tags looks. To create a style, you simply specify either <strong> or <em> as the selector, and then list the parameters. In the following example, I have changed the color value for the <strong> tag to red, and the <em> tag to blue (5.22). The styles are defined as follows. The bold and italic attributes for this style come from the default HTML values, so you must specify only the color change.

```
strong {
    color: #FF0000;
}



em {
    color: #0000FF;
}
```

Creating Bold or Italic Type as Part of a Style

You can also add bold or italic attributes to your page by incorporating the attribute as part of any defined style. Add bold with the following code in a style:

```
selector {
    font-weight: bold;
}
```

Using Type Backgrounds

I touch on creating backgrounds in the previous section of this chapter, but you can do much more with backgrounds. However, after you move beyond highlighting text for links, using a background opens a whole new area of CSS, an area that does not exist with HTML. First, take a peek at the basic background color style. In this code, the background

color for whatever selector is chosen will have a light gray background (5.23).

```
selector {
    background-color: #CCCCCC;
}
```

[**WARNING**]

The term selector is used as a generic placeholder to represent any selector.

Can you see the problem from a design perspective? The background leaves no breathing space for the text. In order to add some space between the edge of the background and the text, you must add padding. Adding padding to the preceding style creates the following style (5.24):

```
selector {
    background-color: #CCCCCC;
    padding: 10px;
}
```

To take decorating text areas a little further, you can add a solid, dark gray border to a style with the following code (5.25):

```
selector {
    background-color: #CCCCCC;
    padding: 10px;
    border: 1px solid #333333;
}
```

You can place an automatic background behind text by assigning a background color to a style.

● 5.23

You can place an automatic background behind text by assigning a background color to a style.

● 5.24

You can place an automatic background behind text by assigning a background color to a style.

● 5.25

Text that is placed between a <strong> and </strong> tag will appear as **bold** with default values. Text that is placed between an <em> and </em> tag displays as *italic* for the default value.

● 5.22

You can set border style and width separately for the top, left, right, and bottom. The next example (5.26) shows a 1-pixel border on the top, left, and right, with a 5-pixel border at the bottom. The code to create this look is

```
selector {
    background-color: #CCCCCC;
    padding: 10px;
    border-top: 1px solid #333333;
    border-right: 1px solid #333333;
    border-bottom: 5px solid #333333;
    border-left: 1px solid #333333;
}
```

[T I P]

See all the possible attributes for CSS styles, including borders at the Web Design Group site at www.htmlhelp.com/reference/css/properties.html.

Finally, you can add an image as a background. The code that follows displays a colored background created with a GIF file (5.27). Note that the borders are the same as shown in the previous example (5.26).

```
.backone {
    padding: 10px;
    border-top: 1px solid #333333;
    border-right: 1px solid #333333;
    border-bottom: 5px solid #333333;
    border-left: 1px solid #333333;
    background-image:
     url(/art/5.back.gif);
    background-color: #99CCCC;
}
```

You can place an automatic background behind text by assigning a background color to a style.

● 5.26

You can place an automatic background behind text by assigning a background color to a style.

● 5.27

[W A R N I N G]

When you work with a background image specifying a background color that is similar to the image color is a good idea. Many people surf with images turned off, and if your text is meant to be read on a colored background, it may not be legible if the image doesn't show. A background color has no effect if the background image is displayed.

Creating CSS with Software Programs

Many excellent software programs exist today that can help to speed up the page-creation process. A few years ago, debates raged about the wisdom of using visual editors, like Dreamweaver. Many felt that hand-coding was the only way to create professional work.

What a difference a few years makes in this industry. Visual editors have become so good that they have been fully accepted into the professional design world. I think designers have also become much better at using the tools offered by a visual editor, and also take more responsibility to know the code behind the visual pages. When you work with CSS, you should also be able to read and troubleshoot the code, even if you're working with a visual editor. That's why I always discuss methods side by side with the code required, no matter how the actual page will be created.

Stand-alone products also exist for creating CSS files. One of the most popular programs, TopStyle, was designed by Nick Bradbury, creator of the well-known HTML editor, Homesite, (http://bradsoft.com). A program that is dedicated to CSS, it writes code for you, in correct syntax, but also presents all the choices. I believe it is an excellent way to learn CSS. If you have a good reference site bookmarked (see Chapter 4, "What Is CSS?"), or a comprehensive book on CSS at your side to check what each selector, property, or value can do for your text, working with a CSS editor can provide you with a map through CSS.

Creating CSS with Dreamweaver MX

You will probably intuitively know that I cannot possibly cover the entire subject of working with CSS in Dreamweaver in one small section of a chapter.

However, I wanted to demonstrate how to create a style and apply it to text in Dreamweaver so you connect the code techniques you have seen here if you're one of the many designers who use Dreamweaver to create your pages.

Adding CSS in Dreamweaver

You can create and link a CSS file in Dreamweaver easily:

1. With any document in a site open, or a new file that has been saved, choose Text ➪ CSS Styles ➪ Attach Style Sheet. The New Style Sheet window opens.

2. Choose Link or Import, depending on how you intend to use the file; see Chapter 3, "Working with HTML Text," for the difference between linking and importing files (5.28).

3. Click the Browse button, and navigate to where you want your style sheet to be saved.
   The Select Style Sheet window opens.

4. Select your CSS file, if you already have a style sheet. If you're creating a file, type in your desired filename in the File name field. Click OK. If you're creating a file, you will receive an alert asking whether you want to create the file. Click Yes (5.29).

5. Click OK again to return to your document.
   If you selected an existing CSS file, that file is now linked to your document. If you created a new file, a blank CSS file with your chosen name has been created, and linked to your document (5.32). You are ready to edit your styles.

To create an embedded style, follow these steps:

1. Choose Text ➪ CSS Styles ➪ New CSS Style. The New CSS Style window opens.

2. To create a <p> style, select Redefine HTML Tag from the Type list.

3. Type p or select p from the Tag drop-down menu.

4. Select This Document Only in the Define In list. Click OK. The CSS Style definition window for p opens. This is the main control panel for Dreamweaver CSS styles (5.30).

5. Select the attributes you desire for this style. The headings in the left menu change the choices displayed at the right. Make all choices for this style before clicking OK (5.31).

[T I P]

You can use the Apply button to show a preview of the effect in the document without closing the window, though much of the document is hidden behind the definition window.

6. When all attributes for your style are set, click OK. Your style is now embedded in the head of your document (5.32). The green highlighting shows the code created to link a CSS file to a document. The pink highlighting features an embedded CSS style.

Adding CSS Styles to a Dreamweaver Style Sheet

After you have a style sheet created, you can add as many styles as you want and edit the styles at any time. To add a style to an existing style sheet:

1. Choose Text ➪ CSS Styles ➪ Edit Style Sheet. The Edit Style Sheet window opens (5.33).

● 5.28

● 5.29

● 5.30

2. Click the New button to add a style to the style sheet. The New CSS Style window opens.

3. Select the tag that you would like to add. If you want to add to a linked file, make sure to select the filename for your CSS file from the Define In drop-down list. If you want to create an embedded style, select This Document Only. Click OK. The Define Styles window for that style opens.

4. Define your style. Click OK.

Editing a CSS Style in Dreamweaver

1. Choose Text ⇨ CSS Styles ⇨ Edit Style Sheet. The Edit Style Sheet window opens.

2. If you're editing a linked file, highlight the filename in the list. Click Edit (5.34)

   OR

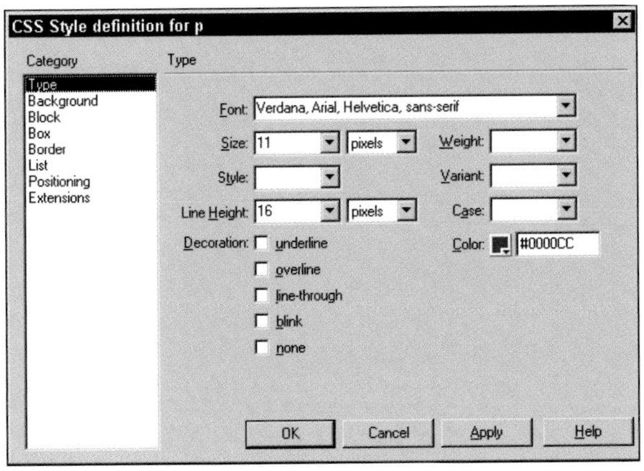

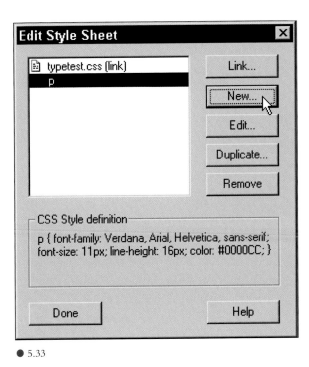

● 5.33

● 5.31

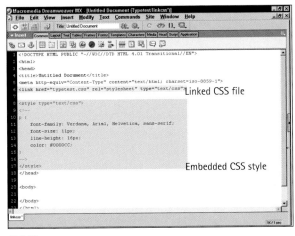

Linked CSS file

Embedded CSS style

● 5.32

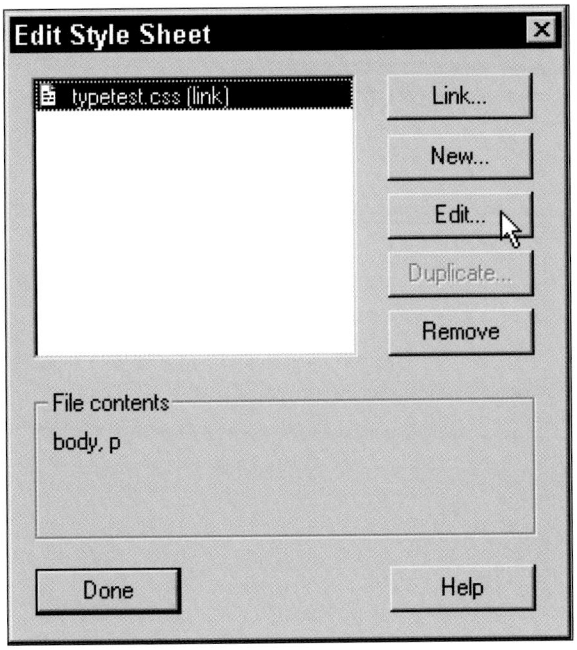

● 5.34

If you're editing an embedded style, highlight the style name and click Edit (5.35). The Define Styles window for that style opens. Skip to Step 4.

[T I P]

When a file is highlighted in the Edit Style Sheet window, the styles included in that file are listed in the File Content area. When a style is highlighted, the properties for that style are listed in the File Content window.

3. **Highlight the style you want to edit and click OK.**
    The Define Styles window for that style opens.

4. **Define your style. Click OK.**

Editing CSS with the Properties Panel

A new feature in Dreamweaver MX allows you to edit your CSS styles from the Properties panel. To the right of the Format list, you can click on the icon to toggle between HTML and CSS mode (5.36).

With the CSS option active in the Properties panel, you have instant access to creating a new style, editing a style, or attaching a CSS file. This route provides a quicker way to access the CSS tools, leading with one click to the methods described in the previous exercises.

[W A R N I N G]

Although you can edit HTML text with the Properties panel, let the icon that toggles between CSS and HTML act as a warning signal for you. There are very few good reasons to be using HTML mode. When you are switching to HTML mode, ask yourself why every time.

[N O T E]

CSS style editing is similar in Dreamweaver 4. However, there are notable differences. With Dreamweaver 4 you must create a blank text file with a .css extension before you can link a file. You must also use the menu route to edit CSS styles, because the Properties panel CSS editing was added with Dreamweaver MX.

Creating CSS with TopStyle

TopStyle is another software option for creating CSS styles. Many designers find that working with a dedicated CSS editor is much easier for complicated style sheets. You move on to creating class styles in the next chapter, "CSS Menus," as well as using CSS for menus, often with several different styles for each menu. Although what we have done to date has seemed fairly simple, when you build a style sheet for a large site, having your styles created in an editor that is watching for slipups or typos is convenient. TopStyle does watch your back as you build your style sheets.

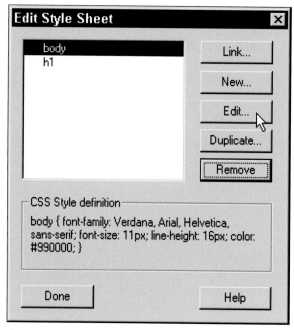

● 5.35

HTML mode

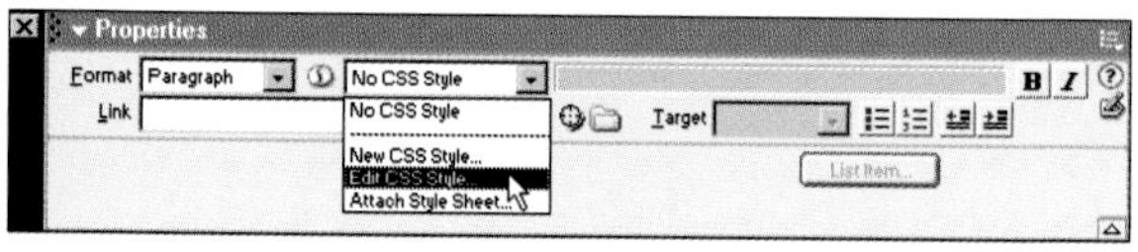

CSS mode

● 5.36

This section is meant only as a basic introduction to creating styles in a dedicated editor. This small tutorial barely scratches the surface of the program's capability. Please download the trial version (full-featured trial allowing 25 sessions) from `http://bradbury.com` and use this mini-tutorial as a starting point.

To create a style sheet in TopStyle, follow these steps:

1. With TopStyle open, choose File ⇨ New Style Sheet.

2. Click on the New CSS selector icon in the CSS Selectors panel at the left edge of the screen (5.37). The Selector Wizard window opens.

3. Click on the Simple tab at the top of the Selector Wizard window. The lower part of the screen changes to present the potential selectors in the simple category (5.38).

4. Highlight the body option from the Select an element list. Click the Add button to place the new style in the Current Selectors pane at the right of the screen (5.39).

5. Click OK. The main screen returns. The selector is placed in the document, with a drop-down list of properties for that selector visible (5.40). Click anywhere to make this drop-down menu disappear.

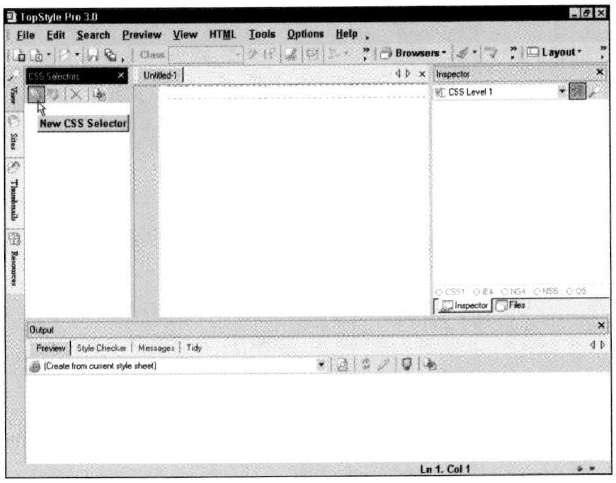

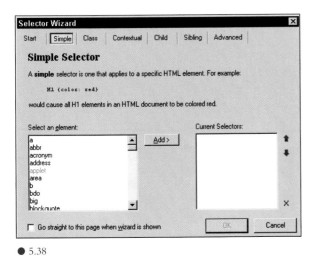

● 5.37

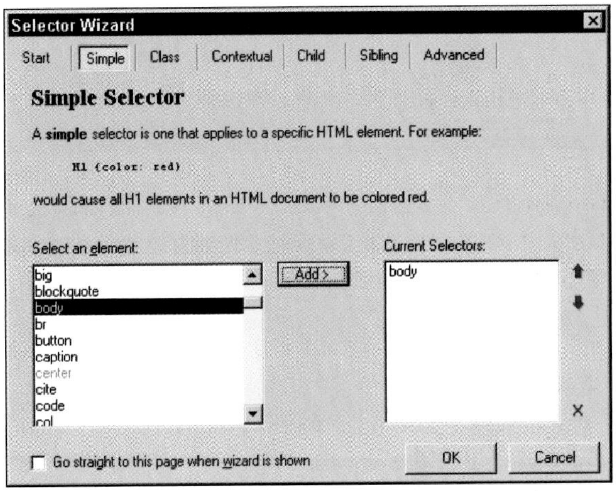

● 5.38

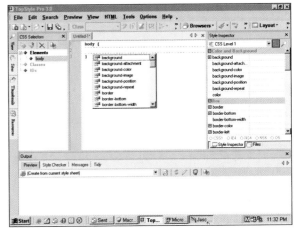

● 5.39

● 5.40

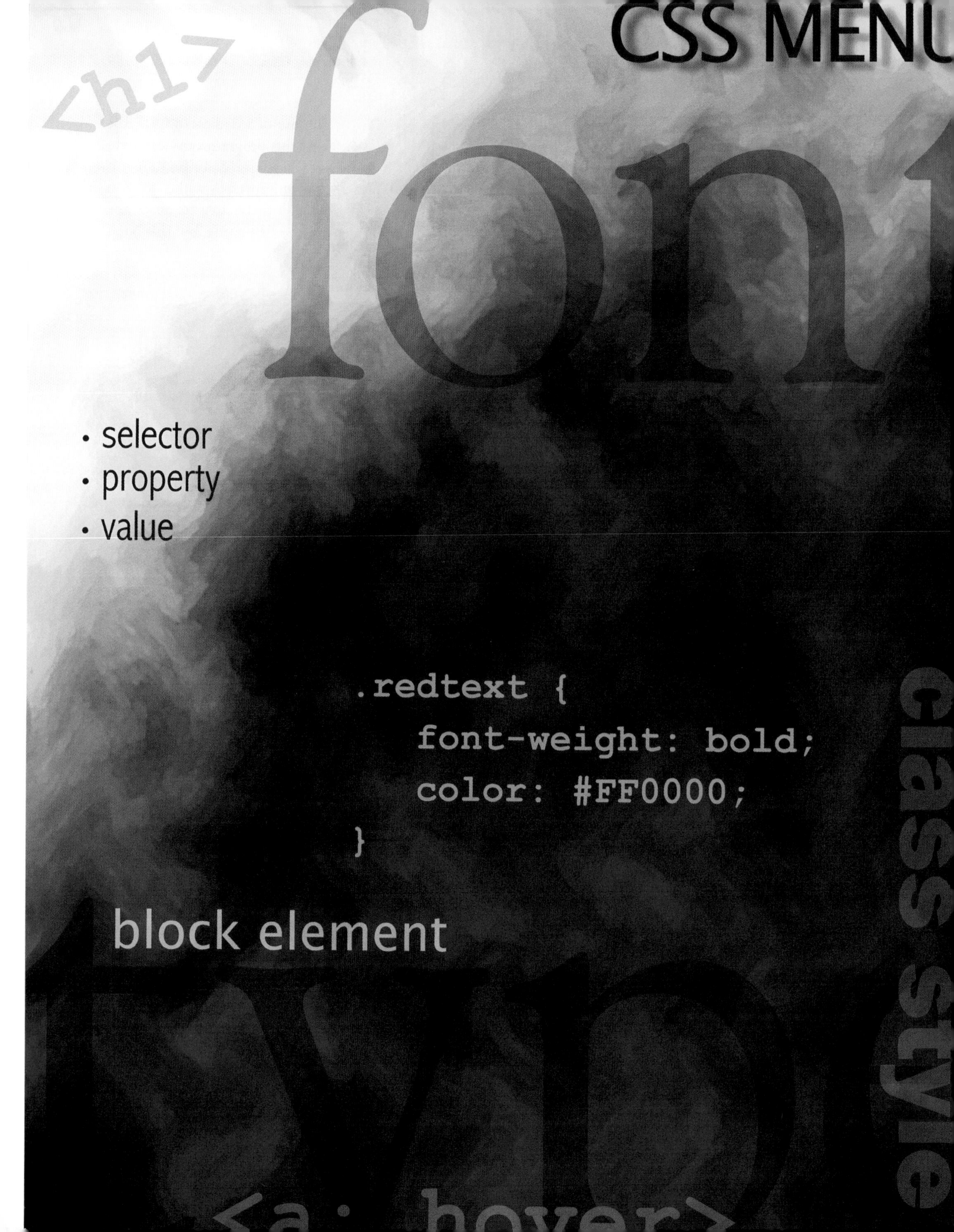

`<h1>`

- selector
- property
- value

```
.redtext {
    font-weight: bold;
    color: #FF0000;
}
```

block element

`<a: hover>`

Chapter 6

CSS Menus

Use CSS menus on just one site. I guarantee you will never look back. If you are looking for professional appearance, easy construction and maintenance, and great navigation for your site, CSS menus are the closest thing to a magic bullet that exists in the Web world.

WENDY PECK

I've brought you some solid reasons to use CSS for your content text in the previous chapters of this book. However, the best is yet to come. Putting the power of CSS to work creating menus is the wisest design decision you can make, for yourself and your visitors. In this chapter you learn how to use CSS techniques to create stylized menus with no graphic assistance. CSS menus offer fast download and exceptionally easy editing, and can be very attractive.

CSS and Menus: A Heavenly Match

The objections are probably already forming in your mind: "But you have to work with a tiny selection of fonts to use CSS-based menus?" True, but it's worth it. "But won't CSS menus look different on different monitors?" Yes, but it's worth it. "But don't I lose the opportunity to have pretty pictures in my menus with CSS menus?" Not completely; but anyway, it's worth it. The overriding theme here is "It's worth it!"

I don't intend to spend a lot of energy trying to explain why you should use CSS menus whenever

possible. I'm not alone in my belief that they are the best solution for most menus. Take a quick tour through the top sites on the Web, and I'm confident that you will find CSS-based menus on almost any that you seek. Try Google.com, with all-text menus, or Amazon.com, with all but the main menus controlled by CSS. IBM.com (6.1) features nothing but

 6.1

CSS menus through the site. FedEx.com (6.2) presents graphic menu tabs for the main menu, but CSS for every other menu item on the site. I don't know about you, but I'm happy to use the same techniques as some of the most innovative companies on the Web, especially when the technique provides faster menu creation and maintenance.

However, it's only fair that I present the pros and the cons for using CSS menus. As in everything bound for the Web, there are compromises. I don't use CSS menus for every menu I create, even today. In fact, my own site (wpeck.com) does not use CSS

for the main menu, although a text menu is at the bottom of each page. My site is very small, and exceedingly simple, with only the menus (6.3) and page titles providing visual interest. Part III, "Graphic Type for the Web," of this book is devoted to text created as a graphic, with a focus on menus. CSS is not the solution for every menu.

Why and Where to Use CSS Menus

Offering definitive "rules" of any type for Web menus is pretty tough. The subject is so complex that I have

● 6.2

● 6.3

---

dS.   **Behind the Scenes**

Eric Dunham and NPR:
Creating a Visitor-Driven Site

Eric Dunham knows the value of team-work. Leaving South Carolina with a Fine Arts degree, he made his way through work with an ad agency in Washington, D.C, and a stint with the Baltimore Museum of Art, before arriving at National Public Radio (NPR). He was hired originally to create button graphics, but by becoming friendly with the programmers, and learning about databases, he worked his way into more Web responsibility.

Today, Eric and Katherine Parker form the design team for the NPR site. Visitor value is top priority, and they do work with outside consultants to test and design the best possible architecture for NPR listeners. This team is driven by visitor feedback, and NPR listeners are a vocal crowd. According to Eric, "our listeners are loyal and very possessive about our service." When the team asks for feedback, they get it. Unsolicited e-mail is a constant report card for the Web team, and they track it carefully. It may be impossible to determine whether the visitors get what they require from the NPR site because

they are a vocal bunch, or if NPR visitors are a vocal bunch because the Web team listens. Whatever the reason, there is a lesson in the NPR experience for all designers.

Q: What is your role for the NPR Web site, and what was your route to working with the NPR Web site?

A: I've been the Senior Web Designer at NPR.org for 3½ years. I'm responsible for page designs, page graphics, interface designs, and online promotional materials. I came to NPR after building sites for other companies in the Baltimore/DC area.

written an entire book, *Web Menus with Beauty and Brains* (Wiley, 2002), devoted to the subject of creating menus. However, I do want to give you some guidelines to help you with your menu decisions.

CSS menus provide:

- Smaller page sizes than graphic menus
- Easy construction — just type after the CSS styles are in place
- Fast, easy editing — type in new menu items or delete unnecessary items as text
- Quick design changes — no saving new images
- Rollover effects with no JavaScript code required
- Dependable links
- A unified appearance because they mix well with content text
- "Food" for search engine spiders
- Recognition as links for visitors — not all graphic menus are obvious

CSS menus are perfect for:

- Menus where content changes frequently (news-based sites are an example)
- Sites where visitor feedback is monitored and changes are made on that basis
- Submenus on interior pages

- Main menus with medium-sized text
- Sites maintained by a team — no graphic files to share
- Sites with huge menus — download speed and editing savings multiply
- Sites that also contain mini-sites for special exhibitions, products, events, and so on
- Sites in testing phase

CSS menus should not be used for:

- Menus that require specific fonts to match corporate style
- Menus using novelty fonts
- Menus with large fonts (no antialiasing)
- Menus with tiny fonts (cannot use specialty fonts designed for tiny size)
- Sites that require special characters in menus
- Menus that require any typography control (kerning, varied character sizes, and so on)
- Varied color menus
- Sites that require menus to have graphics rollover effects
- Sites that must deliver text rollover effects in Netscape 4 version browsers

---

Q: What was the design team asked to accomplish for the NPR site?

A: The design "team" is very small: three to five core designers/programmers. The goals for the site are constantly evolving as we respond to user needs. Initially, the site was news focused. Based on user research, we've moved the design from being "today's news" focused to "content" focused. Recognizing the importance of good search functionality to Web users, we've been tasked with improving search results and search results display.

Q: Why did you decide to do your text control with CSS?

A: We implemented our first CSS with the last major redesign of the site (June '01). A team of writer/editors was being built to create expanded Web-only coverage of radio pieces. With a diverse group creating compelling content many times a day, a central stylesheet was the best route to providing a consistent user experience. For the next rev, we are planning even more layout control with CSS in addition to XML.

Q: Are there any features to the text presentation on the NPR site that should be noted?

A: We made a significant error in our CSS implementation that we plan to correct with the next major overhaul of the site: pixel based font-size properties. Some browsers cannot scale type with a pixel size specified by a stylesheet. A large percentage of our users are older and prefer a larger type size. We unwittingly did them a disservice by "locking" the font-size. On the other hand, we've used CSS

continued

Starting with CSS Menus

Here's the good news. If you have a simple page structure, and require the same color menu items as your links, you already learned all you need to know in Chapter 5, "Creating Cascading Style Sheets." Remember when you were learning to create link effects? They are the ticket to a simple CSS menu. It makes no difference whether text menus are presented horizontally (6.4) or vertically (6.5). That's a layout issue that I cover later in this chapter.

To create menu items as I have shown in 6.4 and 6.5, you simply type the menu titles that you require and assign a link. The code is very simple for the horizontal menu.

[N O T E]

I ignore the code for a vertical menu (6.5) until later in this chapter because the formatting for this layout is mixed with the menu items.

```
<a href="index.html">Home</a>
| <a href="prod.html">Products</a>
| <a href="warr.html">Warranty</a>
| <a href="inst.html">
   Installation</a>
| <a href="down.html">Download</a>
| <a href="contact.html">Contact</a>
```

I'm not making a great argument for CSS menus with the examples in 6.4 and 6.5, however. You can see that the links in the menu and the links in the

Home | Products | Warranty | Installation | Download | Contact

Indignor quicquam reprehendi, non quia crasse compositum illepedeve putetur, sed quia nuper, nec veniam antiquis, sed honorem et praemia posci. Recte necne crocum floresque perambulet Attae fabula si dubitem, clament periisse pudorem cuncti paene patres, ea cum reprehendere coner, quae gravis Aesopus, quae doctus Roscius egit; vel quia nil rectum, nisi quod placuit sibi, ducunt, vel quia turpe putant parere minoribus, et quae imberbes didicere senes.

● 6.4

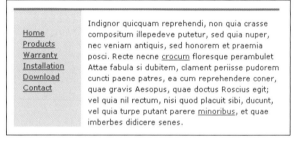

● 6.5

(continued)

text to replace a number of graphics with CSS text, improving site maintenence, site updating, and download times.

Q: Did the team hit any trouble spots with the design, and if so, how were they solved?

A: No significant trouble spots were encountered. We are always adding to and working on an internal list of site improvements based on user, business, and programming needs.

Q: I really like how easy it is to find information on your pages, even though there are many, many links. Can

you talk a little about how the information is presented and what the route was to this format?

A: We adhere to basic best practices for interface design while recognizing our unique position on the Web. Through user research, we found that, generally, our users map their experience of the radio to the Web site. This situation raises some interesting problems (time zones, local vs. national, brand blur, Member station sites and schedules) that a consistent, clear interface can solve.

The site has become more and more modular over time, which helps users quickly find information or parse chunks of the pages. Modularity is achieved by

standardizing the presentation of site elements. For example, a link to audio has its own icon and is placed at the top of an expanded coverage page. In addition, we have formats for particular types of content or features: search results look like program rundowns, which look like news items. This consistency gives the site modularity and improves the user experience: users become familiar with how the site operates across a variety of sections.

Q: How is the site content maintained?

A: There are a number of different types of content on the site. Audio, search, e-commerce, news, Web-only content, and expanded coverage are all handled by body copy are the same. Of course, they are, because the same CSS styles format all the links. Even if the color works for both menus and body copy, it is rare that the same link styles are best for both menus and body copy. I strongly recommend that links in content be underlined, yet menu links, especially in a vertical stack, are better without underlining for easy reading. That sounds like a contradiction to my hard-line "underline links" stance, but menus present themselves as links by formatting and position. I also don't have any color recommendation on menu text, other than it be easily read, and work with the page.

Defining Multiple Link Styles on a Page with Class Styles

Luckily, you have an easy way around links with different requirements on the same page using CSS. A special type of CSS style, called a class style, solves the problem. You create a uniquely named style and assign whatever attributes you desire, including link attributes. You can apply that special style to any selector, and when you use it for links, you have no limit to the number of different type link effects you can place in a page. This example page shows three different link styles and rollover effects all on one page. The rollover effect for the links in the top menu (6.6) and side menu (6.7) are controlled by class styles, named `.topmenu` and `.sidemenu`, respectively (I chose

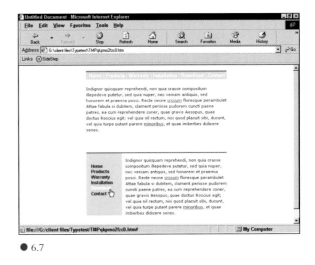

● 6.6

● 6.7

different systems. NPR.org's talented programmers are building a custom CMS that will bring the different types of content under one umbrella.

Q: How important is bandwidth, page download time, and so on, to the Web team at NPR?

A: We work hard to keep the pages small and minimize impact on the users' machines. However, our metrics show that a large percentage of our users access the site over a broadband connection, usually during work hours, which gives us some flexibility. The most important factor is metrics: page views, time on page, user paths, e-mailed stories, and so on. With

strong data, we can make informed decisions about what features need to be improved or highlighted. We also attempt to answer most user e-mail. User e-mail is very powerful for addressing problems with the site that may not have occurred to us or surfaced during user testing. It's also a wonderful tool for ideas!

Q: Is there anything you would like to add about the NPR site?

A: NPR is unique on the Web: It provides content that is deep and rich that listeners/users are passionate about. The audio content is wonderful to serve online: Users can listen while continuing to work, catch a story they missed on their

commute, e-mail links to their favorite stories to friends and family, and enjoy online-specific content that supports and extends their radio experience. Providing a positive user experience in that context is very rewarding for NPR.org's small, dedicated team.

Q: Do you have any tips to pass on about Web design?

A: Always remember the users. Know them, talk to them, and learn from them. Always remember the design community. Network and interact with your colleagues online and at conferences: take advantage of the medium by sharing ideas for creating the best user experience.

Blue, Underlined Links are Never Wrong

I talk in earlier chapters about why you should use underlining for links. Underlined text is an instant link flag for your visitor. As a surfer myself, I find it irritating when I have to use my mouse to see whether links exist, rather than having them presented clearly to me. Even with as much time as I spend on the Web, I'm never sure whether a colored, boldface word in text is highlighted for emphasis, or is a link. The only way I can tell is to move my mouse over the link and see whether I either receive the hand icon indicating a link, or have another mouseover effect signal the link. That uncertainty is frustrating for visitors. Please underline your links. If you have too many links in your copy, and the underlining is distracting from easy reading, perhaps your page would be improved by adding a small menu to direct traffic.

The issue of whether to use blue or not is a little less critical, in my opinion. If you have underlined links, and there is just no way that blue looks good with your body text, then using another color for your links sometimes makes sense. However, and this is a big however, you *are* reducing your visitor's instant recognition of your links. Many blues are available, even within the Web-safe palette. I've not yet designed a site that doesn't work with blue links. The links are not always bright blue. Some sites have blue-gray links, and others feature a blue-green. Finding a blue that works for your site is worth it. You have enough ways to inadvertently slow your visitor's progress through your pages. Why gamble with one of the few truly predictable visitor behaviors?

If you use links without underlining, and a different color than blue — and some of you are not going to like this next statement — you are clearly putting your design entertainment ahead of your visitor's needs. If you are designing a site for your own pleasure, that is acceptable. If you are creating a site that depends on visitors, do so at your peril. Remember, your visitors have the power of the mouse. They can and *will* use that power to leave a site that is even slightly confusing to navigate.

the names). The body copy rollover effect (6.8) comes from the definitions for the default link definition (`a:link`) in the style sheet.

Creating the various states for a menu link style is exactly the same as creating states for the default link style, which you learned in Chapter 5, "Creating Cascading Style Sheets," with one exception. You must first name a class style. You can call the class anything, but using meaningful names makes future editing

much easier. This is not the place to be creative, however. I usually name my styles with literary gems like `topmenu`, `rightmenu`, and `servicemenu`. Resist using mixed-case names (see nearby sidebar on naming styles).

If you worry that you may have trouble identifying a style in the future, you can use a comment within the style to jog your memory. Use the following syntax to include a comment in your style sheet:

```
/* Type any comment here. */
```

Class styles always start with a period (.). A style you want to name topmenu appears in a style sheet as a selector called `.topmenu`. Styles for a menu named `leftmenu` are defined `.leftmenu`. The basic syntax for a style called `topmenu` follows:

```
.topmenu {
    property: value
}
```

I want you to ignore that class styles are often used for menus for a few minutes. Look at the following defined style:

```
.redtext {
    font-weight: bold;
    color: #FF0000;
}
```

If this style is called in your document, the text that is affected by the style will be displayed in boldface and red. The following code displays a portion of the paragraph in red, boldface text, as defined by the CSS style shown in the previous example (6.9). Attributes that are not specified in the class style are inherited from parent tags, in this case <p>.

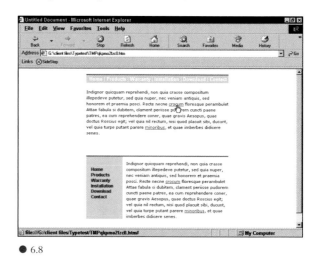

● 6.8

Naming Styles

Eric Meyer, the CSS expert featured in an interview in Chapter 4, "What Is CSS?," lists mixed-case style names, and including illegal characters in style names as one of the common errors he sees on Web sites. He advises using lowercase names for styles you create and name, and understanding which characters can be used. (See www.w3.org/TR/REC-CSS2/syndata.html#q4 for the rules on characters and recommendations on style name case.)

Many designers use class style names like `TopMenu` or `LeftMenu` to make their code easier to read, but this practice is not good. A class style named `topmenu` will always be acceptable. `TopMenu` may cause problems in some documents.

CSS is not case-sensitive, but documents using CSS may be case-sensitive. In particular, although class names are not case sensitive for HTML documents, they are for XML documents. You simply cannot go wrong by using all lowercase names, with no characters other than A–Z and 0–9 in your style names.

```
<p>
You can apply a group of text
    attributes, <span
    class="redtext">as
defined in the CSS class
    style</span>, to any portion of
    text on the page.
Simply enclose that text you wish to
    affect within a style.
</p>
```

In this case, the class style is applied to the `<span>` tag (6.9). This tag allows you to enclose only the text that you want to affect, not an entire block, as with `<p>` or `<h?>` tags.

You can apply a class style to any selector, however. Suppose you wanted this entire paragraph to be formatted with the class style. The following code applies the class style to the entire first paragraph (6.10). The second paragraph has no class style applied, so it is displayed with the defined paragraph attributes.

Specify a class style and you can apply a sets of text attributes, **as defined in a CSS style**, to any portion of text on the page. Simply enclose that text you wish to affect within a style.

6.9

```
<p class="redtext">If you apply a
    class style to a block element,
    like
the paragraph tag, the entire block
    is affected.</p>

<p>This paragraph does not have the
    class style applied, so follows
    the
defined paragraph style.</p>
```

Defining Link Attributes for Class Styles

I hope that your design mind is racing with the possibilities if you have just been introduced to class styles. But remember that you have a lot of design power for menus when you assign link attributes to a class style. This method is how I managed to create the document with three different link definitions that you saw earlier in this chapter (6.6, 6.7, 6.8).

In this section, I step you through creating link styles for three distinct menu styles (6.11). You'll learn to create a simple horizontal menu, a menu

If you apply a class style to a block element, like the paragraph tag, the entire block is affected.

This paragraph does not have the class style applied, so follows the defined paragraph style.

6.10

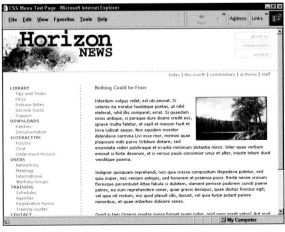
6.11

with decorative border styling, and one that is formatted using a table. These menus can form patterns that you can use for any menu.

First, here is the complete code for a very simple class style named `simple.`, with link attributes (6.12). You can refer to this basic example if you get confused when the number of attributes grow in the more stylized menus.

```
.simple {
    font-family: Arial, Helvetica,
     sans-serif;
    font-size: 12px;
    font-weight: bold;
    color: #003300;
}


.simple a:link {
    color: #006633;
    text-decoration: none;
}


.simple a:visited {
    color: #CCCC99;
    text-decoration: none;
}


.simple a:hover {
    color: #996633;
}
```

[T I P]

The style .simple displays where there is no link in your menu. When you create a menu, most text will be a link, and is controlled by the link styling for the class style. However, the original class style controls the dividing characters between menu items, or headlines that are used to divide menu categories but are not links themselves. You can work with this feature to add extra design savvy to your menus.

home | products | services | contact

● 6.12

Block and Inline Elements with Class Styles

Block elements are HTML elements that have line breaks, including <p>, <h?>, <li>, <table>, and <form> to name just a few.

Inline elements do not have line breaks, and include <strong>, <em>, and <span>.

You can apply class styles to both block and inline elements, and you can use inline elements within block elements. For example, you can enclose any text within a paragraph or table (block elements) with a <span> tag (inline element), and apply a CSS style to the <span> tag. The class style affects only the text between the <span> and </span> tags.

On the other hand, applying a class style to a <p> or <table> tag affects the entire paragraph or table. All text within a paragraph controlled by <p class="redtext"> displays both the <p> tag attributes and the attributes defined in the class style. The styles in the class style override any attributes it shares with the <p> tag.

How do you decide where the class style should be applied? Try to place class styles as high in the layout order of the page as possible to reduce the code required. In other words, use a block element rather than an inline element whenever you can. If all text within a table should have the class style applied, include the class style with the <table> tag, <table class="redtext">. If only a table cell requires the class style, which is common for menu application, apply the class style to the <td> tag, <td class="redtext">.

After you're comfortable with creating a simple class style, and specifying link styles to go with that style, you can move on to using the power of CSS decorative features. This sample page (6.11) contains four separate menus. You cannot see a text menu at the bottom of the page. That menu is controlled by the page link attributes that you learned to create in Chapter 5, "Creating Cascading Style Sheets." In this section, I show you how to create the other three menus on the page.

[N O T E]

Each of you create your CSS in a different way, some with a text editor, some with an on-board visual editor

CSS creation, and others with dedicated programs like TopStyle. I step you through the process with descriptive passages for why and how a technique is done, along with the pure CSS code that is required for that effect.

The main menu (6.13) runs horizontally. This menu is quite simple with a class style applied to the table cell containing the menu, and the dotted line specified as part of the style.

The long side menu at the left edge of the page (6.14) is formatted in a table, with the class style controlling the links. The dotted line to the right of the menu is controlled by this style.

Finally, the upper-right menu (6.15) is created fully with CSS. Class styles containing all the border, margin, and font information are applied to <p> tags to form the individual boxes containing the links.

To give you an idea of how the page is laid out, I created a sample with table borders applied (6.16). The purple border represents the main table for the page. This table has no cell padding or spacing, and provides the overall layout for the page. In the sample shown here, I reduced the table size to 90% from 100% to make the borders easier to see. Note that a cell that spans two cells holds the main menu so that the CSS style in the menu (dotted line) stretches across the page.

The yellow table provides column layout and padding for the content area of the page. Note that the dotted line is contained within the left column, as it is added through the CSS for that cell. These layout tables are the only ones on the page, although the left menu is formatted with a table.

The margin for the page is set to zero through the CSS margin style.

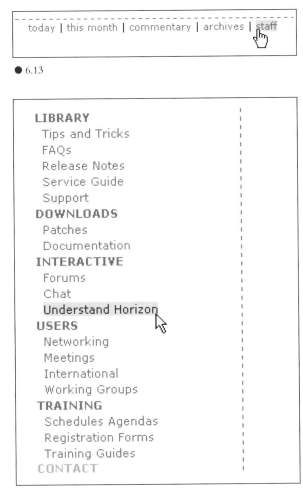

● 6.13

● 6.14

● 6.15

● 6.16

Any

In this view, you can see the text menu at the bottom of the page.

If you want to create this page exactly as I have done, you must add the following CSS styles to your style sheet before you begin to create the menus:

```
body {
    margin: 0;
    padding: 0;
}


p {
    font-size: 11px;
    font-family: Verdana, Arial,
     Helvetica, sans-serif;
    line-height: 150%;
}


h1 {
    font-size: 120%;
    font-family: Arial, Helvetica,
     sans-serif;
    color: #336699;
}


a:link {
    color: #336699;
}


a:visited {
    color: #660033;
}


a:hover {
    color: #000000;
}
```

You can find the HTML code for this page, as well as the completed CSS style sheet in Appendix C, "Chapter 6 HTML Code and Style Sheet."

Creating the Basic Main Menu Style

The main menu is placed in a two-cell span to allow the dotted line to stretch across the page. Text is

typed into the spanned cells, with the cell alignment set to right.

1. **Enter the text for the menu and assign links using the following code:**

```
<a href="today.html">today</a> |
<a href="month.html">this month</a> |
<a ref="comment.html">commentary
    </a> |
<a href="archives.html">archives
    </a> |
<a href="staff.html">staff</a>
```

There is a space following the | character in the previous code.

Your text should be at the right edge of the page (6.17) and have the properties of the `a:link` style for the page. At this point, you have not added any style to the menu, so it is picking up the default values, which includes underlining for links.

2. **Create a class style named** `main menu` **and assign the following values:**

```
.mainmenu {
    font-family: Verdana, Arial,
     Helvetica, sans-serif;
    font-size: 11px;
    color: #000066;
}
```

This code sets the color and font for the style, but adds no styling. Before you address any link attributes, having your menu format in place is

● 6.17

a good idea, so you can see the total effect of the menu as you add effects. In this case, you must add a dotted border above the text, and move the menu away from the margin.

3. **To add the style to the table cell, add the class style to the** `<td>` **tag as follows:**

```
<td class="mainmenu">
```

There will be table formatting attributes already in the `<td>` tag. It doesn't matter where the `class="mainmenu"` goes, as long as it is enclosed in the `<td>` tag. The `mainmenu` class style now controls your menu text.

[T I P]

CSS provides both margin and padding settings for any style. The best way to become familiar with these attributes, and how they interact with borders and background, is to devote some time to playing. I was having a hard time remembering what did what with CSS decorative attributes from the time I created one style sheet to the next. Finally, I spent almost an entire afternoon specifying and previewing backgrounds, various borders, padding, margins, and so on. I tested every "what if" I could imagine. That short timeout from building active CSS style sheets has paid off many times over.

4. **Because you want the style to display right to the edge of the page (remember the dotted line), but want the text to end before the end of the style, padding is the correct attribute to adjust in this case. Add the following value to your** `mainmenu` **class style:**

```
padding-right: 20px;
```

The text has now moved away from the right margin (6.18).

5. **Use the border attribute to create the dotted line. Add the following code to your** `mainmenu` **style:**

```
border-top-width: 1px;
   border-top-style: dotted;
   border-top-color: #666666;
```

These attributes add a gray dotted line 1-pixel wide along the top border of your style (6.19).

6. **The line style is starting to shape up, but the border is a little too close to the text in the menu. Add a little white space by specifying a 2-pixel padding value for the top of the style as follows:**

```
padding-top: 2px;
```

It's amazing what a couple of pixels can do. Your `mainmenu` basic style is complete (6.20).

Adding Link Attributes to the Main Menu

The basic style for your main menu is in place, so now is the time to set the attributes for your links. Nothing in the styling you added in the previous exercise is meant to change as the menu is used. You can let the values from the basic `mainmenu` class style provide the setting for the text, and simply specify the values you want to have for links and mouseovers and to mark pages that have been visited.

● 6.18

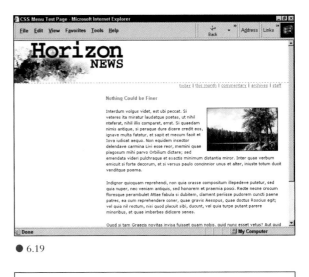

● 6.19

● 6.20

Add the following styles to your `mainmenu` style sheet.

1. **Set your link colors by adding an** `a:link` **style to the** `mainmenu` **class style. The following code removes the underline from links and sets the color (6.21):**

```
.mainmenu a:link {
   color: #336699;
   text-decoration: none;
}
```

2. **Set the specifications for how the links will display when the visitor has already visited the page for that link, in this case as a medium gray (6.22):**

```
.mainmenu a:visited {
   color: #999999;
   text-decoration: none;
}
```

[**W A R N I N G**]

You must visit the linked page and return to the page you are previewing in order to see the visited style in action.

3. **Finally, you can include a mouseover effect for your menu links. Adding a background to a mouseover effect delivers a very clear message that the text is a link, as well as marking clearly which link is highlighted. Add a background as well as confirm the text color for a mouseover effect by adding the following code:**

```
.mainmenu a:hover {
   color: #336699;
   background-color: #CCCCCC;
}
```

today | this month | commentary | archives | staff

● 6.21

today | this month | commentary | archives | staff

● 6.22

[**W A R N I N G**]

You should specify text color again, as a visited link will display the text color for that style. At times, that can cause disappearing text, so covering all your bases by restating the color is best, even if it is the same as the link color.

Your main menu is now complete (6.23). For practice, try applying the `mainmenu` style to a variety of text menus in different forms. Remember that you can add a class style to any selector.

Adding Decorative Styling: Top Menu

If you worked through the previous exercise, you will have no trouble creating the menu that is shown in the top-right corner of our sample page (6.11). The same methods are used to create both the main menu and this smaller menu, but in this case, you work with more border attributes to create a stylized menu (6.24).

today | this month | commentary | archives | staff

● 6.23

● 6.24

To create a stylized menu:

1. **The text for this menu is entered in a separate table cell with top alignment. Enter the code and text as follows:**

```
<td valign="top">
    <p><a href="about.html">about
us</a></p>
    <p><a
ref="employ.html">employment</a><
/p>
    <p><a
href="contact.html">contact</a></
p></td>
```

I included the table cell tags so you can make sure that your cell matches this example. Table cell formatting could interfere with attributes in the CSS decorated style. The text will be tight against the top and left borders of the cell (6.25).

2. **Create a class style named** `toprightmenu` **with the following attributes.**

```
.toprightmenu {
    font-family: Verdana, Arial,
     Helvetica, sans-serif;
    font-size: 11px;
    color: #999999;
    text-align: right;
    text-decoration: none;
```

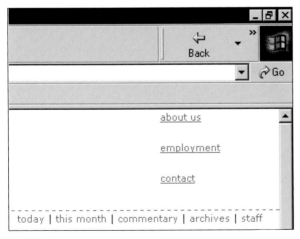

● 6.25

```
}
```

```
.toprightmenu a:link {
    color: #999999;
    text-decoration: none;
}
```

```
.toprightmenu a:visited {
    color: #6699CC;
    text-decoration: none;
}
```

```
.toprightmenu a:hover {
    color: #336699;
}
```

```
.toprightmenu a:visited {
    color: #6699CC;
text-decoration: none;
}
```

```
.toprightmenu a:hover {
    color: #336699;
}
```

These styles control the text formatting for this menu, although you will see no change to the text until you add the style to the text in the next step.

3. **Add the class style** `toprightmenu` **to each of the** `<p>` **tags in the menu text. Your code should look like this:**

```
<p class="toprightmenu"><a
    href="about.html">about
    us</a></p>
<p class="toprightmenu"><a
    href="employ.html">employment</a>
    </p>
<p class="toprightmenu"><a
    href="contact.html">contact</a>
    </p>
```

The text moves to the right margin of the cell, and contains the text formatting and rollover style that you placed in the class style in Step 2 (6.26).

[N O T E]

You add the class style to each paragraph separately so that the borders will surround each menu item. If you applied the style to a `<span>` or `<td>` tag, the border would appear around the entire area, not individual menu items.

4. **Add a border to all sides by adding the following code to the main** `toprightmenu` **style:**

```
border: 1px solid #CCCCCC;
```

The borders are added to the menu items, and extend the full width of the table cell (6.27).

5. **To control the size of the box containing the menu items, and therefore control where the borders display, add the following code to the** `toprightmenu` **style (6.28):**

```
height: 18px;
width: 100px;
```

6. **Now that the box has a defined size, the menu has moved to the left in the cell. The text is still aligned to the right of the box, but the box is following default cell alignment, or left. Change the cell alignment to right (6.29).**

7. **Take a good look at the text within the box, and the box within the page to plan the next steps. You can control where the text appears in relation to the box, and where the box appears in relation to the cell containing the menu through padding and margin attributes. Padding controls the distance between the edge of the box, defined by the border in this case, and the contents of the box (text). Margin values control how far the box is in relation to the element containing it, or table cell in this case.** Use the following code to format the padding and margins for this menu:

```
padding: 1px 5px 1px 1px;
margin-bottom: -5px;
margin-right: 20px;
margin-top: 10px;
```

Your `toprightmenu` style should be as follows.

```
.toprightmenu {
    font-family: Verdana, Arial,
     Helvetica, sans-serif;
    font-size: 11px;
    color: #999999;
    text-align: right;
    text-decoration: none;
    border: 1px solid #CCCCCC;
    height: 18px;
    width: 100px;
    padding: 1px 5px 1px 1px;
    margin-bottom: -5px;
    margin-right: 20px;
    margin-top: 10px;
}
```

● 6.26

● 6.27

Your menu is now complete (6.30). Try creating a new menu, and applying this style. The new menu should look the same as this menu. That's the power of CSS.

Formatting a Menu in a Table

The left menu on this page does not depend on CSS styling for design. The text and rollover effects are created with CSS, as is a dividing line between the menu and page, but unlike the previous sample, you accomplish the formatting for this menu with a table (6.31). The two column format allows you to set an

● 6.30

● 6.28

● 6.29

● 6.31

indent exactly as you require. I've added borders so you can see the table structure (6.32).

[N O T E]

This menu has headlines for categories that are also links. If they were plain text, and not links, you could create the class style with no padding, and add left padding to the link styles for the class, creating the indent.

With headlines as text, you could also achieve this effect by creating two separate class styles, and applying padding to the indented style. However, applying this type of formatting with a table is often easier, and more logical. I prefer to keep only one class style in a menu so that future editing is simple and fast.

The table for the sample menu is 12 rows by 2 columns, with no cellspacing or margins. I used 100% for the table width to fill the menu area. Headline rows are created by a 2-cell span, and are typed in all caps. Menu items are typed with initial caps in the second column of the row. A transparent GIF file holds the indent cell open.

1. **Create the table and linked text with the following code. This code creates a table and adds the links, but does no text formatting. The links will follow the style for the default links on your page (6.33).**

```
<table width="100%" border="0"
    cellpadding="0" cellspacing="0">
<tr valign="top">
<td colspan="2"><a
    href="library.html"><strong>LIBRA
    RY</strong></a></td>
</tr>
```

● 6.32 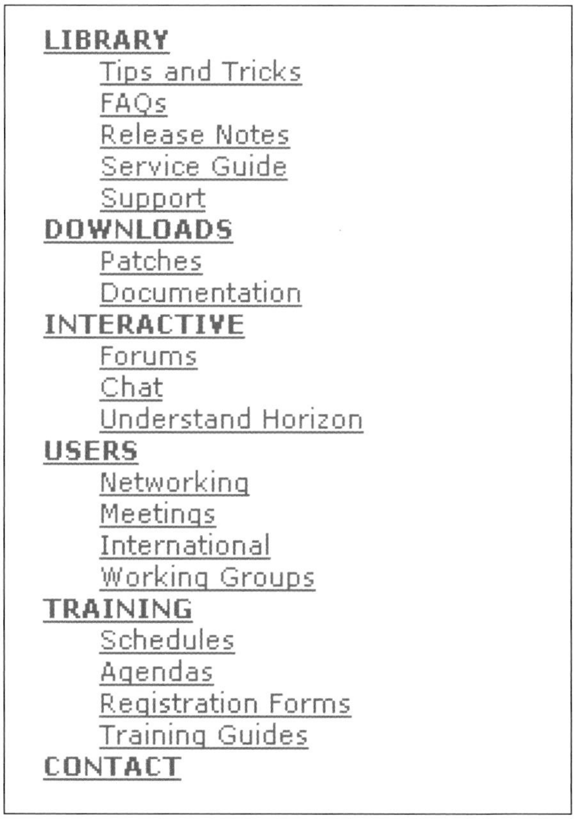

● 6.33

```
<tr valign="top">
   <td><img src="art/spacer.gif"
   width="15" height="1"></td>
    <td><a href="library_tips.html">
   Tips and Tricks</a><br>
    <a href="library_faq.html">
   FAQs</a><br>
    <a href="library_release.html">
   Release Notes</a><br>
    <a href="library_serviceref.
   html">Service Guide</a><br>
    <a href="library_refdocs.
   html">Support</a></td>
</tr>
<tr valign="top">
   <td colspan="2"><strong><a
   href="download.html">DOWNLOADS
   </a>
    </strong></td>
</tr>
<tr valign="top">
   <td> </td>
    <td><a
   href="down_patches.html">Patches
   </a><br>
    <a href="down_documentation.
   html">Documentation</a></td>
</tr>
<tr valign="top">
   <td colspan="2"><a href=
   "interactive.html"><strong>
   INTERACTIVE
    </strong></a></td>
</tr>
<tr valign="top">
   <td> </td>
    <td><a href="inter_forum.html">
   Forums</a><br>
    <a href="inter_chat.html">
   Chat</a><br>
    <a href="inter_understand.html">
   Understand Horizon</a></td>
</tr>
<tr valign="top">
   <td colspan="2"><a href=
   "usergroup.html"><strong>USERS
    </strong></a></td>
</tr>
<tr valign="top">
   <td> </td>
```

```
   <td><a href="user_networkprof.
   html">Networking</a><br>
    <a href="user_meet.html">
   Meetings</a><br>
    <a href="user_international.
   html">International</a><br>
    <a href="user_workgroup.html">
   Working Groups</a></td>
</tr>
<tr valign="top">
   <td colspan="2"><a href=
   "training.html"><strong>
   TRAINING</strong></a></td>
</tr>
<tr valign="top">
   <td> </td>
    <td><a href="train_sched.html">
   Schedules</a><br>
    <a href="train_agendas.html">
   Agendas</a><br>
    <a href="train_regforms.html">
   Registration Forms</a><br>
    <a href="train_guides.html">
   Training Guides</a></td>
</tr>
<tr valign="top">
   <td colspan="2"><strong><a href=
   "contact.html">CONTACT</a>
    </strong></td>
</tr>
</tr>
</table>
```

2. **With the basic formatting handled by the table, your class style is very simple. Add the following class style code to your style sheet:**

```
.leftmenu {
   border-right-width: 1px;
   border-right-style: dotted;
   border-right-color: #666666;
}

.leftmenu a:link {
   color: #336699;
   text-decoration: none;
   font-family: Verdana, Arial,
    Helvetica, sans-serif;
   font-size: 11px;
   line-height: 130%;
}
```

```
.leftmenu a:visited {
   color: #6699CC;
   text-decoration: none;
}

.leftmenu a:hover {
   color: #333333;
   background-color: #CCCCCC;
}
```

You have already added the attributes used in these styles to other styles in this chapter. Now you must apply the style to your menu. In this case, you want the border line at the right to include the entire area of the menu, so the style is applied to affect the full table. Adding the style to the `<td>` tag that contains the table applies the style to the full menu and places the dotted line right at the edge of the cell.

3. **Add the** `leftmenu` **style to the table cell containing the menu table, using the following code:**

```
<td width="200" valign="top"
   class="leftmenu">
```

That's it for the special menus on your page (6.34). Add a text menu to the bottom of the page for easy navigation (6.35), and your page is complete. This page displays consistently in all current browsers, and degrades reasonably well to display in Netscape version 4 browsers (6.36). The links will work, and although the upper menu is out of place and the left menu is missing the dividing line, visitors can navigate easily.

The techniques you used to create the menus on this page give you the tools to create many, many

menu styles. Without CSS, you would have to create these menus in graphic programs, export them, and include them in JavaScript rollover scripts. CSS is a much more efficient way to accomplish many menu styles.

In a different section of your site, you can use the same menu styles with completely different menu items. If you were using graphic menus, you would have to start over and design the second menu, exporting and placing in rollovers as for the original. There is just no comparison in the time required to create a second menu using CSS or graphics. With CSS, you type the menu titles and links, apply the CSS style, and your menu is complete.

Design Tips for CSS Menus

Knowing how to create a menu controlled by CSS is one thing. Creating a CSS menu that looks good is another. I've seen some pretty hideous CSS menus out there. Of course, some of the menus created with graphic text are much worse, as the designer has no restrictions. However, you do need to keep design principles in mind for type, even when using CSS. I've compiled a list of tips to help you avoid most of the errors I have seen.

- **Use identical fonts for related styles.** Make sure all your link styles have the same base font, including type style (6.37). Using a boldface or italic font for one of the link states causes your text to move so that the characters in the different style fit (6.38). At best, these fonts are

● 6.34

● 6.35

uncomfortable for the visitor because the text moves on mouseover. At worst, they can break your page (see the sidebar "One Tiny Error = One Broken Page").

- **Don't use large type for CSS menus.** Remember that HTML text, the type that CSS controls, does not offer antialiasing to keep character outlines smooth (6.39). If you must fill a large space, use a background color or image for

the menu area, or enhance the text with graphic symbols. Bigger is not always better; when it comes to text, large text is rarely the answer to design problems.

● 6.38

● 6.36

● 6.37

● 6.39

- **Don't use overly small text for CSS menus.**
  Text at small sizes will likely fall apart on a Mac monitor. If you must use very small text with CSS, make sure you test on a Mac. Better yet, if the text must be very small, switch to graphic menus, using specially designed fonts for small sizes, often called pixel fonts (6.40). These fonts look better and display consistently on both Mac and PC systems.
- **Watch your spelling and typos.**
  Of course, this tip is not just for CSS, but it seems that CSS menus have errors more often (6.41). My guess is that the text is so easy to create that the same attention does not go into making sure all is perfect. With graphic menu items, you must export and place the files, providing more working opportunity to catch any slips. With CSS text, you just type and run, perhaps never paying close attention to that word again. Be warned!

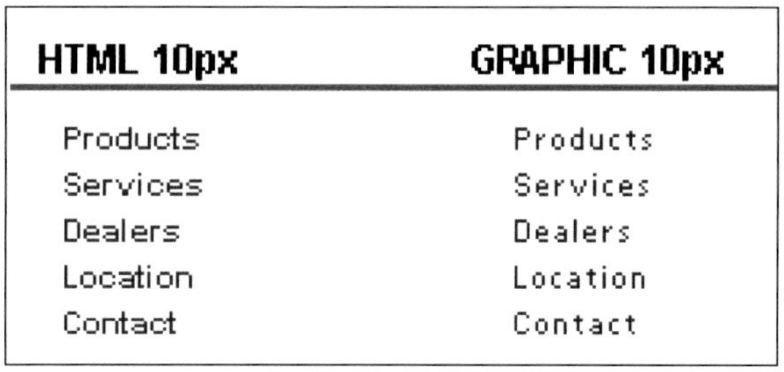

- **Leave enough white space.**
  Again, white space is important for all design, but I have seen so many CSS menus with decorative styling that leave the text gasping for air (6.42). Use padding attributes to ensure that your borders leave text room to breathe. Margin attributes leave breathing room between the edge of your CSS styling and other page elements (6.43). Even if you're not using border styling, you may need to use padding or margins to position your text.

HTML 10px	GRAPHIC 10px
Products	Products
Services	Services
Dealers	Dealers
Location	Location
Contact	Contact

● 6.40

● 6.41

- **Don't leave too much space between related text items.**

  Once again, too much is not good. Menu text items are related, and they are only effective if the visitor sees them as a unit. This is not usually a problem with horizontal menus, as you must work hard with HTML text to include extra spacing. However, with vertical text, seeing the menu items hanging out all by themselves is very

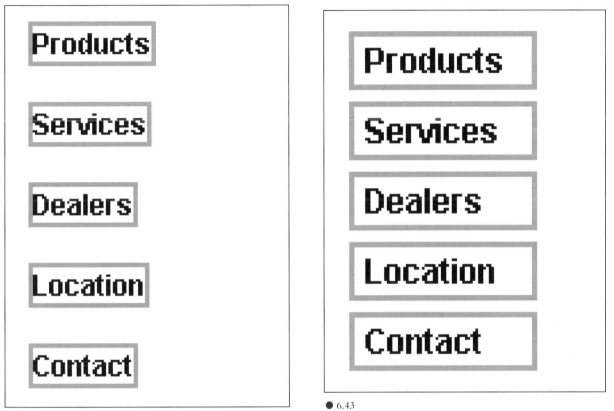

● 6.42

● 6.43

One Tiny Error = One Broken Page

Recently, I saw one small CSS error that initially made me think the page was disintegrating. It was only my curiosity that made me stick around to find out what caused the problem.

The problem page had a normal weight font specified as the `a:link` style, and a bold specified for the `a:hover` style. That can make you a little seasick at the best of times, as bold font characters take more space than the same character with a normal weight font, and the text moves.

In one spot on the bad page, the bold type increased the amount of space required for a long word in a link, and the link jumped to the next line whenever the mouse passed over. Imagine what that did to the display on the screen as a long link was bumped to the next line, then back up when the mouse was removed, down again when the mouse passed over. All the content on the page following this spot moved as the new line was created and returned to normal. Small error. Disastrous results.

Obviously, the designer of this page did not test with the resolution I was using. You must always test your pages with popular resolutions, in all current browsers. Unless you're certain your users will be using current browsers, I do urge you to test your page with a Netscape 4 version browser as well. When it comes to CSS, Netscape 4 version browsers require special attention. Great design is lost if your visitors cannot see your pages correctly.

for your menus. You can accomplish this task by using bold for your menus, white space, background color or images for menu areas, or dividing lines or borders on your menu. Even a

simple, almost invisible dotted line does the job (6.49). But also be aware that the menu should be obvious, but allow visitors to concentrate on the text. Screaming red backgrounds with bold, white text will win over demure content every time (6.50). Keep the balance.

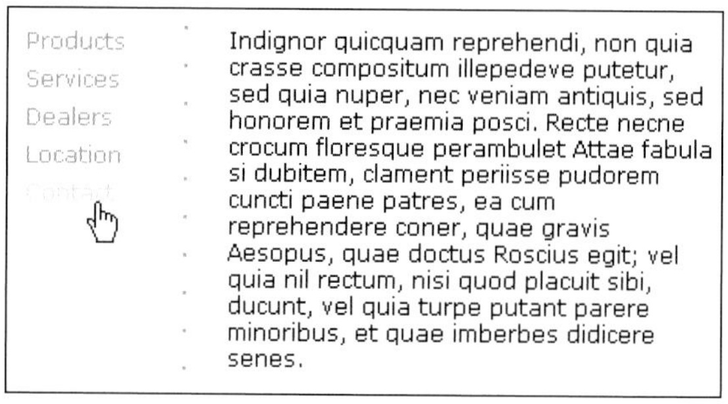

● 6.49

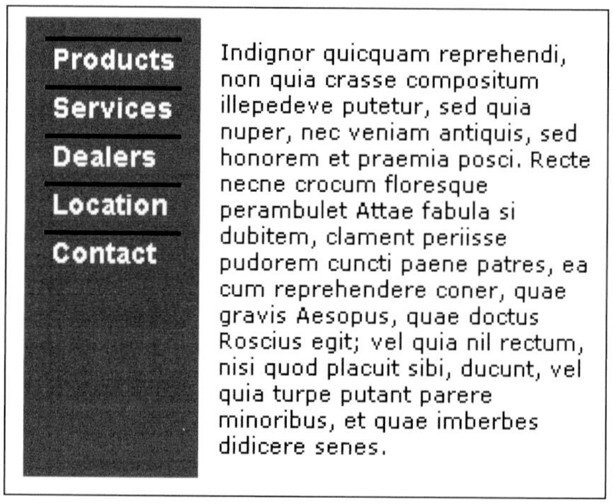

● 6.50

<h1>

HEADLINE

fon1

```
.hotspot {
  color: #FFFFFF;
  background-color: #336699;
  padding: 10px;
}
```

- selector
- property
- value

background

body text

type

<a: hover>

Chapter 7

Designing with CSS Content Text

You should be able to tell the purpose of a page with a quick glance. The visitor is saying, "What's in it for me." Make your page a quick read by using type in a simple way to answer that question.

MICHAEL DEMOPOULOS, RDVO DESIGN

Designing pages with CSS is no different from designing any pages. Basic rules of design, like those I cover in Chapter 2, "Design Principles for Web Type," apply to any page. A good communicative page is a good communicative page. Period. Using CSS does not make it so. Failing to use CSS does not mean your page is bad. Some designers think that using CSS for text control means they are creating great pages. That's not even close to the truth.

What CSS does is offer exceptional tools to create consistent pages that are great. If you put the time and skill into designing the basic page or pages for your site, the rest will follow without much effort. But you cannot skip that first step to make the first page great. Of course, as you build additional pages of your site, you may discover that one of the styles you created for the first page does not work well elsewhere. CSS allows you to change the style sheet, and the change will be made on all pages controlled by that style sheet.

In this chapter I go through how to create that great first page. You've already covered the menus in Chapter 6, " CSS Menus," but as important as navigation is to a page, it is just the start. I discuss using CSS to create headlines and subheads that really stand out, as well as creating customized lists that present your content in a quick and easy format. By the end of this chapter, you will have the tools to create the page described by Michael Demopoulos at the beginning of this chapter.

[T I P]

Although good reasons often exist to create partial CSS files, or to use two style sheets for one site, you get the best results if you keep all styles contained in one style sheet. Keeping track of what styles control which portions of pages can be very difficult, and much of the editing time you save on maintenance is lost trying to keep the CSS files in order. Make sure that there is no other way to accomplish an effect before deciding to use multiple style sheets.

Using CSS for Consistent Pages

CSS helps with consistent layout, but it doesn't guarantee it. If you have worked with templates in a visual editor for Web design, or worked with master pages in print design, you probably understand how important planning is to creating a worthwhile template. Nowhere does the old saying "garbage in, garbage out" ring so true. If your template is weak, the most amazing template technologies can't save the pages that are created from that start.

Consider CSS to be a template for your text control. If you don't put the planning into the initial document, you will find yourself using workarounds to problems, maybe even using — dare I say it — the `<font>` tag to correct deficiencies. After you start "correcting" CSS-controlled text, you have already lost the battle. Changes to the CSS style will not affect all the text in the site, and that is the greatest source of power for CSS. Plan, plan, test, plan, make dummy pages, test, change dummy pages, plan, test . . . I think you get the idea. Even for a small site, like the Glass Loon site, I spend a lot of time working with "dummy" pages (7.1) before compiling the final pages.

Using Content Text to Communicate

Although the design elements and menus are critical to the success of a site, there is usually much more content than design. If your content text is not in good shape, the best menus and design will not make your visitors happy. Remember that visitors to your page are impatient, and ready to move on to the next site with very little reason. You can prevent quick exit, and in fact, guide your visitors through your site with careful attention to content text detail. In this section, I step you through the basics for professional content text presentation. This discussion includes all forms of text and builds on techniques featured earlier in this book.

One of the pages I know best is on my own site, of course. I've had this site for longer than I care to admit, but it has been very successful for me. Every time I feel I must change it — I am a designer after all — I stumble. I've probably spent more time *not* changing my site than most designers do when they constantly change their site to keep it fresh.

The reason I run into such trouble trying to create a new look is that the site works. To return to Michael's wise words at the beginning of this chapter, the message for the page is instantly available. On my Web design page (`http://wpeck.com/web.html`) take a look at what stands out (7.2): **Wendy Peck** (who's page), then **Web Design** (what's on the page), followed by the word **Experience** (vital for a service). Next, the eye catches the phrase, "**You don't need a Web site. You need a Web Presence!**" (unique idea). Finally, you catch my **photo** (real person), and the message that the **look is vital**, which of course implies that you best trust it to me. Within one screen on an 800-pixel-wide display, the visitor gets the whole message. This message creates the desire to read the rest of the copy. I know potential clients read my whole site, because they ask me about many of the features I have there. Run your eyes back over this paragraph reading only the bold type. There isn't much I wanted to say that anyone can escape without hearing. That's what you want.

[T I P]

If you have not already done so, you should read Chapter 1, "Defining Web Type Issues," and Chapter 2, "Design Principles for Web Type," of this book before continuing.

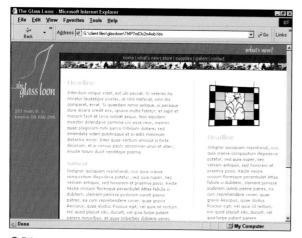

 7.1

7.2

Working with Body Text

By now you should have a good idea which text works on the Web. You know how to create text that appears the way you want it using CSS controls. That's part of the battle, but body text is always presented as a unit, many words tied together in a row. Text that looks great with plenty of space around it, like in a menu, does not look good as body text.

Bold type is a great example. Nothing makes a headline pop out more, and no better way exists to use a gentle color in a menu than with bold text. But for body copy, the thick characters become a problem. Look what happens to the page I showed you in the previous section (7.2) with the same page sporting bold paragraph text (7.3). By logic, even if the text were a little harder to read, the rest of the page should still hold. After all, I didn't change the headlines, the color, the lists at the left. But notice how the whole balance of the page is thrown off. Your eye has no choice but to go to the right, where nothing stands out. Even the photo, which usually demands plenty of attention, is subdued by the heavy text.

I know I'm repeating the bold text for body copy issue, but I see a lot of it. It seems to be a common fix for pages that "need something." When I stop to look at the page, it usually does need something, but bold text is not the answer.

● 7.3

Even the Pros? Especially the Pros!

I think my clients often wonder whether I will ever make a real page when I am working on a project. I will not move ahead until they have signed off on the design completely, and I do mean completely. The last thing I want to do is to be testing hundreds of pages to make sure that adding bold to a style has not messed up the elements anywhere. What do I mean by signing off? I mean they actually sign a form that says that any design changes will incur extra charges.

Beginning designers often think that those who design pages as a career must do things so quickly. Their knowledge and experience must mean that the days of preview, make a change, preview, make another change, somehow magically disappear. If anything, professional designers become more fanatic about testing. The experience that sits heavily on us is the one where we spent eight solid hours working through countless pages to make a correction. You never forget that. It's the reason we tend to embrace CSS as close to a religious principle.

As great as CSS is for making changes across the site, most of us still place CSS-controlled text into HTML layout. Making a change to text can mean making a change to layout. Making a change to layout is outside the wonder of CSS (and into the wonder of templates, but not a subject for this book), and may lead to the situation I described earlier.

I've been known to spend an entire day testing and perfecting the CSS for a medium-sized site. When I start putting the content pages together, I don't want to be making changes to my CSS files. But the pages fly together after I reach the construction stage of a project. With the design and CSS styling working in sync, you can put pages together at an alarming pace. Your content is better, too, because you can concentrate fully on presenting the message. Your tools are all in order, and your focus is not bouncing between message and layout.

The reward for well-designed CSS lasts, too. When your foundation is rock solid, changes at a later time, to update the look, or include new capability, is very quick and rarely presents layout problems. I think I earn as many repeat customers for my "sure, I can do that" response to additions even months later, as I do with the original work.

Body Text Color

Most of the pages I work with look great with plain black text, usually Verdana, less often Arial, at 11 or 12 pixel size. Later I show you some layout tricks that lead to great looking "plain" text, but text itself must sometimes carry some of the design weight. When I designed the Glass Loon site (7.1), I discovered that a medium-gray text blended with the rest of the page, and delivered the result we required — the art was to take center stage (7.4). Notice how strong the black text is in comparison to the gray (7.5). On some sites, the reduced readability of the text caused by the lower contrast between gray and white would be a problem. However, on this site, the text passages are short and are used in a supporting roll for the art images.

Sometimes black text presents the opposite problem, and doesn't have enough impact. Try using a dark color other than black in this case. Although

black is visually stronger, using a dark body text color can often have more impact. Compare a sample of dark blue text (7.6) with the black text (7.5).

[WARNING]

Please be careful when you move from black body text. Few colors can do the job for the main content, which I think leads designers to apply bold. Much of the bold body text I see is not black. It is also critical that the text color fits with the design elements on the page.

Working with colored text can be tricky. The natural, and correct, instinct is to pick a color from the design elements on the page. How can you go wrong when you choose to use an existing color? Actually, going wrong when matching solid color items and text is fairly easy. Text is displayed with tiny amounts of a color. Design elements often have areas of solid color. Even a strong color loses much of its impact when mixed with another color. See how the purple in wide stripes (7.7) seems to be a stronger color than the narrow purple stripes (7.8), yet these samples feature the same colors.

I often use a darker color than is featured in the design elements for body text. The same color often appears to be several shades lighter than the solid color elements on the page (7.9). Using a darker color for the body text gives the illusion of being the same color (7.10). Use the power of CSS to try several different color combinations when you're setting up your basic site pages.

Headline

Interdum volgus videt, est ubi peccat. Si veteres ita miratur laudatque poetas, ut nihil nteferat, nihil illis comparet, errat. Si quaedam nimis antique, si peraque dure dicere credit eos, ignave multa fatetur, et sapit et mecum facit et Iova iudicat aequo. Non equidem insector delendave carmina Livi esse reor, memini quae plagosum mihi parvo Orbilium dictare; sed emendata videri pulchraque et exactis minimum distantia miror. Inter quae verbum emicuit si forte decorum, et si versus paulo concinnior unus et alter, iniuste totum ducit venditque poema.

● 7.4

Headline

Interdum volgus videt, est ubi peccat. Si veteres ita miratur laudatque poetas, ut nihil nteferat, nihil illis comparet, errat. Si quaedam nimis antique, si peraque dure dicere credit eos, ignave multa fatetur, et sapit et mecum facit et Iova iudicat aequo. Non equidem insector delendave carmina Livi esse reor, memini quae plagosum mihi parvo Orbilium dictare; sed emendata videri pulchraque et exactis minimum distantia miror. Inter quae verbum emicuit si forte decorum, et si versus paulo concinnior unus et alter, iniuste totum ducit venditque poema.

● 7.5

Headline

Interdum volgus videt, est ubi peccat. Si veteres ita miratur laudatque poetas, ut nihil nteferat, nihil illis comparet, errat. Si quaedam nimis antique, si peraque dure dicere credit eos, ignave multa fatetur, et sapit et mecum facit et Iova iudicat aequo. Non equidem insector delendave carmina Livi esse reor, memini quae plagosum mihi parvo Orbilium dictare; sed emendata videri pulchraque et exactis minimum distantia miror. Inter quae verbum emicuit si forte decorum, et si versus paulo concinnior unus et alter, iniuste totum ducit venditque poema.

● 7.6

[T I P]

Don't rely on the entry page for your site to set up your CSS styles. Analyze the content that will be included in your site, and prepare as many test pages as necessary to include all different styles. If you have tabular data, or an e-commerce catalog, pages containing that content will have different needs from a page that features the history or other text-based content. Text that looks great in a full paragraph may be terrible when used as a short-line description in a catalog.

You can set up a class style, or use an embedded style for an occasional special text requirement, but if you have distinctly different text styles on many pages, handling the exceptions with an imported style sheet to supplement the main styles may be better. See Chapter 4. " What Is CSS?," for more information on the different ways to add CSS styles to your site.

● 7.7

● 7.8

White Space in Body Text

Color and weight for text is important, but your efforts in that direction will be lost if you don't have a good balance of white space with your text. In fact, the amount of white space affects how color appears. If text is packed tightly into a space, the characters

Interdum volgus videt, est ubi peccat. Si veteres ita miratur laudatque poetas, ut nihil nteferat, nihil illis comparet, errat. Si quaedam nimis antique, si peraque dure dicere credit eos, ignave multa fatetur, et sapit et mecum facit et Iova iudicat aequo. Non equidem insector delendave carmina Livi esse reor, memini quae plagosum mihi parvo Orbilium dictare; sed emendata videri pulchraque et exactis minimum distantia miror. Inter quae verbum emicuit si forte decorum, et si versus paulo concinnior unus et alter, iniuste totum ducit venditque poema.

● 7.9

Interdum volgus videt, est ubi peccat. Si veteres ita miratur laudatque poetas, ut nihil nteferat, nihil illis comparet, errat. Si quaedam nimis antique, si peraque dure dicere credit eos, ignave multa fatetur, et sapit et mecum facit et Iova iudicat aequo. Non equidem insector delendave carmina Livi esse reor, memini quae plagosum mihi parvo Orbilium dictare; sed emendata videri pulchraque et exactis minimum distantia miror. Inter quae verbum emicuit si forte decorum, et si versus paulo concinnior unus et alter, iniuste totum ducit venditque poema.

● 7.10

can appear to be darker (7.11) than if plenty of white space (7.12) surrounds the text. When it comes to color, you can ignore nothing.

However, color is not the only reason to pay attention to white space. The amount of white space on your page, and the spacing between elements is one of the most important factors in good typography. Take another look at the page from my site featured earlier in this chapter (7.13). A lot of white space is on this page. The graphics are bright and aggressive, and the large areas of white around the logo and title gives them enough room to stand out. If the two graphic areas were closer together, they would compete. The black headline is also separated from the text. The yellow text is an integral part of the paragraph.

What happens if all the proportions of text and white space change (7.14)? An easy route through the page no longer exists. The text areas compete for attention. The headlines no longer deliver reading with a glance. The black headline blends into the paragraph below, and the yellow text is not strong enough to stand on its own. It is just hanging there, looking like a lost child. The flow is broken. Reducing the page margins and column padding further reduces how easily the eye can find a path

through the page. I did not make many changes to this page, but it is no longer a page that works.

I can't give you a magic formula for white space. Every page, with every change in graphic elements, font style, font color, and even amount of text affects the "perfect" amount of white space. However, with the Web as a tool, you can be learning all the time. Pay attention when you find a page that flows well, and study how the designer has used white space. Take note when a page makes you think too hard. Chances are that the white space has not been well planned. When you have it right, your eyes will move from area to area on the page, catching the important bits of information, before moving to the next in a smooth motion. It feels effortless.

● 7.13

Indignor quicquam reprehendi, non quia crasse compositum illepedeve putetur, sed quia nuper, nec veniam antiquis, sed honorem et praemia posci. Recte necne crocum floresque perambulet Attae fabula si dubitem, clament periisse pudorem cuncti paene patres, ea cum reprehendere coner, quae gravis Aesopus, quae doctus Roscius egit; vel quia nil rectum, nisi quod placuit sibi, ducunt, vel quia turpe putant parere minoribus, et quae imberbes didicere senes.

● 7.11

Indignor quicquam reprehendi, non quia crasse compositum illepedeve putetur, sed quia nuper, nec veniam antiquis, sed honorem et praemia posci. Recte necne crocum floresque perambulet Attae fabula si dubitem, clament periisse pudorem cuncti paene patres, ea cum reprehendere coner, quae gravis Aesopus, quae doctus Roscius egit; vel quia nil rectum, nisi quod placuit sibi, ducunt, vel quia turpe putant parere minoribus, et quae imberbes didicere senes.

● 7.12

● 7.14

[NOTE]

White space can be green, or blue, or black. The term is a generic title used to describe the space between elements on a page. When on a colored background, elements commonly require more space between each other than when on a white background. A white background with dark text provides the best contrast for readers to separate background and text. Any other combination reduces contrast, and allowing more space between elements compensates for the lower contrast.

Don't forget about line spacing when you're thinking of white space. If your text seems to be too heavy, increasing line spacing is often an elegant solution. The difference can be dramatic. Compare text with default line spacing (7.15) to the same text with line spacing set to 150% (7.16). A word of caution, however. Text with generous line spacing demands extra room between the text and other elements on the page. Because the text is not held together as tightly as text with default spacing, the lines of text must be clearly separated from all other elements to be seen as a unit. You find out more about keeping text together in the next section of this chapter.

Indignor quicquam reprehendi, non quia crasse compositum illepedeve putetur, sed quia nuper, nec veniam antiquis, sed honorem et praemia posci. Recte necne crocum floresque perambulet Attae fabula si dubitem, clament periisse pudorem cuncti paene patres, ea cum reprehendere coner, quae gravis Aesopus, quae doctus Roscius egit; vel quia nil rectum, nisi quod placuit sibi, ducunt, vel quia turpe putant parere minoribus, et quae imberbes didicere senes.

● 7.15

Indignor quicquam reprehendi, non quia crasse compositum illepedeve putetur, sed quia nuper, nec veniam antiquis, sed honorem et praemia posci. Recte necne crocum floresque perambulet Attae fabula si dubitem, clament periisse pudorem cuncti paene patres, ea cum reprehendere coner, quae gravis Aesopus, quae doctus Roscius egit; vel quia nil rectum, nisi quod placuit sibi, ducunt, vel quia turpe putant parere minoribus, et quae imberbes didicere senes.

● 7.16

Using CSS Backgrounds and Borders to Define Text Areas

Perhaps you have started thinking about class styles, and how they could be used to define special areas for your site. You're thinking in the right direction if you came up with this idea. Maybe you need to feature quotes from experts, or offer tips or notes that stand out from the rest of the page. Great design features, answers the challenge to deliver an easy scanned page, and exceptionally easy to do using CSS type control.

I returned to the site I used for the last chapter, "CSS Menus," and added a new class style called "hotspot."

```
.hotspot {
    font-family: Arial, Helvetica,
     sans-serif;
    font-size: 11px;
    line-height: normal;
    color: #FFFFFF;
    background-color: #336699;
    padding: 10px;
}
```

Applying this style to a `<p>` tag creates an automatic style, with a blue background, white type, and indented by padding attributes (7.17). Anywhere on this site that I want to create the same attention to text, I simply apply the class style. Of course, the style can be applied to any selector, so you may choose to use this method to format an entire column.

Change is easy. I think the blue is a little heavy for this page. I removed the background, specified bold text in blue, changed the border to a top and bottom styling, and then reduced the top and bottom

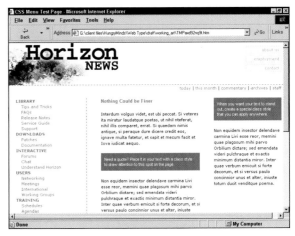

● 7.17

padding for balance. With just a few changes, I have a style that fits more gracefully into the page (7.18).

```
.hotspot {
    font-family: Arial, Helvetica,
     sans-serif;
    font-size: 11px;
    line-height: normal;
    color: #336699;
    padding: 5px 10px;
    font-weight: bold;
    border-top-width: 2px;
    border-bottom-width: 1px;
    border-top-style: solid;
    border-bottom-style: dotted;
    border-top-color: #336699;
    border-left-color: #336699;
}
```

The beauty of this method is that you can add the same style six months from now, and it will look exactly the same as your other pages, without even checking how you accomplished the look. As long as the class style remains the same, your results will be the same.

Once again, I advise that you spend some time playing with borders, backgrounds, padding, and margins until you're comfortable with the effects you can create. When you have a good working knowledge of special CSS effects, you will be more likely to use that power.

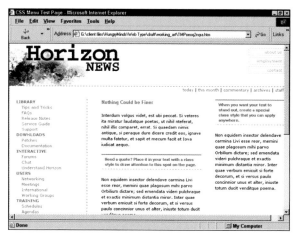

● 7.18

Creating Effective Headlines and Subheads

If you're reading this book in order, you should know that headlines and subheads are very important tools for making your pages valuable and accessible to your readers. The more you deliver your content in small chunks, and make your page message pop into a reader's mind with a quick scan, the more successful your sites will be. Often, simply setting your headlines with a pleasing font that's larger or heavier than the body text is enough to accomplish your goals.

[TIP]

There is no way to add antialiasing to type for the Web, so you should avoid large text (see Chapter 2, "Design Principles for Web Type"). CSS styling can deliver the same impact as large type, without compromising the quality of your text.

But you can do so much more with headlines. You can add backgrounds, borders, or lines to headlines to make them stand out well, as well as add graphic interest to your page. Later I give you a few tips that are outside CSS, as well, because the more tools you have to create great headlines, the more likely you are to apply creative styling.

You've learned how to create class styles, and maybe be tempted to create all your headlines with these versatile styles. Don't do it! Headlines are very important to the search engine spiders, and even though you want to create an effective and beautiful page, don't ignore the importance of search engine placement.

Using Headline Styles Correctly

I rarely define beyond a level 3 <h3> style for my sites, and often only use <h1> and <h2>. This isn't because I don't like the idea of many headlines, but because effectively using more than three headline levels is very difficult. In order to keep your page with the right signals for navigation, headlines and subheads should follow a logical sequence. In other words, a section should start with an <h1> style, with the <h2> heading a sub-point of the <h1> topic. If you need to break down the subject again, that's when <h3> comes in. The headline family should follow a logical order and feature the same subject, or related topics, and so on.

Unless you're working on research reports, or legal or medical content, it is unlikely that you will require more than three levels of headings. Perhaps it will help to think of the <h1> style as the CEO, with the <h2> style taking the role of the manager. After you get to <h3> or lower, you are into a highly subservient level.

[T I P]

I know why many of you would like to use class styles. You hate the spacing created by using block elements like the <h> family. Trust me for a few minutes that you can fix that, or skim down to the next section if you don't trust me, and then come back prepared to create some headline styles.

While you're wandering, you might want to read more about how the search engines use text in Chapter 3, "Working with HTML Type," if you have not already done so.

To edit a headline style, you simply create an <h> style for each level that you require. <h1> is a level-one headline, and highly valued by the search engines. <h2> is a level-two style, still important, but not given the same importance. You no doubt have the sequence figured out, so I will stop and just give you the syntax for a headline style. These attributes create an <h1> style in dark gray, with <h2> a medium blue (7.19).

```
h1 {
    font-family: Arial, Helvetica,
     sans-serif;
    font-size: 140%;
    color: #333333;
}

h2 {
    font-family: Arial, Helvetica,
     sans-serif;
    font-size: 110%;
    color: #336699;
}
```

[N O T E]

Headline styles have bold as a default style. If you don't want a bold font, you must specify normal for the font style.

Working with Color in Headlines

Color on a page, especially when embedded into plain text, can have a dramatic impact on the look of the page. Not only does your eye go to a colored headline instantly, you have the opportunity to bring the design colors for the page into the main content area. Any page looks better when color is woven across the screen. From a pure aesthetic standpoint, color in headlines is valuable.

Nothing Could be Finer

Interdum volgus videt, est ubi peccat. Si veteres ita miratur laudatque poetas, ut nihil nteferat, nihil illis comparet, errat. Si quaedam nimis antique, si peraque dure dicere credit eos, ignave multa fatetur, et sapit et mecum facit et Iova iudicat aequo.

Than to Be in Carolina

Non equidem insector delendave carmina Livi esse reor, memini quae plagosum mihi parvo Orbilium dictare; sed emendata videri pulchraque et exactis minimum distantia miror. Inter quae verbum emicuit si forte decorum, et si versus paulo concinnior unus et alter, iniuste totum ducit venditque poema.

● 7.19

From a navigation and comprehension standpoint, color is essential. Headlines do stand out when they are offered in black type, even with black body copy (7.20). However, just change the color, and the headlines pop off the page (7.21). If you were scanning for information, which color would you choose to help you with your task? The blue headlines are also more

vibrant, exciting. Of course, not all pages should have exciting color in the content area, but any color does stand out.

The design for your page usually determines which colors to use. However, you must be careful to keep headlines legible. You lose all that you have worked for if your visitor cannot read the headline. The good news is that you can use lighter colors for headlines, especially if you can make the font size quite large. Light colors do not show the jagged edges of text that is not antialiased as clearly as dark colors (7.22). Note how the subhead, at a much smaller size, is not easy to read. Save light colors for large headlines. The light-colored headline would look better with a smaller space between the headline and body copy, and that is the next subject.

Spacing Headlines Effectively

You want your headlines to look as if they belong to the content. Large spaces between the headline and the first paragraph often interrupt that connection. HTML defaults display too much space between headline styles and the next element (7.23). Keeping the sections of your page held together as a unit is hard when you have gaps like this.

Luckily, the fix is easy with CSS. You can control the amount of space between one element and the

Nothing Could be Finer

Interdum volgus videt, est ubi peccat. Si veteres ita miratur laudatque poetas, ut nihil nteferat, nihil illis comparet, errat. Si quaedam nimis antique, si peraque dure dicere credit eos, ignave multa fatetur, et sapit et mecum facit et Iova iudicat aequo.

Than to Be in Carolina

Non equidem insector delendave carmina Livi esse reor, memini quae plagosum mihi parvo Orbilium dictare; sed emendata videri pulchraque et exactis minimum distantia miror. Inter quae verbum emicuit si forte decorum, et si versus paulo concinnior unus et alter, iniuste totum ducit venditque poema.

● 7.20

Nothing Could be Finer

Interdum volgus videt, est ubi peccat. Si veteres ita miratur laudatque poetas, ut nihil nteferat, nihil illis comparet, errat. Si quaedam nimis antique, si peraque dure dicere credit eos, ignave multa fatetur, et sapit et mecum facit et Iova iudicat aequo.

Than to Be in Carolina

Non equidem insector delendave carmina Livi esse reor, memini quae plagosum mihi parvo Orbilium dictare; sed emendata videri pulchraque et exactis minimum distantia miror. Inter quae verbum emicuit si forte decorum, et si versus paulo concinnior unus et alter, iniuste totum ducit venditque poema.

● 7.21

Nothing Could be Finer

Interdum volgus videt, est ubi peccat. Si veteres ita miratur laudatque poetas, ut nihil nteferat, nihil illis comparet, errat. Si quaedam nimis antique, si peraque dure dicere credit eos, ignave multa fatetur, et sapit et mecum facit et Iova iudicat aequo.

Than to Be in Carolina

Non equidem insector delendave carmina Livi esse reor, memini quae plagosum mihi parvo Orbilium dictare; sed emendata videri pulchraque et exactis minimum distantia miror. Inter quae verbum emicuit si forte decorum, et si versus paulo concinnior unus et alter, iniuste totum ducit venditque poema.

● 7.22

next with the margin attribute. It's important to remember that the default value for the spacing between elements would be 0. If you want to tighten the space, you must use a negative number. In the example I use here, I want to tighten the spacing considerably, with −15 pixels as the value I need for the heading to appear the way I want it to in Internet Explorer 6 (7.24).

The problem is not yet solved, however. Netscape 4 version browsers ignore the margin command, which

I can live with. Netscape 6 does not ignore it. In fact, the headline is much too close to the paragraph now (7.25). I can't live with that. If I have to choose between too much space and crowding, I will choose too much space every time.

There is a compromise action, of course. If you specify the margin as −10, it is a tiny bit too tight in Netscape 6 (7.26), and though it's looser than I

Nothing Could be Finer

Interdum volgus videt, est ubi peccat. Si veteres ita miratur laudatque poetas, ut nihil nteferat, nihil illis comparet, errat. Si quaedam nimis antique, si peraque dure dicere credit eos, ignave multa fatetur, et sapit et mecum facit et Iova iudicat aequo.

Need a quote? Place it in your text with a class style to draw attention to this spot on the page.

Non equidem insector delendave carmina Livi esse reor, memini quae plagosum mihi parvo Orbilium dictare; sed emendata videri pulchraque et exactis minimum distantia miror. Inter quae

● 7.23

Nothing Could be Finer

Interdum volgus videt, est ubi peccat. Si veteres ita miratur laudatque poetas, ut nihil nteferat, nihil illis comparet, errat. Si quaedam nimis antique, si peraque dure dicere credit eos, ignave multa fatetur, et sapit et mecum facit et Iova iudicat aequo.

Need a quote? Place it in your text with a class style to draw attention to this spot on the page.

Non equidem insector delendave carmina Livi esse reor, memini quae plagosum mihi parvo Orbilium dictare; sed emendata videri pulchraque et exactis minimum distantia miror. Inter quae

● 7.24

Nothing Could be Finer

Interdum volgus videt, est ubi peccat. Si veteres ita miratur laudatque poetas, ut nihil nteferat, nihil illis comparet, errat. Si quaedam nimis antique, si peraque dure dicere credit eos, ignave multa fatetur, et sapit et mecum facit et Iova iudicat aequo.

Need a quote? Place it in your text with a class style to draw attention to this spot on the page.

Non equidem insector delendave carmina Livi esse reor, memini quae plagosum mihi parvo Orbilium dictare; sed emendata videri pulchraque et exactis minimum distantia miror. Inter quae verbum emicuit si forte decorum, et

● 7.25

Nothing Could be Finer

Interdum volgus videt, est ubi peccat. Si veteres ita miratur laudatque poetas, ut nihil nteferat, nihil illis comparet, errat. Si quaedam nimis antique, si peraque dure dicere credit eos, ignave multa fatetur, et sapit et mecum facit et Iova iudicat aequo.

Need a quote? Place it in your text with a class style to draw attention to this spot on the page.

Non equidem insector delendave carmina Livi esse reor, memini quae plagosum mihi parvo Orbilium dictare; sed emendata videri pulchraque et exactis minimum distantia miror. Inter quae verbum emicuit si forte decorum, et

● 7.26

Graphic Type for the Web

CLASSIC

font

DINGBATS

"quote"

design element

type

- kerning
- tracking
- leading

Chapter 8

Introduction to Graphic Typography

I spend a lot of time on the free font sites. I love looking at the variety, but I never use them for corporate work. I think it's usually best to stick with type you know, the classics like Adobe and Monotype fonts.

TRICIA MACGILLIS

In this chapter I move into an area of more control — text used as an image. You have no restrictions as to what you can do with text created this way from a technical standpoint, but I must once again issue a warning about abusing this method. Text that you can offer in HTML format on a Web page should be used for all content text. The next few chapters are intended to teach you to use specialty text, text that you cannot duplicate with HTML — but I urge restraint. Learning to create text with no bounds does not give you license to avoid common sense.

Of course, you can produce text using any font if it will be included in your page as an image. Heed Tricia's words above, however. If you're putting forth a professional image, classic fonts are almost always the best call (8.1). If you're creating a fun site, by all means wander over to novelty fonts, but make sure that your visitors can read your words at a glance (8.2). You cannot expect more than a quick look from your visitor.

With the warnings out of the way, it's time to move into the area of Web type where you actually have some control. Here comes the fun.

Helvetica
Century Schoolbook
Goudy
Franklin Gothic
Garamond

● 8.1

Alley Cat
John Handy
Paisley 02
Times New Random
Ugly Face

● 8.2

Understanding Typography

The word *typography* can be used as an overall, generic term, as I have done through the early chapters of this book. However, it can also refer to a specific craft, one that creates highly controlled text. In the next few chapters, I use the term to refer to the specific craft, plus I include new terms to many of you like kerning and leading.

[T I P]

I recommend that anyone who is interested in great typography obtain a copy of Robin Williams' book, *The Non-Designer's Type Book* (Peachpit Press). Although the book does not have a Web focus, it covers all the important aspects of designing with type, in clear language. If you do no more in the field of typography than adopt the practices outlined in this classic book, you will be far ahead of most Web designers working today. See the interview with Robin later in this chapter.

Proportional Fonts

Until quite recently, like the 1980s, typography was reserved for commercial print operations. Home or office users were restricted to typewriters, which had no ability to alter spacing or the fit of one character to the next. Typewriter characters each took up the same amount of space, known today as monospace fonts (8.3). Desktop publishing programs instantly put typography control into the hands of anyone with a computer. Typography control provides the

exact amount of space required for each character when working with proportional fonts, by far the most common type available (8.4).

Unfortunately, many people treat a computer as if it is a typewriter. Pay attention, and I will step you through using your computer correctly. Right off the top, I want to hit one of my pet peeves — two spaces at the end of a sentence. With proportional fonts, there is no need to use two spaces between sentences. Monospaced fonts are spaced so far apart that a double space is required to separate sentences. Note how the sentences run together with only a single space (8.5). The double space placed between sentences when all characters occupy the same space is required for easy reading (8.6).

● 8.3

Quia

● 8.4

```
Indignor quicquam reprehendi, non quia
crasse compositum. Sed quia nuper, nec
veniam antiquis, sed honorem et praemia
posci.
```

● 8.5

Behind the Scenes

Robin Williams:
Devoted to Beautiful Text

Robin Williams is devoted to typography. She has spent much of her career condensing vast amounts of often obscure information about typography into plain English. Though deadly serious about her topic, Robin's writing is delivered with a lighthearted approach. Many designers instantly "get it" when Robin puts forth a concept or technique to improve text, even when they have been stumbling around in the subject for a long time.

Robin is the author of many books, including one I highly recommend for *every* designer, *The Non-Designer's Type*

Book (Peachpit Press 1998). Robin also writes articles and conducts workshops on desktop publishing and typography, and is a regular columnist for Eyewire, a company supplying images, type, and more to the design community. (Read Robin's columns at www.eyewire.com/magazine/columns/robin/.) Her career keeps her travelling much of the time, but she calls New Mexico home.

Although Robin now hires designers to complete any Web design she requires, I am thrilled to be able to bring this conversation I had with her to you. In my

Compare the same sentences with a proportional font, however (8.7). The text characters are packed in much more closely, and a single space between sentences creates a highly visible break. Any fonts you will use for Web design require only a single space.

[N O T E]

Double spacing between sentences is a habit carried over from typewriter practice. Underlining is another method that stems from a time when there were very few ways to make text stand out. If you're concerned about a professional presentation, make sure you avoid both practices (unless you're presenting a link, of course).

Kerning and Tracking

Typography offers more than just overall proportional character spacing, however. Using a graphics program to create text provides powerful control over how characters relate to each other. Your goal with type should be to create a phrase, or even one word, that holds together perfectly as a unit, yet offers enough that the eye can read the individual characters. Both tracking and kerning are typography tools that you can use to accomplish this lofty type of goal.

Tracking is a common term describing the overall spacing of characters. Loose tracking opens up the characters, and is often used in a decorative way. The example here (8.8) shows the default character spacing first, then loose tracking, and finally, tight tracking.

Kerning is like tracking, but refers to adjusting spacing between individual characters. I have taken some text with tight kerning and adjusted the position of a few of the characters in the lower example (8.9). The arrows show the direction I moved a character

```
Indignor quicquam reprehendi, non quia
crasse compositum.  Sed quia nuper, nec
veniam antiquis, sed honorem et praemia
posci.
```

● 8.6

Indignor quicquam reprehendi, non quia crasse compositum. Sed quia nuper, nec veniam antiquis, sed honorem et praemia posci.

● 8.7

Ave quid haberet.
Ave quid haberet.
Ave quid haberet.

● 8.8

Ave quid haberet.
Ave quid haberet.

● 8.9

opinion, nobody in the design world has done more to teach designers how to create great type. That subject applies to all design, whether for print or Web.

Q : You have devoted much of your career to teaching others about typography. What is it about this subject that captures your attention?

A: Hmm, that's a good question. I've never thought about *why* I particularly love type. I suppose it's just one of those unfathomable passions that doesn't have a clear beginning — like why some people love to collect stamps or build toy trains, or join the Society for Creative Anachronisms. I've always found it fascinating that each one of us finds our little peculiar niche that enchants us. Type happens to be [one of] mine.

Q: Your books, *The Mac is Not a Typewriter* **and** *The PC is Not a Typewriter,* **could be considered a checklist for how to prevent an obviously amateur style in your work. Do you still see work (Web or print) that misses the concepts you address in these books? If so, what** **are the common "flags " that the designer does not understand the concept of typography?**

A: I am constantly flabbergasted at the incredibly expensive posters (like Hollywood movie posters), television ads, or magazine ads in which the designer didn't even know how to create a true apostrophe or quotation mark. How could any designer in the 21st century not know how to type an apostrophe correctly???!!!! How could they not SEE it? Aaarrrgggghhhh!!!! Sorry. I'm calming down. One of my pet peeves. If someone

continued

to equalize the spacing between characters. Note how the *A* and *V* are considerably closer in the kerned sample than in the original. Well-designed fonts automatically adjust the spacing between letters like *A* and *V* to work with the actual shape of the characters, but minor adjustments are often necessary for fonts at large size. Free fonts, or low-cost fonts often do not include character pairing, and manual kerning is required for great results.

[N O T E]

You learn how to adjust kerning, tracking, and leading in Photoshop and Fireworks later in this chapter.

Line Spacing or Leading

Kerning or tracking is used to hold characters together in a sentence for easy reading. Line spacing, or the correct typography term, *leading* (rhymes with sledding), is equally critical for presenting multiple line headings as a unit. Default values for leading in

many graphics programs is too large (8.10). The first line of text hardly seems to be connected to the portion of the title on the second line.

On the other hand, moving the second line quite close to the first creates a unit that leaves no doubt that the two lines are one element (8.11). Pay attention to how close the lines are in this headline. If this proportion of spacing were used for body text, the spacing would be far too close.

Ribicinibus Nunc Gavisa Tragoedis

● 8.10

Ribicinibus Nunc Gavisa Tragoedis

● 8.11

 (continued)

doesn't even know how to set a true quote or apostrophe, it is a HUGE clue that they know nothing AT ALL about any other aspect of typography. On the Web, it is understandable not to have true quotes in body copy because of the variabilities in browser display. But there is no excuse for using straight quotes in any text that has been saved as a graphic. It is the single biggest sign of an amateur designer. And I say "designer" and not just "typographer" because every designer MUST know typographic principles today. (And needs to know *where* to put the apostrophes and quotes! Another pet peeve. Makes me nuts to see packaging in supermarkets that says things like *Cookies 'n' Cream.*)

Another big flag is using two spaces after punctuation. I don't even want to argue about it. It's wrong. That's not just my opinion — it is standard professional typographic procedure.

And the third big flag is paragraph indentation. A first paragraph, or one following a subhead, does not have an indent. And when there is an indent, it's NOT a half inch, nor five spaces. It's about two spaces. And you can choose to indent OR put space between paragraphs, *but not both.*

OH YEAH. AND USING ALL CAPS WHEN THERE IS NO REASON FOR IT. ALL CAPS ARE SOOOO HARD TO READ. ESPECIALLY ON A WEB PAGE, WHICH IS DIFFICULT TO READ ALREADY.

Okay. I feel better now.

Q: Why should a designer, especially a Web designer who faces so many restrictions for where and when typography tools can be used, learn correct typography techniques, especially true professional techniques like those covered in *The Non-Designer's Type Book***?**

A: Many of the typographic principles in print are specifically designed to create

more readable or legible (those are two different things) type. On a Web page, which is intrinsically more difficult to read than paper, a designer must be even more conscious of readability and legibility and do everything possible to make reading on the screen a pleasant and easy experience. The guidelines for what makes type readable or legible on paper must be applied to the screen in an even greater degree (although there are a few differences between readability in print and on the screen).

Half of *The Non-Designer's Design Book* (not the *Type* book) is devoted to choosing different typefaces that work well together. This is just as important on the Web as it is in print. It is a key to creating type treatments that bring a reader's eye to the page, that give the page a dynamic edge and strength, as opposed to a wimpy page or conflicting visual stuff. It's also one of the most fun aspects of design, I think.

[N O T E]

No hard and fast rules exist for how much leading, kerning, or tracking is correct. Each font, and each application of each font, is unique. Applying the correct amount of spacing is a skill that you learn a little at a time, observing what works and what doesn't. Now that you are aware of these settings, your work should improve instantly, however. You may not have been happy with the results you obtained in the past, but simply knowing that these adjustments may be necessary will automatically make you pick up problems and correct them.

Typography Extras

After you master the basic typography spacing tools, you can move to the extras — the techniques that tell the world that you know what you're doing with your type. You learn how to create these effects in Photoshop and Fireworks in the next chapter, "Creating Graphic Text for the Web," but for now, I just want to introduce you to the typography methods I feature in this book.

Quotation Marks

Designers often make mistakes when working with quotation marks. Probably nothing says amateur more quickly than using the quotes that are available straight from the keyboard. Using the quotation marks in many programs creates straight quote marks ("), with opening and closing quotes identical. When used in a quote with a large font, the result is unattractive and can be confusing (8.12).

Using typographer's quotes, which are often referred to in graphics programs as smart quotes, adds a professional touch. These quotes have an opening (") and closing (") style, and have a much more elegant

"Rigicinibus nunc gavisa tratoedis. Avedis quid haberet."

● 8.12

Q: What characteristics do you look for in a headline font?

A: It depends if the headline is a large, major head or smaller ones, like a series of headlines that mark different stories on a page.

Large, major heads can be more playful and juicy, while functional heads that readers need to scan quickly to decide what they want to read need to be the utmost in legibility (not readability). Headlines to be scanned should definitely NOT be all caps or italic or a strange typeface. A bold (but not too bold) sans serif is simple and not too exciting, but works best.

Q: What characteristics do you look for in a font that will be used at a small size, for example, menus?

A: On a Web page, I really prefer the fonts that have been specially designed to fit within the pixels on the screen and

that don't need to be aliased (like those from atomicmedia.net or wpdfd.com). They are so much clearer and easier to read at tiny sizes — just beautiful. Using something like Times in small type on the screen is so bad; Times is designed for high-resolution printing and is a very poor choice for Web type, especially at small sizes.

Q: When and why do you use novelty fonts?

A: Ooh, aren't these the most fun faces to use? But you have to use them like ice cream — as well-deserved treats. Even on a simple Web page with no graphics and lots of text, one lovely treatment with a particularly fun typeface will give a page an attitude. Just make sure it's the correct attitude for the content of the page!

Q: Typography embraces both long-standing tradition with classic fonts and innovation in font design. What

trends do you see in the type design or application over the next few years?

A: Throughout history type has always responded not only to technology but also to the changing social and philosophical trends. For instance, the industrial revolution changed typography, as did the unlocking of the Rosetta stone. The invention of the Macintosh computer put type through the most radical changes since the invention of the movable type printing press in 1450 — for the first time on earth type was in the hands of the masses and wow did type explode. And now the Web is forcing yet more changes. As far as predicting what new trends will appear, I'm no good at that at all — I simply gawk in amazement and delight as the world around me morphs daily.

Q: In your opinion, has the explosion in the size and popularity of the Web affected professional font design? Font distribution? Any other aspect of typography?

continued

Pixels or Points?

Pixels are the best choice for font unit when you're setting fixed size for HTML text controlled by CSS. Because your page is usually designed only to be viewed on a monitor, which displays in pixels, using this measure makes sense. You achieve your most reliable results with pixels.

When you work in a graphics program, you always have the choice to use points, the traditional font measure in print work. However, if your graphic program allows you to use pixels, using that option is best. You will be setting your image size in pixels, and importing the image into a document that uses pixels as the base unit. There is no benefit to using points for Web design, and mixing the units can cause confusion.

Some graphics programs do provide the option to use pixels for font size. Photoshop offers the font unit size on the toolbar whenever the Type tool is active. In Adobe Illustrator you can change the default setting of point text to pixels by choosing Edit → Preferences → Units & Undo.

However, many graphics programs still do not offer pixels as a text size option. These include Fireworks, CorelDRAW, Freehand, and Paintshop Pro. You have to do some experimenting with these programs when trying to match font size in your HTML documents. I usually find that I must use a slightly larger number when I work in points. For example, if I want the text to be close in size to 12 pixels, and must export from a program that does not offer pixel sizing, I specify 12.5 or 13 points to get the right effect. Text from a graphics program usually has antialiasing added, so the softer character edges demand a slightly larger font for the same effect.

Check your program to see whether you can change the font size units to pixels. For Web design, it is the best choice. If this adjustment is available, you will likely find it in the Preferences section, or in an on-screen text attributes panel.

---

shape than the straight keyboard quotes. Also, you should adjust your type so that the first character of each line is aligned in the quote (8.13). There is quite a difference.

[N O T E]

Many graphics programs now automatically convert keyboard quotes to smart quotes. You learn how to set quote preferences in Photoshop and Fireworks later in this chapter.

Character Position and Size

All type sits on a baseline. This term refers to the position of the bottom of most characters. Some characters have portions of the lowercase style that falls below the baseline, called descenders. These characters include *g, j, p, q, y*. In the example of two fonts shown here, the orange line marks the baseline, and the blue line marks the x-height, another common term in typography (8.14). Note how the uppercase *P* does not have a descender, but the lowercase *p* does.

(continued)

A: Absolutely. Professional type designers used to make decent money designing type. It takes years to create a well-designed, professional type family, even with our computers today. But the widespread accessibility and popularity of type, plus the number of non-professional designers using type, has lowered the expectations of the public. Few people will pay $300 or $400 for a great face, or the $1,600 for an extended family. Thus the less expensive, often less well-designed faces are much more popular, as well as all

the free fonts created by people like my daughter when she was seven years old.

Font distribution is fabulous. I LOVE being able to find a font, buy it, then download it instantly. (Remember to always make a backup of those fonts on a disk so you still have it when your hard disk dies!)

Q: Thinking only as a Web user, what would you like to see from designers to make typography, and text in general on the Web, more effective?

A: Readability and legibility are the two aspects of Web typography that most

need to be understood by Web designers. And these two major features are a bit different from print to Web, so if a designer provides a print-friendly version of a page in addition to the screen version, she needs to understand the differences and accommodate them (and fix the quotation marks for print).

Type combinations are important, also (choosing which different faces work well together). And emotive typography (choosing a typeface that emphasizes and supports the attitude expressed in the content). And letterspacing is critical for

[N O T E]

Paying attention to x height is important because a font with a high x height, like Arial, requires extra line spacing for easy reading. On the other hand, a font with a low x height can be harder to read, especially on a monitor. Add this measure to what you study when you see text that works to help you develop an instinct on how to work with varying x height.

You can achieve some great effects by moving text from the baseline, especially when you add color and vary the size of some characters (8.15). However, the most valuable use for adjusting character position is to create professional-looking results for unusual text elements. Typing parentheses does not produce a balanced result. Shifting the opening and closing parentheses characters up to the center of the word looks much better (8.16).

"Rigicinibus nunc gavisa tratoedis. Avedis quid haberet."

● 8.13

People

People

● 8.14

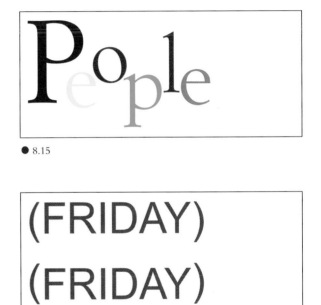

● 8.15

(FRIDAY)

(FRIDAY)

● 8.16

those lovely headlines. And knowing *where* to put the apostrophes and quotation marks is really important so you don't look like an illiterate designer. Understanding letter spacing, line spacing, paragraph spacing, and headline-to-text spacing according to the chosen typeface is intrinsic to readable type, as well as knowing how to control those things using style sheets. And *knowing* which typefaces read best on the screen — not just blindly using the defaults assigned by the Web authoring software. And understanding typographic contrast to help guide a reader through a page is critical. Ah, so much to do!

Q: Is there anything else you would like to talk about with this reader group? You do bring a unique perspective because you have chosen not to design for the Web anymore, but you have experience from before you decided to have someone else do the Web work you require.

A: It's always been amazing to me how typography is often the last thing designers learn about, if they bother to learn it at all. It amazes me because graphic design and Web design is ABOUT type. If there is no type, it's not design — it's something else, such as fine art or ceramics. But *how* to design using the written

word doesn't seem to be a priority with many designers. Isn't that odd? I guess to those who don't have a passion for it, it's not very sexy. But there is no great design without great typography.

"Type is one of the most eloquent means of expression in every epoch of style. It gives the most characteristic portrayal of a period and the most severe testimony of a nation's intellectual status."

Peter Behrens
Included by Robin Williams

Keyboard Shortcuts for Typographer's Quotes

You can create typographer's quotes in any program using keyboard shortcuts on both PC and Mac computers. PC users must use the the number pad to enter the numbers:

PC keyboard shortcuts are

Alt+0147 for opening quotes (")

Alt+0148 for the closing quotes (")

Alt+0145 for single opening quotes (')

Alt+0146 for single closing quotes (')

For the Mac the keyboard shortcuts are

Option +Shift+[for opening quotes (")

Option +Shift+] for the closing quotes (")

Otpion +[for single opening quotes (')

Option +] for single closing quotes (')

This result is even more dramatic when extra editing is used to present a price in parentheses (8.17). Note how the price value is much easier to comprehend in addition to the more professional appearance.

Don't miss the decorative opportunity to be creative with varied text size and position (8.18). In this example, I used a different font for the larger initial character, and moved it down from the baseline. To create a finished look, and add more interest, I added a fine line, which also anchors the smaller characters.

[**T I P**]

When you work with text in a graphics program, try to think of it as a graphic element, rather than simply text. When you create an image, you commonly note that another element is required to bring in a certain color, or to fill in a spot that feels too empty. Text elements are exactly the same, and respond to the decorative practices you use in all your work. Keep your eyes open as you surf the Web or leaf through magazines, for interesting text treatments. Often a tiny line can take your text from yawn to wow. Just remember that you must not interfere with the message of the text.

Web Versus Print: Making the Shift to Monitor Display

Throughout the first two sections of this book, I cover many techniques to help designers keep control of text when possible, but also that Web text was not fully predictable or controllable. The natural answer when you must keep text under control is to create that text as an image. Although you do have complete control over text when you place it on a page as an image, you cannot necessarily just transport your print methods when you design text that will be viewed only on a monitor.

Text is seen on a printed page in a different way than it is viewed on a monitor. The shape and color on a page is presented in a reflective manner. The light hits the page from an external source and reflects back to your eye (8.19). In all but the most unusual settings, you see this reflection from an opaque page.

Viewing text on a printed page is nearly the opposite of viewing your page on a monitor. On a monitor, the color and shape of objects, including text, are seen with the light coming from behind (8.20). Turn off all the lights in a room, and you can still see the contents of a page on a monitor.

The difference in viewing makes a dramatic difference for design. A few adjustments may pop instantly

(249.95)

(249.^{95})

● 8.17

● 8.18

to mind. Obviously, a light color that is illuminated from behind has less impact than the same color viewed on a printed page with reflected light. Be especially careful with light yellow and gold colors. They can disappear completely on a page, and text is rarely legible in yellow at a small size on a white background (8.21). The text shown here is legible on the paper, but is almost impossible to read on a monitor.

You also must be careful with one of the most used decorative techniques for type in print. When you're producing pages that will be printed at high quality, the unit size that creates the picture is very small. Monitor display is quite coarse in comparison.

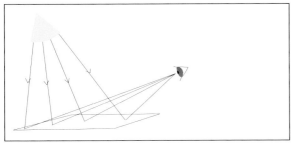

● 8.19

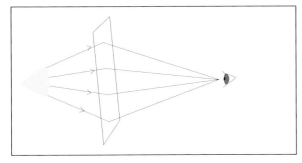

● 8.20

Quod si tam Graecis novitas invisa fuisset quam nobis, quid nunc esset vetus? Aut quid haberet quod legeret tereretque viritim. Ut primum positis nugari Graecia bellis coepit et in vitium fortuna labier aequa, nunc athletarum studiis, nunc arsit equorum, marmoris aut eboris fabros aut aeris amavit, tibicinibus, nunc est gavisa tragoedis; sub nutrice puella.

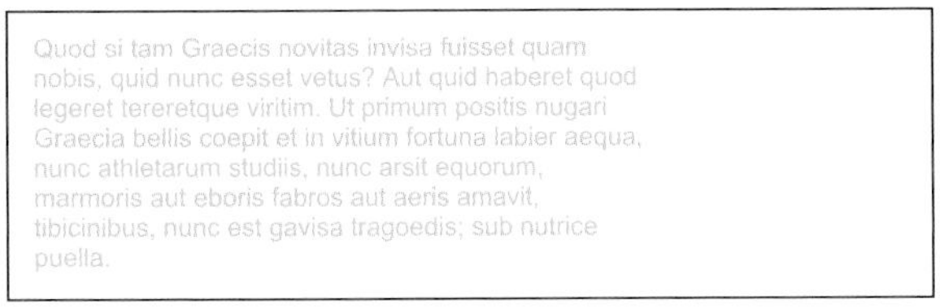

● 8.21

Hairline decorative elements, like lines, or circles around or through text may look great on a high-quality printed page (8.22), but lose much of their impact when exported to an image viewed on a monitor (8.23).

[**T I P**]

Design is not an exact science at the best of times, and text is perhaps the least definable design element. If you come from the print world to Web design, you may not be able to depend on the techniques that you use quite successfully for printed design. Always keep the difference in light source, and coarse monitor resolution in mind when you attempt to borrow from print. Better yet, search the Web for great examples of Web design done well. Many great print designers have learned to work with the new medium very successfully. A site like Cool Home Pages (`http://coolhomepages.com`) is a great place to start.

Selecting Fonts

When you produce text as an image, you can consider using any font you have installed on your computer. The restricted number of fonts for CSS text is

● 8.22

● 8.23

not an issue. However, the opposite problem surfaces. How can you choose the correct font from hundreds, or even thousands of fonts? With so many more choices included with software programs, or instantly available for little or no charge on the Web, the choice can be overwhelming.

Like most designers, I confess to being a fontaholic. This term is accepted in the design world, and rightly so. Like the old expression, "The one who dies with the most toys, wins," designers believe that "The one who dies with the most fonts, wins." A little tongue in cheek, but true enough to bring a smile.

Unfortunately, most of those thousands of fonts are destined to do no more than provide some harmless entertainment as you track them down, download them, and install them. The vast majority of fonts, especially free ones, have no practical use on the Web. In fact, they have little practical use in print. The trouble with fonts is that no matter how innovative, creative, funky, or beautiful they may be, if readers can't instantly read the title or headline you create with the font, it has no value.

I love grunge fonts, the fonts that look dirty and mucked up. Unfortunately, most grunge fonts are barely legible, especially at smaller sizes. I have included samples of two fonts that I really like. The first is Ugly Face, and it has so much character (8.24). At large size, it is quite legible. However, look what happens when you reduce the size to 12 pixels (8.25). The top sample is Ugly Face, and the lower sample is Arial. When it comes to pure legibility, Arial wins hands down.

You can see the same effect with a font named Butterbrotpapier (8.26). Again, at large size, even the impossibly long title is legible. But drop the size to 12 points, and even the shortened title is nearly illegible, especially when compared to the Arial sample in the lower cell (8.27).

Although I usually work in the corporate world, occasionally, I do have the opportunity to work on a fun site for a young audience (8.28). On this site, which is no longer active, I tried my best to use a novelty font. However, as always happens, I found myself falling back to the classic fonts for important page elements. I did get a little novelty font use into the bullet points at the top of the page, but even they are much tamer than my original intent. When it comes right to it, Tricia's quote at the beginning of this chapter holds so true.

Butterbrotpapier

● 8.26

Butter
Butter

● 8.27

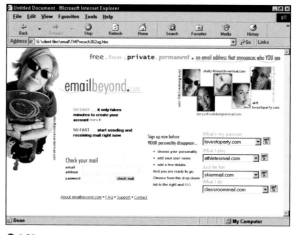

● 8.28

Ugly Face

● 8.24

● 8.25

The classic fonts are usually the best choice for most pages. Of course, there are always exceptions, but as a general rule, sticking to the fonts you know is best. You can dress up plain fonts in so many ways, especially if you become proficient with typography, and rarely does legibility become a problem.

Avoid the Top Ten Errors in Graphic Typography

New designers often spend a great deal of energy trying to identify what is most important in their quest to learn. Of course, any new skill requires building knowledge, but having a tidy list of where to start helps. I have prepared a list of common typography errors to help you improve your pages quickly. If you want to have pages with great text, make sure you avoid doing any of the following:

1. **Using an inappropriate font for the page.**

   It is hard to use a poor font when using HTML text, but when the bounds come off with text as an image, you have many chances to play the "look at the cool font I found" game. Make sure that the fonts you use are appropriate for the mood of the site, and that visitors can read any text without effort.

2. **Appling as many special effects to type as you can manage.**

   Current graphic programs do offer a dizzying array of decorative filters, but most do not belong on type. In fact, when you use an effect on text, you should be able to point to exactly why that effect will help the text legibility. I often use a drop shadow to make the text stand out, or a glow around the outside of the text to make it stand out from a patterned background. If you have an effect on your text, you should know why. If the reason is simply to make it look good, be vigilant in ensuring that you have not reduced legibility in that pursuit.

3. **Creating graphic text only because you want control.**

   A few years ago, many professional designers were using graphic text for this very reason. However, today, a page with unnecessary text as a graphic screams "amateur." Use graphic text only when you need a specific font, or a decorative effect to enhance the experience for your visitor. It's rare that graphic text should be used for more than page titles, menus, and headlines. Make sure a graphic image earns its keep.

4. **Allowing too much space between lines in multiple line headlines.**

   When I see a large gap between lines in any headline, I know that the designer does not understand the basics of typography. Multiple lines should look like a unit, which almost always requires tightening the space between lines in headlines.

5. **Using keyboard quotes in graphic text.**

   I have to put this forth as one of my pet peeves. When you use graphic text, you obviously want to have text that looks great. One glance at a keyboard quote mark, and the whole effect goes down the drain.

6. **Accepting default kerning for your type, especially for lower-end fonts.**

   I admit that this error is a bit on the perfectionist side, but if you're going to add the work and file size of graphic text, you might as well do it right. For as much graphic text as should be included on a page, taking the few extra minutes to make sure that your kerning is in great shape is worth it. Most fonts used at above 12 points (or pixels) can benefit from kerning. Nearly every font at 18 points plus requires at least minor kerning.

7. **Failing to create perfect rollover images.**

   Call me obsessed, but I hate to see the work go into creating images for rollovers, and to have the original and rollover image be off by one pixel. Beyond my obsessive tendencies, having an image jumping on rollover is very uncomfortable, and certainly pulls credibility into question. Along this same line, a rollover effect doesn't have to smash the visitor over the head. A change in color, or background, can do the trick. You don't need to feature a sinking button, and a text color change, and a font style change, and a background change (plus sound if we're talking about Flash) just to get the message across that a link lives there. I've seen some jarring effects. Speak softly to your readers, don't shout at them. Web surfers know that they can click with just a slight change on rollover. Let's face it, if they have their mouse cursor in that position, they already suspect there is a link.

8. Using gigantic text.

Okay, it's true that you can add antialiasing with graphic fonts. Sure large fonts look smooth and clean when saved as an image. But exceptionally large text, especially when used in a menu, falls into the shouting I spoke about in the previous point. Let your white space and balanced page provide the required attention for your menus. A perfect menu will be visible the instant that your visitors want to move, but will fade to the background and let them absorb the content when they have arrived at the right spot. I often see menus that demand so much attention that turning your focus to the rest of the page is almost impossible. Rather than using huge text to say, "Hey, over here," place the menu where visitors expect to find it. It may not be the most creative, but you can guarantee that a visitor can find your menu when it's on the left or the top of your page. The flip side to this problem is hiding the menu in the design of the page. This is a "find the menu" game that everyone loses. You depend on luck that your visitor will find your navigation. Even if they do find the menu, your visitors may feel less confident that they can find their way around. It's your job as a designer to direct your visitors, not send them on a treasure hunt.

9. Using teeny text.

In the next chapter, "Creating Graphic Text for the Web," I feature wonderful tiny fonts that display beautifully on a monitor. They have their place, however, and content text is not it. First, you must create text as a graphic in order to feature these special fonts, and you know what I think about content text as a graphic. In addition, if your message is important enough to be featured on a page, why make your visitors work so hard to read it? It takes a better designer to create a page that is beautiful

and practical than it does to create one that indulges "designer need." Don't forget that the page you're creating isn't for you, it's for others. (Of course, if you're creating a page simply for your own entertainment, you can toss all of my visitor protection techniques out the window.)

10. Treating text as text only or as a design element only.

The wonder of text as a graphic is the possibilities, and the richness of the results come from finding the perfect balance between beauty and function. It is a waste to simply "type" when you are going to the trouble of creating text as an image. On the opposite side, text that loses its focus on communication in favor of being an art element also fails. When you embrace typography principles and apply them to your text, you have a powerful tool for creating design elements that communicate perfectly. It is a challenge, but it is also one of the most rewarding aspects of page design. It's also one of the easiest ways to establish yourself as a talented and experienced designer. Visitors, or even clients may not understand one thing about great typography, but they will notice the quality of the page.

Working with Graphics Programs for the Web

You should now have an idea what effects you can achieve with the graphic typography tool. It's time to take a look at how you can accomplish some of these effects in two popular programs, Photoshop and Fireworks. You can accomplish any of the techniques I cover in this chapter with either of these programs.

Working with Text in Photoshop

Two basic types of text creation are available in Photoshop — Point and Paragraph. With the Type tool selected, click on the screen to initiate Point type, which you use to enter a single line, or a short piece of text (8.29). Click and drag with the Type tool to initiate Paragraph type (8.30). The boundary you set when clicking and dragging is filled with the text you type, with lines wrapping at the edge of the defined area. Because I don't recommend that you create content text for Web pages, the perfect reason to use Paragraph type, I focus only on Point type in Photoshop.

[T I P]

Photoshop automatically creates a new text layer when you create Paragraph or Point text. Text layers remain editable unless you rasterize the layer, which changes the layer information from vector text to bitmap format. Unless you have a specific reason to rasterize a text layer, such as to add a filter effect, leaving the layer in text format is best.

Creating Point Type in Photoshop

You can enter formatting values in the Type toolbar, visible at the top of the screen whenever the Type tool is active (8.31). However, because you will also be using typography controls that are not featured on the toolbar, I show how to do all editing in the Character palette (8.32). In my work I generally use the toolbar unless I'm using the specific kerning tools. Try both methods to enter formatting information, and choose whichever method works for you. For this exercise, if it is not already, open the Character palette by choosing Window → Character from the main menu.

To create Point text in Photoshop:

1. **Create a new document 350 pixels wide and 200 pixels high. Set the resolution to 72 pixels/inch and Mode to RGB Color. Set a White background (8.33).**

● 8.31

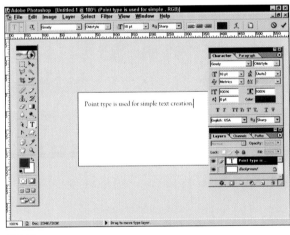
● 8.29

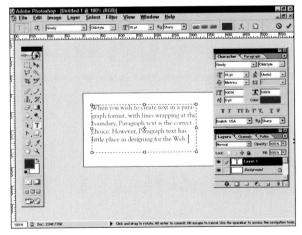
● 8.30

● 8.32

● 8.33

2. In the Character palette, click the color well and set the color to a dark blue. This color is the type color.

3. Set the font to Arial, the font size to 36, and antialiasing to Sharp. The remaining selections should show default values (8.34).

4. With the Type tool selected, click at the left side of the canvas, roughly halfway down the canvas. Type Downtown Venue. A new layer is created with the text you entered as a title, and the typed text appears on the canvas (8.35).

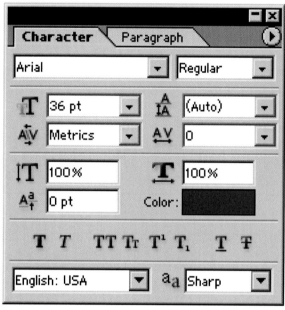

● 8.34

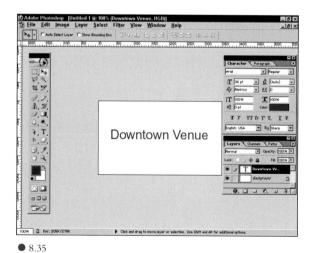

● 8.35

5. Save your document, but keep it open for the next exercise.

[NOTE]

I use Arial for this example, because most computers have this font installed. If you prefer to use a different font, go ahead. It is highly unlikely that the kerning of a different font will be the same as for this example, however. In fact, depending on your computer system, and the particular version of Arial you have installed, your spacing requirements quite possibly will be different from my example. You have to determine where you can adjust the text for your sample.

Adjusting Kerning and Tracking in Photoshop

Perfecting type spacing is easy in Photoshop:

1. With the file from the previous exercise open, and the Type tool active, click and drag over the text to highlight it. Set the value to 50 in the tracking field (8.36). This setting creates text that is too open. Select 5 in the tracking field. This may not be the correct setting for your text. Change the value until you are satisfied.

[NOTE]

I had you select a value that was too high in the previous step simply as an example. Changing the tracking by a value of 5 is barely visible, but I wanted you to use a temporary larger value to clearly see the effect of this setting.

2. To adjust the spacing between individual characters (kerning), insert your cursor between the characters you want to affect. In this case, I have inserted my cursor between the *D* and the *o*. Select –25 from the Kerning field. If this setting does not provide the correct look for your example, select another value. Notice how the tracking field grays out when you place the cursor in the text. Tracking is only available for multiple characters.

Continue kerning between characters until you're satisfied with the results. If the preset values in the drop-down list are not perfect, you can type any value in the Kerning field. You may find setting the values easier if you use a zoom view (8.37).

That's all there is to tracking and kerning control in Photoshop. It truly only takes a minute or two to create perfect text.

[T I P]

If you want to make the identical changes to character attributes for all text on a layer, you can select the layer in the Layers palette, and specify the new attributes in the Options bar or Character palette.

Adjusting Leading in Photoshop

To create two lines for this exercise, add a hard return at the beginning of the second word. The leading is set to Auto as a default. This value is a standard preset for body text size fonts. However, headline size type usually requires much closer spacing. Adjust the leading, or line spacing as follows:

1. **Drag over both lines of text to select. Type** 32 **in the Leading field (8.38). If this setting does not work for your sample, test different values until you are satisfied.**

Adding Creative Effects in Photoshop

With kerning and leading in hand, you can look to more ambitious text effects. For this exercise, you add a character, adjust the font size and color for a single character, and adjust the vertical position for the edited character.

1. **Insert your cursor at the end of the second line of text. Type** 2 **(8.39).**

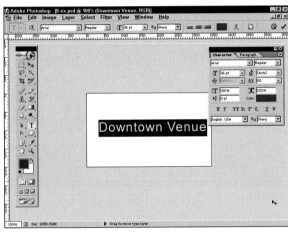

● 8.36

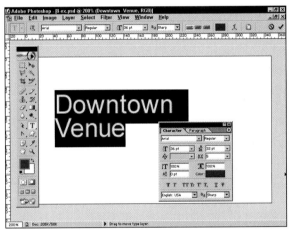

● 8.38

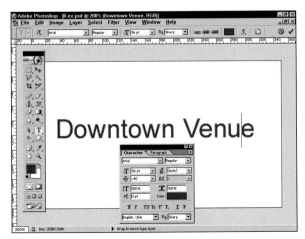

● 8.37

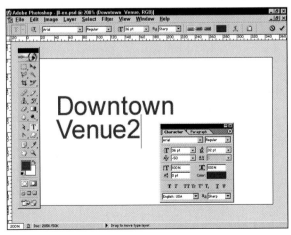

● 8.39

2. **Drag to highlight the character 2. Click the color well and select a red color. Set the font size to 12 (8.40).**

3. **To raise this character, make sure it is still highlighted, and type 15 in the Baseline shift field. The text will raise 15 pixels above the baseline (8.41).**

4. **Finally, if desired, insert your cursor between the *e* and the *2*, and set the kerning to a lower value to bring the raised character closer to the text (8.42).**

Believe it or not, that short list of techniques is all you need to create professional results with typography in Photoshop. Think of a few creative text applications, and use the techniques in this chapter to make your idea come to life. After you create a few pieces of text with great typography, I'm confident you will never again accept default values for your graphic text.

Working with Text in Fireworks

Macromedia Fireworks is one of the most popular Web graphics preparation programs. You can choose to use it as a stand-alone graphics program, or in conjunction with Macromedia Dreamweaver. It has many powerful Web graphics features, but in this exercise, I'm only concerned with the text creation options.

You enter all text in Fireworks into a text block (8.43). This block controls the area the text will cover, and is editable. You can define the area of the text box by clicking and dragging, or you can determine the text wrap manually by entering hard returns. Text control is handled through the Properties Inspector (8.44). If it is not already open, open this window by choosing Window → Properties from the main menu.

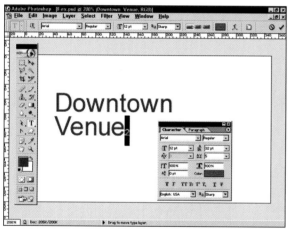

● 8.40

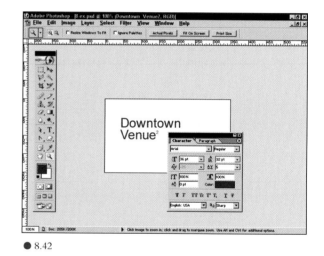

● 8.42

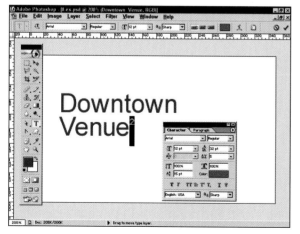

● 8.41

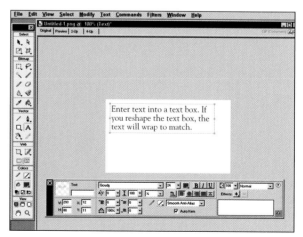

● 8.43

[T I P]

Fireworks creates a new text layer for each text element that you add. This layer maintains the text in vector format, both editable and scaleable. However, if you add filter effects to the text, Fireworks converts the layer to a bitmap layer, and the text is no longer editable. Make sure that you have done all typography adjustments to your text before adding any filter effects. In fact, duplicating the vector layer and keeping an invisible copy of the original layer before you add special effects is best.

Creating Text in Fireworks

To create text in Fireworks, follow these steps:

1. Create a new document 350 pixels wide and 200 pixels high. Set the resolution to 72 pixels/inch and Mode to RGB Color. Set a White background (8.45).

2. In the Properties Inspector, click the color well and set the color to a dark blue. This sets the type color.

3. Set the font to Arial, the font size to 36, and antialiasing to Crisp. Leave all other attributes set to default values (8.46).

4. Set the text alignment to Left, and click the icon to the left of the Left alignment button, selecting Horizontal Left to Right if it is not already selected (8.47).

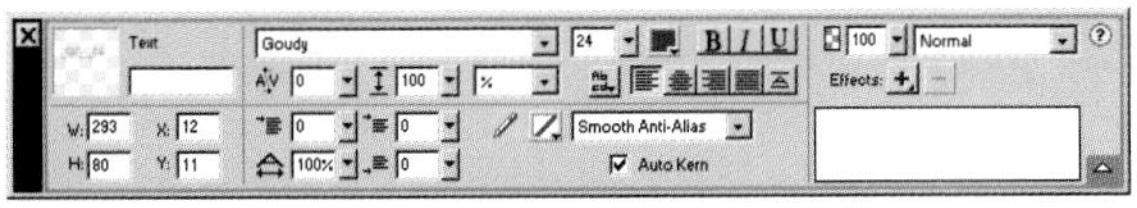

5. With the Text tool selected, click the cursor on the left side of the canvas, roughly halfway down the canvas. Type Downtown Venue. A new layer is created and the typed text appears on the canvas, contained in a text block (8.48).

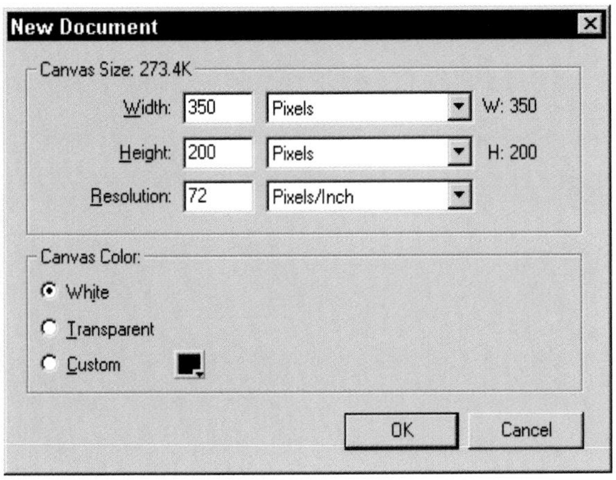

6. Save your document, but keep it open for the next exercise.

[N O T E]

I used Arial for this example, because most computers have this font installed. If you prefer to use a different font, go ahead. It is highly unlikely that the kerning of a different font will be the same as for this sample, however. In fact, depending on your computer system, and the particular version of Arial you have installed, quite possibly your spacing requirements will be different from my example. You have to determine where you can adjust the text for your example.

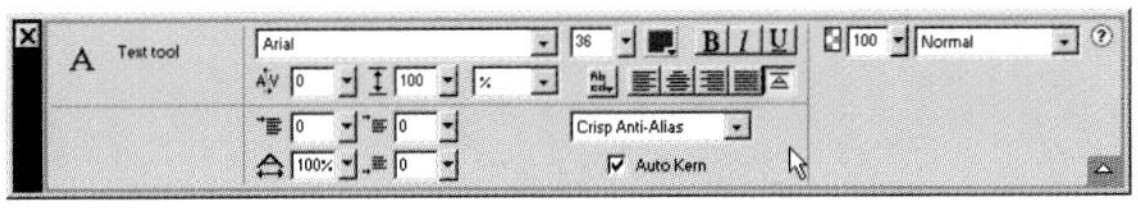

● 8.44

● 8.45

● 8.46

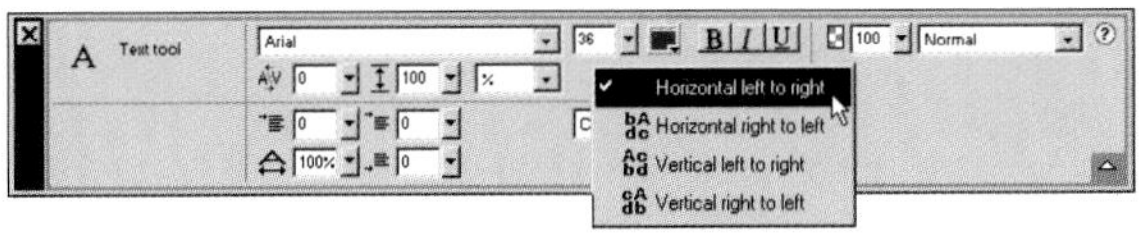

● 8.47

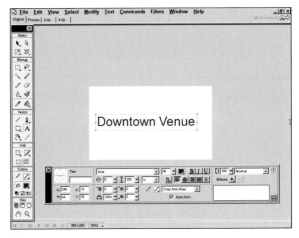

● 8.48

Adjusting Kerning and Tracking in Fireworks

1. **With the file from the previous exercise open, and the Text tool active, drag over the text to highlight it. Set the value to 11 in the Kerning or range kerning field (8.49). This setting creates text that is too open. Select 1 (or type 1, if it is too hard to select with the slider) in the same field. This setting may not be the correct one for your text. Change the value until you're satisfied.**

[**N O T E**]

I had you select a value that was too high in the previous step simply as an example. Changing the tracking by a value of 2 is barely visible, but I wanted you to use a temporary larger value to clearly see the effect of this setting.

2. **To adjust the spacing between individual characters (kerning), insert your cursor between the characters you want to affect. In this case, I have inserted my cursor between the *D* and the *o*. Select –1 from the Kerning and range kerning field. If this setting does not provide the correct look for your sample, select another value. Notice how the tracking field grays out when you place the cursor into the text. Tracking is only available for multiple characters.** Continue kerning between characters until you're satisfied with the results. If the preset values in the drop-down list are not perfect, you can type any value in the Kerning field. You may find setting the values to be easier if you use a zoom view (8.50).

That's all there is to tracking (range kerning) and kerning control in Fireworks. Creating perfect text truly only takes a minute or two.

Adjusting Leading in Fireworks

To create two lines for this exercise, add a hard return at the beginning of the second word. The leading is set to 100% as a default, which is a better setting for headlines than provided by many graphics programs. However, so that you know how to adjust the leading, I'll have you tighten the spacing just a bit. Adjust the leading, or line spacing by dragging over both lines of text to select. Type **96** in the Leading field, and make sure that the % option is active in the units for the Leading field (8.51). If this setting does not

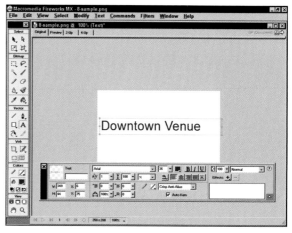

 8.50

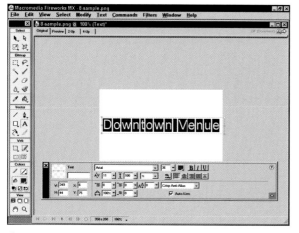

 8.49

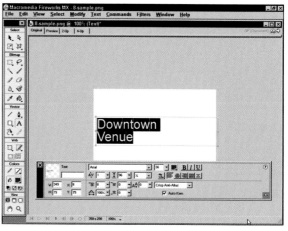

 8.51

work for your example, test different values until you're satisfied.

Adding Creative Effects in Fireworks

With kerning and leading in hand, you can look to more ambitious text effects. For this exercise, you add a character, adjust the font size and color for a single character, and adjust the vertical position for the edited character.

1. **Insert your cursor at the end of the second line of text. Type** 2 **(8.52).**

2. **Drag to highlight the character** 2. **Click the color well and select a red color. Set the font size to 12 (8.53).**

3. **To raise this character, make sure it is still highlighted, and type** 15 **in the Baseline shift field. The text raises 15 pixels above the baseline (8.54).**

4. **Finally, if desired, insert your cursor between the** *e* **and the** *2,* **and set the kerning to a lower value to bring the raised character closer to the text (8.55).**

With the typography tools you have just used, you have all that you need to know to create great type in Fireworks. Think of a few creative text applications, and use the techniques in this chapter to make your ideas come to life. After you create a few pieces of text with great typography, I'm confident you will never again accept default values for your graphic text.

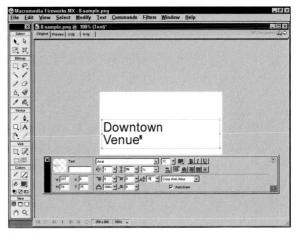

● 8.54

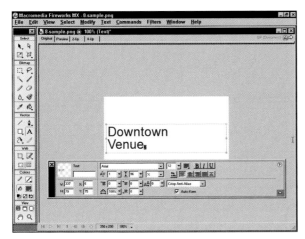

● 8.52

● 8.53

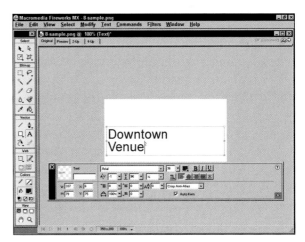

● 8.55

Chapter 9

Creating Graphic Text for the Web

Great typography is not lost on anyone. Even if they cannot say why something looks great, they still know that they are looking at professional work . . . it adds a high credibility factor.

ROBIN WILLIAMS

In the previous chapter, "Introduction to Graphic Typography," I introduced you to typography principles. You also learned how to apply basic typography controls in popular graphics programs. There is a lot more to producing terrific type for the Web than just understanding typography, however. The Web demands type practices that are rarely seen in print, like creating menus, and there is the big leap from graphics program to HTML page. This chapter moves into the finer points of designing with type, and then helps you to move your type to the Web.

[T I P]

If you're wondering where the fancy stuff is, check Chapter 10, "Customizing Graphic Type for the Web," and Chapter 11, "Graphic Type Special Effects." But please come back. The basics are so important to typography that the special effects and design tips that follow this chapter will not lead you to great type unless you spend the time to understand the entire subject.

Creating Great Text for Export

In earlier chapters, I have briefly mentioned two antialiasing concerns that can be solved by creating text in a graphics program. The ability to add antialiasing is one reason that you may choose to move from HTML text to graphic text. Text that is not antialiased, like any HTML text, can have very jagged edges. Graphics programs can add antialiasing, producing much higher quality text at larger sizes.

On the other hand, when you work with very small sizes, antialiasing is not good. The fuzzy edges interfere with legibility. Luckily, special fonts exist that are designed to be crisp and clear, and they definitely do not sport jagged edges. The trouble is that you can't take the chance that these specially designed fonts will be available on your visitor's computer, so you must use them only in a graphics program.

Working with Antialiasing

Any element that is displayed on a monitor is made up of thousands of little squares, or pixels. When you look at a rectangle on a monitor, many little boxes add up to the shape you see (9.1). Because the sides of the object are straight, they appear crisp and clean to your eye.

A curve or diagonal shape does not fare as well, however. There is no such thing as a half pixel, so the curve must be approximated with square pixels (9.2). Without intervention, the result is jagged edges.

Antialiasing compensates for the square nature of pixels by adding pixels at the edge of an object to blend the color of the object with the background

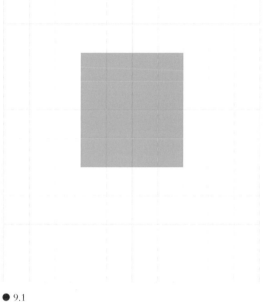

● 9.1

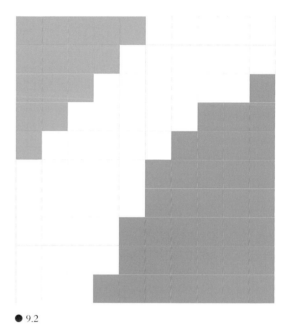

● 9.2

Behind the Scenes

Joe Gillespie: King of the Crisp, Clean Font World

If you have ever worked with a pixel font, the odds are great that the creator of that font was Joe Gillespie. Joe lives in London, England, just a few yards from the River Thames, overlooking a 16th century church graveyard. He works from a home office, mainly doing consulting work now. He came to the Web design world first from a traditional graphic design back-ground, leaping to multimedia just as it started. Joe's clients have included Apple Computer, Canon, Sony, and Microsoft, and he was the driving force behind a project for the *Daily Telegraph*, a major London newspaper. This project resulted in

the launch of the Electronic Telegraph, the first major newspaper to publish on the Web, early in the 1990s.

Joe's background in both traditional and multimedia have meshed perfectly for creating the fonts that have made things much more clear on our Web pages. He understands how important traditional typography is to communication, but has pioneer experience with the demands that monitor display places on fonts. Designers are lucky that Joe chooses to relax from his "work" by designing fonts for the Web.

color. Your eyes see a blend of the high and low contrast pixels between the edge and the background, and are tricked into thinking they see a smooth line (9.3). The examples I show here are grossly exaggerated for illustrative purposes. However, a severely magnified view of an object edge with antialiasing working shows the process in action (9.4). The original object is shown at actual size, with a section of the magnified edge included for comparison.

Although antialiasing is a vital part of creating excellent images in graphics programs, it also has a downside, especially with text. One of the characteristics that makes text easy to read is how crisp the edges are, and how much contrast exists between the outer edge of the text and the background. Antialiasing deliberately blurs this contrast. At large text size, the antialiasing effect only affects a small percentage of the total character size. Notice how the

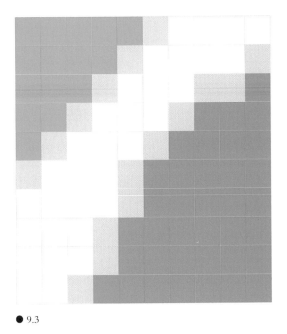

● 9.3

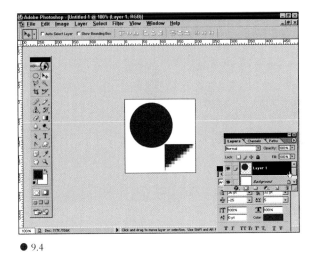

● 9.4

Q: How did you come to graphic design and/or Web design?

A: As a child, I was good at art, music, and practical things, and hopeless at math and foreign languages. I did a one-year foundation course at art college, where I got to try everything, and gravitated towards graphic design. I then did the three-year graphic design course in the mid-'60s. The college I went to was heavily biased towards the printing industry so I got hands-on experience with real metal type, which taught me the "mechanics" of typography, but not much about typographic design. I then spent another three years at the Royal College of Art in London where the emphasis was very much on design and conceptual thinking and got my master's degree in visual communication.

Seven poverty stricken years of art college!

Q: You are the pixel font expert, probably of the world. How did you become interested in this one aspect of type design?

A: Necessity, mother of invention and all that. When I worked in multimedia, I needed small type for buttons and interface elements. Fonts designed for printing never work well at small sizes on a comparatively low-resolution screen. I had been involved with font design for text display on television at one stage in my career and was very aware of the problems – and solutions. I designed a couple of small fonts specifically for computer screen display, one of which was MINI 7. MINI 7 is the smallest font possible. Being only 5 pixels high, you just can't form an *A* or *E* with any less. You need one pixel for the tail of commas and the letter *Q*, and there is another pixel of line space, making seven pixels in total – hence MINI 7.

continued

large text, 72 pixels, in this example (9.5) is crisp and clean, yet the small text, 14 pixels, is quite fuzzy. Both of these samples were created with the same font and the sharpest antialiasing available.

You can see what is happening in the magnified view of the same words (9.6). Note how only a few pixels on the edge of the large text have been affected by antialiasing, yet on the smaller text, nearly all the pixels have been included. The effect is so disruptive that finding one pixel remaining in the original color is difficult.

So, why not just leave the antialiasing off smaller text? One look at that result provides the answer (9.7). All the elegance you can see in the larger version of this font has been stripped away. The small gray box in this sample contains a magnified version

of the smaller font so you can see exactly how the characters have been shaped.

[T I P]

All fonts are not created equal when it comes to antialiasing. In fact, the fonts that will react well at smaller sizes are fairly predicable. Fonts with fine detail, and many changes in direction through the vertical and horizontal portions of the characters are more affected by antialiasing. They simply have more edge area to adjust. Thin fonts with curved lines are especially hard hit, because the antialiasing works on the curve, and because it has so few pixels to work with, the results will not be good. The best fonts for small sizes are blocky and relatively straight. Less antialiasing is required, and when it is, enough pixels exist to change the edge without wrecking the main shape.

Many graphics programs offer varying degrees of antialiasing, which can help to create the best results. Photoshop offers None, Sharp, Crisp, Smooth, and Strong as options. Fireworks offers Crisp, Strong, or Smooth, along with no antialiasing. As with so many techniques in graphics, no set rule exists, though for

Headline

● 9.5

(continued)

Q: You have created many pixel font sets that you offer for sale at reasonable prices (see `http://wpdfd.com`**). How did you venture into creating commercial fonts?**

A: I had been using MINI 7 on sites that I'd done and people kept writing to me and asking what that small font is. At that stage, it was only a Macintosh bitmap screen font with no vector outline so it only worked in Photoshop on a Mac. So, in December 2000, I was in the usual pre-holiday work lull and decided to draw-up MINI 7 as a TrueType font and generate a few more variants — condensed, expanded, and so on. I put them on sale on WPDFD in January 2001 and by the end of the month had sold about

2,000 copies. I believe it is better to sell 2,000 copies at $15 than 500 at $30, and that's what usually happens, or people just "share" them if they are too expensive.

MINI 7 is only capital letters and I had another font that was called MINI 10 at that stage, which was based on the minimum 5-pixel height for lowercase characters. I launched that as Tenacity and it sold very well, too.

Needless to say, the response to my fonts encouraged me to do more and eventually I launched a dedicated site — minifonts. com — to sell them, although WPDFD, with its large traffic of Web designers, is still the main store window. There is now a whole range of pixel fonts going from 10 to 22 pixels. At sizes larger than that, printer fonts usually work just fine.

Q: Do you have any pet peeves about how text is used on the Web?

A: The most common mistake, by far, is for people to allow lines of text to flow the full width of the screen. This result is lines of text that are too long for optimal readability and, when combined with inappropriate fonts and almost no line spacing, become very difficult and tiring to read.

I also hate this concept of database-driven pages where the text is "poured-in" with no consideration for typography whatsoever. I know they are necessary, but I'd rather not be involved.

Q: With so much attention turning to CSS generally, and menus in particular, in the past couple of years, do you

Web design, the first setting offered is often the best choice. With some fonts, telling the difference between the antialiasing settings is difficult, whereas with others, the text may be great with one setting, and terrible with another. If you're not happy with how your text looks, try a different one.

● 9.6

If you require small text that is clear, you're better off looking to pixel fonts, as described in the next section.

Creating Pixel Text for Menus

You've seen the result when you add antialiasing to small text, but at times, you want smaller text to use for menus, or perhaps for directional elements in your pages. With pixel fonts, you can use small fonts that will fit into a smaller menu area, leaving you more room for content, and helping your menu to be a background element when not in use. Because these fonts are designed for use at a small size and

● 9.7

think that graphic menus, a common place to use pixel fonts, will become a thing of the past?

A: No. With CSS, you are still stuck with generic fonts, the same ones used for body text. At the moment, small GIFs are the only way to introduce the non-generic fonts that give a site character and identity. Pixel fonts can be saved as two colors (1-bit), as they don't need all the extra colors required for antialiasing, so they are very small in file size.

You have to recognize that CSS is only a means to an end and that a Web site usually has a much higher purpose than merely satisfying some "rules". Again, we are on the borderlines between pushing and fighting. With my background in advertising, corporate, and brand identity,

it is more important for me to produce a compelling site with a unique character and message than to fight the medium — with one arm tied behind my back.

CSS fundamentalists interpret the "standards" in their own extreme ways without standing back and asking, "What are we really trying to achieve?" The point of taking your car to the supermarket is to allow you to carry home vast amounts of groceries; it is not to demonstrate how well you know the highway code or to brag about the accuracy of the cogwheels in your gearbox. If a Web site validates as squeaky clean, that's fine, but if that becomes the *purpose* of the exercise, then something more important has probably been overlooked. It's the tail wagging the dog!

I am very happy to use the extra layout possibilities that CSS offers, although strictly compliant code diminishes those possibilities somewhat. The CSS box model has no equivalent to the depricated table cell `valign='middle'` and `valign='bottom'`, which is a major omission in my view. For some layouts, I am forced to use non-compliant markup as there is just no alternative. If I want to center an image or line of text vertically in a browser window, I can set a table to 100% height and `valign='middle'` — but the W3C validator doesn't like it. I reckon that is their oversight, not mine!

I also think that the W3C standards are hopelessly inconsistent and confusing; even the browser manufacturers and programmers are confused, so what hope is there for us poor designers?

continued

without antialiasing, the results are excellent (9.8). The secret is in the specially designed characters with a minimum of diagonal lines, to ensure a smooth appearance without the assistance of antialiasing.

You must use pixel fonts without antialiasing and at the exact size that is specified for that font, or multiples of that size. Most fonts are scaleable, meaning that you can use them at any size with good results. Pixel fonts are literally customized pixel by pixel, so even one size larger or smaller breaks the perfect engineering. See how the font Tenacity, designed to be used at 10 pixels, falls apart at other sizes (9.9). In this sample, the first menu item is shown at 8 pixels, the second at the correct 10 pixels, the third at 12 pixels, and the fourth at 14 pixels. Only the 10-pixel

sample looks crisp and clean. The characters in the 8-pixel sample have broken up because there is character shape information that cannot be included. The larger samples show extra pixels that are added to the characters, throwing off the delicate balance in the character shapes.

Pixel fonts can range from very tiny to 22-point size (perhaps higher that I have not seen). Thinking of pixel text only as small text is common. I do it myself. And it does come in small variations like MINI 7, designed to be used at 7 pixels (9.10). However, don't miss the great text you can create with larger pixel fonts. Maxxi is meant to be used at 20 pixels (9.11).

● 9.8

● 9.9

   (continued)

Q: How do you use pixel fonts in graphics programs that only offer point sizing for type, when pixel fonts are dependent on pixel sizing?

A: I only know of one such program, PaintShop Pro — even with a page resolution set to 72 ppi, it insists in setting type at 96 ppi. All the other graphic programs can handle both pixels and points. (Well, actually, the Windows version of Flash has a problem, too. It can handle font sizes in pixels just fine, but its line spacing is in points, which means that multi-line settings shift off the pixel grid. Dumb!)

For people who have problems with font sizes in pixels, I have written a little utility called SimpleSetter, which lets you set the type in pixels, and then the setting can be copied and pasted into any program. It has

several other nice features for setting text and pictorial fonts and is available free for Windows and Mac users from www.minifonts.com/simplesetter, but does require the user to have Tenacity installed, as it needs at least one consistent font for its interface elements.

Q: You have a great new site, Fun with Fonts (www.funwithfonts.com/). It is well named, as you do have fun designs featured, yet it does feature serious typography methods. What was your reason for starting this site?

A: There are a number of reasons. Firstly, it is a test-bed for CSS-P techniques. Again, I'm pushing to see how far I can go before it starts fighting. As it transpires, the main browsers can handle even the trickiest CSS-P pretty well, but the Web page editors like Dreamweaver and GoLive are lagging somewhat behind. This

means that designers, at the minute, have to use text editors to do such layouts.

If you are a "right-brainer" who thinks and works in terms of images, as most graphic designers do, it is a major hurdle. They think in pictures, probably working out their ideas in Photoshop, and then they have to translate that into markup code so that the browser can change it back into pictures. That, to me, constitutes "fighting."

The work flow from concept to final production is not as transparent as it could be. The problem, of course, is that the programmers who write these programs are "left-brainers" themselves and don't understand the visual side of the equation. I even count in pictures; that's why I was so bad at math and good at art!

Joe Gillespie of Web Page Design for Designers (http://wpdfd.com/) designed Tenacity, MINI 7, and Maxxi. Joe is known as *the* pixel font guru, and offers hundreds of pixel font variations. In fact, Joe has created a special site devoted to pixel fonts (www.minifonts.com/). You can find all the fonts and a great deal of information about pixel fonts at this site. You can learn more about Joe and his work in the interview in this chapter.

The secret to using pixel fonts is to follow the instructions. I have already mentioned how important setting the size as required by each individual font is.

● 9.10

Many pixel fonts come with special spacing characters, although I have had good luck using the typography controls in graphic programs. Usually, a well-designed pixel font doesn't require much adjustment.

Turning off antialiasing in your graphics program is also critical. Remember clean and legible Maxxi (9.11)? Turn on antialiasing, and the clarity disappears (9.12). MiniHaHa is a great small-case font at 10 pixels

● 9.11

● 9.12

So, Fun With Fonts explores Web typography using GIFs, Flash, and CSS, and the results of the experimentation are detailed at www.wpdfd.com/editorial/wpd0902.htm showing how well (or badly) the various browsers and WYSIWYG editors cope.

I often find that designers have preconceptions when approaching a new project and will work the job around an idea that they have in the backs or their minds regardless of whether it is the best solution for the task. This site gets some of those situations out of *my* system harmlessly before I inflict them upon someone else's site!

Q: All designers have favorite tricks to create great type in their own style. Would you care to share a trick or two with us?

A: For me, the "trick" is using type that adds to the communication of the message it is spelling out. This is the way I was taught: Imagine you are driving along a country road and on one side there is a crudely, hand-lettered sign that says "Pick your own strawberries" and just beyond that is a huge Plexiglas sign that says "Flying Lessons." Both are acceptable and believable communications in their contexts. If you reverse the situation, where the "Pick your own strawberries" is a big plastic sign and the "Flying Lessons" is chalked on a piece of wood, you would rightly be suspicious of both.

The style of the type can either enhance or detract from the communication, or it can be neutral and add nothing. The designer's job is to communicate in the most effective and concise way so it is a matter of matching the type style to the

message. That, of course is a lot easier when you have a reasonable palette of typestyles to choose from.

Q: Do you have a favorite non-pixel font for headlines? Body text?

A: For headlines, I will use anything that I think is appropriate to the message. Every typestyle says someting subliminally, be it "precision," "informality," "classic elegance," or whatever. The range of typestyles available to Web designers is very restrictive if they stick to "available fonts" like Times, Arial, and Helvetica. For other fonts, that means making GIFs or using Flash at the moment.

I have to say that these are fonts I would *never* use out of choice. Times Roman was designed for a specific purpose — narrow columns of text printed on newsprint. Helvetica suffers from gross overuse and

continued

(9.13), but turn on even the lowest antialiasing set-ting, and you have a fading font (9.14).

Spend some time experimenting with pixel fonts. If you want a crisp clean type that packs tightly into a defined area, you won't find a better solution.

[NOTE]

Not all graphics programs can deliver good results with pixel fonts. Illustration programs like Adobe Illustrator and CorelDraw do not offer a way to turn off antialias-ing. These vector programs work in a completely differ-ent way than programs like Photoshop or Fireworks. Generally, using a program that offers options for pixel-by-pixel control and antialiasing options when working with pixel fonts is best.

Macromedia Flash does not offer an acceptable method to turn off antialiasing for type. See Chapter 13, "Creating Basic Type in Flash," for special ways to han-dle small text when designing with Flash.

Understanding the Trip from Graphics Program to the Web

Creating great type is only the first step in the process of creating graphic type for the Web. You must know how to save the files you create in the best way, at the right size, and often with several nearly identical ver-sions of the image. I begin by discussing saving files to the correct format, because the best text in the world falls flat on its face if you don't save it correctly.

GIF or JPG?

Two image formats are in common use on the Web today. Any browser that has ever been in use for the modern Web can view GIF and JPG. Although PNG is a format that most browsers can view, it is not an especially good choice because GIF and JPG are so universal. In fact, for type, the only really great for-mat is GIF. Keep an eye on PNG format in the years to come, but for now you would be better off spend-ing your learning time fully understanding the two

● 9.13

● 9.14

(continued)

was originally associated with very clinical "Swiss typography." Arial is a poor copy of Helvetica. There are much better serif and sans-serif typefaces, but people don't have the fonts on their computers.

When it comes to body text fonts, we are even more restricted. There are only one or two fonts that have been designed for the medium — Verdana and Georgia are the most common. I find it very difficult to use anything other than these for text on Web pages because I know that the others are less good.

I will usually spec my type as `Verdana, Geneva, Arial, Helvetica, sans-serif`' or `Georgia, Times, `Times Roman`', serif`', the reason being that if the first choices are not available, the next choice is the best one for the platform. Arial and Times Roman are not good choices for Mac users, and ordering them this way gives them a better experience without impact-ing on the Windows people. The Helvetica is only there for UNIX systems where it is the default sans serif.

There are a few font-embedding tech-nologies around, but they are not very successful and poorly supported.

There are several other excellent screen fonts. Espy Sans is probably my favorite Mac screen font, but it is not widely avail-able and can't really be contemplated.

Q: Anything else you would like to add?

A: Someone once asked me what my idea of a good Web site was, and I said that it was "compelling content, delivered pain-lessly." It is surprising how many sites fail on both accounts.

The other thing I'm asked very often is "Where is all this headed?" With the Internet, the world has been given the ability to communicate, but it has also

formats that are universally accepted.

So what's a GIF and what's a JPG? Many articles are written on how GIF and JPG are constructed and processed, but what matters most is how they are put into correct use. As this is not a graphics book, but a type book, I skip over the technical babble, and concentrate only on the techniques that count to create great type.

JPG format images are best for photographic type images. These images blend gradually from one color to the next, and in order to create files with reasonable file size and full color inclusion (GIF files contain a maximum of 256 colors), the compression method employed by JPG format images is required. JPG images literally remove information from an image, tossing out that information to reduce the amount of information required to display the image, and therefore reducing file size. Using JPGs is a great way to create photographs with good quality and reasonable file size. However, this compression method is not kind to text.

GIF format is the best format for text because it works with solid color areas. Plain text is usually a solid color image. You optimize GIF files by reducing the number of colors that an image contains when you save the file. When you export a text image, you can usually use very few colors, creating an image with a small file size. When you work with pixel fonts in a solid color, you can reduce file size to two colors and create a tiny file. Text that uses antialiasing requires a few more colors because of the edge blending.

So, GIF format creates the smallest files for text, but what about quality? Because GIF format images are optimized by reducing colors, as long as you specify enough colors to account for edge blending from antialiasing, the quality is perfect. This sample, shown in Photoshop's Save for the Web window (9.15), provides a preview of the original file (left pane) and the results of the specified settings, 8 colors in this case. The file size is very small for an image that is 249

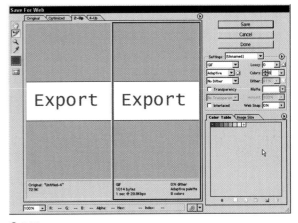

● 9.15

been given the ability to fly-post. A local hit-and-run, fly-poster selling some dodgy furniture can inflict a lot of damage. On a global scale, it becomes horrendous. The amount of data flowing around the Internet is snowballing day by day and the amount of *useless* information we all receive is rising exponentially. The trouble here is that that "Flying Lessons" company is blissfully unaware that they are getting no business from their inappropriate hand-scrawled sign because it is just plain wrong. So, they put up more hand-scrawled signs instead of replacing them with ones that would work. If you think in terms of "hand-scrawled" Web sites, you'll see what I'm getting at.

Web sites communicate something other than what the words say, and so do spam mails. I always put it down to body language. You can usually tell if someone is not to be trusted by their attitude and demeanor — the way they dress, the way they stand, they way they nervously stroke their noses. Web sites send similar subliminal messages, and if the people who produce them are unaware of these undertones, they are dead in the water.

It is the quality of the communication that counts, not the quantity. If you are the only source of Product X and it does something useful, you won't have too much trouble selling it. If you are in

competition with other companies selling similar products or services, then you have to try a lot harder. At the moment, the infrastructure is in place; it's just that people don't know how to use it effectively yet. It will take time.

The Web has been with us for less than ten years. There was a lot of toe-dipping to begin with, then came the hype, then the big bubble burst. Now, the true possibilities are starting to become apparent and things are taking a more sensible and achievable perspective. We still need to improve the signal-to-noise ratio and I think that is the next major hurdle that needs to be crossed.

pixels by 100 pixels, thanks to the low number of colors. Virtually no difference exists between the quality of the original and the optimized image. However, if you reduce the colors too much, you lose the antialiasing effect (9.16).

You also lose quality when you save text as a JPG image. JPG images compress file size by removing information from the file. Artifacts, or pieces of undesirable color, are a common side effect of compression. For photographs, this effect is often invisible or barely seen. In text, JPG format text is never as crisp and clean as GIF format text files (9.17). I have zoomed in on the sample here to show the dramatic loss of quality from the original when JPG format is specified. To add insult to the quality injury, the file size is much larger.

So what do you do when you have text that is placed on a background that is best saved as JPG?

First, try to avoid that scenario. Successful designers think several steps ahead of where they are, and planning file formats is an important part of forward thinking.

You can also use some creative ways to keep the GIF format requirements separate from the JPG format requirements of photograph-style patterns. Text filled with a pattern evokes the GIF/JPG dilemma (9.18). Do you save the image in JPG format to ensure a smooth pattern, or do you save it in GIF format to keep the text outlines crisp and clean?

I suggest saving it in both formats. Save the pattern as a JPG image that will be used as a background in a table (9.19). Then create a reverse copy of the type, with the background color that you desire, with the text as a transparent area (9.20). I have magnified this example, which illustrates the image in Photoshop ready to export to a GIF format. To create the effect, place the image in the table cell that contains the background. The white portion of the image, cleanly outlining the text area, blocks out the unwanted

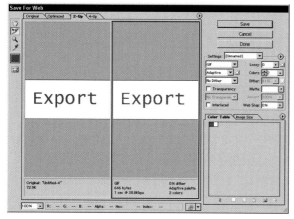

● 9.16

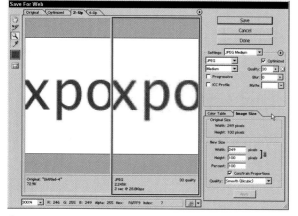

● 9.17

● 9.18

● 9.19

● 9.20

portions of the background (9.21). I have allowed the cell to be wider than the image to illustrate the background.

In a reverse scenario, with the pattern forming a background for solid text, you can use a slight variation. Create the background as in the previous sample, but create a positive text image with a transparent background (9.22). The example here is the image ready for export in Photoshop. The solid-color text image is placed on the background, creating the desired effect, and no compromise in quality (9.23).

What's a Slice?

Text that you create in a graphics program is rarely created in isolation. Many designers complete a mockup of the final page in a graphics program, and export the required images from this full-page image (9.24). This page is a mockup for the interior pages of a client site, shown in Fireworks. All the design elements are in place.

Designing the look for a Web page is much easier when you have the flexibility that a graphics program

offers. As long as you're careful to make sure that your page can be reformatted for HTML, using a graphics program is an excellent way to start a site. However, after you complete the design, you want to be able to harvest the images from the mockup page.

Most current graphics programs provide a method to slice the full-page image into the images you require. Using a special tool, usually called a Slice tool, you draw boundaries around the areas that will eventually form individual images (9.25). You can optimize these images individually. You assign a name and specify GIF or JPG format for each slice, as well as the level of compression or number of colors. When you save the results for the Web, many customized, individual images result. In the example shown here, seven individual images will be saved.

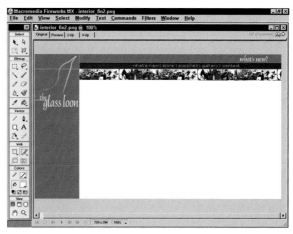

● 9.24

● 9.21

● 9.22

● 9.23

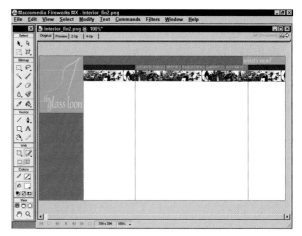

● 9.25

[NOTE]

I have not included the menu bar collage as a slice, because I created that element as a separate image earlier in the process.

Software-Generated HTML: Good Idea? No Way!

Automated HTML generation from graphic files is very popular, and many of the best software manufacturers are investing a great deal of expertise into creating "slice-and-go" type Web-page creation. The idea is that you create your entire page in the graphics program, and then click your mouse a few times. Magically, a completed Web page, HTML, and images are ready to pop onto the Web.

Although I'll admit that the graphics program developers have done an admirable job of cleaning up many of the nightmare results that early versions of this technique created, I am still opposed to *any* automatically generated HTML. Unless you fully understand HTML and how it works in all browsers and across computer platforms, you should never use automatically generated HTML. Tracking down problems that can be created when you make a simple one-pixel error when lining up your slices is just too hard. And if you don't understand how HTML tables work, creating a page that is not easily formatted into HTML layout is highly likely. Plus, you're guaranteed to create much more code with automatic HTML than you will if you create your own pages.

The irony is that most people who truly understand HTML, the ones who could do a great job of using automatically generated HTML, find it *much* faster to create pages of their own HTML design. You have total control over how the page is structured, often keeping exceptions to the standard layout in mind as you design your tables. HTML-generated programs cannot think about what you may have to fit into three of the 50 pages you require.

Do yourself a favor, and learn to create stable pages with your own skill. The only benefit I can see with automatically generated HTML pages is the learning you will gain in troubleshooting. There are much easier ways to gain HTML skill, however, and you will end up with a lot more hair if you bite the bullet in the beginning and learn to create your own pages.

Creating Rollover Images

A natural extension of the slicing technology is creating rollover images from slices. The idea is quite simple. Create a slice, and then create a different look for that slice that will appear as a rollover effect (9.26). You export the results, and a separate image is created for the original and the rollover state (9.27). The naming of the rollover state is automatically generated from naming preferences you set, and based on the original slice name. This process is a little confusing in the beginning, but it is as slick as it sounds after you master your programs exporting function.

[NOTE]

I won't go into saving images as rollovers in specific software programs. Each program features a unique way to create additional states for a slice. Check your software manual and help files to establish the best way to create multiple states for your slices. I concentrate instead on designing great rollovers. You'll find little information on what you should do for successful effects.

● 9.26

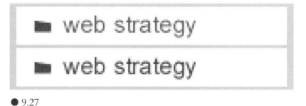

● 9.27

When you create a rollover image, you must imagine how the effect will work when it is in action. Consider what your visitor will be thinking and doing when the effect is initiated. The best link, which is what a rollover signifies, is one that is obvious before the user brings his or her mouse over the spot. You should not be forcing your visitors to roll the mouse all over the page, seeking links, so by the time they do invoke the rollover effect, you're simply offering a confirmation that their mouse is over a link.

If you keep that in mind, you are unlikely to make the biggest mistake that I see in rollovers — overly aggressive effects. I tend to stick to a text color change for my rollovers. This subtle effect does the job, and has no shock effect. It is also easy to create, and easy to match to the page.

[WARNING]

Remember that your rollover effect must also blend into your page. You spend a lot of time making sure that your page is balanced and that the color works. Don't blow your work with your rollovers. When you create a menu, you must make sure that the rollover effect looks good with the original state. Your visitor will only see one rollover image at a time, usually tucked closely with the other links, which display the original image. Most designers are careful to make sure this works. However, your rollover must also maintain the balance on your page. This is a tiny detail, but the little things are what add up to separate an ordinary page from a great one.

Rollover Effects You Should Use

What rollover effects can you use? The list is endless. You can change the background color of an image. This effect is best used when a natural border exists for the background color change. In the example shown here (9.28), the left edge of the rollover effect reaches the edge of the page. Because the background effect fades completely at the right, you don't need a boundary. However, when the background gradient fill is reversed (9.29), the right edge should come up against another design boundary, or it won't

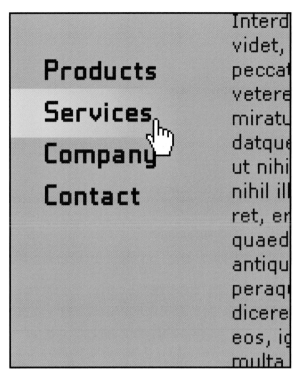

● 9.28

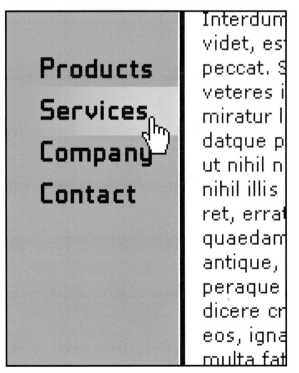

● 9.29

have an integrated look (9.30). Try to avoid having anything on your page appear to be floating alone.

Adding a simple graphic element like a bullet point (9.31) or underline (9.32) are subtle methods for marking a rollover action. Rollovers are also a perfect opportunity to use a graphic program's effects, like a drop shadow (9.33) or outer glow (9.34), but please be subtle. The default values for many effects are too strong for most images.

[T I P]

I have an article on creating professional drop shadows at WebReference.com (www. webreference.com/graphics/column38/). Although this article is specific to shadows, many of the principles apply to other effects.

You can add information with a tiny description for a rollover effect (9.35). This example was created entirely with pixel fonts, and although it does not take up much space, the text is clear. Note also that I have tied the rollover color to the text color, plus added a short line to connect the menu item to the description. If you do a little thinking at the design stage, your visitors won't have to think about what they are doing to use your site. That's what you want.

Although the variety of rollover effects you can use is endless, please don't work too hard to be different. Most of the work I do includes very simple text color change for rollover effects. It's simple, and it works.

[T I P]

You can use an animated GIF as a rollover image. Again, I urge that you keep the word *subtle* in the front of your mind. A gently blinking bullet appearing as a rollover effect allows you to add a little motion to your page, yet you are not inflicting an annoying, constant flash on them. The effect is not active unless the visitor is actually holding the mouse over the link, so they are in control. I used this effect quite successfully on a sight for teens, providing a tiny bouncing ball over the link on mouseover. It was fun, added almost nothing to file size, and did not take away from the rest of the page.

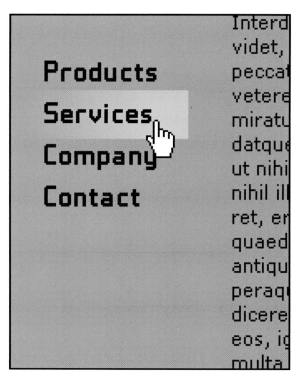

● 9.30

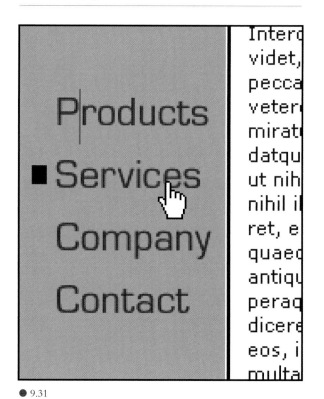

● 9.31

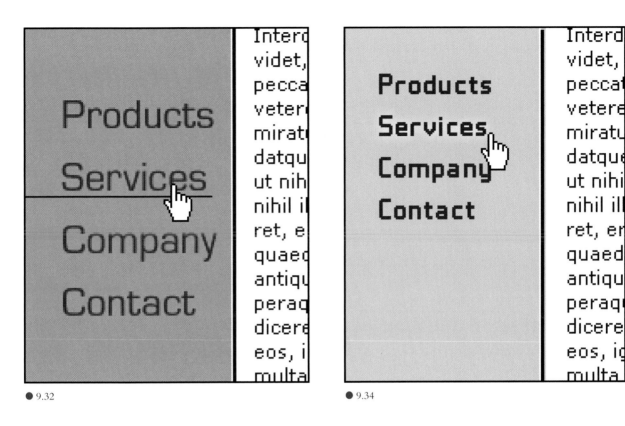

● 9.32

● 9.34

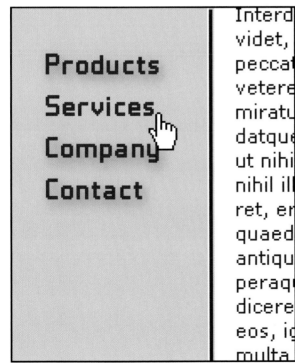

● 9.33

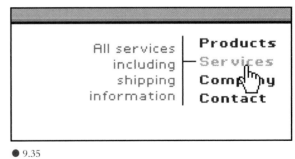

● 9.35

Rollover Effects You Should Never Use

I could talk for hours about some of the horrible rollover effects I have seen, but a list of the worst of the worst doesn't hold much learning power. Instead I list the most common errors I have seen. Please check this list every time you create rollovers. Don't be caught saying, "Seemed like a good idea at the time." Make sure you don't:

• Use bold text for the rollover when the original text was not bold. At best, your rollover will seem jumpy. At worst, especially if you're not creating your images from a slicing program, your rollover may be larger than the original image. Jumping text and position could cause an unpleasant physical reaction for your visitors. Think seasick!

- Use italic text when the original text was not italic. See the previous point for why. And for goodness sake (yes, I have seen this), don't use italic and bold on your font for the rollover when the original text was plain. That's almost into the worst of the worst category.

- Use bright blue background with bright red text, or vice versa. I'll admit that catching attention seems like a good idea, but this method is like tapping someone on the shoulder with a sledgehammer. I am not sure why this combination is so popular, but it threatens to give me an instant headache when I see it. To make it worse, it seems that the more discordant the color combination, the larger the designer thinks the font/link image should be. If you don't have a great eye for color, please make sure that you gather some people around you who do, and test your ideas with them.

- Use sound, especially loud sound for a rollover when designing in Flash. I don't have a huge problem when a click brings a sound, but using even a gentle pop for a rollover effect often turns into pop, pop, pop, as my mouse lazily trails over a few links to get where it needs to be. I'll admit that this item is not in the least about text, but this is my pet peeves list, and this method is right up there.

- Use a glaring effect for rollover text. Adding a gentle drop shadow does add a little movement, and certainly lets visitors know it's a link. However, blasting a huge emboss setting or glaring color around text is overkill.

If you avoid all the preceding effects when creating a rollover effect, at least you will not be making one of the errors that screams amateur on a page. Once again, I advise you to be on the lookout for great rollover effects. There is no better learning method than filling your mind with great examples.

Planning for Liquid Design

The term *liquid design* refers to Web pages that stretch to fill the browser window, and shrink when a window is reduced. The technique depends on using flexible tables in the HTML page, and prevents too much white space when the page is viewed on a high-resolution monitor. Most designers today design pages to look great, with no scroll for monitor resolutions at 800 pixels wide. They also test the page at 1024-pixel-wide display to make sure that it still looks good.

The first sample of the Mobyz.com site is shown with an 800-pixel-wide display (9.36). The next view shows the liquid page at 1024-pixel-wide display (9.37). Note how the line lengths are a little long, and there is more white space than I would like to see, but generally, the page looks pretty good. If this page were designed with fixed tables at 800-pixel-wide display, the page would look very close to the first image (9.36). However, look what happens when the same fixed page is viewed at 1024-wide-display (9.38). A large white area appears to the right of the content.

This tutorial is not about how to create liquid pages, but a warning to plan ahead if you want to use text images as part of a liquid page. As you create the mockup of your page, or create your graphics, make sure that you keep the final destination in mind. I

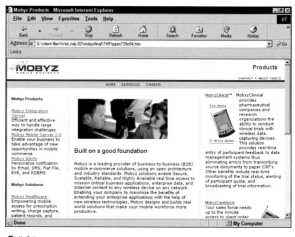

 9.36

often test an image in an HTML mockup before I create the final graphics for a page. Requiring a margin to be placed at the edge of the first or last graphic in a horizontal menu is not unusual.

You also want to watch for opportunities to use table or cell backgrounds for the color behind your text. An image cannot expand and contract as the browser window changes size, so you must depend on background colors to create a flexible line of color that extends to the edge of the page no matter what the browser display size may be.

You can also work with images as table backgrounds to create liquid design that could not be

accomplished in any other way. Table backgrounds and images with transparent backgrounds are the key. To create this flexible menu (9.39), a background image (9.40) is applied to the table cell. Then the individual menu items, with a transparent background (9.41) are inserted into the cell. No matter how much the browser window is enlarged or

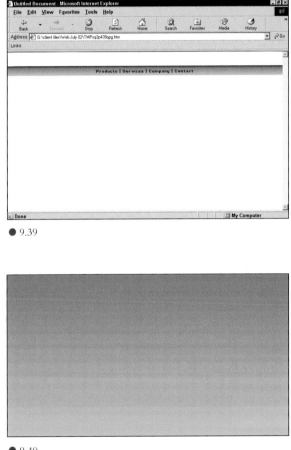

● 9.39

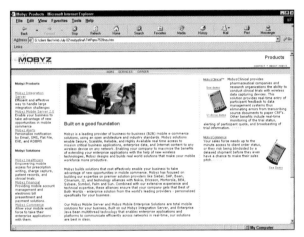

● 9.37

● 9.40

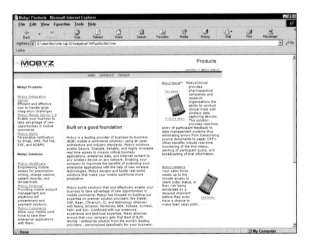

● 9.38

● 9.41

reduced, the background pattern stretches from edge to edge, and the menu items remain in the center of the cell (9.42).

[N O T E]

I have a brief tutorial on liquid design for menus in a series of articles called "Menus with Beauty and Brains: Graphics" (www.webreference.com/graphics/column43/5.html). Also, my books, *Web Menus for Beauty and Brains* (Wiley 2001) and *Dreamweaver MX Crash Course* (Wiley 2002) have an entire chapter with step-by-step directions for creating liquid pages.

Keeping File Size Down

Here are a few tips for reducing the size of your files.

Optimizing Image Files

I've stepped through the basics you require to create graphic text for the Web. Before I move on to specialized text techniques, and stretch the focus beyond the graphics program and into the HTML page, I want to focus on a very important part of creating effective graphic text: file size. If you don't know how to keep your file size down, it doesn't matter how great your pages look, how well balanced they are, or how perfect your navigation. If your visitor patience is shorter than your site's download time, you lose.

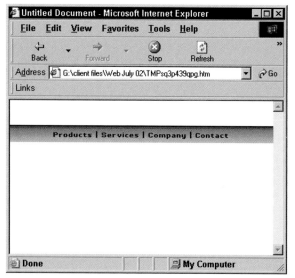

● 9.42

[W A R N I N G]

Graphic file size is an important component in the display time for a Web page, but it is not the only consideration. If you're using complex table layouts, especially with many layers of nested tables, even when your visitor has high-speed Internet connection, your pages may still be very slow. That's one of the key reasons I don't like automatically generated HTML from a software program, as the result is often a complicated layout and table structure. Keeping your page structure simple and your graphic file size down are important. Fast-loading pages not only keep your visitors, they also present a professional image.

Earlier in this chapter, I outlined GIF and JPG format files, and how they were compressed. I would like to take that discussion one step further here, and delve into creating images that compress well. In other words, thinking about compression as you create your design is better than arriving at the finish line only to discover that the images you want to compress will not cooperate. A few times I have run into what I call "brat" images. Every bit of knowledge I have about compression and graphic creation does not help to create an acceptable file size. I've learned to accept the exceptions to logic, and concentrate on the vast majority of images that follow the rules.

Any image can benefit from one overall concept. When you can reduce the number of sharp color changes in any image, whether it's destined to be saved as JPG or GIF format, your file size will be smaller. The file size in this original image is 9.8k (9.43). The design of this sample is not conducive to creating small file size. It has sharp changes in color, and many of those changes are vertical. Vertical color breaks create larger files than horizontal patterns. One small change, applying a blur effect to soften and blend the edges, results in a file size that is 6.9k (9.44).

Adding a slight horizontal color direction to this image with a light wind filter has little effect on the overall appearance of the image, but reduces the file to 8.1k (9.45). A few bytes may not seem like much, but they do add up.

I'm not suggesting that you design your images completely around optimization, but if you're providing a background for your text, why not consider using a horizontal direction for your color, or less contrast in your pattern? Lower contrast is better if it's behind your text anyway.

[WARNING]

Don't, under any circumstances, take these file-size-reduction suggestions to your text. To heck with file size when it comes to creating text with clear, crisp

edges. You might be able to reduce your file size by blurring your text, or running horizontal lines through it, but then your visitor could not read it. Nothing has been gained. Crisp, vertical edges on text earn their keep.

Working with Background Colors

You should never be saving files that have a large, solid color area between elements. Although solid color blocks do create the smallest file sizes, HTML color specification code is much smaller than the smallest graphic file. When you design your images for export to a Web page, always watch for opportunities to use background color instead of the image.

The bubbles mockup has plenty of graphic elements in the top area (9.46). You may be tempted to

● 9.43

● 9.45

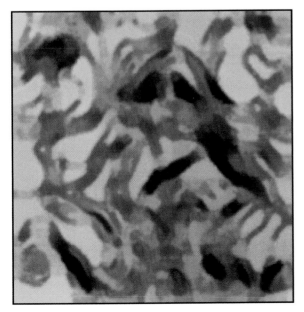

● 9.44

● 9.46

create the full light green area as an image, and place it in a Web page (9.47). However, you lose any chance to use liquid design by saving the entire heading, but more important, you create a larger file than is necessary for this design.

You can break this design into two or three small images. The version with three images, shown here with blue tagged Photoshop slices (9.48), would create the smallest overall size, but would require a more complex table in the HTML page to reconstruct. Combining the images at the left of the heading allows a simple two-cell table to be used to place the images (9.49). In this case, I would choose to use three images, not for file size, but because I could float the center set of bubbles to reduce the empty effect of a wide display. I've turned on the borders in the HTML table to show the structure (9.50). All green showing in the background is created by background color.

● 9.47

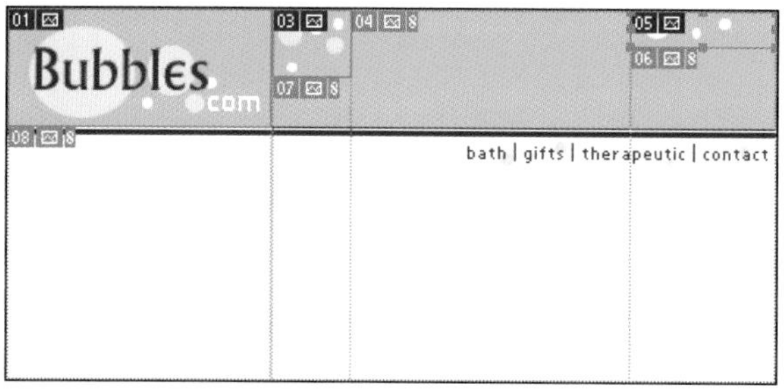

● 9.48

If you're creating GIF files that will be used with background colors, then specifying all background areas in the images as transparent is a good idea. The graphics program can create slight shifts in the color, compared to the HTML-specified color. This difference is rarely enough to have an effect on the page appearance, but images that are one or two shades off from the background color that is creating the rest of the look does jump out at you.

Blending Graphic Text into the Page

You may remember my touching on this topic for HTML text in Chapter 2, "Design Principles for Web Type." Bringing your attention to blending your text with the page when you create the page in a separate program may be even more important. You may want to take a trip back to Chapter 2 before you move on to the next two chapters, and designing with text.

In fact, I just give you a little reminder in this section. Make sure that the colors, shapes, and textures in your graphics blend with the HTML portions of

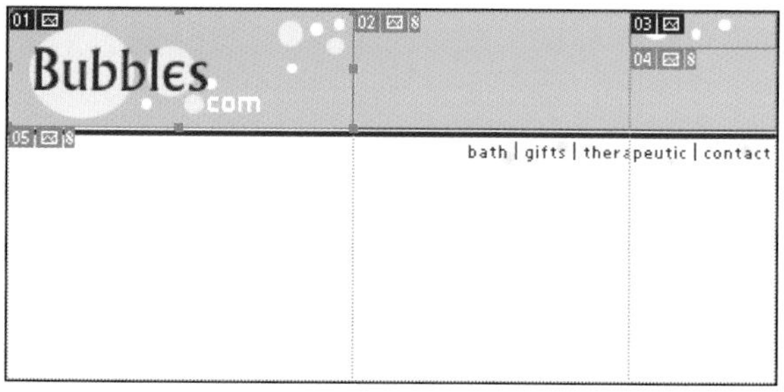

● 9.49

your page. You can easily create your comp (layout proof of the entire page) image in a graphics program, export your text, but forget that the great design you created in the comp has a few design elements missing. I often refer to my comp, especially if the HTML page just does not have the life I expect.

Usually, I find that I have missed one black line to tie in some utility text that I have exported, or one colored line to tie in another graphic. It's rarely a huge design element that is missing when I check the comp.

I also tend to do some fine-tuning in the HTML page. Although you can come up with a good representation of HTML pages in a graphics program, the two results are never quite the same. Graphics programs are especially good at fine detail. HTML is a little clunky when it comes to adding that perfect little touch. I sometimes find myself returning to the graphics program to create a colored GIF to use for lines in the HTML page. In the sample shown in the previous section (9.50), I used HTML backgrounds to create the fine lines at the lower edge of the heading. If you're using tables with cellpadding, HTML background color won't work for fine lines, because the cell is twice the width of the padding value before content is entered.

In the next section, I move on past the basics, and start putting the techniques and ideas you have learned in this chapter, and Chapter 8, "Introduction to Graphic Typography," to work. I hope you have paid attention to the basics, however. I love to rush ahead, getting to the good stuff, and delving back to the basics only when I run into trouble. This technique is not a great idea with Web design, however. Basic knowledge of HTML, plus solid understanding of how images, and for this book, text as images work, free your creativity and reduce the time you spend on every page you design. Even with my personality, I have to admit that "they" were right, when "they" told me to slow down and make sure I understood the basics.

● 9.50

[T I P]

Suzanne Stephens has an excellent tutorial on selecting and perfecting color schemes for Web pages by drawing the color from the images for the site. You can find a wealth of information on color, blending elements, and pure design in Suzanne's tutorial. It's well worth the trip (`www.wpdfd.com/editorial/wpd0802.htm#feature`).

subtle

font

- normal
- over
- visited
- active

menu

optimize

export

Chapter 10

Customizing Graphic Text for the Web

If you've read the last two chapters, you've had a good trip through the basics of typography, and getting type onto the Web. I want to cover a few more basic techniques to ensure that your toolbox is well rounded, and then we can get into the area that delights designers — beginners and experts alike. Working with text to create decorative effects while communicating is challenging, but always immensely satisfying. In the next two chapters, I stretch past the basics, and teach you typography tips and skills that are hard to find in a Web context. Prepare to have some fun, because the skills you require are already in your hands (or will be after the first section of this chapter). You're heading into the application phase of your typography learning.

Exporting Images from a Graphics Program

I introduced creating slices in a graphics program in Chapter 8, "Introduction to Graphic Typography." You should know how to create a slice and understand that separate images are saved for each slice. In this section, I move ahead to setting the preferences for saving slices, and finally, teaching you how to create rollover effect graphics from slices. The concept is slick, and really quite simple if you take it step-by-step. After you have worked through a simple example like the one I use (10.1), you can apply the same methods to save graphically complex effects. Your software program does not know whether it is exporting the most brilliant graphic effect, or plain text.

[WARNING]

At the risk of sounding like a broken record, I do want to once more discourage you from using automatically generated HTML. Both Fireworks and ImageReady (Photoshop), the programs I feature in this exercise, offer the option to save images and HTML. Both programs deliver acceptable results – as acceptable as can be for this technique. Your pages will be much better if you focus only on the capability that I outline in this chapter, and create the HTML for your rollovers separately.

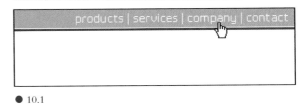

● 10.1

Automating Rollover Images in Photoshop (ImageReady)

Photoshop offers sophisticated tools for creating rollover effects. Based on powerful layers that Photoshop perfected long ago, you can create any effect for many states of your graphics. The key to working smoothly with Photoshop rollovers is to use layers effectively. If you do not have a solid grasp of the layers concept, you should pause to get that information before you go on with this section. Unless you understand layers, creating a rollover could be confusing, especially when you create each rollover image in separate layers.

[**T I P**]

I have a tutorial devoted to using Photoshop layers on WebReference.com (`www.webreference.com/graphics/column32/`). I wrote this article for Photoshop 5.5, but little has changed with layers, except

you can now create layer sets. The basics still apply, and you need this the knowledge to create rollovers.

[**N O T E**]

You can export images from Photoshop, using the Save for the Web feature, and for simple, one-image exports, I do. However, the power of rollovers and slices resides in ImageReady, the program that ships with Photoshop. For almost all my work, I use ImageReady when I am preparing a sliced document, and always if I am creating rollover effects. If you are new to creating slices and rollovers, I highly recommend you do all your design work in Photoshop, and all your slicing and exporting in ImageReady.

To do this exercise, you need to create a navigation bar, with a few menu items entered. The example I created has four menu items, separated by a bar. To

Behind the Scenes

Suzanne Stephens: Type Evangelist

(c) Christopher Flick, `www.csfgraphics.com`.

Suzanne Stephens is passionate about great type, a statement that should be considered an understatement. Like many Web designers who came from the print world, type has been Suzanne's art form for much of her life. Growing up with a Mom who created custom-designed monograms with a hand-controlled machine, and creating store display posters by hand, Suzanne learned about the beauty of letterforms at a tender age. Her Dad and brother are engineers, and an aunt is an accomplished painter, influences that Suzanne credits with creating "an ideal background for ending up doing graphic design on computers."

Suzanne drew constantly as a child, and private art lessons with Clara Zimmerman Clayton, provided composition and design techniques that she uses today. A false start in Fashion Design was quickly thwarted by a dislike for sewing, but Suzanne found her way to the world of typography soon after. As is so often the case, Suzanne's future work was influenced by yet another exceptional teacher, Evie Chang Henderson, Visual Communications instructor at Central Piedmont Community College in Charlotte, NC. Through Evie, Suzanne learned to work with, and love classic type faces, an interest that has never duplicate this example **(10.1)**, create a Photoshop document and type **products | services | company | contact** on the canvas. I used Maxxi Thin font at 20 pixels, and adjusted the baseline on each of the dividing bars by −1 px. The menu bar has a drop shadow effect with Opacity on the effect set to 30%. Any menu bar will work for this exercise, but make sure that your Layers panel resembles mine **(10.2)**. I merged the stripes on the menu bar for simplicity, so you may have more layers.

[NOTE]

I prefer to keep my text for rollovers on one layer. The help files included with ImageReady place each rollover on a separate layer. My menu items, the only rollovers I do on a page, are never buttons or individual design elements, common designs for professional sites. Try

my method, then step through the Adobe method. With the two methods in hand, you can choose the best route for each project.

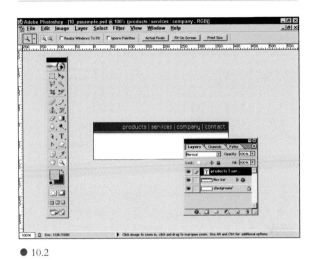

● 10.2

---

diminished, and was carried into her work as a freelance graphic designer. Her freelance work evolved into ownership of a full-service ad agency, specializing in health care and retail advertising. Finally, a move to California, and soon after Oregon led Suzanne to her Web work.

Q: What made you move to Web design from your print business?

A: I moved to the San Francisco area in 1989, and met my graphic designer husband Dave on AOL in 1994. Soon after meeting, we moved to Ashland, OR. Soon after our arrival, some graphic designer

friends told us about a meeting of people volunteering to do a Web page for the City of Ashland. "What's a Web page?" we asked. "We don't know but we figure we'd better find out," our friends answered.

Most people at the November 1994 meeting were local geeks such as instructors from Southern Oregon University and guys who ran small local ISPs. They excitedly demonstrated the first public release of Netscape Navigator, speaking a foreign language among themselves, with words like "you are Ell" and "Ech tee tee pee colon slash slash" and showing us some really ugly Web sites.

Lost and confused, I finally gathered my wits about me to ask, "how much does it cost to have a Web site?" When Alan Oppenheimer, a former Apple engineer who operates Opendoor, a Mac-based ISP service, answered, "about $40 a month," the hair on the back of my arms literally stood on end. I was stunned, since I knew from my ad agency experience that communicating worldwide through print or advertising media could cost millions of dollars. I still wasn't exactly clear about what a Web site was, but I instinctively knew I was witnessing the beginning a major paradigm shift in communications.

continued

In this exercise, you create four separate rollover image sets to serve as a menu:

1. **Select the layer containing your text. Click the menu icon at the top right of the Layer palette and select Duplicate Layer. A duplicate layer is created (10.3).**

2. **Double-click on the name of the new layer and type** Over **to rename the layer (10.4).**

3. **With the Over layer highlighted, double- click the word** products **in the menu to highlight. Change the text color to gold. Repeat for the remaining menu items. (10.5).**

Menu flyout

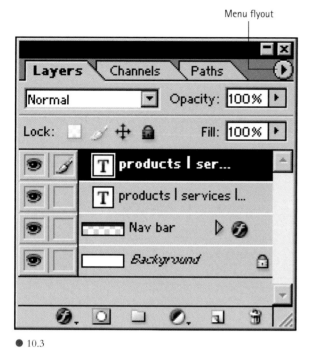

● 10.3

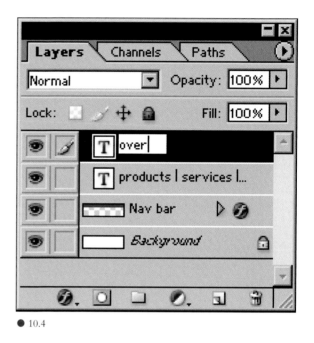

● 10.4

(continued)

Immediately, Dave and I got off AOL and onto the "real" Internet. Dave supported me for several years while I obsessively taught myself Web design and tried to sell Web sites to people who had no idea what I was talking about. I eventually quit doing print design altogether when, unable to juggle the technical details for both media, I made some costly mistakes on a print job.

Learning HTML was easy for me, since I immediately recognized it as a derivative of SGML, the code I had used to set type at the newspaper. I was lucky to have started when there was little to learn, since I was able to add skills as new features were added to HTML. For example, when tables came about, they had only limited use because AOL didn't support them. I learned HTML from a few pages of tags that I printed from Netscape's site, far different from the 1300+ HTML 4 reference book that's on my desk now. And I'm proud to say that I never, ever used a `<blink>` tag.

Eventually I lucked onto sites where Lynda Weinman and David Siegel shared all they knew for free before they figured out they could make money writing books. From Lynda, I learned about the Web safe palette. From David I learned about spacer gifs and using borderless tables for layouts, gaining a new sense of pixel-by-pixel control over page layout.

Q: Print designers are type and typography fanatics. How have you adjusted to the restrictive working conditions for typography on the Web?

A: CSS is so widely supported now that I hardly think of the restrictions any more. Before CSS came into wide use, the problem that drove me nuts was the huge difference in font size display between Macs and PCs. I was shocked the first time I saw one of my Mac-designed projects on a PC!

Now that CSS has helped wrestle that font size alligator into submission, I've been able to use basically the same approach to typography that I used in pre-digital typography. Back in my ad agency days, we used expensive hand-set phototypositor type for display type

I do not want the separating bars to change color with the rollover effect, so they are left white in both text layers. If there were no separator bars, or if you did want the bars to change color, you could highlight the entire text block and change the color once. You can also apply a color overlay layer style to change the color on the entire layer.

4. Click the eye icon for the Over layer to turn off layer visibility. Your menu items appear in white again (10.6).

5. Save your file. You're now ready to move to ImageReady to create your slices and rollovers.

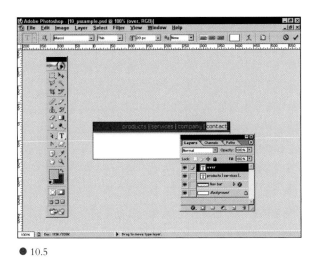

● 10.5

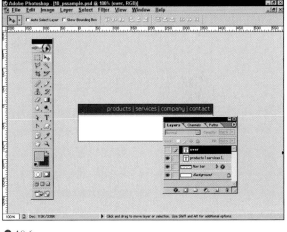

● 10.6

(headlines and subheads). Almost any legible body text style could be mixed with a headline style, since the designer is dealing with the block of type as a whole rather than with individual letterforms. The phototypositor display type set the mood and feel for the page. The body text had a less dramatic effect on the overall design, lending a solid or open, light or heavy feel or color to the page.

We used to pay $1/line for body copy and $2.50 per word for headline type, plus extra for edits and alterations. Because typesetting was so expensive, we habitually used combinations of type that we knew from experience would work well. My ad agency assistant art director used to tease me by asking which of my five typeface combinations I wanted to use, but she exaggerated. I used at least six. When I first discovered Quarkpress in 1990 I thought I had died and gone to heaven! I could hardly wait to get my hands on a Mac so I could play with type to my heart's content!

In Web design, I use Photoshop type the same way I used to use phototypositor type — to establish an overall feel and mood for a site. Just as with print I handle body copy with an eye towards mass, weight and color. Knowing that I have little control over what font the user will see on his or her own computer, I specify some safe combinations and try not to obsess over it any further.

Q: You are a color expert, and have a new series on the Web Page Design for Designers site (http://wpdfd.com) designed to help Web designers create great color on their pages. Can you let us in on a few of your secrets for working with color in type for a Web site?

A: Actually, with Joe's [owner of wpfd.com] encouragement, instead of doing a series on WPDFD, I've been working on getting my own new site ready for launch. So the first secret I want to let your readers in on is to watch for the launch of SharpenYourDesignSkills.com later this year!

My site will offer downloadable tutorials focused primarily on pure design issues,

continued

6. **Click the Jump to ImageReady icon at the bottom of the toolbar (10.7). ImageReady opens, if it is not already, and the current document appears in ImageReady.**

● 10.7

You use a lot of palettes when you create rollovers in ImageReady. This program is one of the few where I minimize open palettes. Usually, I close palettes I'm not using, or get used to them on the screen if I use them all the time. With ImageReady, I found I was opening and closing palettes all the time, so I started to minimize palettes as the more efficient choice. I don't always have them open in the screen shots for this exercise, as screen shots are easier to follow if they are not too busy.

7. **With the slice tool selected, click and drag the area for your first slice. You may find selecting the correct area easier if you zoom in on the area you want to slice. If you want to include a drop shadow or any type of feathered effect, make sure that you include enough area to completely enclose the feathered color. The Optimize window enlarges as soon as you create a slice, even if it is minimized. Just ignore it for now (10.8).**

8. **Repeat Step 7 for each of your rollover elements (10.9).**

Your slices are complete. Now you're almost ready to move on to creating the rollover effects, but first you must tell ImageReady how you want the slices named and optimized.

To optimize images in ImageReady, follow these steps:

---

dS.   *(continued)*

such as color theory. While I may offer a few techniques specific to one computer program or another, the focus will be on teaching design, not on computer programs.

Q: What color warnings do you have for designers on the subject of Web type?

A: Color is free on the Web. Don't be afraid to use it, as long as you make an effort to use it with style and elegance. All elements on a page should relate to each other in some way, and that includes type colors. Avoid too little or too much contrast between type and background colors.

Q: How do you decide whether to use CSS type or graphic type on a Web page?

A: I prefer to use graphic type for subheads and headlines over about 14 to 18 pt in size. However, since they tend to be a high maintenance item and I don't like doing site maintenance, I've scaled back my use of Photoshop type.

Q: How much of your typography knowledge do you use when you are creating a site? What methods have

you found to be especially useful for the Web?

A: I've probably forgotten more than I use, and I sure wish CSS was as intuitive and easy for me to learn as HTML.

Q: Do you have any pet peeves with what you see in Web type use?

A: Do you really want me to go there? My list is endless! Among the things that really set my teeth on edge, are the use of: inch marks instead of curly apostrophes; italicized type, which is usually illegible and ugly on Web pages; aliased type in Web graphics (with the exception, of course, of graphics using the special Web mini fonts).

1. If it is not already open, choose Window → Optimize from the main menu to open the Optimize palette.

2. Click and hold on the Slice tool icon in the toolbar to expand the tool choices, and select the Slice Select tool. Click on the first menu item to select the slice (10.10).

[T I P]

I find that the Options window gets in the way, and usually close it. ChooseWindow → Options to deselect Options. Also, having your image set to 100% magnification when optimizing is best so you can see the true results of your optimization. My sample is enlarged for clarity.

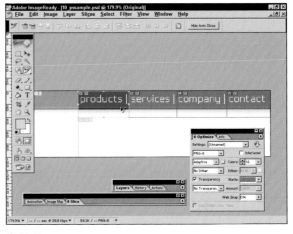

● 10.9

● 10.8

● 10.10

The list continues with: poor letterspacing or kerning in graphic type, especially really gaping holes between the worst offenders, such as capital "T" and neighboring letters; excessive word spacing; random use of Capitalized letters FOR EMPHASIS when there's Really no grammatically valid reason For Capitalizing a word. People apparently do it for emphasis, but it just looks silly and amateurish to me.

And more: excessive use of bold type, caps, big type, and other misguided attempts at emphasis (the net result being to turn readers away instead of enticing them to read important content) or the most common typo of all, "It's" instead of "Its."

In both Web and do-it-yourself print design, the most common typographic design errors are those related to excess, as in use of: too many colors; too many type styles; type that's too large (especially text copy); paragraphs that are too long to be easily legible; too many or improperly placed capitalized letters; overly decorative typefaces, especially script and "swashy" typefaces; gee-whiz colorizing effects and of twisted, distorted type effects; too many drop shadows, especially drop shadows that aren't needed because there's already enough contrast between the page background.

Finally, over use of those ugly tired typefaces that come installed with operating systems, especially Helvetica, Arial, Zapf Chancery (possibly the ugliest typeface ever created besides Bookman Swash and Cooper Black).

Q: Anything else you would like to add?

A: If I were the King of Computers, I would require every person to submit proof of having read Robin Williams' "The Mac [PC] Is Not a Typewriter" before being licensed to drive a computer. Since I'm not likely to assume that throne anytime soon, I'll just settle for my husband's pet name for me, "The Type Bitch."

3. Click on the Optimized tab at the top left of the screen. This tab presents a real-time preview of the image with the optimization selections you make.

4. In the Optimize window, with the first slice still selected, set the file type (GIF or JPG) as well as color depth or quality, and transparency, checking the actual image for the results (10.11).

5. Repeat for each of the slices. Each slice can have its own optimize settings, although in my example, the same settings are right for all slices.

[N O T E]

Although the text and background for this example uses only two colors, I had to specify 16 colors for the GIF format in order to keep the shadow looking good.

6. Minimize or close the Optimize window. Click the Original tab at the top of the screen.

7. Open the Slice Palette if it is not already (choose Window → Slice). With the Slice Select tool active, select the first slice. Highlight the name in the Name field. You will replace this name with one that makes sense for you. For my example, I used the actual menu item, or products. This name will be used as the filename for this slice (10.12).

8. Repeat Step 7 for each slice.

Your slices are now defined, optimized, and named. You're ready to move on to creating rollovers. Working with one slice at a time, you specify how the rollover is to look in normal state and for the rollover state. You then tell ImageReady to save the images, and a separate image is saved for each state, ready to go into your rollover code.

To create a rollover state, follow these steps:

1. Open the Rollover palette (choose Window → Rollovers) if it is not already. You should see a layer named Normal, plus one for each slice you created. If you followed the instructions in the last exercise, the layer names will correspond to the names you created in the Slice palette. Note that clicking on a layer selects the corresponding slice. Clicking on a slice highlights the corresponding layer (10.13).

2. Open the Layers palette (Window → Layers) if it is not already. The original text layer should be visible, and the Over layer invisible (10.14).

3. With the Slice Select tool active, select the first menu item.

4. In the Rollovers palette, click the Create rollover state icon, the second icon from the left at the bottom of the palette (10.15).

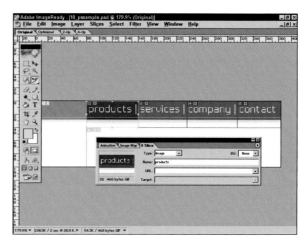

 10.12

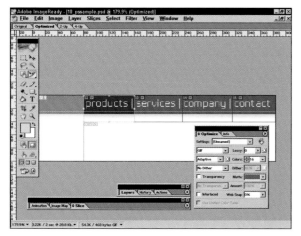

 10.11

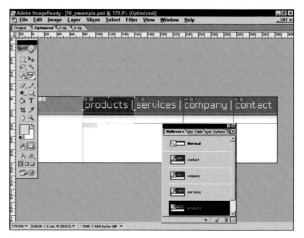

● 10.13

5. Ensure that the Over State for the first menu item is highlighted in the Rollover palette. Turn off the visibility for the Original text layer in the Layers palette, and turn on the visibility of the Over layer. The text on the canvas should now appear in the over color, and the thumbnail in the Rollover palette reflects the new text color (10.16).

6. Repeat Steps 3–5 for each slice requiring a rollover. Each slice should now have a rollover state in the Rollovers palette (10.17).

[NOTE]

You can specify more states for each slice. Simply add another rollover state, and choose the appropriate layer effects to create the different look.

That's it. Your rollovers are automated. Now all that remains is saving the images. You must first set up your preferences, and then save the files.

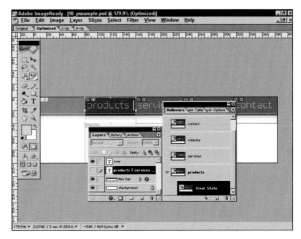

● 10.16

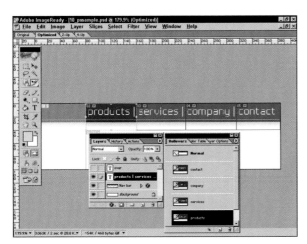

● 10.14

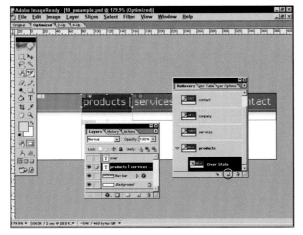

● 10.15

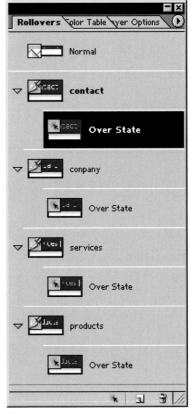

● 10.17

To save automated rollover images, follow these steps:

1. Choose File → Output Settings → Saving Files from the main menu. The Output Settings window opens, with the Saving Files options presented. You can choose how your filenames will look from this screen. I like very simple names, so I select just the slice name plus the rollover state. Each field offers a drop-down selection of values. Select none in any field that you want to exclude. Do not click OK yet (10.18).

2. In the lower portion of the window, you can specify a folder where ImageReady will place your slices. If the folder you specify in the Put Images in Folder field does not exist, ImageReady will create it for you. In this example, I specified that the images should be saved in a folder named menu.

[N O T E]

Although creating a folder for menu images adds extra steps to the image path, the separation from your other files can really help to organize your work, especially if you have several states for each rollover.

3. Uncheck the Copy Background Image When Saving option. If you have specified copyright information through File → Info in either ImageReady or Photoshop, and have the Include Copyright option selected, each image will be saved with copyright information embedded (10.19).

4. Click OK to save these settings. You're now ready to save your files.

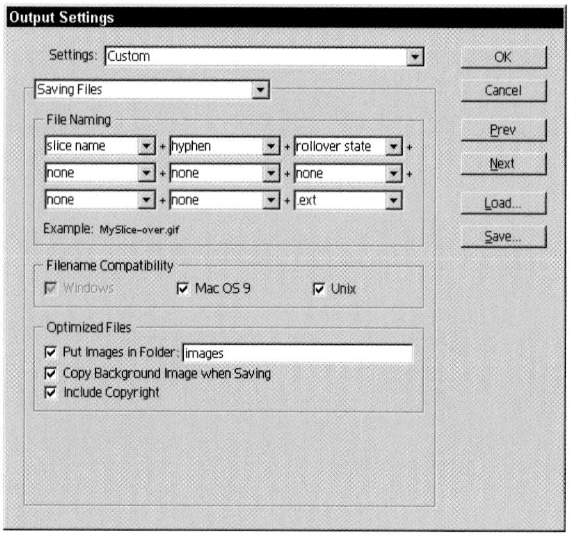

● 10.18

5. With the Slice Select tool active, Shift+click all slices you want to save.

6. Choose File → Save Optimized As from the main menu. The Save Optimized As window opens.

7. Navigate to the folder where you would like to save your files.

[W A R N I N G]

Remember that ImageReady will place your files in a folder in this directory if you specified that setting in the Output Settings window. A common error is to navigate all the way to the folder created for the rollover files. ImageReady creates a new folder within that folder. In my case, I would end up with a menu/menu path for my images.

8. In the lower part of the screen, select Images Only for the Save as type option.

9. Choose Selected Slices for the Slices option. Your settings should resemble mine (10.20).

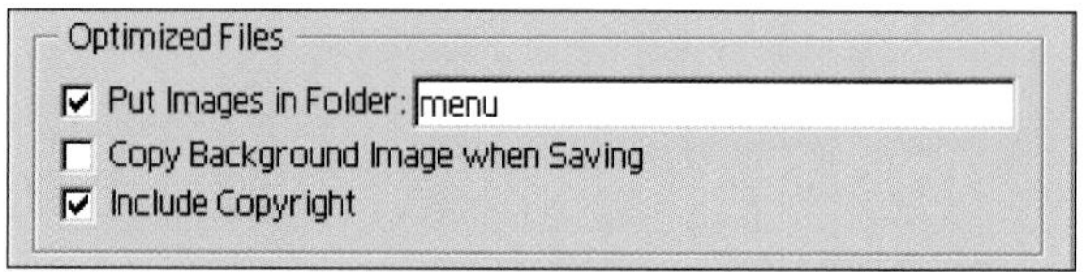

● 10.19

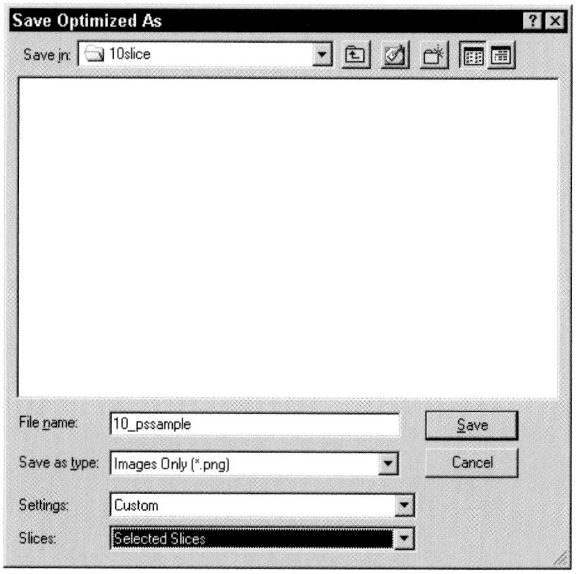

● 10.20

[N O T E]

Don't worry about the filename field, or that the image type specified in the Save as type field is not what you have chosen for your slices. Slice names will be used if you have chosen that option, and the files will be saved in the format you specified when optimizing each image.

10. **Check the folder that you have specified for your images. You should have a set of images for each slice. You can make a quick check by choosing File → Open. Do not open the files; just use this command to confirm that the images are in the right place. This window gives a preview of each image as well (10.21).**

Getting to this point took a lot of explanation, but exporting images really is quick and easy. As long as you work carefully on the basic setup for the page, you will find that saving rollover images is easy. The benefit comes when you have to make a change. Simply save again, and any changes you made to the objects in the slice will be saved for all states automatically.

These images are ready to place into your HTML page.

Automating Rollover Images in Fireworks

Fireworks was one of the first programs to offer automated rollover image creation, and it shows.

Slicing, optimizing, and saving various states for rollover images is fast and easy.

To do this exercise, you need to create a navigation bar, with a few menu items entered. The example I created has four menu items separated by a bar. To duplicate this example (10.22), create a new document in Fireworks and type **products | services | company | contact** on the canvas. I used Maxxi Thin font at 20 points, and adjusted the baseline on each of the dividing bars by −1 px. This menu bar has a drop shadow effect with Opacity on the effect set to 30%. Any menu bar will work for this exercise, but make sure that your Layers panel resembles mine (10.23).

[T I P]

I have a tutorial devoted to using Fireworks layers on WebReference.com. (www.webreference.com/graphics/column35/). I wrote this article a few years ago, but the basics remain the same. The article does contain the knowledge you need to create layers, and as a bonus, introduces you to frames, which you use for rollovers.

● 10.22

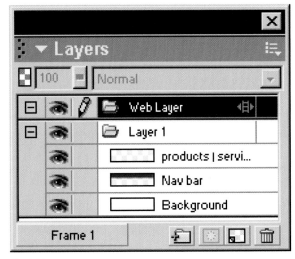

● 10.23

● 10.21

To get started, you must create the slices that will create your rollover images. For accuracy, zoom in on the area you will be slicing.

1. Select the Slice tool from the toolbar, and drag over the first menu item to define the slice area. A green area defines the slice, and a new layer called slice appears in the Layers palette, which you can see by choosing Window → Layers (10.24).

2. Repeat Step 1 for all menu items.

3. To name your slices, with the Pointer tool active, select the first menu item. Type a name for the slice in the Slice field of the Properties palette. This name will become the name of your image file for that slice. Note that the name you added for the slice is now reflected in the Layers palette (10.25).

4. Repeat the preceding step for all menu items, assigning a unique name for each slice. The Web

Layer section of your Layers panel should contain only named layers (10.26).

Your slices are now complete. But you only have the original image prepared, and must now create the rollover effect. Fireworks uses frames to prepare different states for images. The work you have done so far has been added to the default frame, Frame 1, automatically. Now create a second frame and set the rollover effect on this frame.

5. Choose Window → Frame to open the Frames palette (10.27).

6. Click on the menu icon at the top right of the Frames palette and select Duplicate Frame. A new Frame, Frame 2, is created (10.28). It is identical to the original frame, so you have to edit this frame to create the rollover effect.

7. Click the Hide Slices and Hotspots icon (10.29) in the toolbar to make the slice indicators invisible for easier editing.

8. With Frame 2 active, using the text tool, select the first menu item. Change the text color to gold. The text for this item is now white when Frame 1 is active, and gold when Frame 2 is active (10.30, 10.31). Repeat for each menu item.

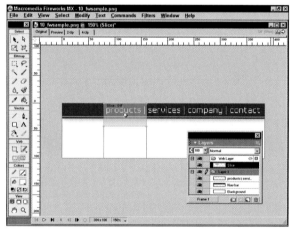

 10.24

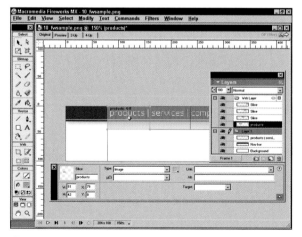

 10.25

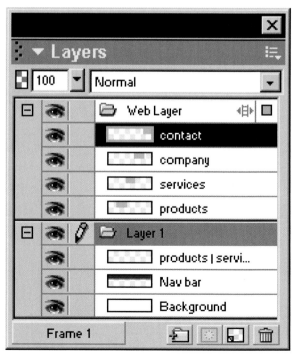

● 10.26

[NOTE]

I don't want the separating bars to change color with
the rollover effect, so they are left white in both text
layers. If there were no separator bars, or if you did
want the bars to change color, you could highlight the
entire text block and change the color once.

Your sliced images are ready to use, with the rollover
effect in place. All that remains to create finished,
individual images is to optimize the slices and save
them.

To optimize and save sliced images:

1. **With Frame 1 active, turn the Slice visibility back on
   by clicking the Show Slices and Hot Spots icon in
   the toolbox. Select the first menu item. You are
   going to optimize each slice (10.32).**

2. **Click the Preview tab at the top of the screen and if
   it is not already open, open the Optimize window
   (Window → Optimize).**

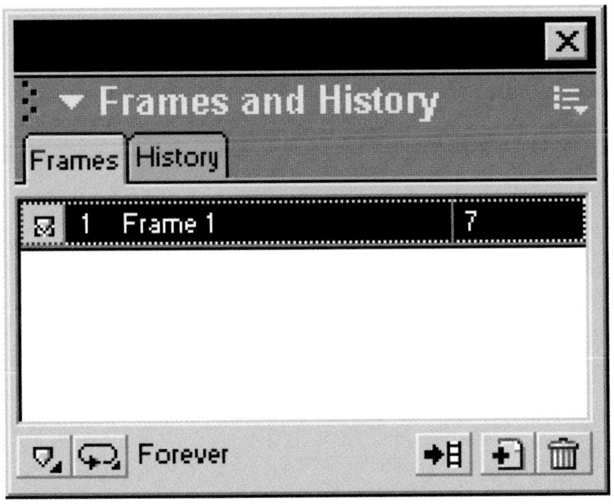

● 10.30

● 10.31

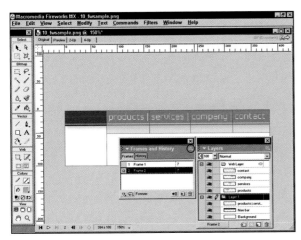

● 10.27

● 10.28

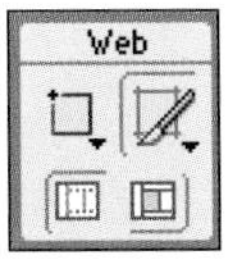

● 10.29

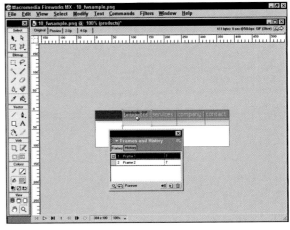

● 10.32

[NOTE]

Working at 100% view when you're optimizing an area is best, because gauging the final quality is difficult unless you can see any compression or color reduction effects on the actual size images.

3. Set the file format and optimization settings required for your example. In this case, I have used GIF format, with 16 colors. Repeat for each slice (10.33).

[NOTE]

You can select multiple slices and apply optimization when they require the same settings. Simply Shift+click on as many slices as you want to select.

4. Click the Original tab to return to the editing screen.

5. Select all slices with the Pointer tool. Choose File → Export Preview. The Export Preview window opens (10.34). Don't worry about the settings in this screen, because the slice settings override the overall settings.

6. Click Export. The Export window will open. Navigate to where you would like to save the images.

7. Select Images Only for Save as File Type. Make sure Export Slices is selected for the Slices option.

8. Activate the Selected Slices option. Make sure that the Include Area Without Slices is not checked. The filename does not matter, as the slice name will override this name. (10.35)

9. Click Save. Your files will be saved in the folder you specify, with the slice name for the normal state, and _f2 added to the slice name for the over state.

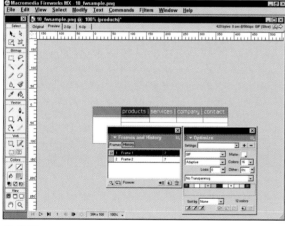

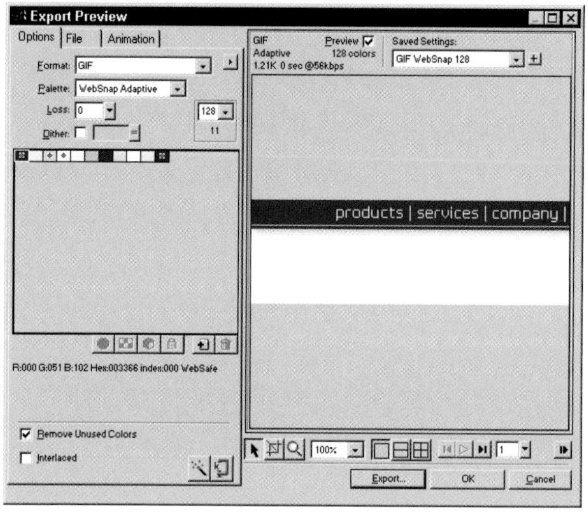

● 10.33

● 10.34

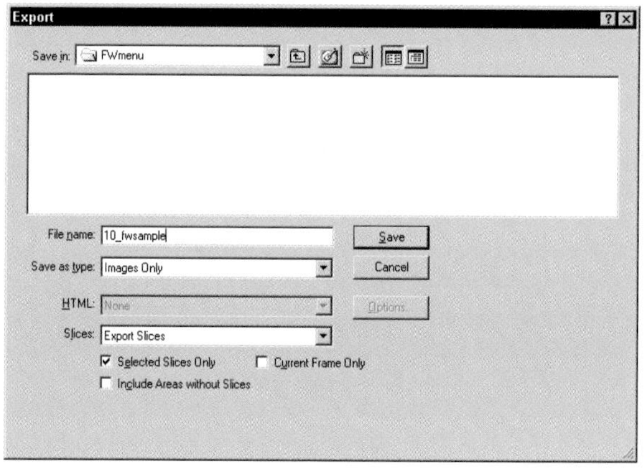

● 10.35

Planning for Consistent Typography on a Site

When you're jumping between HTML pages and graphics programs, keeping your look consistent can be hard. Add the variety of content that is included on a single site — pages with pure text, pages with returned data, some with images, some without — and the task becomes daunting. So how can you keep consistency from one page to another, especially with text, when a one-pixel change in size can affect the entire look?

Unfortunately, there is not one secret to keeping your type consistent, but you can put some practices in place that will help.

Use CSS for ALL content: Part II, "Controlling Web Type with Cascading Style Sheets (CSS)" is devoted to the best type consistency technique available, or CSS. When you use CSS for all text, using only the `<strong>` or `<em>` tags for emphasis, you strip the number of elements you must worry about to two: the CSS file and your graphics program files. Not a single trick can add consistency to your work more effectively than using CSS.

Keep all relevant graphics files open as you work: I came to this method of operating over years of experience. Coming from the days of low RAM on my computer (my first computer had 2MB — cutting edge at the time), and never one to upgrade quickly (I hate changing my equipment when I have it running well) my practice is normally to close files I am not actively using. However, with Web design I find that my work is much more consistent if I keep all working files open during the page-building phase of a project. The added benefit is that I tend to use fewer documents now, preferring to add elements to the open main or interior comp, rather than creating a file just for page titles, as an example. With the files open, I am much less likely to assume that I have the font, font size, exact color, and so on, memorized. Checking makes sense when I can get to the file in question with a keystroke.

Use a template concept for all work: Don't restrict the concept of templates to a program, like Dreamweaver, that has an official template function. I do heavily use program-based HTML templates, and urge you to learn how to use your editor's template capability. But beyond that, I always base a new document in my graphics program on one that exists for that site. I usually create a proof for the entry page on a site as a first step. At least one interior proof is always required, and I always base subsequent proofs on the original entry page. In practice, that means I save the original page as a new name, and build my interior proof with the elements on the page. Even if the layout is completely different, I do have the active text blocks right on the page, and often make drastic changes in appearance, yet use the original text block. Making a consistency error is hard when you're editing the exact element that has been used to create all the pages. No matter what element you're working on, watch for opportunities to base new work on old. You'll save plenty of time, too.

Keep a notebook handy: I have a cheap, spiral notebook sitting on my desk. This notebook would make my former teachers scream, because it is an unholy mess of reminder notes, dates, phone numbers, color notes . . . there is nothing that does not belong in this book. This tool is not one to put my life in perfect order (actually, it was intended that way, but it didn't take). It simply replaces my notes on the back of envelopes, proof pages, even the back of (usually) unimportant photos when I was really desperate. I've tried sticky notes, leather-covered planners, just about every fancy organizing tool available, and this tool is the most effective I have found. I never lose anything. I'll admit, at times it takes me more than five seconds to find what I need, but find it I do. When I'm working on a site and need to note a color number, font size, padding value, whatever, it goes in the book. Try it! I promise you this is the best 99-cent tip you'll ever adopt.

10. To check that your images have been saved correctly, choose File → Open. Click on any file for a preview (10.36). Cancel the window when you have confirmed the images.

That's it. You now have a set of images ready to place into an HTML page. If you make changes to the file, you simply export the affected file again, and it will overwrite the current file.

Creating Graphic Headlines

Even if you use CSS menus on your site, you may choose to create your headlines with a graphic image. Although using image headlines is considerably more work than text menus, you have much more font choice. If you're careful with optimizing your files, you won't add too much weight to your pages. I often use images for page titles, and occasionally as main titles in the content. I don't recommend using an image graphic as a subheading. It's just too much work, and really unnecessary. HTML text works well for minor headings, which tend to look best if they match the content text.

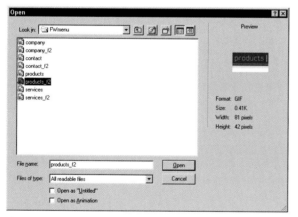

● 10.36

[W A R N I N G]

Don't forget that you lose the search engine food of the `<h1>` tag for your most important and relevant headings when you use graphic text for headlines. Adding the `alt` attribute to the graphic headline `<image>` tag helps the search engines to find you, but it doesn't deliver the high score that an `<h1>` tag delivers for search engine placement.

If you go to the extra work of a graphic headline, make sure that you do it right. No point exists in creating a graphic element when a text version can do exactly the same thing. In this example (10.37) note how no difference exists between the HTML text and the image that features text with no antialiasing. Access to antialiasing is a reason to use a graphic headline, but in this case, the text with antialiasing does not look good. The font is too small to handle the edge blurring. (See Chapter 9, "Creating Graphic Text for the Web," for more information about antialiasing.) Of course, if you use a font that is not available on the Web and add a decorative effect, the benefits outweigh the drawbacks (10.38). This process is one that you should always work through when deciding whether to use HTML or graphic text for headlines.

Typography is very important for headlines. You lose every benefit of graphic text if your type kerning or spacing is weak. If you're new to typography, becoming proficient with the skills required to create

New this week!	Text
New this week!	Image no antialiasing
New this week!	Image with antialiasing

● 10.37

great type will take you a little time. You reach a point where kerning becomes second nature, and perfecting your type adds very little time. The difference is subtle, but good typography does really count in the overall look of your page. The headline shown here (10.39) has only a few adjustments to the kerning values in the lower example, but the entire element is much better balanced.

[T I P]

People who are new to typography are always skeptical that the subtle difference that constitutes most typography control doesn't really matter. I can jump up and down and holler about how important kerning is, but you must experience it. Commit to using the principles I have brought to you in Part III, "Graphic Type for the Web," for one site. Your text will be better, of course. But your attention to detail on the entire site will go up. That's the main difference between an amateur and a professional designer — attention to detail. If the site where you focus on typography is not the best site you have ever done, go back to your old ways. I guess I don't have to tell you what to do if it is the best. That's why you're reading this book, right?

You also want your headline to stand out. But please, don't take that statement to mean that you need BIG, **BOLD**, LOUD!!!!! Headlines. A headline is like a menu — it should be there when your visitor wants to skim the page, or find the right information, but bow out and sit in the background when they are reading content text. Remember, if your site is designed well, your content is what the visitor is seeking. Not headlines, not menus, not graphic elements, but content. Don't ever lose sight of the purpose.

You can make a very small headline stand out with little more than a line. In this gentle example (10.40) the text is not big or bold, or even capitalized. It is in a soft color. Yet the thin line, also a soft color works with the type to make the headline stand right out. This headline is a perfect example of one that would leave center stage as soon as its job was done.

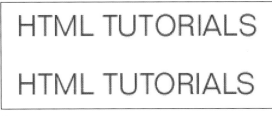

● 10.39

● 10.38

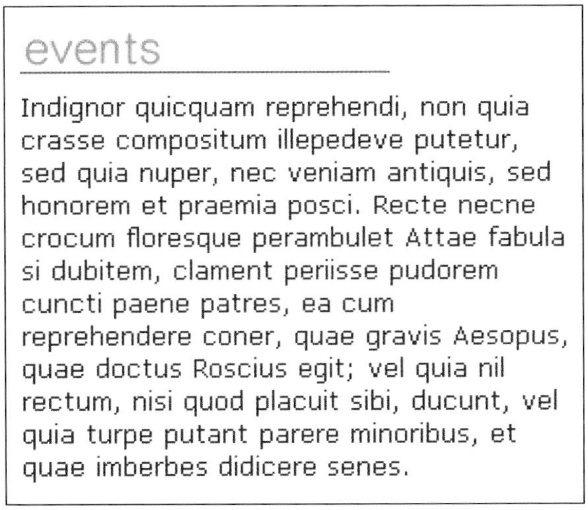

● 10.40

Demure headlines can be quite effective. Look at the effect that a soft background color has on this small text headline (10.41). The information is crisp and clear; the color background stops the eye, but it does not permanently chop the content.

Adding a design element is an effective way to make a headline stand out. I've included a sample of a light headline with and without a design element (10.42, 10.43). Isn't it amazing how much more the headline stands out with that tiny addition? Besides providing more graphic impact, design elements also perform as guides on your page. If you consistently use an element throughout your site, visitors will soon be taking their navigation clues from your design elements.

The next section takes you deeper into the design element subject. Keep headlines in mind as you read through it, but there is much more you can do with a solid set of elements for a site.

Creating Graphic Type Elements for Your Pages

Graphic elements are like the spice of a page. Like spices, design elements come in many variations, from bold and spicy, to soft and sweet. Like spice enhances a meal, so should the extras on your page. However, like spice, if you use too many, or the wrong type, you will ruin your page, just as garlic would ruin apple pie.

Graphic elements are generally very small. I'm not talking about photographs that advance the message, but small additions used to bring color through the page and help direct the visitor's eye to the right places. I'm talking about lines, dots, squares, triangles, and so on, usually in tiny sizes. Most of the graphic documents will measure less than 10 pixels in width or height, and may be as small as 1-pixel square. Although they are often taken from the logo or heading design, they are a separate part of the page.

I design many of my design elements as I create my pages. In the proofing stage, I usually use a few design elements to balance the page, and I create the obvious elements as I slice my rollovers and any other graphics. Many times, though, I don't decide to use a design element until I reach a stage of the HTML construction. These include files to use as bullets, and a selection of 1-pixel files filled with a solid color. I'll start with that valuable little trick.

events

Indignor quicquam reprehendi, non quia crasse compositum illepedeve putetur, sed quia nuper, nec veniam antiquis, sed honorem et praemia posci. Recte necne crocum floresque perambulet Attae fabula si dubitem, clament periisse pudorem cuncti paene patres, ea cum reprehendere coner, quae gravis Aesopus, quae doctus Roscius egit; vel quia nil rectum, nisi quod placuit sibi, ducunt, vel quia turpe putant parere minoribus, et quae imberbes didicere senes.

● 10.41

❖ **events**

Indignor quicquam reprehendi, non quia crasse compositum illepedeve putetur, sed quia nuper, nec veniam antiquis, sed honorem et praemia posci. Recte necne crocum floresque perambulet Attae fabula si dubitem, clament periisse pudorem cuncti paene patres, ea cum reprehendere coner, quae gravis Aesopus, quae doctus Roscius egit; vel quia nil rectum, nisi quod placuit sibi, ducunt, vel quia turpe putant parere minoribus, et quae imberbes didicere senes.

● 10.42

events

Indignor quicquam reprehendi, non quia crasse compositum illepedeve putetur, sed quia nuper, nec veniam antiquis, sed honorem et praemia posci. Recte necne crocum floresque perambulet Attae fabula si dubitem, clament periisse pudorem cuncti paene patres, ea cum reprehendere coner, quae gravis Aesopus, quae doctus Roscius egit; vel quia nil rectum, nisi quod placuit sibi, ducunt, vel quia turpe putant parere minoribus, et quae imberbes didicere senes.

● 10.43

Have you ever wished you could just draw a line in your HTML page the way you do in a graphics program? You can, if you create a 1-pixel GIF file. Most of you will be familiar with the idea of creating a clear GIF file, to create invisible placeholders for table cells. But if you make the same file with a color, instead of transparent, you have a very effective tool for creating lines or other design elements.

You create a single-pixel color image in a graphics program. I usually start with an image that is 10 px by 10 px just because I like to see what is going on, confirm a fill, and so on (10. 44). The sample here is created in Photoshop and magnified to 600%. Before exporting, I simply reduce the image size to 1 px by 1 px. I rarely even save the file, because I can create it so quickly.

Look what you can do with nothing but CSS text and a red 1-pixel image (10.45). I've included the code that creates this effect. Note that the 10reddot.gif file forms the 6-px square dot and the 300 px by 2 px line.

```
<tr>
   <td align="center"><img
    src="10reddot.gif" width="6"
    height="6"></td>
   <td><h1>EVENTS</h1></td>
 </tr>
 <tr>
   <td colspan="2"><img
    src="10reddot.gif" width="300"
    height="2"></td>
 </tr>
```

I hope that sent your idea-creation mind into overdrive. The wonderful thing about the 1-pixel image is that the tiny file size is loaded only once for your whole site, as the browser will have it in the cache every time it is called. That is close to graphics for free. For most sites that I do, I have at least two of these color files on hand, in each of the main colors for the site. I use them for lines and dots whenever a little extra touch is needed. To show how versatile this concept is, I have included another sample of the same headline, this time with a yellow dot, and sized to 8 px by 8 px because the yellow does not have as much weight as the red (10.46). I wonder if there would be a little more energy if I made the design element elongated, like 12 px wide and 4 px high (10.47)? What do you think? You have amazing power to customize design elements for every need on a site. Just make sure that you do keep consistency in mind. I would not use both the square and elongated element on the same site. I may use a square in a different application with an elongated element in the headline, however.

■ EVENTS

Indignor quicquam reprehendi, non quia crasse compositum illepedeve putetur, sed quia nuper, nec veniam antiquis, sed honorem et praemia posci. Recte necne crocum floresque perambulet Attae fabula si dubitem, clament periisse pudorem cuncti paene patres, ea cum reprehendere coner, quae gravis Aesopus, quae doctus Roscius egit.

Vel quia nil rectum, nisi quod placuit sibi, ducunt, vel quia turpe putant parere minoribus, et quae imberbes didicere senes.

● 10.45

■ EVENTS

● 10.46

▬ EVENTS

● 10.47

● 10.44

Of course, this method provides only square elements for your page, and at times, a circle is more appropriate. Circles are easy to prepare in a graphics program, and you should create them with an uneven number of pixels; that is, 5 px by 5 px, or 7 px by 7 px. In most programs, creating a circular selection with antialiasing, and filling with a solid color delivers excellent results. I have included a sample 7 px by 7 px file, magnified to 1600% (10.48). The same file is shown in an HTML document (10.49).

The circle is not as flexible as the square element, however. As soon as you add antialiasing to an image, it should be used at exact size in your HTML documents. The circle image with a 5 px by 5 px HTML-specified size loses its shape and clarity (10.50). Compare that to the result when I created a new image at the correct size (10.51).

Don't stop with simple shapes, either. You can add extra design lines, create open circles — whatever will fit within a small image. I've included a few ideas to start you off (10.52).

[TIP]

There is no limit to the number of different elements you can create to enhance pages. However, I do advise that you keep them simple and small. An image over 10-pixels high can interfere with text line spacing, and much of the power of design elements comes from being able to use the extras as inline images.

Finally, don't stop with simple or more complex images with this idea. You can create little text messages that can be ready to go for any page. I often create a "more" image to use in introduction type text sections on a page (10.53). The graphic file that creates this look is shown at 600% magnification (10.54). The font is Helvetica, 9 pixels, with no antialiasing. The triangle is drawn on a separate layer and uses antialiasing.

Using Dingbat Fonts as Graphic Elements

Creating the right graphic elements for a page can be a frustrating effort. At times, you have the concept in

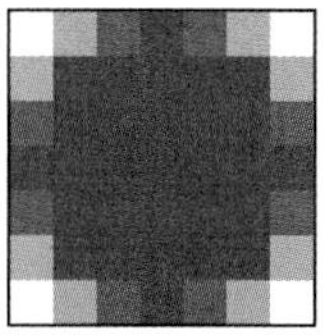

● 10.48

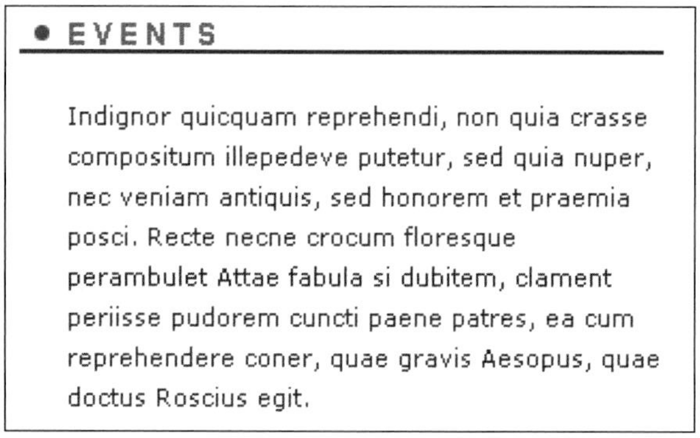

EVENTS
Indignor quicquam reprehendi, non quia crasse compositum illepedeve putetur, sed quia nuper, nec veniam antiquis, sed honorem et praemia posci. Recte necne crocum floresque perambulet Attae fabula si dubitem, clament periisse pudorem cuncti paene patres, ea cum reprehendere coner, quae gravis Aesopus, quae doctus Roscius egit.

● 10.49

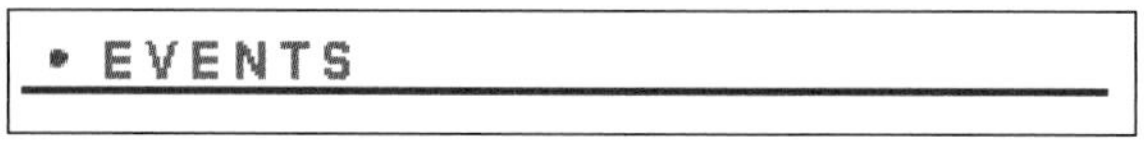

EVENTS

● 10.50

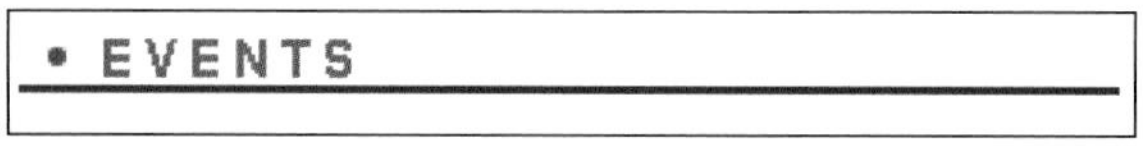

EVENTS

● 10.51

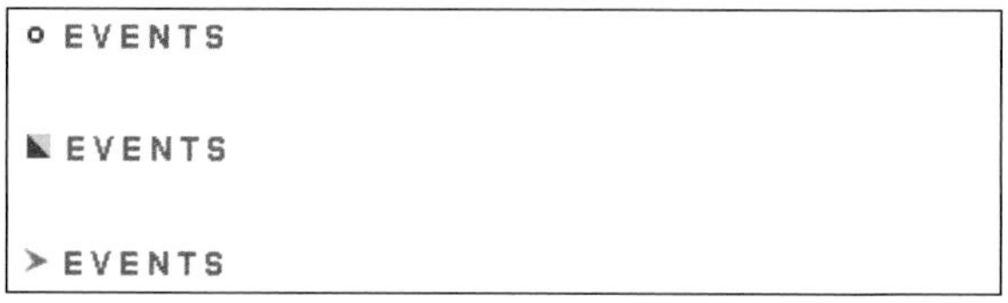

EVENTS
EVENTS
EVENTS

● 10.52

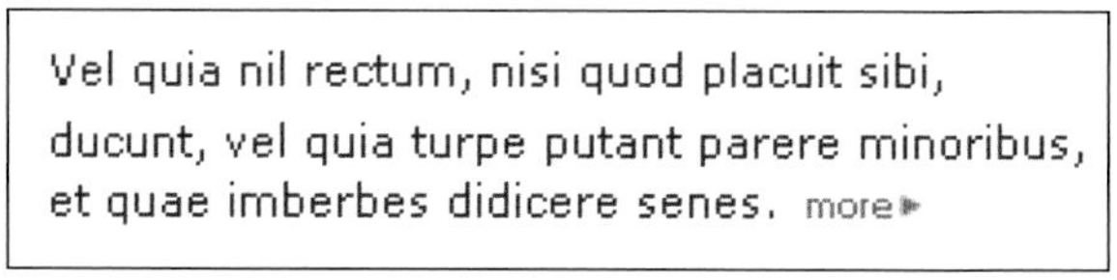

Vel quia nil rectum, nisi quod placuit sibi, ducunt, vel quia turpe putant parere minoribus, et quae imberbes didicere senes. more

● 10.53

more

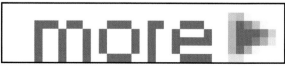

● 10.54

your mind, not quite solidly enough to sketch it, but you will know it when you see it. Perhaps you're looking for a shape, a mood . . . or an inspiration.

Enter dingbats. These little graphic element collections, disguised as fonts, can be the most valuable tool in your design element toolbox.

Dingbats can save you hours when you stop thinking of them as text, and see them as graphic templates. What is a dingbat, if not an outline? An outline just begging to have your style applied to it. And they come in sets. Find one that sets the right tone and you usually have many other outlines in the same style to choose from. Design the first one, save a set of actions and click, click, a design set — in your style (10.55).

Dingbats *are* fonts. This is both their power, and their problem. You install them on your system in the same way as you install fonts. Choose the dingbat font as your font choice, type a letter, and a picture appears on your page.

However, with a font, when we type an *A*, an *A* appears — it may be straight or curved depending on the font style, but it is an A. With a dingbat, the first problem emerges when you want a shape in the middle of a font set, but you don't know which letter will give it to you. The dingbat character shown here is an *e* as you can see in Photoshop's Layer palette (10.56). Note the cursor on the canvas, and that the layer containing this character is a Text layer. Unless you have all the time in the world, and the patience of a saint, you will require a font viewer to use dingbats. See the nearby sidebar "Viewing Dingbats Easily."

Although dingbats are entered into a program as type, they do not have to remain in that state. If you use a raster program like Photoshop, you can convert the layer containing the dingbat to raster format, and the dingbat becomes a regular bitmap image.

If you have access to a vector illustration program like Adobe Illustrator, Macromedia Freehand, or

CorelDraw!, you can convert a dingbat shape to a vector by converting to curves. In the CorelDraw! example shown here (10.57), I converted a dingbat character into curves, and further separated the image into three separate objects. Each of the objects has been treated to a different effect. After the dingbat is a curve, you can edit the points freely as with any other curve. The editing possibilities are endless.

You enter dingbats in the same way you enter text in any program. Choose the dingbat font and type the appropriate character. If you're using a font viewer to make your choice, copying the chosen character is often faster. In most cases, only the character, not the font specification, will copy, so you must select your dingbat font in the application. All font viewers have copy capabilities, or use keystroke copy (Ctrl+C for PC or Command+C for Mac).

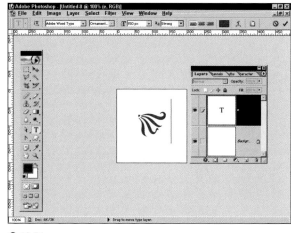

● 10.56

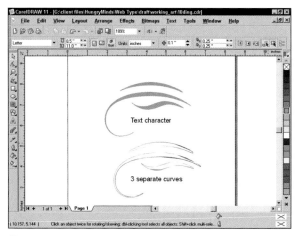

● 10.57

● 10.55

Viewing Dingbats Easily

You will not realize the full power of dingbats unless you have a way to view and use dingbats easily. Both Macs and PCs offer onboard viewers that are especially handy for dingbats. The Mac uses Key Caps, and the PC uses the character map (charmap.exe in the Windows directory). You may want to copy the character map to your Start menu for convenience.

You can also find third-party character viewers. Some of you may already have font-management programs if you have come from, or are still in print production. They are overkill for Web design use, though, and these little programs are a good value if you want more convenient dingbat viewing.

For the Mac, check out PopChar Pro (www.macility. com/products/popcharpro/), or for a freeware viewer, Get Char (www.geocities.com/Silicon Valley/Way/6897/).

For the PC, Font Xplorer (www.moonsoftware.com/ fxplorer.asp) and Font-ABC (www.abc-ware.com/ fontabce.htm) are worth checking out. All have trial versions.

Entering the text into your program is as simple as pasting a copied character and changing the font. Alternately, if you know which character you require, you can simply set the font and size, and type the character. In the Photoshop example shown here, I have set the type to Zapf Dingbats font, and typed the ^ (Shift+6) character. The font size is 150 pixels, and antialiasing is set to Strong (10.58).

As long as the dingbat is text, you can apply any effect to the dingbat that you can add to text. I added a gentle bevel effect to the dingbat to achieve a slightly puffy appearance (10.59). Because the image is a font, you can easily change color and even character — much more easily than for a bitmap image. To achieve this image, I changed the font color, and replaced the ^ with an *h* (10.60).

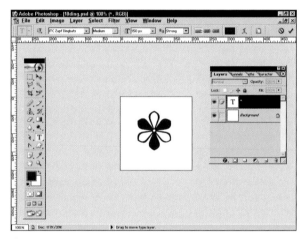

● 10.58

[N O T E]

In Photoshop, when you rasterize a layer that has a layer style applied, the layer style remains separate. Only the original character is converted, which means that you can edit the Layer style, or remove it at any time before and after rasterizing the layer.

● 10.59

● 10.60

In most graphic programs, you cannot use the full range of filters with a text layer. When you are happy with the general appearance of your dingbat character, you can change the font to a bitmap, and apply any filter to the layer. I converted this dingbat character to a bitmap, and applied a twirl filter, and then a torn edges filter to change the look completely (10.61). This example should give you a good indication of how many different options are open to you when using dingbat fonts.

[T I P]

Many free and very low cost dingbat fonts are available. You can find a list of Dingbat sites in my column at WebReference.com (www.webreference.com/graphics/column18/9.html). Also, Websitetips.com has a rich section on fonts in general, including many sites that feature free dingbat fonts (http://websitetips.com/fonts/index.html).

● 10.61

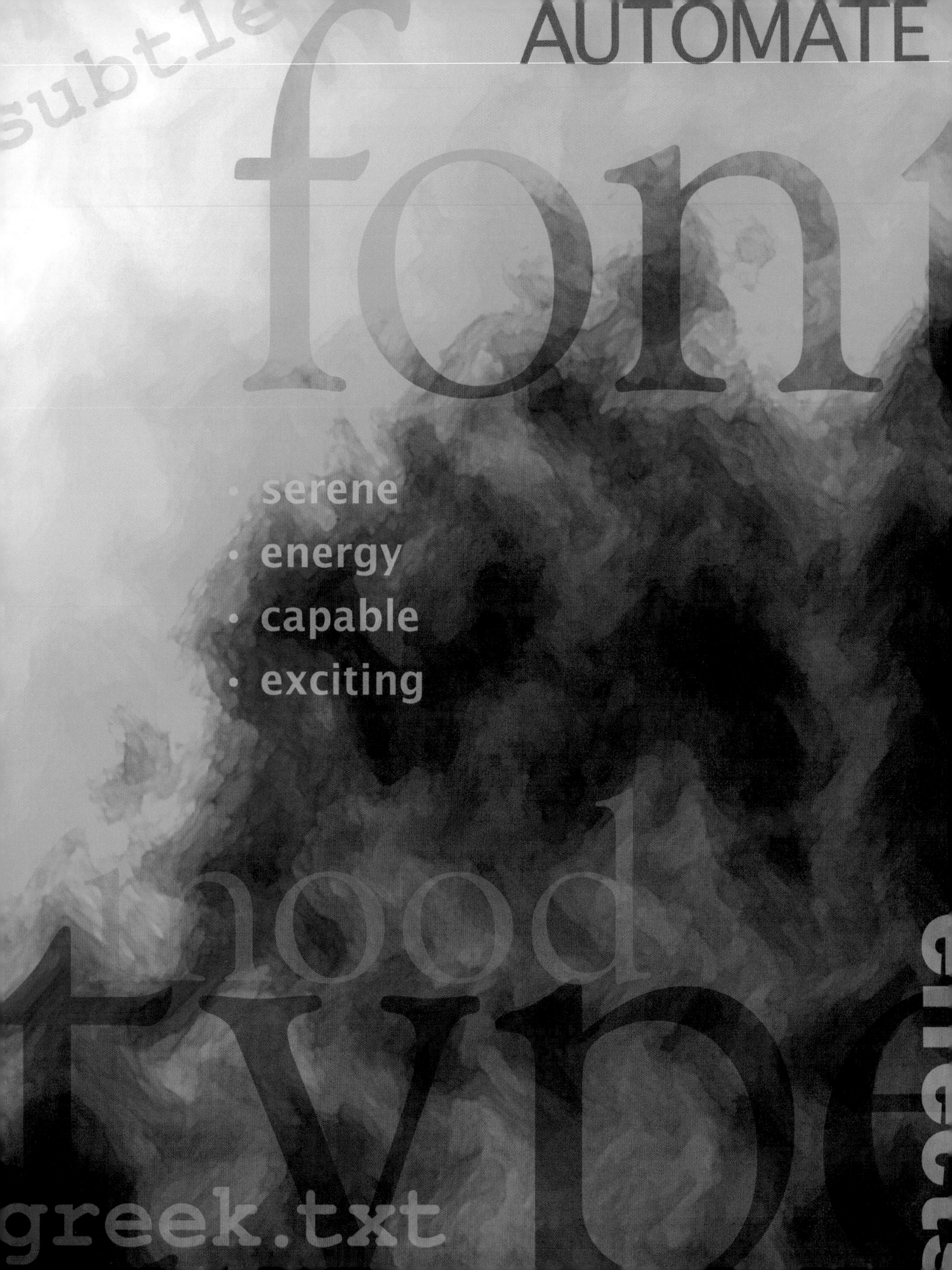

AUTOMATE

font

- serene
- energy
- capable
- exciting

mood

type

greek.txt

Chapter 11

Graphic Type Special Effects

Color is free on the Web. Don't be afraid to use it, as long as you make an effort to use it with style and elegance. All elements on a page should relate to each other in some way, and that includes type colors. Avoid too little or too much contrast between type and background colors.

SUZANNE STEPHENS

I promised you fun, and this chapter is where I really deliver. I've hammered home dire messages about type quality, download time, visitor needs, and so on. You know to use HTML text whenever you possibly can. But when you arrive at the point that you need a good design element, and know that graphic text is the only way you can reach what you need, you should focus on creating dynamic results. After all, you don't get to really play with text much if you follow what I have been telling you.

Setting a Mood with Text

One of the first things that an experienced designer tackles for a new site is the mood. Hopefully, you already know the site goals, and understand what the content requirements for the site will be, but the design decisions you make on mood will affect the entire site. Are you looking to create excitement? Is your message serious and serene, requiring the matching mood? Or are you selling an idea or concept, like relaxation, beauty, or function? The answers to questions like these provide the mood. Every element you use on the pages for a site must match the mood, or the site won't have continuity throughout. So before you dive into using text to create mood, I want to make sure you understand the overall concept.

[**T I P**]

I have a series of articles, "Menus with Beauty and Brains," that takes a brief look at site purpose and mood. (`http://productiongraphics.com/column42`). My book, *Web Menus with Beauty and Brains* (Wiley 2002) is an expansion of this series and goes into the subject thoroughly.

What Is Mood?

Mood is a tough concept for many new designers to grasp. It's hard to define exactly what creates a site's mood. Yet, it is the foundation for presenting your message, vital to the success of your site. Creating mood is a skill that becomes easier as your experience grows, and you get a better "feeling" for how to adjust your style to evoke different responses from visitors.

Like balance and color work on a site, with much of the success depending on the designer intuitively knowing where to place things, or which color will balance a page, there are also learnable skills that will help to create mood. These skills are what I introduce you to in this section. The most valuable part of the information I have here is the sidebar exercise, "Match the Site with the Mood." Don't skip it if you want to create better pages.

Match the Site with the Mood

Here's a little exercise for you. I've listed six URLs for you to visit (yes, visit — I'm not including screen shots because you need to see the site, check a few pages, find the flow and mood of the site). Six words are listed below the URLs. Assign one of these words to each site, a different word for each site. Make sure that you go right to the URL I've listed so you will bypass any Flash introductions (makes it hard to compare apples to apples).

```
http://tiffanys.com/html/
```

```
http://oxygen.com/
```

```
www.deltaleisure.com/index.asp
```

```
http://cbc.ca/
```

```
www.designbeef.com/index.php
```

```
www.designiskinky.net/
index_main.html-
```

Choose a different word that best describes each listed site:

Irreverent, Corporate, Young, Luxury, Current, Information

This is very much an opinion exercise. I want you to observe all the elements that make up a site — the navigation, colors, fonts used, content, tone of content. You need to look at every aspect in order to separate a couple of them and assign the word that fits best. I give my opinions later in this chapter, but don't read them before you visit the sites and make your own decisions. This highly valuable exercise will only really sink in if you do the thinking to identify the mood.

[WARNING]

I continue from here as if you have completed the exercise in the "Match the Site with the Mood" sidebar, and checked my opinions in the "Match the Site with the Mood: My Opinions" sidebar later in this chapter.

I hope you noticed as you picked through the sites just how important text was in delivering the mood. Even though the content text on all the sites was more or less the same style (we have so little choice) it was presented in a different way on each site. The amount of white space around the text, the way the headlines fit, the colors of the headlines — all contribute to the overall look and mood of the site.

The graphic text presentation, in all cases, worked with the content text delivery to present a unified front. Compare the Oxygen site to the CBC site. Although classic fonts are used for both sites, they are prepared and presented in a very different way. The text on Oxygen is always surrounded by color. On the CBC site, the text is clear, but placed in a much more subdued setting. The Design is Kinky site puts the headlines right in your face — more impact, and more likely to draw a response from a youthful audience. Some amazing sites are out there for younger adults — you must deliver impact or you will be lost.

[NOTE]

There was a wonderful television ad several years ago that perfectly captured mood. I wish I could show that ad to anyone struggling with this concept. The ad was for CBC radio, Canada's national radio station, famous for news, national stories, and music/entertainment geared for more mature adults than most stations — at the time, probably 35 years old and up. The ad featured a man getting into his car to go to work. He starts the car, and acid rock music blasts him back in his seat. With a desperate look on his face, he scrambles for the controls and soon the soothing sound of great voices delivering national news, then classical music takes over. He relaxes and smiles, instantly serene. It was a great ad — using mood to almost wordlessly deliver the benefit of the product to the intended audience.

Using Text to Set Mood

How do you match your text to the mood? You don't! That's the wrong way to approach text and mood. Text is a critical part of the team that creates the mood, not a piece that comes in after the fact. When you're creating your proof page ask yourself what mood you must achieve. Establish what colors, design elements, and text styling will work together to present the mood that you require.

You need to consider both graphic and content text at this stage. If you don't have one already, obtain a copy of Greek text, the text I have been using throughout this book for examples. Greek text has no message, which makes it perfect to use as a design element, rather than "real" words, which can distract us from the pure design concept. Try to estimate the amount of text that will appear on the final pages, and break the text into headings and subheads to approximate the final appearance of the content for your site.

[T I P]

You can download a copy of the Greek text I use at `http://wpeck.com/greek.html`.

While I stress that content text is important to the mood, you can manipulate text in only so many ways. You saw that in the mood-matching exercise. Although there are differences in font size, white space, and color, clear content text on the Web must stay within pretty rigid boundaries. Refer to Part II, "Controlling Web Type with Cascading Style Sheets (CSS)" for a full discussion of how to present content text using CSS.

Graphic text, on the other hand, is a perfect tool for presenting mood. You can use any font that remains legible, add effects, jumble the letters, and play with decorative kerning and tracking — all methods that have a dramatic impact on mood.

Your font choice is obviously the first step. How seriously would you take a bank or trust company site with pretty, curly headlines (11.1)? Does this look give you the confidence that this company should look after your financial well-being? Compare the curly sample to the same headline in a classic font, Century Schoolbook (11.2). Another choice might have been Palatino (11.3). Note that I also changed

the color. Even with the more appropriate font, the light blue did not offer the solidity that I sought.

But font choice is not the only factor that contributes to mood. Dare I say, font choice may not often be the most important factor. A great exercise is to take one font, and see how many variations in mood you can create. I've done just that with one of my favorite fonts, Eurostile (11.4). This is the font delivered straight up, no color, no kerning. I like this font because even without any work, it delivers a great look that fits many moods.

Open the tracking on the font, however, use all lowercase, change the color, kern to remove gaps (note that the space between the characters and the punctuation is reduced), and the mood changes dramatically (11.5). This arrangement would work for an artistic site, or perhaps a special interest news site — anywhere that a light, open feeling is desired.

A change to all caps with bold style changes the mood of this font completely (11.6). I changed it back to black for full impact. It's hard to imagine that this is the same font as the previous example, and harder to imagine the page that could hold both versions of the font. To further illustrate how versatile one font can be, I took the same all caps arrangement and assigned a soft, classy color (11.7). What happens when you remove the bold style, and create a small

● 11.1

Trust Us

● 11.2

Trust Us

● 11.3

What's up?

● 11.4

what's up?

● 11.5

WHAT'S UP?

● 11.6

WHAT'S UP?

● 11.7

caps version of the same expression (11.8)? Different again. This look could pass as a quasi art deco mood.

Finally, I went in the opposite direction and tossed characters all over the place, with different sizes and colors (11.9). Check back to the plain, out-of-the-box sample (11.5) to compare how much a few changes can affect the mood of a font.

Mood cannot have standards applied to it. What you find dark and foreboding may be what I call serious. You run into that with all design issues. Your job as a designer is to be in touch with your visitor's translations. Often, just by the fact that you're interested in creating a site for a specific group gives you a good understanding of how your group reacts. Professional designers often create sites for groups of people they have never had any contact with. A great deal of research is required so that you can understand how these groups think and what they want. It's not an easy part of a design career, but discovering the perfect mood for a completely new group can be exciting.

If you were hoping that I would have a list of 25 fonts that would deliver a, b, or c mood, I hope you understand now why that is not possible. When I came up with so many different looks from one font . . . there is just no way to create that list. I suppose an entire book, maybe the "Type Designers Mood Selector," could cover the basics, but even that would only be a guide.

I do recommend that you take a font you really like, preferably a clean or classic font, and experiment with many variations like I did for Eurostile. You will no doubt come up with some effect that you will use in the future. Even if you don't discover a great combo you can use, the exercise will sharpen your instincts for what effect each change in a font makes to mood.

I also recommend that you build a list of fonts that come through for you. I don't mean a list of fonts you really like. I've mentioned before that I love the font Ugly Face (11.10), but it does not reside in my main font file. Eurostile certainly does (11.11). This font has done the job for me many times on the first try. If you have ever spent hours trying to find exactly the right font among the thousands of possible choices, you know how much that means.

Adding Effects to Text

Creating the right mood often means adding effects to text. You should enter this section repeating the mantra: subtle, subtle, subtle. Although graphics programs offer the wonderful opportunities to add effects to any element, you are dealing with text. And text must be read. Text that is manipulated to non-legibility is no longer valuable. Shoot to create an "effect" rather than producing text with an obvious effect.

I'll show you what I mean (11.12). In this example, the top word obviously has an emboss effect added.

● 11.8

● 11.9

● 11.10

● 11.11

● 11.12

Match the Site with the Mood:
My Opinions

This is part two of the exercise I presented earlier in this chapter. Please note the word I have used throughout my discussion on this exercise: opinion. That's what makes mood such a slippery target, and why I wanted you to concentrate hard before I prattled on about how I see each site's mood. Being "right" isn't the point. Nor is whether I agree with you, or vice versa. What's important is that you take a magnifying glass to the site elements, and "get" how everything in a site adds up to a whole.

Luxury

`http://tiffanys.com/html/`

This was quite a giveaway. However, I don't feel bad. Everything about this site drips quality and the finer things in life. I pay less for a car than many of the jewelry pieces featured on the Tiffany & Co. site, but I still love to be here. Everything on this site works towards the same goal, which makes it a comfortable place to hang around.

Current

`http://oxygen.com/`

This site could have gone into news, and maybe, if you did not pay attention to the content, young. But the colors, and the topics, even the (dare I say it) rolling marquee message adds to a feeling of NOW! The content is definitely for women, but not for young women, exclusively. While it has a youthful appearance, note that the site has an underlying corporate feel to it, as well. The colors are bright, but the fonts are all classic.

Corporate

`www.deltaleisure.com/index.asp`

This site has achieved something that is hard to do — putting forth a corporate image yet capturing the idea of fun. Here, the product is actually fun (vacation), but the provider of the service can't afford to be lighthearted. You want your airline to be stodgy, concerned with rules and doing things right. The nightclub that the same customers go to when they arrive at the destination has the luxury

of putting forth a 100 percent fun face, but an airline must make you feel that they can keep you in the sky so you can reach the nightclub.

Information

`http://cbc.ca/`

You may have mixed this up with current, as CBC is the national radio service in Canada. But the site is presented more as a news provider than cutting-edge current. Compare this site to the Oxygen site, and I think you will see the difference. Had the Oxygen site not been in this list, perhaps CBC would have ended up as a current one, but I would not have included it in that category because it is missing the immediacy that I demand to call a site "current." I expect my senses to come alive, and while CBC does have an excellent site for what it is intended to do, it's a stretch to call it "exciting" — a word I associate with current.

Irreverent

`http://www.designbeef.com/index.php`

I struggled with this one for quite a while. It felt irreverent. My instant reaction was that it is irreverent. Yet, it felt too corporate to be irreverent. Had I been surfing, I know I would have instantly felt it was irreverent. Then I "got" it. It's very corporate appearance is one of the strongest pushes towards irreverence. I'm not sure I would have been as bright if faced with the challenge to create this site.

Young

`www.designiskinky.net/index_main.html`

Did you put this one in as irreverent? But it's not really. Read the content. Some serious stuff is here. Some fun for sure, even some humor that could be called irreverent, but as it is directed at a young crowd, I'm not sure that it even qualifies on that score. The topics, images, and layout are all youthful. My final decision is that it is a young site? When "get your arse over there" is tossed in casually with news about great new sites from talented designers, I'm pretty sure it is geared to a younger crowd.

The lower example, however, has an effect, but it is hard to identify what it is. Note how it actually pops off the page better than the one that has been obviously altered. I used a plain emboss effect to create the top example, and three subtle effects to create the lower example. I used a little embossing to create dimension, a slight inner glow in yellow to add a

little light excitement, and finally, a tiny, nearly invisible drop shadow that helps to complete the dimension and pop it off the page a little. I think that it stands out better, and the effect interferes less with the shape of the characters, which is very important for maintaining legibility.

Whenever you work with the effects function of your graphics program, think half and double. Start with half of the default values, and double the number of effects. I usually find I get better results by reaching a look deliberately, one step at a time. Add a little texture, add a little light, and add a little shadow. Later in this chapter you learn how to automate your effects, so after you have the first sample done, you can apply the same effect easily to the rest of your graphic text.

Manipulating Text as Text

At one time, not all that long ago, even in computer terms, you had to convert text to a bitmap image before you could add any filters or effects. That is no longer true. Most programs allow you to add some effects to your text while it remains as editable text. The previous example (11.12) remained as text when I applied the effects. I simply typed new text to create a new image (11.13) — a feature you want to maintain as long as you can.

Most of the effects I use regularly are available to editable text in most programs. Photoshop offers Layer Styles (11.14). You can add the styles shown here through the Layer Style window (11.15). These styles are just a basic selection of what you can accomplish by adding a layer style. When you combine effects, or consider that each effect has many, many potential variations with distance, opacity, blend mode — you truly can create an infinite number of effects with layer styles.

Fireworks offers many options to add effects to editable text. You add effects through the Properties palette, by clicking on the + (plus) icon in the effects section (11.16). A small selection of the effects that you can produce are shown here (11.17).

Try to achieve the effect you seek with a method that leaves text editable. As soon as you convert text to a raster format, you lose all ability to edit it as text.

● 11.13

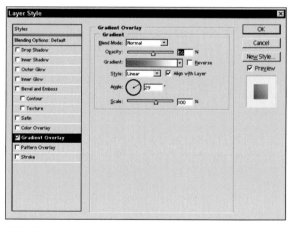

● 11.14

Using and Creating Styles to Automate Effects

You have the option with many software programs to use prefabricated styles that you add to text with one click. Open the Styles palette in Photoshop or Fireworks by choosing Window → Styles. Using these styles could not be simpler. Highlight your text, or text layer, and click on a style. I'm really not under-playing the difficulty. Take a look at the Photoshop

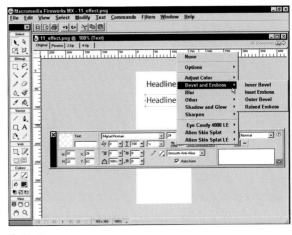

● 11.16

● 11.15

● 11.17

Styles palette (11.18) and the Fireworks Style (11.19) palette. With any element selected on the canvas, one click on a style applies all the attributes to create that look.

In Photoshop, you apply styles to layers. I have applied a variety of styles to the same text entry as an example (11.20). I've selected one of the samples, and you can see the effects that have been added in the Layers palette. You can edit these effects after you apply the style in the same way that you can edit a Layer style you apply manually.

If you create an effect manually, using your own layer styles, you can save your own style. With the layer highlighted, simply click on the menu icon at the top right of the Styles palette, and select New Style. Assign a name and you have a style that you can retrieve at any time, even months down the road. Photoshop places your style into the Styles palette for easy retrieval.

Fireworks applies styles to objects and works in the same way as Photoshop's styles. Select the object and click on the style you desire. I have included a few

applied samples (11.21). The styles in the lower portion of the Styles palette are designed for text. When you apply a text style, the font size may change. Simply reset the text to the size you desire.

You can edit styles in Fireworks after application in the Properties palette. The Properties palette containing the properties for the selected object shown previously (11.21) is shown here (11.22).

You can also create and save a style in Fireworks. Create your style, and click the menu icon in the top right of the Styles palette. Select New Style, and choose the properties you want to include in your style (11.23). Your new style will be placed in the Styles palette, and is available at any time you need to repeat the effect.

Setting Text in Motion

At times, setting text into motion can be fun. Text leaving the straight and narrow adds energy and motion to a page — as long as it is still legible, and matches the mood (11.24). Long ago I saw a page that had wavy headlines through the site. They were

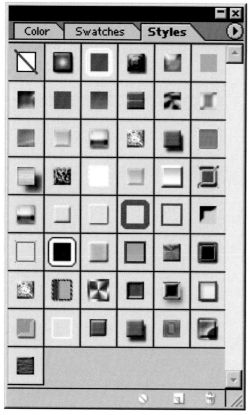

● 11.18

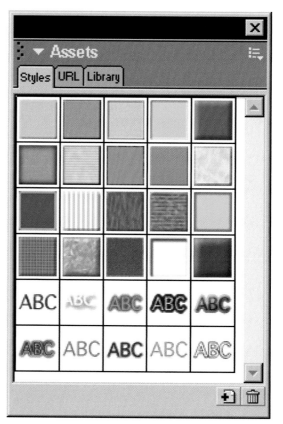

● 11.19

very well done, all in different, bright colors, and this technique really made the site. That site is long gone, but I do remember that there was very little else for design on the page. The message was easily available, but the pages made me smile, which was perfect for the subject.

Where I hate to see text in shapes is the oh-so-overdone text in a circle (11.25). At times, it can be very effective, but generally, I think text is placed in a circle because the designer has seen it before and figures he or she has to do something to make it look like it was "designed." The worst is when an illustration is surrounded by circular text, a common logo technique. But please don't do it. You can integrate text with an image in so many other ways. If you want to use text in a circle, make sure you have answered the question, "Why?" If the answer is that you want to make it look good — don't. If the answer is that you want to put forth a circular mood for a defined reason, go ahead.

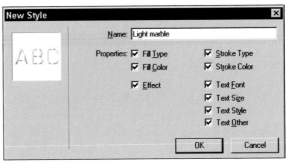

● 11.23

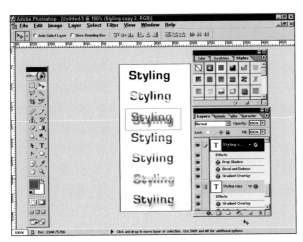

● 11.20

● 11.24

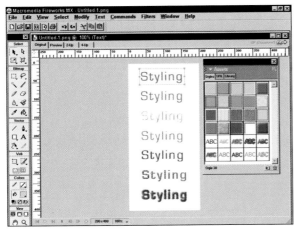

● 11.21

● 11.22

● 11.25

Software programs vary widely in how they create text on a path. This is one rare area where I have to say Photoshop falls short of almost every other program in the graphic world. When Warp Text was added to Photoshop 6, for a few short minutes, we old-time Photoshop users thought we had text on a path capability. Unfortunately, while Warp Text did add a tool to distort text, this feature is not close to providing text on a path. Warp Text can make text wiggle, but the text is distorted as if an envelope is applied around the text, and the envelope is distorted, taking the text with it (11.26). Compare this result to the one created in Fireworks (11.27), which provides powerful, true text-on-a-path capabilities.

[T I P]

Illustration programs like CorelDraw! or Adobe Illustrator have terrific text-on-a-path capabilities, so if you're a Photoshop user who also has one of these illustration programs, create your text on a path in the Illustration program, and export the results for use in your Photoshop document.

To create text on a path in Fireworks, which is a similar method for all vector illustration programs, you create your text and shape separately. Select both the text and the object you want to shape the text around, and choose Text → Attach to Path (11.27). Easy! Text remains editable, though having your text in great shape before attaching to a path is best.

Moving Beyond Simple Effects

If you're prepared to leave text editing behind, most graphics programs offer many more choices for adding effects (11.28). I try my best to create text effects that you can apply to editable text. However, if an effect I want cannot be applied to text, I always plan to use the program's automatic effect capability, like Actions or styles in Photoshop or Styles in Fireworks (see more about this topic later in this chapter).

[W A R N I N G]

Always plan ahead. Perhaps you cannot imagine another word or phrase that you will need to match the ones you create today. Trust me — as long as you have no easy way to replicate your results, you *will* need to repeat. Murphy's Law applies to this topic more often than not. At the very least, keep a record of how you achieved an effect in a safe place. Capturing the exact steps in a saved and automated way is much better than any other method to replicate an effect. *Do not* assume you will never forget how you created an effect. You will, and sooner than you could ever think possible.

Text is converted for use with filters by a process known as rasterizing. When it is still text, the characters are defined by mathematical coordinates. When you rasterize text, the mathematical coordinates are tossed out, and pixels are used to display the shapes. The text becomes a bitmap image. It's almost right to think of vector text as a floating object that can be manipulated freely, in contrast to pixels that are glued

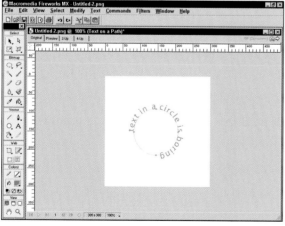

● 11.26

● 11.27

● 11.28

to the layer. To change a bitmap image, you must select an area and apply the desired edit. All typography and editing controls are lost.

Working with Filters in Photoshop

In Photoshop, you rasterize text by converting the layer containing the text (Layer → Rasterize Type). The text looks the same after you rasterize the layer, but the change appears in the Layers palette (11.29). Note that the *T* icon, signifying a Text layer, is missing from the upper layer containing the word "Wow!." I duplicated the original text layer and rasterized the copied layer. Now I can apply any filter effect that Photoshop offers to the rasterized layer.

You do give up more than just text editing, however. Like text, you can enlarge or reduce vector objects at will with no quality loss. Not so with bitmap objects (11.30). In this example, to enlarge the top sample, a text layer, I simply increased font size. I enlarged the lower sample in the only way available for a bitmap image — to transform the object. Note the quality difference.

Working with bitmap images has its drawbacks, but oh, the freedom! The full power of Photoshop filters is in your hands. You are limited because text must remain legible, of course, but you can still use many great effects to customize text (11.31).

● 11.30

● 11.31

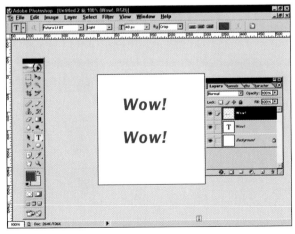

● 11.29

With a little creativity, you can create an effect that renders the text difficult to read, but find a way to add legibility. In the sample shown here, I wanted a blurred look, but the top sample is too hard to read. By adding a layer in the original font, and playing with a Layer style and opacity, I was able to keep much of the mood of the blurred sample, yet make the text outlines much more clear (11.32). The orange layers compile the new text, and the blue layer is the original.

Automating Effects for Consistency

You've already seen some automation with styles, and learned how to save styles. For many of the effects that you want to save, automated styles do offer the power that you need. Styles are easy to create and very easy to use.

Graphics programs usually offer more powerful methods to save the steps that you use to create an effect, however. In Fireworks, you can save the steps that you use to create an effect, and recall those steps at a later time. Photoshop offers a sophisticated way

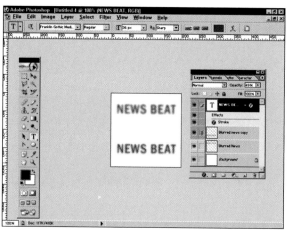

● 11.32

to save any group of steps and play them back at any time. Photoshop's Actions are extremely powerful, and you can even find sites on the Web devoted to sharing saved Actions.

[N O T E]

You may think that I am bringing you automation information to save you time. In fact, in my opinion, the time saved is a nice side effect to the real benefit of using automated features: consistency. When you find a page that looks great, no matter how closely you examine it, the one thing you will always find is that the details are immaculate. All the headlines are identical in size, color, effect, and spacing. The design elements are exactly the same every time they are used. This consistency comes automatically when you place all relevant information in a retrievable form. Computers may not have the power to think, but they are masters at remembering.

Automating Steps in Fireworks with the History Palette

When you need to save all details for your text effects in Fireworks, including typography effects, the History panel offers the best features. (Open the History palette by choosing Window → History.) As you work, the History palette, whether it is open or not, tracks every move you make. You can save the steps you require from the History palette, and replay them at a later date.

Including as much information as you can when saving your steps is best. I've always found that my results are better when I do a test run for my effect before actually committing the steps to a saved command. Although Fireworks will save an error and the correction — for example when you set the wrong kerning value, and return to change it — why clutter anything with a forward and backwards path to the result?

To save a series of steps in Fireworks:

1. **Create a new document in Fireworks, and type** Saving the History **on the canvas to use as a starting point. This text will not be included in the steps you save and should not have any of the type effects in place that you want to include in the automated steps.**

[**T I P**]

Although you can save the actual typing with this method, it is highly unlikely that you will require the same words over and over. When I work, I generally type the word or words I require, and then consider formatting and effects. For this work pattern, omitting any actual typing from the set of steps you will save is much better.

2. **Open the History palette (choose Window → History) if it is not already open. Click the menu icon at the top right of the palette and select Clear History. Click OK if an alert appears, warning you that clearing the History also clears Undo. The History palette is now empty. Selecting the correct steps when only the desired steps are displayed is much easier (11.33).**

3. **Change the font to Verdana, font color to brown, text size to 24, and kerning to 10.**

4. **Add a drop shadow with Opacity 35% and distance 4 px. You're now ready to save these steps. Your History palette should be the same as mine (11.34).**

5. **Select the top item in the History palette. Shift+click the last item in the list. All items should be selected (11.35).**

 11.34

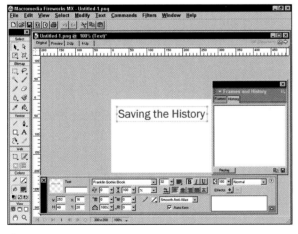

 11.33

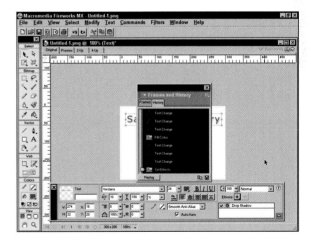

 11.35

6. Click the icon at the top right of the History palette and select Save as Command. The Save Command window opens.

7. Type History test in the Name field. Click OK. Your steps have been saved. The History test command appears at the bottom of the Commands window in the main menu (11.36).

8. Type a new text entry with attributes that are different than the ones you just saved to test the command. Make sure to select the text with the Pointer tool (11.37).

9. Choose Commands → History text; your text should be identical to the first text (11.38).

[T I P]

If you want to remove or rename a history command, choose Commands → Manage Saved Commands and make your changes.

Automating Steps in Photoshop with Actions

Photoshop Actions can automate much more than text effects. Becoming very comfortable with this feature is well worth your while. Actions are sets of saved steps that you can replay an endless number of times. If you think of recording a CD, you have the correct concept. When you want to play a song from a CD, you insert it in the player and press Play. To play a set of Actions, you select the set and click Play. Of course, the effect is only as good as the information that was saved, so this area is one in which you must work carefully and accurately. Perfecting an action is worth the few extra minutes, especially when it will be played over and over.

[T I P]

You should plan out where you would like to have your action begin. Do you want the action to begin after text is entered? Do you need the freedom to choose color before the action begins, or can you insert a break to choose color as the action plays? Pre-planning is critical to your success with Actions.

To create an Action in Photoshop, follow these steps:

1. Type Saving the Action to use as a starting point.

2. Open the Actions window (Window → Actions).

3. Create a Set (folder) to hold your Action(s). Click on the menu icon at the top right of the Actions palette. Select New Set. Name your set Action test (11.39).

● 11.36

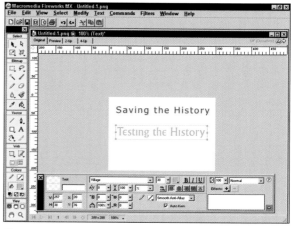

● 11.37

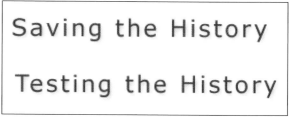

● 11.38

[T I P]

When I test a process, I always add the word "test" to any names I must supply. After I have perfected the technique, if I forget to delete the test work, I always know it is not valuable. I tend to be sloppy at times, and when I do clean up, I always know that I can safely delete "test" items. Of course, if the test turns out to be perfect, you must change the name, or at least remove the "test" designation.

4. Click the menu icon in the Actions palette and select New Action. The New Action window opens.

5. Type Test text in the Name field. Ensure that Action test is selected in the Set field. Click Record and the Action starts recording every keystroke you make. The red icon at the bottom of the Actions palette is the signal that recording is turned on (11.40).

6. Select the text and apply the following attributes: Verdana, 24 px, 24 px leading, 75 tracking, and green color.

7. Add a Layer style drop shadow with a 35% Opacity.

8. Click the Stop Recording icon at the bottom of the Actions palette. Your action is complete and saved. Click on the arrow beside the Action name to expand it if it is not already (11.41).

9. Create a new text layer. It doesn't matter what you place in this layer, but it must be a text layer.

10. Click the Play icon in the bottom of the Actions palette and watch the magic as the identical text is created.

11. Highlight the text and type the desired words (11.42).

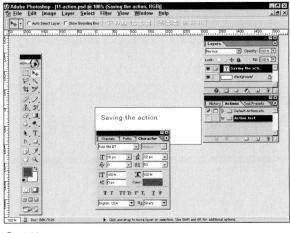

● 11.39

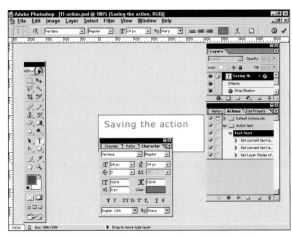

● 11.41

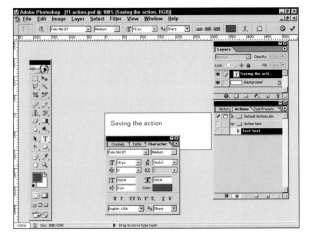

● 11.40

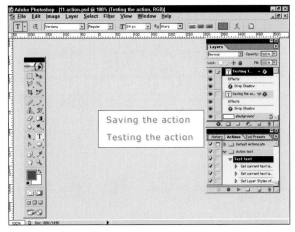

● 11.42

[T I P]

You can stop the action by clicking the Stop Playing/Recording button and resume with the Play Current Selection. You can also create Actions with stop points to allow you to enter steps that will vary, so the range of what you can accomplish with Actions is endless. If you find yourself doing repetitive steps, look to Actions.

The Wow! Factor: Exceptional Type from the Web

If you have followed this book from the beginning, you have a bulging toolbox of techniques and tips to help you create great type. To help you know how to put your tools to use, studying how other designers have handled problems, and to watch text creativity at work is a valuable exercise. I spent a long time searching the Web to bring you samples of great text. Each of the following sites made me sit up and take note because of the text. Obviously, the great typography caught my attention, but in all cases, you'll see that the entire package is noteworthy. These pages hold together because the attention to text detail is high. They are presented in no order other than they were next in line by the sometimes erratic way I name my graphic files.

[W A R N I N G]

I present these sites as great examples of the points I mention in the descriptions. In most cases, I have not even looked at the code behind the page. It is entirely possible that I have included examples that look great but have highly questionable code structure (or perhaps I have THE perfect page in every way in this group). Some pages in this group do not meet my minimum standards for navigation simplicity, a subject I have written a book on. I encourage you not to worry about what's not here. Too many developers specialize in one area, whether it is clean HTML, extremely tight JavaScript, or perfect CSS application, and they reach a point where that area is all they see.

I learned to create clean code from primarily butt-ugly examples. I learned to communicate effectively with text on the Web by studying the mood of pages that were miraculous in that they displayed correctly. Don't hold yourself back by only offering respect to pages that have the same strengths as yours.

This collection of sites, in my opinion, can teach any of you some terrific things about text use, communication, color use, and page balance. If you catch yourself viewing the code and saying, "Yeah, but . . . ," you're missing the point entirely.

Cyber NY

Cyber NY (www.cyber-ny.com/) has used one of the techniques that is a pet peeve for me — a Flash introduction page — and made it work (11.43). So, what makes this one work? For me, on my slow connection, it's access to the menu. Although the introductory movie does take a little time to load (very little), I have access to the menus nearly instantly.

The menus are presented in light gray type, over a lighter gray pattern, which should present a legibility problem. However, the heavy font and excellent line spacing solve that problem, and although the effect is a subtle menu presentation, it is easily read. Also, the mouseover effect adds color to the menu item, as well as adding a description of what will be found at that link (11.44).

When you move to the interior pages, the site switches to 100% business (11.45). Text is presented in short, snappy pieces, and bullet points further create easy-to-skim information. I had an overview of the company in about five seconds. That's successful content presentation. The menus nearly disappear at the top of the page, but when you want to move,

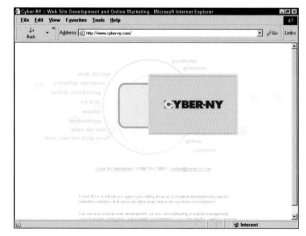

● 11.43

pointing your mouse in the right direction is an automatic process.

Headlines are graphic images, but they are so skillfully blended into the pages, it is hard to figure out what is text and what is an image. Scroll down on any page, and you will find text menus and graphic text messages to help direct the visitor to another page. This page is an excellent example of presenting great design without sacrificing function.

netdiver

http://netdiver.net/whatsnew.php

[NOTE]

The images and the content on this site changes regularly. You will not see exactly what is depicted here when you visit.

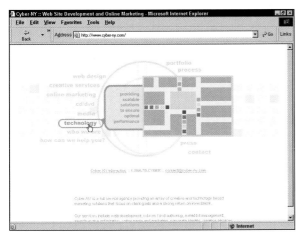

 11.44

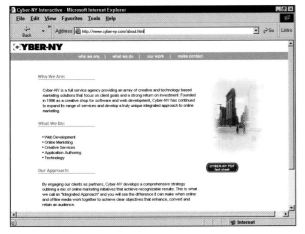

 11.45   All images © Cyber NY. Used with permission.

netdiver (http://netdiver.net/whatsnew.php) describes itself as "a new media culture_magazine + portal" (11.46). I would not have wanted the job to define this site. It is a combination of great design, news, and opinions, and it is all very well done. I love the mood of this site. The best I can come up with as a description is that it is a place where creative people feel at home. (It's no wonder that left-brain thinkers have trouble understanding us creative sorts.)

The text use is amazing. In this screen shot are nineteen menu items and four graphic teaser links. Just fitting all that into one screen is a feat. When you consider that the page is light and airy, that many links is miraculous. The top menu items are created with CSS control (love the mouseover effect) and the menu just below is created with graphic text.

How about that link effect? It's underlined — so it passes my acid test, but it sure doesn't look ordinary, and it matches the page exactly. Even though it is not blue (something I like to see) there are so many links that I really don't think that the lack of blue reduces the usability of this site one bit. Don't forget that most who would be interested in this site are Web savvy, which reduces some of the need for clear "click here now to proceed" instructions.

The dotted lines continue through the page and provide definite structure without boxing in the page. Perfect for designers — we know we need bounds, but are much happier when we can pretend they are not there. It's not often you find a page that is both functional, pretty, and perfectly suits the visitor group. I think netdiver has done it.

 11.46   All images © netdiver. Used with permission.

DotContent

DotContent (`www.dotcontent.com/dotcontent.html`) is another Flash site, and much of what I said previously about Cyber NY holds true for this site as well. This site is completely done in Flash, but once again, the menus appear very quickly (11.47). All menu information is in place before the small movie starts to play, probably accounting for the quick feeling for me.

This site is a wonderful source for lowercase text ideas. All the text fits into small, clearly defined areas, and until you move to content text, most is presented in all lowercase characters. They use color wisely to keep text phrases legible, the biggest problem when you leave capitalization behind. And you have to love the logo for this company. You don't get much simpler than this for a corporate mark, but it is highly distinctive, and mostly text (is that a parenthesis graphic?).

The interior pages continue with the great text look (11.48). The movie and menu are in the same places as on the entry page for consistency, yet the addition of large type blocks still looks great. Note the bold text in the content text, a great help for skimming visitors. If you can only get a limited number of words into your visitor's mind, you should choose which of those words make it. Take a tour to see how the DotContent designers incorporated the artistic look of the entry page with the content text through the site.

Endless River Adventures

And now for something at the opposite end of the scale, just to prove that you do not need to do clean and spare to create a great site (11.49). Endless River Adventures (`www.endlessriveradventures.com/whatsup.shtml`) is an adventure company, supplying a range of products from boats, to kayak training, to adventure tours. This company sells adventure, no matter what the product may be to deliver that adventure. The site reflects that idea perfectly.

This one page could be the project for a typography course. The typography is varied and perfect. It takes an experienced designer to be able to use this

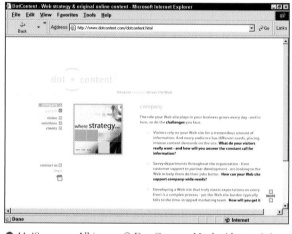

● 11.48   All images © Dot Content. Used with permission.

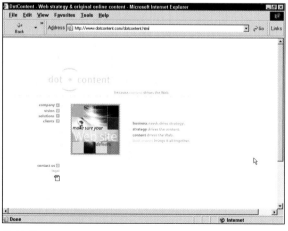

● 11.47

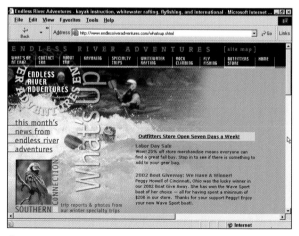

● 11.49   All images © Endless River Adventures/ Suzanne Stephens. Used with permission.

number of elements on a page and have it work. The menu area is obvious, depending on the stark black to attract attention, even on the busy page. The compact font style of the menu allows plenty of white space (black space) around each menu item, making the items easy to focus on. The black menu background also lets the menu fade to the background when not in use. Any color that would have been strong enough to hold up against the image would likely have commanded more constant attention than a menu should. I also love the color bar between the menu and the image. How perfect to blend the solid black into the rainbow of colors in the image.

Note the semi-transparent vertical text that forms the page name. Not knowing exactly where you are is pretty hard, but the text enhances, rather than distracts from the image. Another notable use of text is around the bird photo. If that text had been placed in the traditional place, above or below the image, it would have been boring, and perhaps would not have had a clear enough connection to the image on the busy page. By wrapping the title around the image, a border between the background image is formed, and there is no doubt that this text belongs to this image.

You may want to spend some time at this site. It has many pages with creative, professional typography in use. Even if your style tends to lean to the more Spartan side of design, you can learn plenty about type and defining areas on the pages of this site.

Marc Klein

I've followed Marc's work (`www.marc-klein.com/main/index.html`) for quite a while, and it is always clean, always fresh, and at the same time absolutely classic. If you want to see great pure design, this is the place to do it. Marc's site is 100 percent an artist's site. Selling millions of books in this format would be hard, but that does not make this design less valuable for the Web, or those who create pages for the Web. Like the Tiffany's site you saw earlier in this chapter if you did the mood exercise, this site is so consistent with its purpose that it makes visitors very comfortable.

The typography is the best you will see. The kerning and spacing of the main fonts are perfect. Note how Marc has used color to separate elements into subtle, but easy-to-recognize areas of the page. He uses color to separate the page name from his name on each page in a brilliant way. On a primarily black-and-white background, any color can make an element stand out. Rather than hitting us with a large title, Marc has used a slight drop of color to make the small page title stand out.

You'll want to click on the artwork samples at the bottom of the page. Some stunning examples of art typography are tucked away in these samples. You may not have the luxury of creating an art site like Marc has created, but any designer will be better for studying why this site is so stunning. It is not any one thing that makes it great. It is the compilation of carefully designed, perfectly executed elements that makes this site a "Wow!" site.

Mando Group

My breath caught when the Mando Group (`http://mandogroup.com`) site came up on the screen (11.50). It was partly the color on the entry page — the fuchsia color is difficult to work with and still maintain a professional look. And there was no mistaking that this was a professional site from the

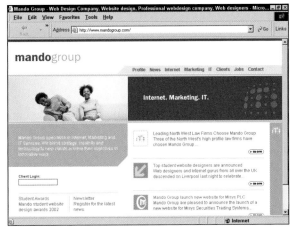

 11.50

first glance. But it's not just the color. When you move to different pages in the site, the color changes, and it is still a wonderful treat for the eyes (11.51).

This site uses shape especially well. Note how the elements of the page are all elongated rectangles. Seeing this shape repeated over and over is not especially common. It works very well.

The text work is also excellent. Note how the color and font change in the name separates the words with no help from capitalization, creating a small package that not only carries the name message, but provides a design element to enhance the pages. I love the pink headlines, with no bold applied. They serve as headlines in that they stand out, but they also become part of the paragraph when you start to read.

I was quite surprised when I started to analyze why this page was so good, at how few design elements actually occurred on these pages. What is there is perfect. The color for each page occurs just often enough to blend in the strong color of the heading. Don't miss the color line tucked right at the top of the page. Also, the design elements use negative space (the white shape that is outlined by colored objects) and reversed shapes very effectively.

On the interior pages, an extra menu is tucked just below the heading. The placement and design make sure you don't miss it as a menu, but the placement and design also let it fade into the background when not in use. I see more little details every time I look at this site, which falls right into what I have been telling you through the book — that great design is all about the details. You'll learn plenty about details with a slow trip through this site.

Ken Mayer

Ken Mayer's site (www.kenmayerstudios.com/) shows the beauty of black and white (11.52). Perhaps the photographers of this world are those have always understood the power of absence of color. The perfect irony is that photographers are also the ones who often best know how to exploit color in its finest forms. That this site uses both black and white and color to perfection is fitting.

The entry page for this site is powerful in its simplicity. Coming upon this page and just sailing by without a reaction would be hard. The stark simplicity and almost harsh use of the full scale of grays available assure that "whoa" quality that designers always try to capture.

The type is excellent. I've studied the kenmayerstudio element at the top of the page to try to decide why it works. I'm still not sure. Using all caps with no spacing is quite common, but usually you need to change the color a tiny amount. This has no such change between the ken and mayer. Yet, from the first time I saw it, my mind read it as Ken Mayer. Perhaps the exact balance between the two names allows this exception to the rule. Perhaps Ken was lucky that the *N* and *K* provide a solid vertical element to place back to back. I tried this exact style in my own name and the two words definitely blend together and make it hard to read. However, the *Y* does not provide a vertical boundary between words. I do know that you cannot carry off a look like this without perfect typography. When your type is your design, you had better do it well. I really like the boxy, all-caps presentation of the details in the lower section

● 11.51   All images © Mando Group. Used with permission.

● 11.52

of the entry page. Plenty of space makes it easy to read, and it reflects the square nature of the rest of the page perfectly.

The interior pages are perfect for showing off great color photography (11.53). Note that the page details continue with the neutral color scheme, and definitely allow the images to take the spotlight. The studio name is now featured in reversed type because it is now on a gray background. If the white had been carried on to this page, the contrast would have taken away from the power of the images. Great typography, with an understanding of exactly what is important on each page makes this a must-see site.

Maria Roth is the Web designer for this site, and the graphic design was done by Kim Wolf, of Hanger 18.

Michaela Sucha

A collection of sites for type would not be complete without a sample of type blended into a vital part of the art on a site (11.54). Michaela (`www.mishka.cz/`) has used type exceptionally well to create a legible page that seems to be only concerned with art. But take a close look at the identity art. Before you focus, I'll bet that you already knew that the site featured Mishka's Web design and graphic design.

While the design seems to be art focused, some great typography principles are at work here. The flow of the identity design leads you right to the important words. The site is set up in a horizontal format, and horizontal lines lead you from the art into the content. The menu is obvious from the start, and reflects the horizontal movement to the rest of the page. Of course, the dark borders also lead you to a horizontal orientation.

As I said about Marc Klein's site earlier in this section, this format would not be an appropriate look if you wanted to sell a million books. But it is absolutely perfect for the site that it is. Detail, detail, detail. Wonderful color. Exceptional typography. Texture. A wonderful experience.

While you're at this site, treat yourself to more of the same on the portfolio page. The sites do not always feature English, but don't let that stop you. When you're studying great typography, language is no barrier.

Moonrock Paper Company

I've found another great example of understated design — spare, but perfect in detail (11.55). The Moonrock Paper Company (`www.moonrockpaper.com/pages/moonrock_main.htm`)

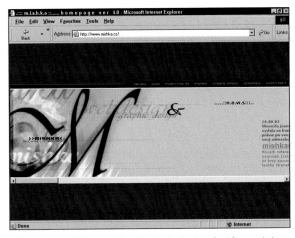

● 11.54   All images © Michaela Sucha. Used with permission.

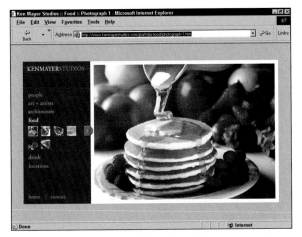

 11.53   All images © Ken Mayer. Used with permission.

 11.55

presents a definite image, and it seems to match perfectly with their products.

I think the logo was what caught my attention in the first place. Using a script font successfully is hard. Many of them look great, but cannot be read. Others are easy enough to read, but impart an amateur feeling to the page. This script font certainly does not look amateur, and while it could have a legibility problem in many settings, the designer has allowed plenty of white space around the script words. The white space gives our eyes enough room to resolve the character shapes, and voilá — we can read it. It also breaks what could have been too corporate a look for this product line. What could be more perfect for a line of paper products than part of an identity that looks like an elegant signature?

The photographs on each page lead right to the two menus: the dots at the top of the page that give a description on mouseover, and a housekeeping menu at the right. The spacing for all the text is excellent, and is often the success of a mainly white page like this. If you try to pack the text in too tightly, you lose the open look. If you try to spread it apart too much, you lose the connection between elements. It's a fine line to walk, and they have done it well.

It's worth a trip to the product pages to see how they have presented each product (11.56). It's hard to find a great example of data presented in a stylish and easy-to-use format. You can just see the beginning of the tabular data here, but take a trip to a product page for the full impact. I also wanted to show you how

the details, photos, and descriptions work so well together.

Susan Sweeney

I'm still presenting these sites randomly, but this site is the perfect one to follow the Moonrock Paper Company. Susan Sweeney (http://susansweeney.com/) has a commercial site, but one that has a very different product (11.57). Susan offers Internet marketing books and training as well as consulting services. This is not the place to be sweet and soft. Visitors to her site are looking for a no-nonsense, knows-what-she's-doing mood. I think her site delivers that message perfectly. Susan's image on the page is friendly, but also gives off the impression that she is a confident, competent leader.

The typography is perfect for the mood. Check the number of menu items, and then note how they don't seem the least bit crowded. The compact font was an excellent choice to solve the problem of many menu items. The white space below the menu helps with the open look, and also provides an area for a descriptive mouseover effect.

In an unusual feature, Susan Sweeney's books are available right on the front page. That presents a long front page, but in this case, I think perfectly appropriate. Susan's clients are busy people, and have probably arrived with a goal in mind. If that goal can be met on the front page, for this group, all the better. If they want to go further, the menu is easily accessible and ready to take them where they need to go.

● 11.56   All images © Moonrock Paper Company. Used with permission.

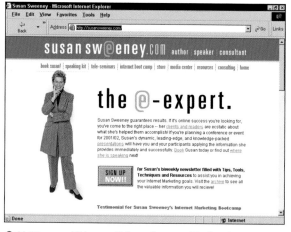

● 11.57   All images © Susan Sweeney. Used with permission.

Take a quick scroll down the entry page, and you will see how well the information is presented. Even scrolling fast, you're not likely to miss anything that you might be seeking. This is an excellent, utilitarian site that perfectly matches the product. Had the designer tried to add a more artistic look, the effect would not be anywhere near as strong. Many designers should spend some time on this site to learn from one of the best examples of appropriate mood for a product. And how could this site be more perfect for a woman who has designed a popular series of workshops called Internet Boot Camp? Well done!

Wanda Cummings

[N O T E]

I know Wanda, and have not only brought you her current Web site, for obvious reasons, but also forced her to dust off her old design so I could bring you the Flash intro that featured great typography and a powerful message.

There is so much great typography on Wanda's new site (11.58) that it is hard to know where to start (www.wandacummings.com). Start with her name. Look closely. Wanda and .com are in all caps. Cummings is in all lowercase. What a great technique to present the ever-challenging Web address. It also creates a shape that reflects the menu on the bottom gray bar.

Then we move to the word *perception*. The font is beautiful, no doubt. Lots of white space makes it easy to read, but look at the design element directly below. The beautiful, flowing tails on the font are carried on in the design element. When you can capture that type of connection, the elements cement together and present a perfectly unified presence on the page.

Did you catch the typographer's quotes? What a wonderful way to bring the green in the page to the center section. You can barely tell that the quotes are green, but if they were gray or black, the page would not have the great flow that it does. The photo perfectly marries with the gray borders. The menu is presented simply in all caps, as are the housekeeping details on the page. There is nothing on this page that does not have a place and a purpose. I'm back to the mantra: details, details, details. And Wanda is one of the best for details.

Wanda Cummings (2000)

Although this site is no longer active, I wanted to give you the chance to see this Flash presentation (www.wandacummings.com/creative/). Wanda used type effectively in this introduction, which was featured by Macromedia shortly after it was released. I've tried to bring you enough to give you an idea of the piece, but I do urge that you see the presentation. When you see the way that the type moves onto the screen, it is much more powerful.

The introduction starts with some great type (11.59). Look how "one second" and "audience attention" pop from the page. To enforce that idea, the eyes of the drawing blink — driving home the one-second measurement.

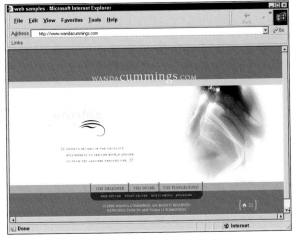

● 11.58   All images © Wanda Cummings. Used with permission.

● 11.59

The type then morphs from one phrase to another, exceptionally well. For example, creative answers (11.60), morphs to creativesolutionsdesigns.com (11.61), the Web address of Wanda's business at the time. (Wanda is now operating under her own name — see previous example.) Following this screen, creative solutions morphs into the Web address, and then smoothly into position on the static Flash site.

Although the concept was great to start, it was the masterful delivery of type, and the powerful image of eyes blinking, that really drove home the message, and proved that this designer understood what marketing on the Web is all about.

Web Page Design for Designers (WPDFD)

I've been a long-time follower of Joe Gillespie's work, though I just came to know him a bit as I was writing this book. (See my interview with Joe in Chapter 9, "Creating Graphic Text for the Web.") However, I had never really considered just how effectively he used type on his page until I began the search for sites in this section.

WPDFD (`http://wpdfd.com/`) is a site devoted to design, with a heavy tilt towards text and typography (not surprising, because Joe recently launched a new site: Funwithfonts.com). In addition to all the great type information on the wpdfd.com

site, visitors can learn by example. (11.62). The typography is excellent, innovative, and communicates perfectly, starting with the site logo. After a set of type like this is complete, it looks so simple. But this effect is not easy to create. You not only have to fit in many words, but make the words read in the correct order. This example is great. Quick — read the words. The large font pulls you all the way through the "web page design" phrase before you settle on the "for designers" phrase. Try to read it in any other order, and it just does not work.

I love the menu area at the right of the page. No, it sure is not a traditional menu. And it's in a funny place for a menu. So why is little Ms. "put menus where they 'belong' so people can find them" (that's me) so happy with this menu that breaks all the rules? I'm happy for several reasons. One is the audience. The "for designers" phrase is a strong clue to the visitor base. I mentioned earlier in this section that you can get away with wandering from standards when the visitors are likely to have high Web savvy. It's also the nature of the topic. I'm not sure that this menu is really an official one or not. I could make a case that the links list to the left is a menu . . . a weak case, but a case nonetheless. The list of links (getting careful now) is also so well done that this entire discussion is a little irrelevant. It's pretty hard to miss what is going on — especially when you're probably very interested

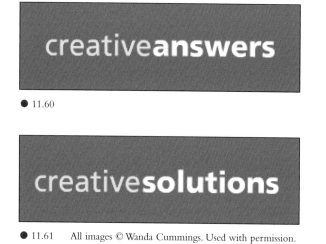

● 11.60

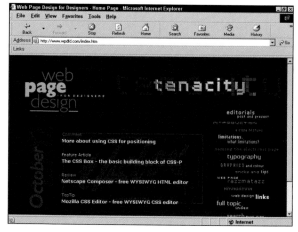

● 11.62   All images © Joe Gillespie. Used with permission.

● 11.61   All images © Wanda Cummings. Used with permission.

in type if you are visiting the page. Finally, as I am nearing the end of the reviews, maybe I can be a little careless with my words.

Don't miss the date at the left edge of the page, either. It shows a wonderful use of text — it adds a design element, yet fulfills a purpose. Even the ads on the page (and these may be different when you visit) feature great type. Visit for the information, because there is much here anyone interested in type should see. But don't forget to drink in the fine features that the site itself presents.

Netymology

The Netymology site (`http://netymology.com/`) features a unique blend of exceptional subtle effects, and colorful, energetic enhancements. I've seen many sites that offer each of these styles, but it's rare to find both subtle and knockout color working so well together. Compare the subtle rollovers in the top menu, with a tiny marker creating the effect (11.63) to the red rollovers in the menu at the right of the page. (11.64) I love it. Note the gentle shadows that provide a three-dimensional effect to the main menu, in contrast to the bright color in the decorative image. Just for fun, fold a piece of paper and cover the color image. Isn't that a sedate, decidedly corporate appearance? Yet with the image showing, there is nothing sedate about this site, but the corporate background does shine through to provide a feeling of competence. Without the muted areas of the page, the color could put forth an impression that was not serious enough to indicate competence. Brilliant.

You must appreciate the type details. I love the font for the date stamp in the upper-right corner. The menu items are all created with non-antialiased fonts, quite legible even at the small size in the main menu, and very crisp and clean for the right menu. Note that the designer used antialiased fonts for the "Design. Develop. Deploy." entry. The red > symbol adds a wonderful touch. Once again, try covering it and see the results. The text is aligned and looks fine, but the effect is not nearly as exciting as it is with the small red addition. The same symbol occurs in two forms in the right menu as well. Isn't that the marker for the main menu rollovers the same shape (11.63)?

To complete the set, you'll find the same shape in the small Flash movie at the top of the page.

This is a site that you should visit and study. I see new things every time I look at this page, and the interior pages offer the same attention to detail. There is no doubt that this site has been created with loving attention to detail.

Elevista

I love unusual color on a Web site, when it is used well. Elevista (`http://elevista.com/`) features bright gold boldly in combination with shades of

● 11.63

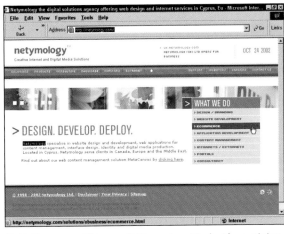

● 11.64   All images © Netymology. Used with permission.

Finding Your Style is Like "Finding" a House

Several years ago, I lost my home to fire. Whether you share this experience or not, I'm sure you can imagine the resulting chaos. One of the greatest stress points was that I had to plan a new house. I live in winter country, and the start date was critical. The new house absolutely had to be started less than two months from the fire date, or we would have been gypsies for an extra six months.

So amidst rental nightmares, stints in hotels with three young teens (not recommended) and battles with the insurance company, I had to find the plans for my house. Luckily, I had experience with "finding my style" through many artistic pursuits, and instinct took over. I bought as many books of modest home plans as I could find. Whenever I had a minute, I would flip through the books. I liked many designs, but occasionally, one jumped out at me. I would rip that plan from the book, and place it in an envelope. For all the plans I perused, and I had a four-foot stack of books by the time I finished, not that many qualified.

Finally, I had to make a decision within a week, or I could not hit the start date. I brought out the envelope containing the "good possibility" plans, not having seen any of them once they went into the envelope. I had no idea how much agonizing I faced before my final decision.

I spread the pitifully small collection of eight plans out on the table and started to laugh. The plans were nearly identical. There were slight proportion differences, but the basic layout was identical. I had successfully used old and familiar patterns of behavior to "find my style." I didn't design a house; I found it. The house was started on time.

That was over seven years ago, and I still live in the same place. The success of the method I used to "find" my house is evident every day I live here. Even today, after all those years to think about it, I would change almost nothing. I have never been accused of thinking far into the future, but my kids are all away in university now. The house that easily contained three teens, and all that entails, has converted perfectly to a small house with a fabulous studio area. I wonder whether my subconscious was planning ahead without my knowledge.

Perhaps when I give you tips to find your style, I should be wording it another way: "Do this so your style can find you."

gray for a dynamic site (11.65). This site presents the confidence that only comes with choosing a concept and going forth with gusto. If the designer had held back on the amount of gold, or tried to weaken it with texture, the effect would have been lost.

The site color is carefully planned, however. Note that only a tiny touch of red accents the gold, black, and gray color palette. Study the images on the entry page (11.65) and an interior page (11.66). These images are not simple black and white photos, but rather are duotone images. Duotone images are similar to grayscale images, but have one additional color added. In this case, I suspect the extra color is the same gold that appears on the rest of the page. Using a touch of the design color in the duotone images ties the gray, black and gold together on the page.

The all caps presentation of the text on this site works well, as does the square font with generous spacing. The text presentation adds to the energetic feeling created by the color and active images. The menu, placed in an usual setting near the middle of the page on the entry page, and near the bottom of the interior pages, is clearly visible. The white type contrast on the submenus for the interior pages should be hard to read, as there is little contrast between the gold and white, but the designer has used excellent spacing, and a fine black line to guide the readers eye. Although the text is a smaller size for the content text than I like to see, it works here because there is so much white space on the page.

● 11.65

You should try squinting at these pages to blur the detail. The balance details for the pages will pop right out at you when you view the page without detail. Note how important the little touches of color at the right edge of the page become when you are not distracted by the images and text.

This site is well designed, beautifully balanced and presents a dynamic mood that projects confidence and competence. It is not necessary to stick to "corporate blue" to present a professional image. This vibrant gold, black, and white site is living proof.

That concludes the sites that I have for you, but don't let it be the end of your search for great type use on the Web. A little of your design time should always be set aside to keep your mind fresh. This exposure is especially important if you're a new designer.

Developing your own style takes a while. Most early designs are all over the place with style, and this is part of the natural learning process. The more styles you can observe, the more your own style will develop. That's why taking a tour of other sites is so important, purely to see what others are doing, at least once a week. Create a folder for your favorite sites and visit them often.

It takes a while, but soon patterns of what you like will emerge, and before you know it, pieces of everything you have seen will combine to emerge as your style. It will be evident in everything you do. After your style is established, you can really start to create dynamite sites. Make sure you feed the process.

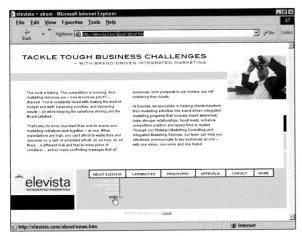

● 11.66   All images © Elevista. Used with permission.

<h1>

VISITOR

font

content
layout

Embed? Link?

atmosphere

font

<link href="12type.css" rel="stylesheet" type="text/css">

Chapter 12

Putting It All Together

There is something ... almost beautiful ... about the restrictions that HTML places on you as a designer.

TRICIA MCGILLIS

Piece by piece I have guided you through everything you need to know to create great typography for the Web. You have the skills, and have had some reference for how one technique works with another. Now it's time to see how it all works together.

Through the book, I have given generic information when possible. You can create most techniques that I have used in any HTML editor, or any graphics program. For this portion of the book, I work with Dreamweaver and Photoshop, with a short stop in CorelDRAW. This decision is based partly on my own working patterns, but not as an endorsement of one product or to discredit any other program. It's also because it includes the two best-known software companies in this field: Adobe, publisher of Photoshop, and Macromedia, publisher of Dreamweaver. I could just as easily use Macromedia Fireworks for graphics, with Adobe GoLive as an HTML editor, or HomeSite for HTML and Paint Shop Pro for graphics. There would be no difference in the final result. In fact, I have sites where I have designed all the graphics in Adobe Illustrator or CorelDRAW. It's not the program that matters, but the process. I am narrowing down for simplicity.

In this chapter I walk you through the steps for creating an entire project, and in the end, you'll have a completed page to file for future use.

I've designed a site especially for this chapter (12.1). I take you through the entire creation process, in a smooth line, from creating a logo to testing the final site, referring you to the appropriate chapter as necessary for more information.

● 12.1

Preparing a New Site

As you learned in Chapters 1 and 2, many site details are in place before you ever move your mouse. Starting the design process without an understanding of where you are going is like starting on a trip with no idea whether you are going east or west. Preparation may seem like a waste of time, but it is time that comes back to you many times as you work through the project.

Establishing the Purpose and Creating a Site Map

This site is a simple one, with an easy-to-define purpose. I have had an online diary (Blogger) for many years, and although it is probably the most boring blog known to humankind (like a continuous Christmas newsletter), I have friends and family all over Canada and the United States who keep up with what's going on in my life through this site. This is a classic example of a professional not looking after her own presentation. The design would be embarrassing if I just played with Web design (12.2). I threw it together in under an hour "to test the concept," and have never managed to find time to create a decent page. Considering my profession, I should have been shot years ago for this presentation, even for a personal site — perhaps especially for a personal site.

However, the changes I want to make are not just about appearance. The site needs to be reorganized because my visitors are there for many reasons (see the nearby sidebar "How to Get What to Whom"). I also want to be able to write more about specific topics. Right now, I hold the volume down because there is no way to separate who gets what. My goals for this site are not being met by the current format. The original idea was to be able to keep up the e-mail correspondence with a large number of people, yet not have to type the same information over and over. Unfortunately, with the diverse group I serve, I still end up including highly specific topics in individual e-mail messages. My goal is to include only truly person-to-person topics in my e-mail, with the "news" available through the blog.

![Wanderings and Wonderings - Microsoft Internet Explorer screenshot showing a blog page titled "Wanderings and Wonderings" with Photo Pages section and a Thursday, October 03, 2002 entry.]

● 12.2

Behind the Scenes

Tricia MacInnis

Like many of the designers I talked to while writing this book, Tricia McGillis started with print graphic design. I didn't focus on print-turned-Web designers on purpose, but I think it makes sense. I talked to designers because I thought their Web type work was excellent — a common print industry skill that always shows through in Web work.

Tricia was "talking type" by the late 80's, graduating from Yale in 1991, with a focus in graphic design and sculpture. After working for two book publishers, at first as "the one and only computer user" she turned her focus to the computer graphic design field in a big way. Tricia was the first designer for Wired magazine in 1992. As the first on the scene, she was not only responsible for layout and design (award winning layout and design), but also for production of portions of the magazine and collateral material like flyers and brochures.

By 1994, Tricia was putting her energy into the Web. She was a founding partner and Creative Director for Cyborganic Gardens, a "a pioneering community-based Web site that provided tools for geeks to meet on- and off-line." This site brought high-level media attention to Tricia's work, including a profile in Rolling Stone magazine. Today, Tricia offers Web design, print, and corporate identity

Having thought through the process, I was ready to create a site map. I decided that I wanted all pages easily available from any other page. Many of the people who visit my site are not especially Web savvy, by choice. That I can get them to visit is a miracle in some cases. If the information is not right in front of them, I might as well save my fingers. The site map I created accomplishes this goal easily (12.3). The secret is bringing the individual topics for the essays to a submenu on every page. These submenu items are actually search links. A search may be easy for those of us who spend a great deal of time on a computer, but clicking "kids" is a lot easier for someone who has little experience than thinking to type kids into a search box.

Establishing the Mood

The structure is in place, but how will it look? I go back to the site purpose to answer that question. This site is primarily for information. It must be clean and easy to read. A good percentage of my readers connect to the Internet by modem. The site must be fast, so I have to be careful with images, and keep the layout structure clean and simple. (Complex tables add to download time.) You may feel like I am getting a little ahead of the program, but I want to show you the table structure now, so you can follow the image production (12.4). Table borders have been turned on to show the cell structure for the two tables. I decided on a two (text) column format to keep things very simple.

To keep line length to a reasonable size in the main content portion of the page at higher resolutions, I

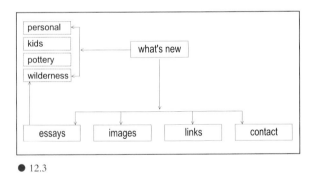

● 12.3

● 12.4

services to clients from her office in Berkley, California.

Q: Your business site, McGillis.com caught my attention because you have used type for the entire look. How did you decide on this route for your site?

A: I was fretting about the design for my front page. I was stunned by some of the graphics I saw, and was struggling with what picture would represent what I wanted to say. I love type, and what better descriptor? I love the classic fonts with modern touches, like Trade Gothic. This design let's you get up close and see the

detail. The rounded shapes and tiny curves are elegant. I knew I wanted to fill the entry page visually with type without it looking crowded. Why not do huge menu items? I tried it in three different versions, bright, light and dark blue, and the gray with a dark orange rollover. With the white rectangle and lots of white space, it just fell together.

Q: Do you think that your print background helps with Web design?

A: I tend to organize and think ahead when I am working on a design. I think that comes from print. Unlike the Web,

print pages have only so much space, and you have to work within that space. I also think I learned to pay a lot of attention to type, always doing little tests to see what benefits each font can add to the

continued

opted for generous margins (12.5). To keep the open look, and help direct the reader's eye when the line length gets longer than it should be, I also decided to use a very large line spacing. I don't have to worry about too much vertical scrolling. My visitors are a captive audience, as long as they can get to the page containing the information they seek.

[W A R N I N G]

The planning stage is exactly when you should start thinking of how your page will be constructed. If you don't keep structure in mind from the beginning, you may end up with many nested tables and a complex layout that you must support and control by heroic means. That's just asking for trouble, plus slows the page load time considerably.

So . . . I have the content text area sketched out, I know where I am going with the layout, but I still need to choose the color and font for the decorative area of the page. I have my menu items, but not the style, or location. I do know that I want a bright and cheery look. I tend to be a Pollyanna personality, so the content is almost always upbeat. My tone is conversational, usually sprinkled with comments that are

● 12.5

meant to be humorous. (Efficient English would have been to say "humorous comments," but the same conservative upbringing that taught me to write prevents me from declaring that my blog is funny.) The look should reflect the tone — lighthearted, upbeat, optimistic. Words like these help to guide me to the look.

I must mention one site goal here. Remember why I'm creating this new site? I have had a clinically boring page up for a long time. One of my personal goals with the redesign is to create a page that reflects better my profession, and my artistic side. I want to make a really nice page. My style is never dramatic, so that most certainly wouldn't fit on a personal page, but I do want a page that is more than utilitarian. Oh yes, I am also lazy with maintenance. This site must roll with the punches.

Finally, no matter what content I may decide to include, and that can be from pure text, to images, to tables, to showing off my latest Flash project, the page must be a good showcase. Although I often include images, I don't want the page to be dependent on images to look good. Keeping up regular postings is hard enough. No way do I want to come up with images for the main page every time I post.

Now I'm ready to start creating the true look of the page. You know the colors that I chose, but follow along as I work through creating the logo, which defines the final look.

Creating a Logo

Finally, it's time to get to the typography that you worked through in Part III, "Graphic Type for the Web." I needed a logo that would act as the primary design element on the page. I've known for a while that the new name would be My View (IMHO),

---

(continued)

page. When I moved to the Web, that continued, and studying what Arial might offer over Verdana makes a difference when you are looking for the best design.

Q: Was the switch from print to the Web difficult for you?

A: I think I had a natural sensibility for the Web from the start, almost as if I was born to it. When I first started, there was

not even a `<center>` tag, so we looked for every trick we could find. It was a shock at first — there were not even any tables for layout. All you could really do was place images. The limitations were so vast, that every addition was so exciting. At the same time, there is something . . . almost beautiful . . . about the restrictions that HTML places on you as a designer.

Q: Unlike many print-turned-Web designers, your work seems to have

a focus on clear navigation and fast download times. Why?

A: I don't want my work to be design done for the sake of the designer. A Web site is not supposed to be artwork unto itself. Every page has a job to do. When you have seen many pages, the ones that have clear navigation and load quickly stand out. That's what I think my job as a designer is. It's rare that a client is a designer, but they have seen a lot of pages. However, they don't necessarily

How to Get What to Whom

Along with a better look, I also want to change the format of my blog from a straight chronological diary to an essay format that I can enter into a database, and have content returned dynamically through link searches. I've had people ask me where they can find certain entries. Although my readers know me, they know me for different reasons, and want different information. The grandmas want to hear about the kids. My artist friends want to see what I'm up to with my pottery. Some people know me through canoeing, and could care less what I am doing for art. I'm pretty sure my kids read it all (or they do well when tested), but I'm not sure anyone else does. The current chronological format is not great for most of my "customers."

The other area of information that has been all but lost in the past are the links and images that I scatter through the essays. The news may be old, but at times someone does want to see pictures again. Recently, I have been pulling photos that I think may have future interest onto a separate page, and listing them in the left, static side of the site, but this setup is not at all efficient. I definitely need more organization of the gems I sprinkle through the text.

You may worry that I suddenly think that you are interested in my life enough to know all about my blog. But that is not why I am sharing this portion of the site preparation. Everything in this section is critical to the final design. My menu categories are a direct result of working through this process, and analyzing how I can best get the information my visitors want efficiently.

which, of course, is Internet-speak for In My Humble Opinion. I didn't know exactly how it would be placed into a graphic, but I did want My View to be obvious. Remember that many of my visitors won't have a clue what the IMHO means.

Beyond the title requirements, however, I had no idea what I wanted. No idea of color, or shape, or font. When I face that number of variables, I tend to turn to an Illustration program. I designed this logo in CorelDRAW, but any vector program would have done. I like the way CorelDRAW handles text. Fireworks has the same capabilities that I used to create this piece, and there is no reason it could not be done in a raster program like Photoshop. The important thing here is the process, not the program.

Font choice is usually where I start. I create one text object, with the text I require, and duplicate it many times. I then go through my font choices, applying any that seem at all promising. I try not to make judgements until I have many choices (12.6). I also like to work in black to start. I look for font shape at this point. Note that I have included samples in lowercase and uppercase separately. When you're

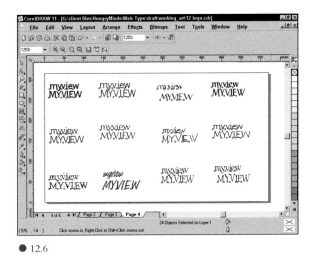

● 12.6

know what makes a great page. It's our job to take their ideas and make them work on the Web.

Q: Do you have any pet peeves with design you see on the Web?

A: Long download times and needless animation. There was a period on the Web when new things were just like TV. There was fascination in who was doing what. But that's not interesting now. If a visitor has not asked for entertainment, they should not be subjected to it invasive, annoying, pointless gimmicks.

However, in the last year, I've noticed a real improvement. The average company now has a good site. You can find what you are looking for.

Q: Do you have any tips to pass on about type or design?

A: Make sure you kern your type. That is one thing that really stands out. I have even seen poor kerning on type for big corporations, which should never happen. Also, don't use too many, or fancy fonts. I spend a lot of time at the free font sites, always looking but I almost never use them. It's best to stick to type that you know, which for me is type from Adobe or Monotype.

choosing a font that will be worked into a high-profile graphic element, every character counts. You want to make sure that you don't choose a font that has one character that just will not work.

Are you looking for the font I used? Picking it out is hard unless you're very familiar with fonts (12.7). Franklin Gothic Medium is the name of the font, but I did not use it as is. I don't have a narrow version of this font installed, but I wanted a taller look for the uppercase presentation. So, I stretched it (12.8). Please see the nearby sidebar, "You Did *What* To that Font?" for an important consideration.

While I was searching for my font, I accidentally discovered the dingbat that eventually found its way into the design (12.9). CorelDRAW shows a preview of the fonts as you scroll down the list, and this character is the uppercase *I* from the Cairo dingbat font. I liked it, so I placed a copy on the page to consider later.

The actual design for the logo came together quickly. When I can use any color that I choose, and at times, even when corporate colors take away almost all choice, I try to start the design process in grayscale (12.10). Color can get in the way of your design. When working only with shades of gray, you are much more likely to come up with a balanced design, no matter what colors eventually replace the gray.

Choosing the color was not hard once I found it. I started with colors I liked, but just did not feel right (12.11). Remembering the color on the entry page for the Mando Group (see Chapter 11, "Graphic Type Special Effects") was what nudged me to the pink. After I placed the color on the page, I instantly made the decision to use it. The teal and gray followed naturally. It fit the mood perfectly.

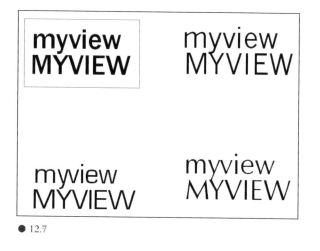

● 12.7

● 12.9

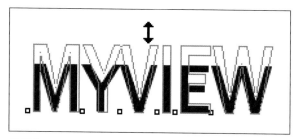

● 12.8

● 12.10

The samples shown here are still rough, however. I did some initial typography adjustment, like centering the parentheses, and lining up the upper and lower characters. Some areas still need attention however. I've marked some of the changes with yellow (12.12). The guideline setup shown in this sample (12.13) illustrates the meticulous work that makes

● 12.11

● 12.12

You Did *What* to that Font?

If I want my font taller or wider, I stretch it. I can hear my type mentors screaming from the past over this issue. First that I would dare do it, then that I would confess, and finally, that I would corrupt those I am supposed to be guiding.

Here's the official line: **Thou shalt not corrupt the balance of a character set under any circumstances.**

The reason? It's a good one. High-quality commercial fonts are carefully designed. Every mark on each character has a place and a purpose. Font designers spend unbelievable amounts of time adjusting detail one point at a time. However . . .

First, the chance that you're working with a meticulously designed font goes down with every free or low-cost font you install. Second, even if you are working with a good font (and Franklin Gothic is definitely one of them), starting with a well-designed and balanced font is better than finding a lesser-quality, compact font with the features you need. (For this project, buying a narrow or compact version of this font could not compete with a mouse move.) Third, you could spend all day trying to find a font that has all the right characteristics *and* is exactly the right proportion for your project. Finally, if you have a good eye, you will find an acceptable balance for the adjusted font. If you don't have a good eye, using a perfect font probably isn't going to save the project, anyway.

However, before you break a rule, you should be at least aware that the rule exists. You've been duly notified. And all tongue-in-cheek tone aside, it is a rule that should make you at least proceed with caution if you do adjust the proportion of a font.

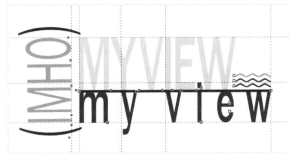

● 12.13

the final product the best it can be (12.14). I converted the lowercase text into a curve (bitmap in a raster program) to adjust the size of the dot on the *i*. See how it now demands less attention than in the original (12.11), and lines up with the characters in the upper line.

Creating a Site Proof

You know where you are going with a site, your site map is in place, and you have your logo ready to go. It's time to move to page design. This is where the true skill in Web design takes place. A page that is well designed for Web use converts to an HTML page easily. Making a great-looking page in a graphics program is easy. However, if that page will not move easily to HTML, it's not a good Web design. Period. It may be stunning . . . as a poster. But this is the Web, and you should be working with, not against, the bounds of HTML layout.

[WARNING]

If you spend hours trying to get the design you created in a graphics program to work in an HTML page, you're not doing your job at the design stage. Every step of the way, ask yourself how this element fits into HTML layout. If the answer involves a convoluted slicing structure — well, I can't stop you, but I sure can warn you loud and strong to reconsider.

I set up my proof pages at 700 px by 450 px. This size fits well onto my screen at 800 px by 600 px display, with a 100% view. Working at 100% magnification is best. Even small changes in magnification can seriously affect the screen display, but not the final image. I have my Photoshop work screen shown

● 12.14

Moving Between Design Programs

To bring the logo for this site into the layout image, I exported the logo as a TIFF file, ready to bring into Photoshop. If I had created the logo in Photoshop, obviously that would not have been necessary. For a simple design (I did a lot of adjusting to this one) I often export the element, but place it in Photoshop or Fireworks only as a pattern to trace. In fact, creating the basic outline for a page in an illustration program and exporting the entire page is not unusual for me. I place the exported page on a Photoshop layer, with a reduced opacity (usually 50% or less), and rebuild it in Photoshop.

Why? For pushing and prodding and throwing things all over the page, you simply cannot beat an illustration program. I don't think any program comes close to CorelDRAW's text manipulation features. Plus, if you must prepare design elements from the page in higher resolution, perhaps for print material, an illustration program can handle them with no problems, because they are vector based.

However, I am still not as happy with the Web features in any of the illustration programs as I am in either Photoshop or Fireworks. (If you do not have an illustration program, but do have Fireworks, it does offer many of the benefits that the illustration programs do.)

I'm really not trying to confuse you. Because I came from the print world, where illustration programs and Photoshop are used hand in hand, using both is natural for me. However, moving back and forth between programs is not necessary. Either Photoshop or Fireworks (and a few other programs) will do all that you need.

But, in case you do happen to have an illustration program, and know how to use it, I would be remiss not to point out where you may find it a good option. I *do not* suggest that anyone purchase a high-end illustration program for Web design. They present a long learning curve, and are expensive. Unless you plan to learn print design, purchasing and learning an illustration program is simply not a good investment.

with the logo visible (12.15). My Layers palette is always open. I usually drag the palettes that I'm most likely to require into the Layers group. I will be working with a lot of text for this sample, and want my Character palette handy. Here I show it grouped with the Layers palette (12.16).

[T I P]

When you're working on a big project, like a Web proof page, do not underestimate how much time you save by setting up an efficient workspace. Your work will be faster, less frustrating, and more accurate. Keeping an eye on the details of your page is hard when much of it is covered with palettes.

Creating Menu Areas

The menu areas usually follow the logo placement for me. The menus are the most important usability element for any page, and, in my opinion, should be created when you still have many options. As you progress through your page, your options narrow. Color becomes fixed, spaces on the page are assigned, and changing will upset the balance. I see the process as an ever-narrowing shape (12.17). Make sure that the important elements of your page are near the top, before your choices become too constricted.

The first decision, of course, is whether to use graphic text or HTML text for your menus. For a menu that is likely to change, I always use HTML/CSS. I knew I wanted options to change my search links, or create more as I received feedback from my visitors. Perhaps my occasional rant is what brings them back. I don't like it when I have to return to a graphics program, rearrange the menu items, make it all fit, rearrange slicing, and export and create new rollovers. I prefer to simply type in a new category.

The search links menu had to be HTML, which left me with basically one choice: color (12.18). I don't

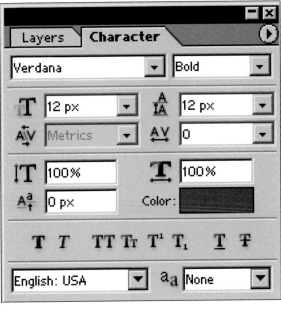

● 12.16

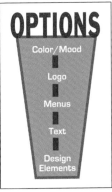

● 12.17

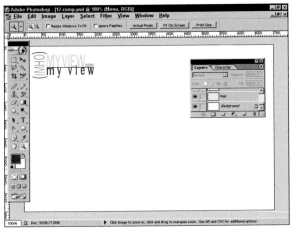

● 12.15

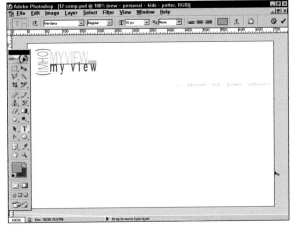

● 12.18

need this menu to announce itself loudly, so I opted for a soft teal. Note that the ~ (tilde) characters between the menu items (12.19) reflect the same shape as the dingbat design element I found earlier (12.9).

[WARNING]

When you place text that is destined to be HTML text in a graphics program proof page, make sure you specify an effect that you can achieve in the final document. If you're not certain about CSS effects, this is a good place for a test in an HTML page. You don't need perfection. Create the menu in an HTML page (copy the text from the graphics program for speed) and create a CSS style. An embedded style is fine as you are simply testing, not building, a CSS file you will keep. Of course, if you create a brilliant effect with many properties, you may want to save the CSS code to place in your final file.

My main menu is unlikely to change. These are the only topics I have on this site. If I go on a Flash binge, and want to give visitors access to my work in that line, I can simply add a new search link. Because one of my goals is to create a page that is crisp and clean, I wanted a pixel font for this menu. I chose MiniHaHa, another 10 px font from Joe Gillespie (http://wpdfd.com). The font certainly answers the crisp and clean call, and by using bold style, certainly stands out, even at a small size (12.20).

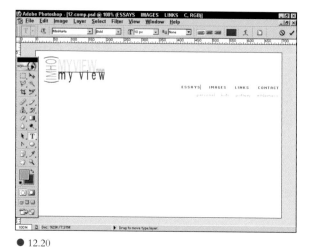

● 12.19

I like the type in the menus, but they are not working as a unit. The whole menu area is hanging in midair, with nothing to anchor it. Nothing divides the two menus, which can be confusing for visitors. It's also dull, dull, dull. Just because menus are important, and must first answer usability, does not mean they should be boring.

A simple line fixes the lack of menu separation (12.21). It also magically binds the menu area to the page. Although this line does an impressive job, I try to tie in design elements at every opportunity. I also want a slightly playful feel for this site to enforce the upbeat nature of the content.

[TIP]

I use a lot of lines in my work. They serve as dividers and design elements, tie elements together, and often point visitors to what I want them to see. Lines can be any color, rough and casual, heavy and demanding, or a hairline, but their power on a page is amazing.

Enter the dingbat (12.22). The top sample here is still in text, the character *I* in 120 px Cairo font. The lower sample shows a duplicate copy of the character, with the layer rasterized, and one portion of the element selected, moved, and filled with a different color. Dingbats are powerful design elements. To make my line more interesting, I borrowed one of the wavy lines from the dingbat, manipulated it a little, and positioned it at the end of the line. In this magnified view, you can see the wavy end of the line on one layer, and the plain line on another (12.23). I like to keep my elements on independent layers, at

● 12.20

● 12.21

least until the design process is complete. The line has much more character now (12.24).

[T I P]

You can convert any dingbat from a font to an editable design element. In a raster program, like Photoshop, you rasterize the layer containing the dingbat character to enable editing. In an illustration program, convert the character to a curve, and edit it like any other curve. After the conversion is complete, you can use one part of the dingbat, color or resize parts of the original design, add filters, or distort all or part of the element.

I decided to run with the wavy line theme a little longer, and use a wavy divider between the menu items. This divider is simply a variation of the wave line from the dingbat character, with a pink fill. I decided to cut the bottom wave off in mid-flight, partly to create a true center for the element (12.25) and I like the slightly chopped look, which sends the

wavy line into the gray line below, rather than trailing off to the left (12.26). Details, details, details. The

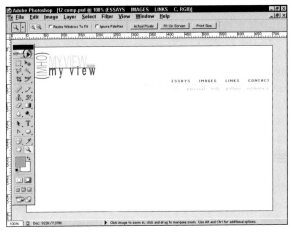

12.24

12.25

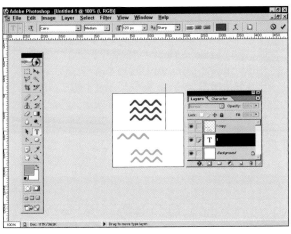

12.22

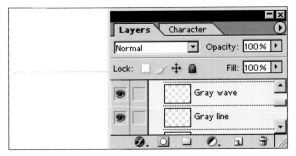

12.23

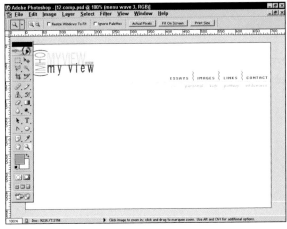

12.26

Preparing the Content Text Area

The content area for this site was really set in the planning stage. Remember that I wanted to present my content in two columns for the best flexibility. This format really reduces my options, and makes planning the content area very simple. In fact, the table layout was included in my Guides layer (12.31) before I turned my attention to the lower section. The dividing line and, to some extent, text choices, are the only variables.

[N O T E]

I do include Greek text of my content text, and take a close guess as to how it will appear in the final page, but at this stage, I only try to get a general idea of how the page will look. I do the fine-tuning of my text attributes when the page is in HTML format, and I can see the actual results as I build the CSS file.

With the table guides visible, I placed Greek text into the main content area (12.32). Here is where I made the decision to keep the line spacing very open. Although I knew that line length in a two-column format could be a problem, seeing the lines at the ideal length in a 700-pixel-wide document really drove home the concept in a visual way. I have to allow for more than 300 extra pixels being added to the width of this page. Extra line spacing is one way to provide a very well-defined horizontal element to help readers follow longer lines.

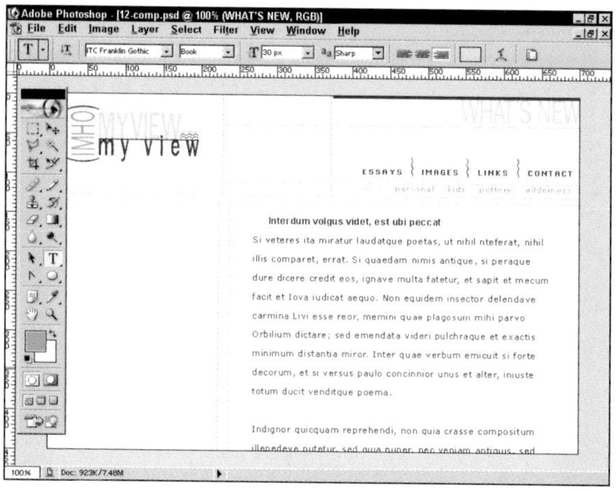

When I designed the logo, I used dark gray, rather than black for the dark elements. That usually means that dark gray text will be the best for content text. Although the black text isn't dramatically different (12.33), the text does sit into the page better as gray (12.34).

[N O T E]

The difference between the black and gray text may not show up well in the printed version. If it does, you will clearly see what I mean. If it does not, please don't just roll your eyes and discount all of my detail talk. Try it on a sample page. Create design elements with dark gray as the darkest color, and then both black and dark gray text. Trust me, there is a difference.

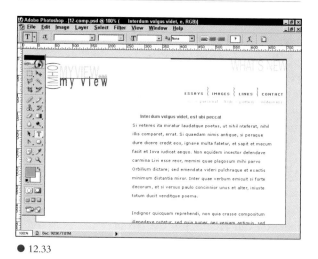

● 12.33

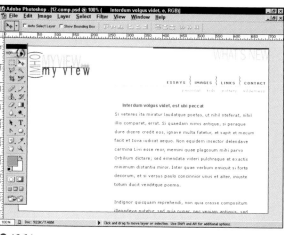

● 12.32

● 12.34

For the left portion of the page, I actually typed real content (12.35). Doing so is not uncommon for me. Guessing exactly how many Greek words to use as a test is hard, and dummy text can take me as long to do as placing real items into short text pieces. Also, for short pieces, the format becomes very important. Working towards the best format is easier when you use actual samples of the material that will appear. I had originally planned to have a much tighter line spacing in this section. There are no long lines that need help here, and I wanted more items to fall above the fold of the page. However, that made the page instantly too heavy on the left (12.36). Text that is close "weighs" much more than open text. Matching the text to the main content text brought back the balance (12.37).

Finally, I needed a dividing line between the left and content text. It is separated, but there is no clear division. This was not much of a challenge. I simply created the same line as the line that divided the menus, but in a different color, and ran it vertically, not horizontally (12.38).

[T I P]

You may be wondering how I can create a vertical line with a decorative top. You may even think I will have to create a special line for each page, customized to be the correct length. Not so. In HTML, and you see this technique a little later in the chapter, you can place one image directly below another. That's how

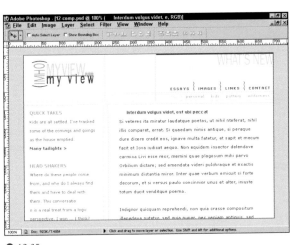

● 12.35

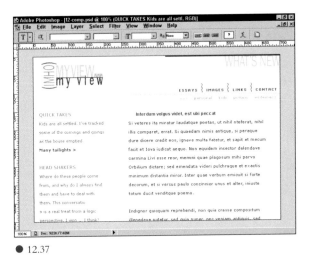

● 12.37

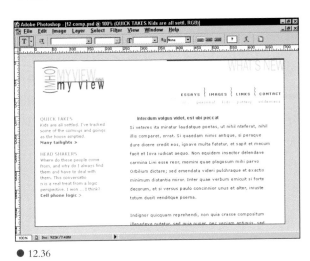

● 12.36

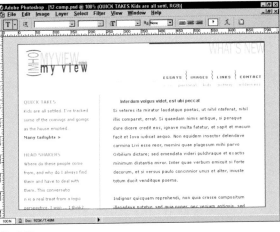

● 12.38

I accomplished this look. The wavy part of the line is an image that is placed in the top of a cell. The straight part is a single-pixel GIF file that is adjusted to be as long as I want — using an HTML length value.

The secret at the design stage is to make sure that the single-pixel GIF can align to perfect center with the top element. That's easy if you keep the top element to an uneven number of pixels (5 px in this case), and the element has no extra pixels on either side of the colored pixels.

Slicing the Image for Export

The proof is ready. You can prepare to export the required images now.

This page has a simple layout, and many of the elements on the page will be created in the HTML document. I've prepared the slices that are required, and selected them to give you an overview (12.39). Although it looks like quite a mess at first glance, there is perfect order.

Slices 01 (12.40), 03 (12.41), and 09–12 (12.42) are the basic images for the top section. I have prepared a simple rollover for slices 09–12, (12.43) where the text changes to medium gray. Slices 04, 06, 17, and 20 require explanation.

In order to have a page that stretches from edge to edge, or a liquid design, there are times when you require a background image that will allow a line or other element to stretch. In this example, slices 04 and 06 work in partnership to create a flexible line (12.44). Slice 06 is a background image saved to allow the line between the menus to stretch with the page width. Slice 04 is the static end of the line, but

it must match exactly with slice 06 in order for the effect to work. I've magnified all the slices mentioned to this point to 200% for clarity.

Slices 17 and 20 are also design elements (12.45). This view is shown at 300% so you can see the elements. Slice 20 is a little design element I created to use with the headlines. I'm not sure whether I will use it, but I wanted it there for experimenting as I created the CSS file for the page. Slice 17 is the top of the wavy line. To make sure that I had an uneven number of pixels for the width, I magnified the image to 600%, and opened the Info palette (12.46). Note that I have also included a little of the straight-line portion of this element in the slice. This helps to make a clean line when I match this image to a single-pixel line.

The sliced images that I will use for this site are ready. I also prepared a single teal pixel file, and a pink triangle, which is shown at 1600% magnification (12.47) to use for bullets and link endings. The full set of files is shown here in Photoshop's file browser (12.48).

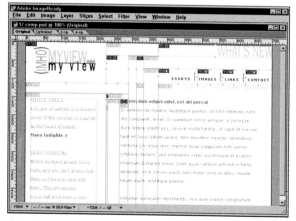

● 12.39

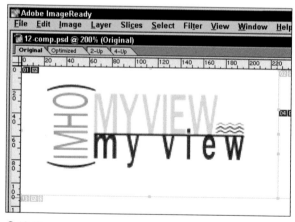

● 12.40

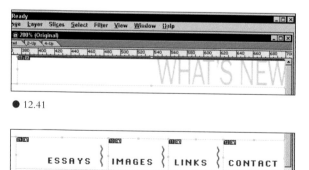

● 12.41

● 12.42

This section completes the proofing stage. From here, I move on to creating the HTML proof page. If the graphic program proof stage has been well done, the layout will be easy to create. I'll then build the CSS file, and voilá — a template. Although I have spent a lot of time getting here, the time will be repaid as I move forward.

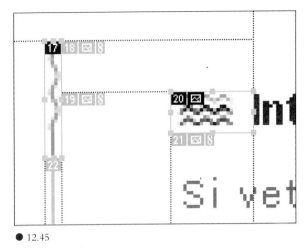

● 12.45

● 12.46

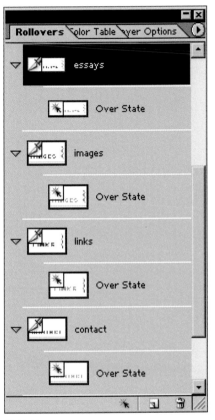

● 12.43

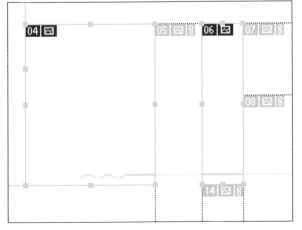

● 12.44

● 12.47

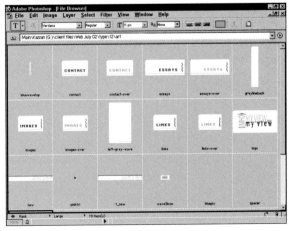

● 12.48

Creating HTML Layout

As I mentioned in the introduction for this chapter, I feature Dreamweaver as I put this page together in HTML. I include the code when necessary. For the CSS portions, to keep this section as generic as possible, I work strictly in code. I do use a combination of Dreamweaver's on-board CSS editing, TopStyle and straight text editor entry, when I build my CSS. By using code only for illustrations, you can accomplish the effect in the way you usually create your code without any software instructions interfering.

Creating the Basic Page

I like to start with a saved document with an attached CSS file, even though the CSS file is empty. For this example, I've created a document called indexwork.html and a CSS file named 12type.css. The CSS file is linked to the HTML document.

```
<link href="12type.css"
    rel="stylesheet" type="text/css">
```

My very first action is to set the margins for the document. I like to use zero margins, which I set with CSS in the <body> tag. While I am in the <body> tag, I add the background color, plus the generic font family and color, in case a visitor's older browser cannot interpret other styles. With the font specified, the content should at least display in the correct font.

```
body {
    margin: 0px;
    font-family: Verdana, Arial,
     Helvetica, sans-serif;
    background-color: #FFFFFF;
    color: #333333;
}
```

Building the Top Table

Next, I want to establish the table layout. Referring to the Guide layer in Photoshop (12.31) shows that I need a table for the top content that is three rows by three columns. It must stretch across the page, so the width is 100%. I rarely have padding or cellspacing for top element tables. The left column requires all rows to be merged. The basic table is shown in Dreamweaver (12.49).

I place all the images for the top in the appropriate cells. I place all the menu items into the middle cell of the right column. I place the wavy line into the middle row of the middle column. I place the title image into the upper-right cell. I turned the borders on with a blue color so you can see how the images are distributed.

[TIP]

I do not use one cell for each menu item, but rather place them side by side in one cell, or stacked with only a <br> tag between menu items for a vertical format. I have found this method to be a much more accurate way to keep images together, and of course, there is much less code, and far more flexibility should a change be required.

I also place my menu items as simple images to perfect the page, then add the rollover effect. Working with a plain image is much easier should any adjustments be necessary. After you're satisfied that the menu items are in the right place, and the layout is stable, deleting each image and replacing it with a rollover, or adding the rollover code to the image code is an easy matter. The alignment for each cell is listed here (12.50), with the Horizontal alignment listed first, with vertical alignment as the second listing.

The layout is nearly complete as you can see in this preview (12.51). I've left the borders turned on so you can see exactly how the images are placed. The

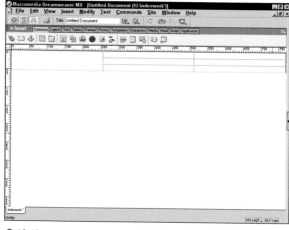

● 12.49

only spot that needs attention is the gap in the line between the menu items and the end image. This area is filled in with a background image, specified in a CSS class style:

```
.lineback {
    background-image:
       url(art/greylineback.gif);
}
```

The class style is applied to the cell containing the wave image as follows:

```
<td width="100%" valign="bottom"
    class="lineback">
<img src="art/left-gray-wave.gif"
    width="63" height="110"></td>
```

This cell is set to 100% width to tell the browser that this cell is the one I want to expand. This cell expands as the page width increases, but because the line is placed as a background, the line expands as well (12.52). Pretty slick, huh? I also added the class style to the cell containing the menu items. That way, if that cell expands for any reason, logical or not, the line will still be seen in the empty area.

The last part of the top section is to enter the text menu items, and apply CSS. I did add the type (12.53), but want to define my basic CSS values before I specify the menu CSS. The menu can wait for a little while, while I create the lower table and place some content text.

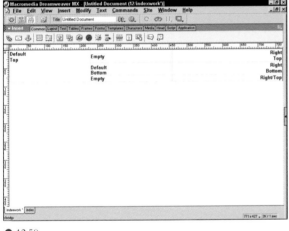

● 12.50

● 12.52

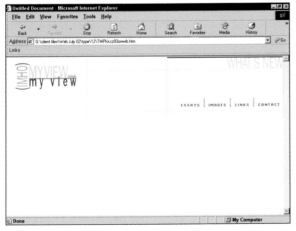

● 12.51

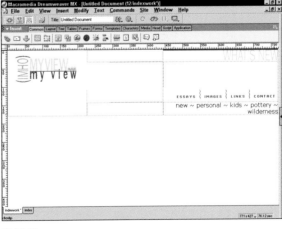

● 12.53

The full code for the top table is shown next. The rollovers have not been added to the menu items at this point, nor had the CSS menu style been applied to the text menu. However, the structure is all here.

```
<table width="100%" border="0"
    cellpadding="0" cellspacing="0"
    bordercolor="#99FFFF">
  <tr>
    <td rowspan="3" valign="top"><img
    src="art/logo.gif" width="227"
    height="110"></td>
    <td> </td>
    <td align="right"
    valign="top"><img
    src="art/t_new.gif" width="325"
    height="34"></td>
  </tr>
  <tr>
    <td width="100%" valign="bottom"
    class="lineback"><img
    src="art/left-gray-wave.gif"
    width="63" height="110"></td>
    <td align="right" valign="bottom"
    class="lineback"><img
    src="art/essays.gif" width="112"
    height="42"><img
    src="art/images.gif" width="72"
    height="42"><img
    src="art/links.gif" width="66"
    height="42"><img
    src="art/contact.gif" width="75"
    height="42"></td>
  </tr>
  <tr>
    <td> </td>
    <td align="right">new ~ personal ~
    kids ~ pottery ~ wilderness</td>
  </tr>
</table>
```

Building the Content Table

Table construction does not get much simpler than the table I needed for my content text. The table is two rows high and three columns wide, with a 10 Cellpadding value, and 100% width. I always place one row at the bottom of my content table to act as a sizing row. Here I have specified that the left column is 195 px, and the right column is 100%. I placed a 195-pixel clear GIF file in the left column to hold the size. Placing a clear GIF file in the right

column, with a width of 300 to 500 pixels, depending on what screen width you use as your minimum, is also a good idea. Technically, it should not be necessary, but Netscape 4 browsers often decide to share the screen space between columns, even when a fixed width is combined with a 100% width. The clear GIF file placed in the right column convinces Netscape version 4 browsers to respect your specified column widths.

All cells are set to Top for vertical alignment. The top center column requires Center horizontal alignment. All other alignment is left with default values. Here is the completed table, with the clear GIF image in the left column selected to illustrate where it is, along with the code (12.54).

```
<table width="100%" border="0"
    cellspacing="0" cellpadding="10">
  <tr valign="top">
    <td> </td>
    <td align="center"> </td>
    <td> </td>
  </tr>
  <tr>
    <td valign="top"><img
    src="art/spacer.gif" width="195"
    height="1"></td>
    <td valign="top"> </td>
    <td width="100%" valign="top"><img
    src="art/spacer.gif" width="450"
    height="1"></td>
  </tr>
</table>
```

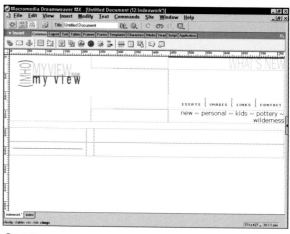

● 12.54

With the table in place, I can add the dividing line images. The wavy line is placed first, followed by a `<br>` tag. Then the one-pixel blue GIF file is placed, and the desired length specified. I've used a length of 300 px, as the division is only required until the left content runs out (12.55). Although a slight gap shows in this Dreamweaver view, you will see in the next few examples that the gap disappears in a preview.

Building the CSS File

This proof page is nearly complete. Adding the CSS controls, first for the content text, then for the menu areas, is all that remains.

As always, I place Greek text to use as a filler, apply an `<h1>` style to the headline, and add `<p>` tags to the paragraphs. I have the correct text for the left side, so I'll simply paste that into place. I also have the

triangle images placed in the left column. I added dummy links to some text to test link appearance. I also added the links to the text menu (12.56). Don't worry — it always looks this bad.

To start, the `<p>` style code is as follows:

```
p {
    font-size: 11px;
    line-height: 24px;
    margin-right: 15px;
    margin-left: 24px;
    font-family: Verdana, Arial,
     Helvetica, sans-serif;
}
```

I have added space at the right and left of the content text area by adding right and left margins to the `<p>` tag. I have cell padding in the table, but I need less space for the left section and the cell holding the dividing line. Applying margins to the `<p>` tag solves the problem.

The `<h1>` style code is as follows:

```
h1 {
    font-family: Arial, Helvetica,
     sans-serif;
    font-size: 100%;
    color: #990066;
    margin-bottom: -10px;
}
```

I have added a negative margin value to the bottom of the `<h1>` style to tighten the space between the headline and the text. Also, because the `<h1>` style

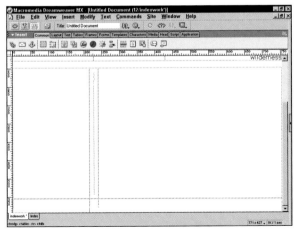

● 12.55

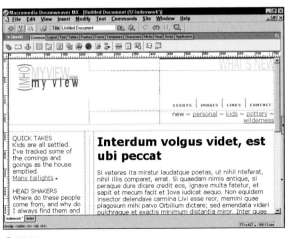

● 12.56

does not have a left margin value, it will start to the left of the <p> tag (12.57).

The default page links are as follows:

```
a:link {
    color: #006666;
}
a:visited {
    color: #990066;
}
a:hover {
    color: #990066;
}
```

I rarely use an a:active style, and for the page defaults, usually leave the underlining. These links are teal, with the rollover effect pink. I think this color is close enough to qualify as my required blue (12.58).

The page controls are finished. Finally, I get the top menu under control, and set the styles for the left content text area. The top text menu styles are part of a class style. The code for the styles is as follows:

```
.menu {
    font-family: Verdana, Arial,
     Helvetica, sans-serif;
    font-size: 10px;
    color: #999999;
```

```
    padding-right: 10px;
}
.menu a:link {
    color: #669999;
    text-decoration: none;
    font-size: 11px;
}
.menu a:visited {
    color: #999999;
    text-decoration: none;
    font-size: 11px;
}
.menu a:hover {
    color: #990066;
    text-decoration: underline;
}
```

The style is applied to the cell containing the menu:

```
<td align="right" valign="top"
    class="menu">new ~ <a
    href="#">personal</a> ~ <a
    href="#">kids</a> ~ <a
    href="#">pottery</a> ~ <a
    href="#">wilderness</a></td>
</tr>
```

Both the application in the HTML page and the styles are standard menu control practices. Of note in this sample is the padding added to the menu style.

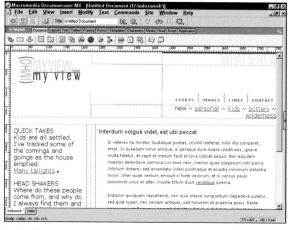

● 12.57

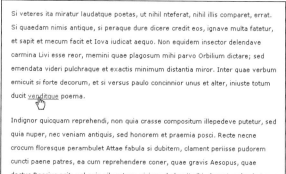

● 12.58

This attribute provides a space between the text and the right edge in a table that has no padding (12.59).

[N O T E]

I fully explain the menu styles featured here in Chapter 6, "CSS Menus."

The left side CSS styles are created in the same pattern as the menu:

```
.leftside {
    font-family: Verdana, Arial,
     Helvetica, sans-serif;
    font-size: 11px;
    line-height: 24px;
    color: #333333;
    padding-left: 20px;
}
.leftside a:link {
    color: #990066;
    font-weight: bold;
    text-decoration: none;
    border-bottom-style: solid;
    border-bottom-width: 1px;
    border-bottom-color: #CCCCCC;
}
.leftside a:visited {
```

```
    color: #990066;
    border: none;
    text-decoration: none;
}
.leftside a:hover {
    background-color: #CCCCCC;
}
```

However, I added one extra style for the type in the left column, a style for the headlines in this section:

```
.lefthead {
    font-size: 12px;
    font-weight: bold;
    color: #006666;
}
```

I like to have headlines defined for a section. You are much less likely to resort to the `<font>` tag if you have a style fully developed and ready to go (12.60).

[N O T E]

There should be a text menu added to the bottom of the page, but I have already covered all the skills required for that menu.

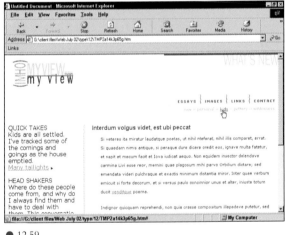

● 12.59

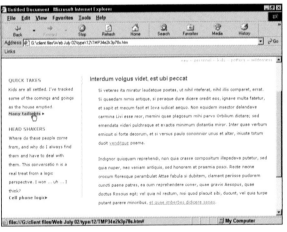

● 12.60

And one final touch — I've added the small triple wave design element that I saved when I was creating the slices for the page. I've inserted the icon into the `<h1>` style, allowing it to line up with the `<p>` tag (12.61).

Add a page title, and that's a wrap as far as this exercise goes. The page must be tested in several browsers, and across platforms, of course (12.62). You should also go to `http://w3c.org` to validate both your HTML and CSS code. The page that I created for this exercise was validated for both CSS and HTML.

[N O T E]

You can see this finished page at `http://wpeck.com/type`.

You've now completed both the CSS and HTML portions of this book. However, don't stop. You have worked through so much, you should continue on to find out why Flash requires its own section in a type book.

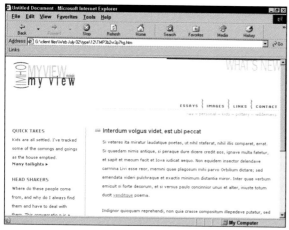

● 12.61

● 12.62

Typography for Flash

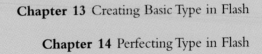

rolley

VECTOR

f

font

n

Pixel font

- static
- dynamic
- input

embed

Chapter 13

Creating Basic Type in Flash

Flash type is a whole new world. Forget most of what you know about type if you want a sporting chance at producing great type in Flash.

WENDY PECK

Creating a Flash movie is at once the most exhilarating experience you can have when developing work for the Web, and one of the most frustrating. The learning curve is long, the mines along the path, many. But, oh how wonderful it feels when you sit back and watch that movie play. The rewards do outweigh the often high cost along the way.

I would love to tell you that the next two chapters will clear the way for you to produce great movies with little pain. Nothing could be further from the truth. I will not pretend that I am teaching you Flash. The focus of this book is typography, and what I offer in this section of the book is how to create *great type* in Flash.

The focus is fully on type. Not type that fades, or hops, or turns somersaults. After your type is created in Flash, it is no different from any other object, and you will have to turn to other sources to learn how to make Flash objects perform. I spend very little time on fantastic effects for type. Again, a wealth of information is available, most of it free on the Web, for turning lights on and off, laser effects — imagine it and a tutorial will be available. I help point you in the right direction for that knowledge.

But what good is the most amazing effect, if the base type is not great? That's where this section of the book comes in. I'll teach you to create type in many ways, type that delivers when you want it, and that

remains crisp and clear. You'll find information here that is hard to track down elsewhere.

Understanding Flash Type

Through this book, I have talked about two kinds of text: HTML text controlled by CSS, and text created as an image. Flash type combines the characteristics of both HTML and graphic type in that you can use any font you have installed (like text produced in a graphic program) but it is editable and scaleable (like HTML text). But that comparison is only for reference to set the stage. You are better off to consider Flash type a new skill, and not compare it to either HTML or text created in a graphic program.

Comparing Vector and Raster Formats

Flash is the only widely accessible vector format in use on the Web, and to grasp how Flash works, you must start by understanding the basic difference between vector and raster formats. Raster formats display information pixel by pixel: This pixel is one color, the next pixel is a different color, and so on. Vector format displays objects with a mathematical formula: display a blue rectangle with the coordinates at a, b, c, and d.

The samples I include here show how the formats differ. A raster format display of stripes (13.1) looks like the sample at the left on the screen, but is actually a series of pixels. A vector image looks the same, but is constructed with objects (13.2).

[T I P]

I have a short, illustrated article on the difference between raster and vector format in my column at WebReference.com (`www.webreference.com/graphics/column31/`).

Although there is no apparent difference in appearance between the same object in vector or raster format at original size (13.3), the difference shows instantly when you enlarge the image (13.4). Vector format coordinate information changes, allowing the same quality as in the original size image. Raster format pixels simply get bigger when you enlarge the image, resulting in jagged edges and overall quality loss.

A vector image that measures 100 px by 100 px produces the same file size as the same image enlarged to 200 px by 200 px. A raster image that is 200 px by 200 px produces a file size that is many times the size of the same image at 100 px by 100 px. Flash is a vector-based format, which presents the opportunity to create exciting Web content with small file size.

[N O T E]

If you don't associate Flash movies with small file size, it is not the fault of the format. Flash movies operate on the same principles as an animation, or showing many images in rapid succession. If the same movie were created only with raster images, the resulting file size would be far too large for Web use, even with the fastest known connection.

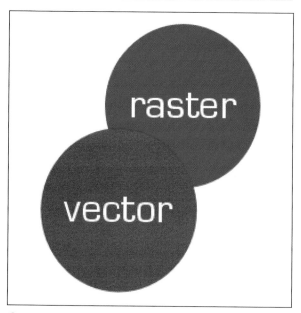

● 13.3

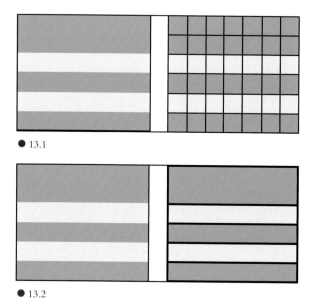

● 13.1

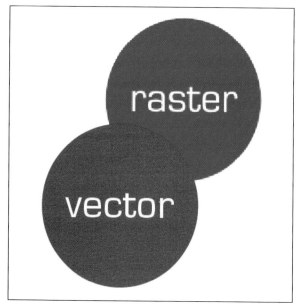

● 13.4

● 13.2

Including Fonts in Flash Movies

Flash offers Web designers the opportunity to work with a wide range of fonts. When you publish your movie, Flash embeds the font information required in the SWF file. A visitor can view the movie with the fonts you specified, even when the font is not installed on the visitor's computer. Sounds perfect? Or have you been working on the Web for long enough to know that there is a "yeah, but . . . " coming? You're right! There are a few cautions that come along with the freedom to embed fonts in movies.

The first caution is that the fonts will be embedded only in the SWF version of the movie. If you want to share FLA files with another designer, they must have the same fonts installed in order to have the document display as designed.

Some fonts cannot be embedded in the SWF files. If you are working with the option View → Antialias Text selected, and the type is jagged on the screen, that font does not have an outline included with it, and cannot be embedded.

Embedded fonts add to movie file size, so please limit the number of fonts you use. Limiting the number of fonts on a page is good design practice, but when you add the baggage of a new embedded font in your file for every font you include, the incentive for restraint multiplies. Static text blocks embed only the characters you use in your movies, but for dynamic text, Flash will embed all characters for each font used in the movie, unless you specify otherwise. You choose which fonts to embed in the Properties inspector, with the dynamic text block selected. Click the Character button, and specify which characters of that font you want to have included.

Antialiasing is a concern for small type (see "Beating the Fuzzies" later in this chapter). All type is antialiased in Flash, unless the movie is exported with low quality specified, which adds more problems than it solves (see sidebar. "Antialiasing Type in Flash").

If you are prepared to give up control over text in your movie, you can use device fonts for horizontal text. There are three device fonts in Flash, one each for serif and sans-serif fonts, and a typewriter font. When the movie displays, the visitor's computer displays the default fonts for the type you specify (serif, sans serif, or typewriter). You certainly lose control over font display, but the file size is considerably reduced because no fonts are embedded in the movie. In addition, the type is not antialiased, which improves the appearance for smaller type. For static text, specify device fonts by selecting your text block, then checking the Use Device Fonts option, and selecting one of the device font styles from the font field in the Properties inspector. For dynamic text, select one of the device fonts as for static text, and click Character in the Properties Inspector. Specify No Characters for the Embed Font Outlines For option.

Finally, if you are running several movies containing the same fonts, you may want to consider using font symbols. Font symbols are stored on the site, and called on when the movie requires a font. The font contained in the symbol is not embedded into the movie, saving file size. Of course, a little time is lost as the movie requests the font informaiton from the symbol, but in some settings, the file size savings can be significant. See "Creating font symbols" in the Flash help files.

Vector files are not always smaller than raster files. Vector format puts raster format to shame with file sizes on solid-color objects. However, the same is not true for photographic type images. Because vector images must specify a new object for each color change, file size explodes for images containing frequent color changes. Take a look at a photo magnified to 800% of the original size (13.5). The inset includes the image at 100% magnification. For this image, raster format simply specifies a different color for each pixel. Vector format must specify a new object for almost every pixel, which takes more file size than a simple pixel color declaration.

● 13.5

Now that you have a tiny overview of vector and raster format, you can move on to the basics of creating Flash text.

Understanding How Flash Type Works

Before I move on to how to actually create text in Flash, and the various options available to ensure quality, I want to provide a short overview of how text goes from entry in a Flash document, onto the Web.

Macromedia Flash, the program, creates documents in FLA format. This is a proprietary format, unique to Flash, just like Photoshop produces PSD files, or CorelDRAW creates CDR format files. Flash files containing all construction information for the movies are saved in this format. FLA files cannot be viewed with a Web browser. However, with the FLA document open in Flash, you can export an SWF format file. SWF format files can be included in an HTML file and viewed on the Web. To create a Flash movie and make it available for viewing on the Web you will have three files: an FLA file, an HTML file, and an SWF file (13.6).

You add text in the FLA document (13.7). Then you export the movie to an SWF format file, which you then place in an HTML document. This Dreamweaver sample shows the movie placed in a table, with a caption added in HTML text (13.8). When you preview the HTML document, the movie plays (13.9).

Although this process sounds like a cumbersome route to placing content on the Web, Macromedia has done a great job of making the export process,

referred to as publishing, simple. Flash has eight different export formats, but for this discussion, I talk about exporting to Flash format, or SWF. You set the publishing settings once (13.10), and as long as the settings do not change, choosing File → Publish creates an updated SWF file. The publishing process can produce an SWF file for placement in an HTML document, or an SWF file and the HTML markup required to display the movie.

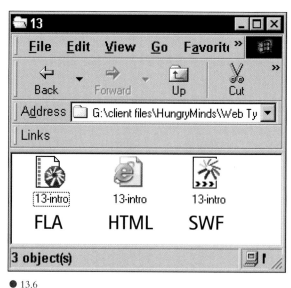

● 13.6

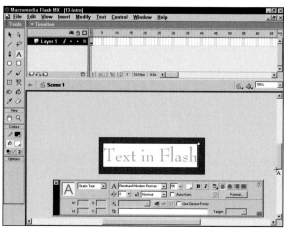

● 13.7

The Flash default settings for publishing create SWF and HTML files using the same name as the FLA file, and placed in the same location. If you're creating your own HTML page to contain the Flash movie, it is a good idea to use a filename that is different from the FLA file to prevent a Flash-generated HTML file from overwriting the one you have created. All things being perfect, you will not have the HTML option checked when you publish. But all things are rarely perfect. I am always careful when checking one option can cause an entire page to be lost. You can, of course, change the name for the file in the Publish settings, but I prefer to have SWF filenames match the FLA files to prevent confusion for future edits.

That's how text entered in Flash finds its way to the Web. This process does not change no matter which of the many choices for text production in Flash you choose. I'll start with basic text entry, and then move to some of the more interesting options you have for including text in Flash.

Entering Text in Flash

You enter text into Flash in three basic ways. The first is static text. You enter the text on the screen, and perhaps add effects to it, but that is the end of it. To edit static text, you must open the FLA file and make changes.

You can also provide a spot for dynamic text to be entered in your Flash document. Dynamic text comes from sources external to the Flash movies, such as text files, ColdFusion or ASP, and is called on when the movie is played on the Web. If you are familiar with Server Side Includes (SSI), the concept is similar. The beauty of this method is that you can edit the text outside the FLA file.

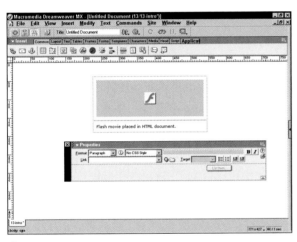

● 13.8

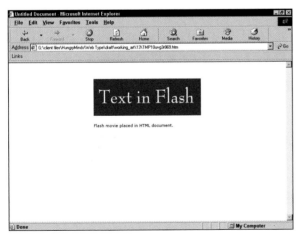

● 13.9

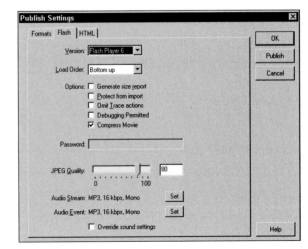

● 13.10

Finally, you can enter text fields, which visitors will fill in, into a Flash document. Because I won't be discussing functional documents in Flash, I do not cover Input text.

Creating Static Text

The basic, or static text entry method in Flash is similar to other graphic programs. With the Text tool selected from the Toolbox, click on the canvas to create an expandable text block, which is marked with a circular icon in the top-right corner of the text bounding box (13.11). This text continues across the canvas until you enter a hard return to start a new line.

To create text with a fixed width, drag to create the text block (13.12). This form of text block is marked with a square icon in the top-right corner of the bounding box.

You create vertical text in the same way as horizontal text, but with a vertical format selected in the Properties Inspector (13.13).

Editing for text in Flash takes place primarily in the Properties Inspector, a wonderful new feature in Flash MX. Selecting the text block with the Arrow tool applies changes to the entire block (13.14). Highlighting text with the Text tool applies changes only to the selected text (13.15).

Paragraph controls are also available for Flash text. The Format button on the Properties Inspector opens the Format Options window. Selecting text with the Arrow tool applies the changes made in the Format Options window to the entire text block. With the Text tool active, changes to paragraph settings are applied to selected paragraphs. In this example, a section of text is indented by adding a 30 px margin on the left and right (13.16). The full block

 13.11

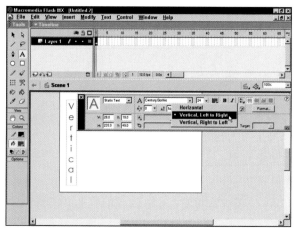

 13.13

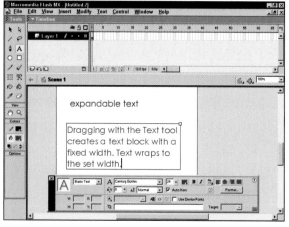

 13.12

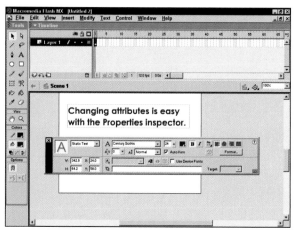

 13.14

of text has a first line indent of 15 px, a setting that was removed from the indented section of text.

[T I P]

You can paste text into a Flash text block. Simply copy the text from another application, create a text block of the desired style, and choose Edit → Paste. You can also use the keyboard shortcut Ctrl+V (PC) or ⌘+V (Mac).

Creating Dynamic Text

You've seen how to enter static text. Now you can move on to the sophisticated, and exponentially easier-to-maintain method of calling text from a file. My plan was to deliver just the basics to whet your appetite. Remember, my responsibility in this book is to teach you about type, not programs. However, I found a wonderful tutorial, written by Kirupa Chinnathambi, for creating a scrolling text block that uses text from a simple text file. The original tutorial is available at www.kirupa.com/developer/mx/dynamic_scroller.asp (13.17). I urge you to visit and read through the original tutorial, especially because you can download the completed file to see exactly how the effect is accomplished.

[T I P]

Kirupa's site (www.kirupa.com/) is an excellent stop for anyone who wants to learn Flash. The tutorials cover sensible topics, and are very clearly written and well illustrated. In fact, although very young, he already has one book to his credit: *FrontPage 2002: A Beginner's Guide* (McGraw-Hill Osborne Media 2001).

I've changed nothing in the structure of this tutorial, but simply walk you through the steps as I went through it. My words are not better than Kirpa's, but you are used to me. The technique depends on a click-and-drag scrollbar addition to the text box; the ActionScript code is provided, so adding a dynamic text area could not be more simple.

To create a scrolling text block and import remote text, follow these steps:

1. **Create a new Flash movie of any size. Make sure you take into account whether you want this text area to be the entire document, or if you want it to be part of a full movie.**

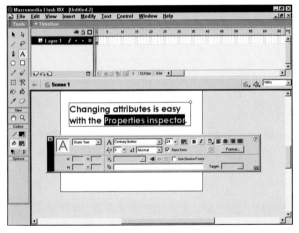

● 13.15

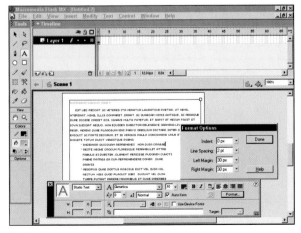

● 13.16

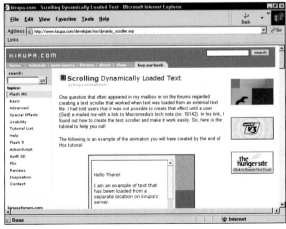

● 13.17

2. Select the Text tool and drag a text block to the desired size. The scrollbar will be added to the outside of the right edge, so make sure you leave enough room (13.18).

3. Select Dynamic Text from the Text Type selector, if it is not already selected. Type Scroller in the Instance field. Choose your font, font color, and size. Select Multiline from the Line Type selector. Activate the Selectable Text and Show Borders icons. Each of the fields that need to be set are marked with red dots (13.19).

4. Click the Format button in the Properties Inspector and set the Left and Right margins to 10 px (13.20). Your text block is now complete, but you need to add a scrollbar to it.

5. Choose Window → Components to open the Components palette if it is not already open. Click the ScrollBar option and drag to the right side of the text block, on top of the text field (13.21). On release of the mouse, the scrollbar will be placed at the right edge of the text block (13.22).

That's the end of the text block creation portion. All that remains is to tell the Flash movie where to find the text to place in the block. You do so through ActionScript — onboard programming to create effects and actions.

[T I P]

ActionScript is the heart and soul of Flash, especially for menus and interactive screens. Learning the basics is not that difficult when you focus on the subject, but it is beyond the scope of this book. Thanks to Kirupa, I can hand the script to you and make creating a dynamic text area easy.

6. Type the following code into a text editor and copy it. I've shown it here in Notepad (13.23). There is no need to save this file.

```
loadText = new loadVars();
loadText.load("greekimport.txt");
//creating the loadVarsText function
loadText.onLoad = function() {
    scroller.text = this.greektext;
};

//creating a new object
loadText = new loadVars();
//Load text from the external text
    file
loadText.load("greekimport.txt");
```

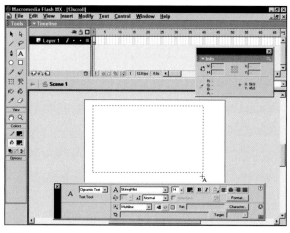

● 13.18

● 13.19

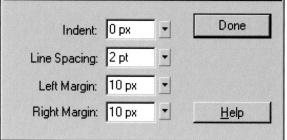

● 13.20

```
//creating the loadVarsText function
loadText.onLoad = function() {
//set the scroller text field to
   contain the greektext from the
   text file scroller.text =
   this.greektext;
};
```

7. **Open the Actions window (choose Window → Actions) if it is not already open.**

8. **Click on the first keyframe in the Timeline. Paste the code you copied into the Actions window by right-clicking (PC) or ⌘+clicking (Mac), and selecting Paste (13.24).**

[TIP]

If you click on each line of code in the script, you can follow how it was constructed through the fields above the pane containing the script.

Your Flash portion is now complete. The script is calling for a text file named greekimport.txt, which you complete in a moment. The text file that you create contains the text you want to appear in the text block you just created in the Flash movie. You must give a title to this text, however, so that the movie will know that it has the right text. Take a peek at the script again, and see the reference to

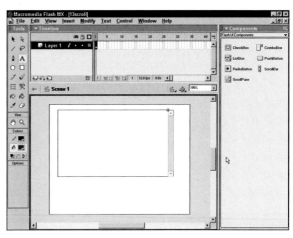
● 13.22

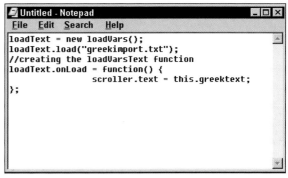
● 13.23

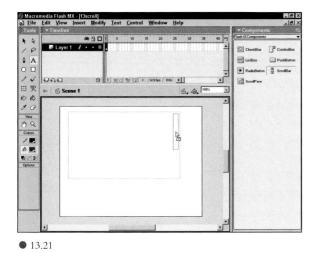
● 13.21

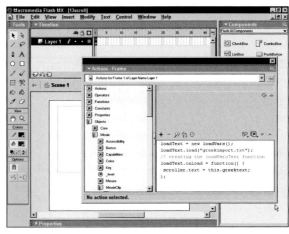
● 13.24

greektext. You insert this above the desired text in the text file, and your project is complete.

9. **If you do not already have the file, download the** greek.txt **file from** http://wpeck.com/greek.html.

10. **Open** greek.txt **in a text editor. Type** greektext= **at the very beginning of the text (13.25). Save the file as** greekimport.txt **in the same directory as the Flash file containing the text block for this text.**

11. **Choose Control → Test Movie to see the results (13.26).**

That's it. You have a scrollable text block in Flash that is connected to a text file. To edit the text, simply open the text file, make your changes, and save. The next time the Flash movie is played, it will load the new version of the text file.

Go ahead and make some edits. There is an extra space at the end of each paragraph, and I don't like the gap at the top of the text. Open the text file and remove the extra spaces. Remove the line break

between the entry code and the rest of the text (13.27). Save the file, and test the movie again. The changes will show in the movie (13.28).

You change the text content in the text file, but the attributes, such as color, font, and so on, you control through the Properties Inspector, in the same way as any other text block (13.29). You can also change the scale of the text block without adjusting the text file. The text will pour into the new shape quite happily the next time it is requested by the Flash movie.

If you want to see this text block in place in a page, I have placed an adjusted copy of the file I created in the previous exercise into the page that I created for Chapter 12, "Putting It All Together" (13.30). Remember, to edit the words in this file, all I have to do is open the text file, change the content, and save the file — and this page is updated.

[T I P]

You could edit this file from literally anywhere in the world with Internet access. Download the tiny text file, edit it on any computer (all computers have text editors,

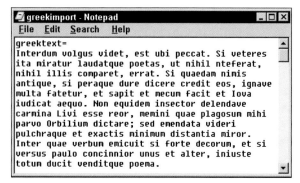

● 13.25

● 13.27

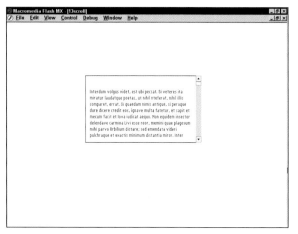

● 13.26

● 13.28

and whether the computer is a Mac or PC doesn't matter). Upload the edited file, and you have new content. It's an exciting concept, and very easy to put into action.

Beating the Fuzzies

I have deliberately delayed bringing this subject to the table. I wanted you to understand how text was placed before I started talking about exact pixels, but now is the time.

Text is a problem in Flash. Large size text performs beautifully (13.31). You don't have to do anything to settings to have smooth, clean edges. However, that

is also a problem in Flash. At smaller sizes, as in all programs, text becomes fuzzy (13.32). With other graphics programs, you can turn off antialiasing. Unfortunately, you really cannot do that in Flash, because taking antialiasing away from small text takes it away from large text, too (see the nearby sidebar "Antialiasing Type in Flash").

Aligning Text Perfectly

One trick makes all of your text look better in Flash. Where you place the text block is important. If the text lines up exactly with a pixel, the result will be better (13.33). In this example, two blocks of identical text are shown at high magnification. The top example is not placed exactly on a pixel (top-left corner), but the lower example is. When viewed at 100% magnification, though neither sample is crisp,

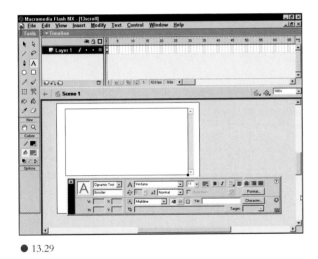

● 13.29

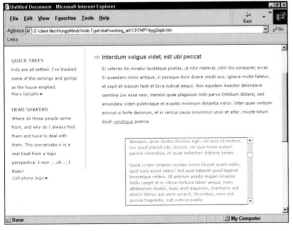

● 13.30

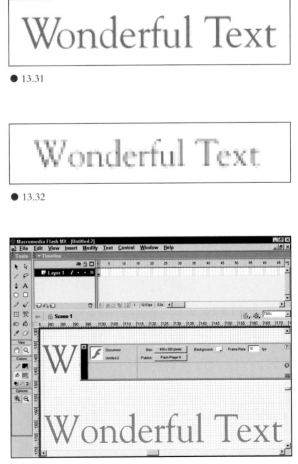

● 13.31

● 13.32

● 13.33

the lower sample, with its precise alignment, is considerably clearer (13.34).

You can accomplish this alignment in a couple of ways. The first, and easiest, is to turn on automatic alignment directly with a pixel. Choose View → Snap to Pixels to force Flash to place all elements exactly aligned to a pixel. You can see this in action at magnification of 400% or more when this option is turned on.

You can also manually set the position for a text block, and this method is usually the easiest, if you have not placed text with the Snap to Pixel option turned on. Open the Info palette by choosing Window → Info. If the numbers in the x and y fields in the Info window are not whole numbers, that is, only 0 (zero) behind the decimal point, change the number to be a whole number (13.35). The same information and adjustment opportunity is available in the Properties panel when you select the text block with the Arrow tool (13.36).

You can also learn which fonts are best. I have found this process to be one of trial and error. The more I

try to use logic to decide which fonts will work well at smaller sizes, the less luck I seem to have (13.37). Some fonts do react well to this environment, however. Keep your eyes open for the good ones.

Using Pixel Fonts in Flash

Ironically, pixel fonts, which are specially designed to be used without antialiasing, can deliver great results at smaller font sizes (13.38). The top example is SkinnyMini, a pixel font. The lower example is Arial. While there may be irony in this fact, there is also logic. In a magnified version of this example (13.39), you can see the lines of the characters clearly. The

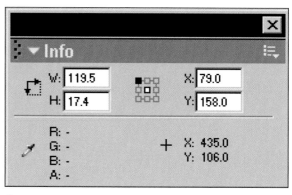

● 13.35

● 13.34

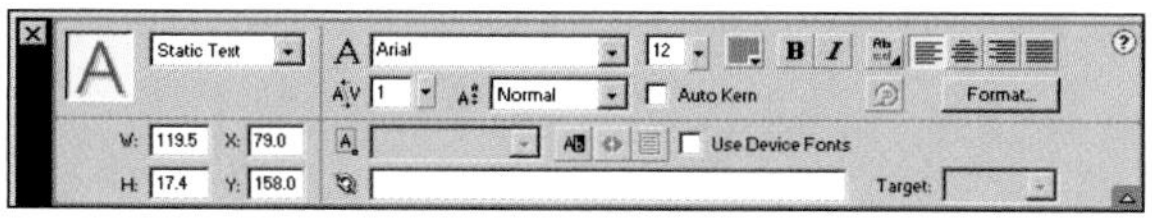

● 13.36

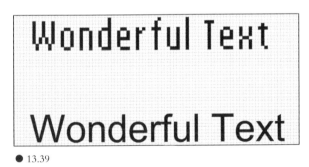

● 13.37

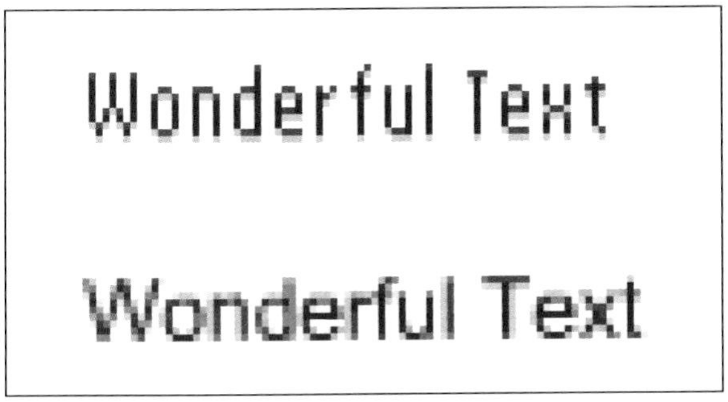

● 13.38

● 13.39

Antialiasing Type in Flash

Technically, you can turn off antialiasing in Flash. You can set the Quality option to low in the Publish Settings window to effectively stop any antialiasing. Unfortunately, this setting makes everything else in the movie look like garbage. Antialiasing is necessary for any diagonal or curved line, or the edges will be obviously jagged. If you turn off antialiasing to increase the quality of small text, your vector objects will suffer the opposite effect.

You also lose the quality that Flash *does* deliver with text, which is the large-size text. Remember that when working with HTML text, as the font size increases, the quality goes down, because there is no antialiasing for HTML text, either. Publishing at low quality for small font quality negatively affects any font above approximately 12 pixels, depending on the font.

Flash offers one solution that works quite well at small sizes: device fonts. Three fonts are included in Flash that look great. These fonts do not embed in the document — they use fonts installed on the viewing computer. The file size is smaller because the font is not embedded, but — Yup! Caught it didn't you? You're right back to the no-choice problem that HTML text presents — device fonts cannot be used with dynamic text.

So what's the answer? No Flash-based solution exists for creating text at small sizes. However, a few tips, and some third-party solutions do make great text possible. Read all of this section to get the solution for most problems you will encounter.

antialias

pixel

embed

device

CHARACTER

font

OBJECTS

· kern

· range kern

· line space

align pixels

Chapter 14

Perfecting Type in Flash

You learned how to get text into a Flash documents in Chapter 13, "Creating Basic Type in Flash." You're also wise to the pitfalls that come hand in hand with Flash text. Now I can bring you the finer points of working with text in Flash. Like any graphics program, you have typography controls available to you, and you can create terrific effects for text before you ever consider what you can do with motion and other effects.

Using Typography Controls in Flash

Flash offers most of the controls that are available in graphics programs for typography. For large type, the type that would normally have antialiasing applied, little difference exists between creating perfect type work in Flash and Photoshop or Fireworks. However, for small type, the type where you reduce antialiasing as much as you can, some special rules apply. I begin the discussion with the simple stuff — the large type — and then move on to the cautions.

Text is often used at very large sizes in Flash. You can move the text on, and then off the screen, so you can make a great impact with size. If your text is moving, or otherwise showing off on the screen, and you have a gap between letters that stands out, you risk all viewer attention being drawn to the flaw.

How's that for a scary thought? Try it. Cover the huge *Wow!* here (14.1) and then pull your hand away and recover it quickly. I'll bet the gap between the first *W* and the *O* is what is imprinted in your brain when the image goes away. Try this test again with type that operates as a unit because the spacing is even (14.2).

[N O T E]

I just want to remind you to place all text on whole pixels. Check the Properties panel or Info window to make sure the x and y values are on whole numbers. Read more about this important aspect of Flash text in Chapter 13, "Creating Basic Type in Flash."

● 14.1

● 14.2

Behind the Scenes

Michael Demopoulos: Flash Master with Feet Firmly on the Ground

When I'm surfing with my impossibly slow modem connection, and I stumble on a site that makes me sit right up in my chair, and then I realize that it is a Flash site, let me tell you, I want to know who

did that site. The site belongs to Radius Product Development (www.radiuspd.com/), and the designer, Michael Demopoulos, of RDVO Interactive Marketing Solutions in Somerville, Maryland. I think the magic in the site is in the way that Flash is woven seamlessly with HTML, offering the best that both

formats have to offer. Michael, and his constant work partner, Art Director, January Spalatro, created a site well worth studying for any designer.

Michael has been working in Web design for six years, following many years as a musician. His band was together for five

Now that I have your attention, I can show you how to create great type in Flash. If you're familiar with type controls in other graphic programs, you're halfway there, although Flash does present some interesting little quirks.

Kerning and Tracking Control

The starting point for typography control is always spacing between characters. Flash has only one control for tracking (overall spacing of characters) and kerning (spacing between individual characters). In the sample I have here, both tracking and kerning must be adjusted. The characters are too tight overall, and some characters need special attention (14.3).

To adjust the tracking in a text block, you can select the block with the Arrow tool (14.4), or with the Text tool selected, highlight all the text you want to adjust (14.5). The result will be the same if you select

● 14.4

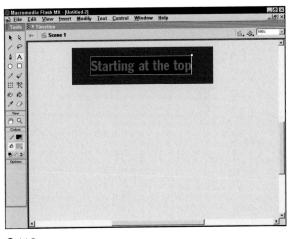

● 14.5

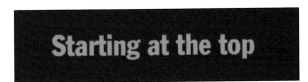

● 14.3

---

years, crossing the United States many times, traveling to Europe, and producing three albums. Michael wandered into Web design out of necessity when the band needed a site, then another band needed a site, then a CD project came along . . . like so many in this profession, he ended up in Web design, rather than setting a course for this career.

Accidental though his entry may have been, Michael and his colleagues have certainly mastered a special corner of the field. A nomination for a 2001 MIMC award (http://mimcawards.org) was thought to be the most exciting thing by this small team, with their site, Stop the

Hate (http://stopthehate.org). Then they won their category (Non-Profit/Government). Then they were announced as the winners of Best Concept. But the best was yet to come. RDVO, with competition like 7up, Microsoft, Harvard Business School, and the Smithsonian Institute, to name a few, took the top prize — Best of Show. It changed their business in an instant.

When this team can deliver work like the Radius site that caught my attention so strongly, it is obvious that they were in the right company. I'm pleased to bring you the conversation I had with Michael Demopoulos soon after the Radius site was released.

Q: How did you get started with Flash?

A: It's hard to recall exactly when I started using Flash. I know I used Flash 2 as a method to play gags on friends. Then I worked on a CD-ROM project for another band. I tried to learn Director, but it was difficult, and was beyond what I needed, and Flash was the answer. By the time I turned to the Web, I was already starting to focus in that direction.

Q: It was your hybrid HTML and Flash approach that caught my attention. How did that style come about?

A: I like getting the best of both worlds. A lot of our clients are asking for Flash, but I have yet to build a site entirely with it. There are some usability issues when

continued

all the text with the Text tool, or use the Arrow tool to select the entire block.

To increase the overall spacing for this sample, I've selected the text block and specified a value of 1 for Character spacing (14.6). The upper example is the original. Carefully compare the two examples to see how much difference this small adjustment can make. If I had tried to correct this text with kerning alone, I would have had to adjust nearly every character.

The word *Starting* requires some adjustment, as you can see in this magnified example (14.7). The space between the *a* and *r* is too wide, and the space between the *r* and *t* is far too close. The rest of the type is adjusted as well as can be done in Flash.

To kern the problem characters, select the single character that lies at the beginning of the space you

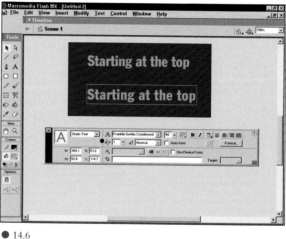

● 14.6

   (continued)

Q&A columns:

menus than DHTML. When you test Flash on a few computers, you know what it will look like everywhere. With DHTML, there is always the question of how it will look on other computers. Flash is faster to create, lower risk, and the download size is smaller.

If there is no other Flash on the site, I use static, HTML menus.

Q: How do you deal with text in Flash?

A: You only have two choices for fonts in Flash. Embedded fonts at high quality will have antialiasing and may be fuzzy. Make sure you align type on pixels to help with that. Device fonts solve that problem, but are limited by other drawbacks. There is no guarantee on kerning, and device fonts

the visitor has delved deeply into the site, and they see that the address is still at the root of the site. That causes problems with bookmarking as well, and the solution is clunky. I like the easy bookmarking of HTML. We've also tried to "componentize" content management for our clients, and HTML is better at that. Both technologies have little things that make them the best for certain tasks.

Q: You seem to use Flash menus a lot. How do you decide whether to use Flash or HTML menus?

A: If there is any other Flash on the site, I use Flash for menus. I feel that there is a lower risk using Flash for drop-down

look different on Mac and PC computers. Also, you can't mask device fonts. If there is no other way, you can always bring in non-antialiased text as a graphic without adding too much to file size.

Q: Do you have any favorite fonts?

A: I like Aveneer, an Adobe font. It works well in menus. I discovered it when working on a cooperative project, and bought a copy.

For HTML, I like Arial. It is easy to read and renders well. Verdana is good, too. It's important not to have too many fonts on a page. Stick with one or two.

Q: What do you think is important in a Web page?

want to correct. To reduce the spacing between the *a* and *r*, select the *a*. I selected a lower value in the Character spacing field, 0 in this case (14.8). The space between the *r* and *t* must be increased. Again,

you select the character ahead of the space you want to affect, but instead of specifying a value, you can move the value slider and see a preview of the result on the screen (14.9). This slider is very handy when you're snuggling one character against another. I settled on a value of 2 for the separation between the *a* and *r*, although it was a tough call between 2 and 3. I chose 2 because at 3, I felt the space was causing a

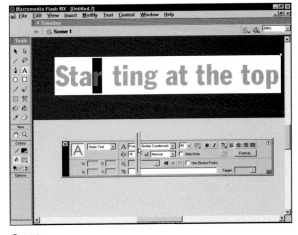

● 14.7

● 14.8

● 14.9

A: One thing I think is very important is that a visitor should be able to glance at a page and tell the purpose of a site. They want to know, "What's in it for me?" Make the page a quick read by using type in a simple way.

It's also important to start with the user, not the technology. Find out who's there, and use the technology to achieve the site goals. If you are selling something, hold the visitors' hands and guide them. Don't leave them to fend for themselves through the site. Make an obvious, clear path for them.

Q: Do you have any pet peeves with what you see on the Web?

A: I think that the trouble with the Web is that there is too much emphasis on design, and not enough about message. Is the Web art or info? Everyone seems to give raves about a site being gorgeous, but does it really deliver? What is it giving the user?

Q: How did the Stop the Hate site come about, and why do you think you had such success with it?

A: The Request for Proposal came to us cold. We could see it had the potential to be a difficult project, and the budget was low. But we decided to bid on the site. When we won the contract, we knew it could never be a profitable project, so we just decided to put our energy into

making a great site to give back to the community. We really threw our best behind this project.

I think part of the success was a timing thing, as well. The awards came shortly after September 11, 2001, and the message of the site really hit home.

Wendy's final comment: The timing for RDVO's MIMC award may not have hurt them in light of the social atmosphere at the time, but I urge you to visit the site. This was not an award won on hitting the right chord at that right time – this is a truly exceptional site that delivers what the visitors are seeking (`http://stopthehate.com`).

break in the fluidity of the word (14.10). The call could have gone either way — such is typography. Here are the original and the completed versions for comparison (14.11).

[TIP]

Although I do a lot of typography work with my view magnified, I always (and you should, too) check the result at 100%. What looks perfect at 300% may not look as good at 100%. The 300% view may be technically correct, but the only thing that counts is how it looks in the final view, or 100%.

Adjusting Character Position

Things get a little interesting when you want to control how your type moves up and down in Flash. Creating an automatic subscript or superscript position for your text is easy. But if you want to control the vertical position of your type, you must break apart the text. First, I show you a superscript addition. Simply select the character that you want to place into a superscript (or subscript) position. Select Superscript (or Subscript) from the Properties Inspector. The character will automatically become smaller and be placed above (below) the rest of the text (14.12). I also adjusted this sample to move the superscript character closer to the next character, and reduced the spacing around the *x* considerably.

But suppose you want to raise an entire word, and you know exactly where you want it to be? You have to break apart the words into individual characters. I've prepared an example to illustrate this technique, selecting individual characters to reduce and enlarge the size. I also adjusted kerning to create the basic idea for the look (14.13).

I want to move the words vertically, however, to enforce the message, and add more interest. The only way to do so is to break the words into individual characters. Activate the text block with the Arrow tool, and choose Modify → Break Apart (14.14). Each of your characters is now separate from the

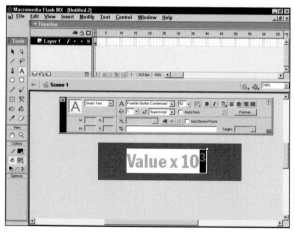

● 14.12

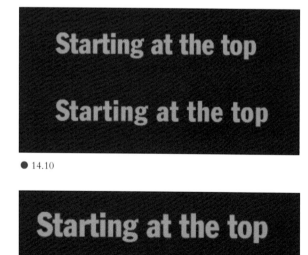

● 14.10

● 14.11

● 14.13

● 14.14

next. You can select any number of characters and move them. Here I have selected all the characters of the word *small* and moved them down (14.15). There is no limit to what you can do after the characters are separated (14.16). The individual characters are still text. In this example, I have added to the separate *g* character to create the word *bigger* (14.17).

[WARNING]

After you have created separate characters with the Break Apart command, you cannot put the characters back into word states, even though you can edit the individual characters as text. You can, however, select all the characters in a word, and choose Modify → Group. This command groups the characters as objects, and you can move or scale them as a unit.

● 14.15

● 14.16

● 14.17

Creating Objects from Characters

This section is perhaps not where I would choose to place the topic of creating objects from characters, but I came so close to it in the previous section, that I want to carry on. You can apply only so many effects to text. For example, you cannot fill text with a graduated fill when it is in text state. You can't even fill text with a graduated fill when it is broken into individual characters. But you can convert the text into an object and apply any effect that you can apply to any other object in Flash.

Starting from entered text, converting text to objects is a two-step process. First, you must choose Modify → Break Apart. As you already know, the text breaks into individual characters (14.17). Choose Modify → Break apart again, however, and the characters convert to objects (14.18). When the objects are not selected, they look just as they did before conversion (14.19). However, by using the Arrow tool to select the characters (the Text tool no longer works), you can fill the characters with a graduated fill (14.20).

● 14.18

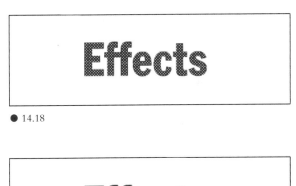

● 14.19

● 14.20

[W A R N I N G]

Breaking text into objects increases the final file size, which is always a concern with Flash files.

You can also add an outline to text when it is an object, which you cannot do when it is just text. Activate the Ink Bottle tool. In the Properties Inspector, set the stroke width, color, and style. Click on each object that you want to have filled (14.21). Several preset brush styles are available, but you have the opportunity to create a custom brush, as well. Click the Custom button in the Properties Inspector, and select the options you desire for your custom style (14.22). I have outlined the final two characters with a custom pattern (14.23).

For an interesting variation on an outline, try setting the background color as the outline color. When the outline is added to your object, the outline disappears into the background. You can use this method to create a ragged effect for a plain font (14.24).

[W A R N I N G]

Outlines are separate objects. If you click a character to select it, and then move it, the outline remains behind. You can select both the outline and character by using a marquee selection (with the Arrow tool, drag over the entire character) and choosing Modify → Group to group the outline and the character together.

Adjusting Paragraph Settings

When you're creating type for the Web in a graphics program, you're not usually concerned with paragraph controls. Content text should be created in HTML. However, that is not so with Flash. Building your entire site with Flash is possible and, in some cases, practical. Paragraph type is important in this setting. In Chapter 11, "Graphic Type Special Effects," you saw several sites that were created entirely in Flash, like the Dot Content site (14.25).

The paragraph settings in Flash are fairly basic, but will do what you need. In fact, when you consider antialiasing issues, any fancy work, like bulleted lists, should be done manually anyway. All paragraph settings are available through the Format button in the Properties Inspector. Again, if you select the text block with the Arrow tool, all text will be affected by the formatting choices you make (14.26). With the Text tool selected, the paragraphs containing selected text (or even the cursor) will be affected (14.27).

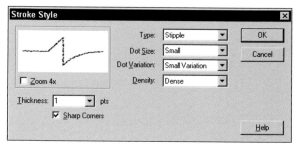

● 14.22

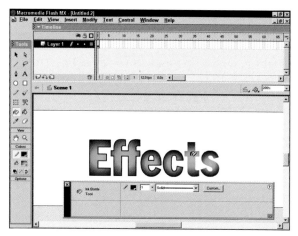

● 14.21

● 14.23

● 14.24

If you set a border around your text when using dynamic text (14.28), you should set both left and right margins with paragraph formatting. With the text block selected, click the Format button in the Properties Inspector, and type the desired margin value in the Left Margin and Right Margin fields (14.29). You can set the top margin using a hard return before text begins (14.30).

[T I P]

If you want to use an indent to separate paragraphs, do not use an extra line between paragraphs. Choose one method or the other to separate your paragraphs. Using both creates an instant amateur look to your work, and makes reading more difficult for your visitors.

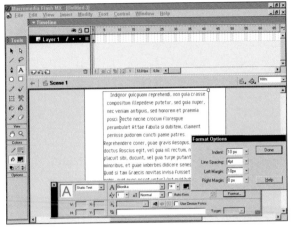

● 14.27

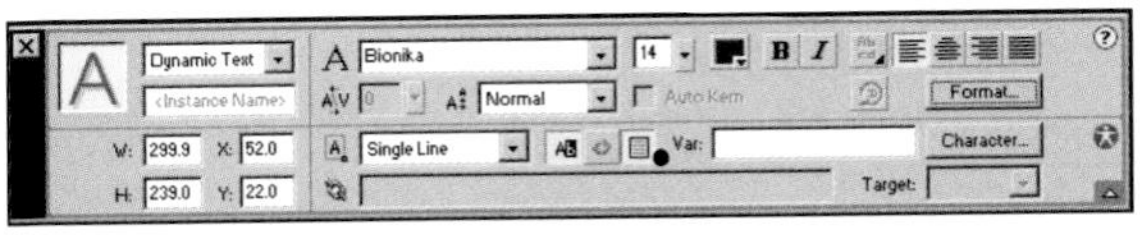

● 14.28

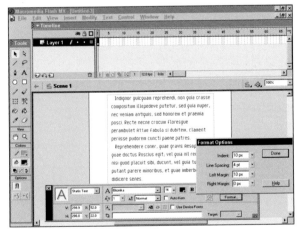

● 14.25

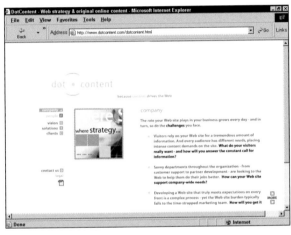

● 14.26

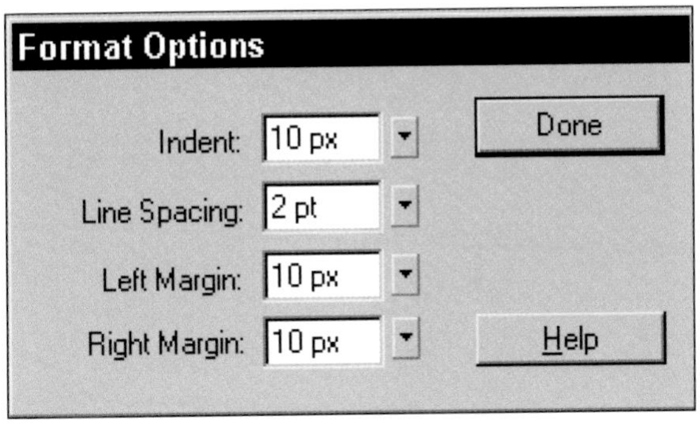

Format Options

Indent:	10 px	Done
Line Spacing:	2 pt	
Left Margin:	10 px	
Right Margin:	10 px	Help

● 14.29

Indignor guicguam reprehendi, non guia crasse compositum illepedeve putetur, sed guia nuper, nec veniam antiquis, sed honorem et praemia posci. Recte necne crocum floresque perambulet Attae fabula si dubitem, clament periisse pudorem cuncti paene patres.

Reprehendere coner, guae gravis Aesopus, guae doctus Roscius egit; vel guia nil rectum, nisi guod placuit sibi, ducunt, vel guia turpe putant parere minoribus, et guae imberbes didicere senes.

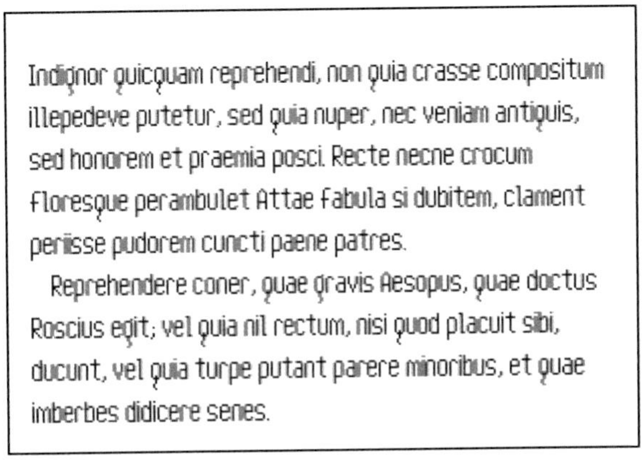

● 14.30

Line spacing is a little confusing in Flash. There is a default amount of line spacing that varies depending on the font. For example, when you set line spacing to 0, a space of 2 to 3 pixels appears between the lowest point on one line of text and the highest point of the following line. Setting the Line Spacing value to 1 increases the default spacing by 1 pt (at 72 ppi, 1 pt=1 px). A setting of 2 increases the default spacing by 2 pixels, and so on. This example shows line spacing set to 0, with 3 pixels between the lines (14.31). The green guides mark the lowest and highest points between the lines. Changing the line spacing to 3 increases the spacing to 6 — the original 3 plus the line space setting of 3 (14.32).

● 14.31

● 14.32

Exactly how you create the line spacing is not important, because the visual spacing between lines is what counts. However, because this system of line spacing is unique, I wanted to show you how it was calculated so you have an idea of which settings to try.

[N O T E]

Many of the fonts used in this chapter come from Atomic Media, a font design company that specializes in fonts for Flash and other multimedia. You can see their selection of fonts at www.atomicmedia. net/am/. You will find a surprising selection of styles, considering their focus. I have yet to find one of their fonts that fill in open areas in the characters when used in Flash, a common occurrence with other fonts used at small sizes.

Creating a Bulleted List in Flash

Finally, I wanted to leave you with a suggestion for how to create a bulleted list in Flash (14.33). You have just seen the full paragraph control options, and the options for creating any type of list are not there. In many programs, that would be a real inconvenience. However, because Flash is based on objects, the fix is quite simple, and the options for list style are unlimited.

Quite simply, you create a text block with the list items in separate paragraphs. Because you want multiple line list items to be lined perfectly on the left, the edge of the text block creates a perfect setup. I like to place the list and bullets on separate layers, so place the list on a layer named List (14.34).

I create a layer named Bullets, and create a bullet, in this case a tiny circle (14.35). When I'm satisfied with the style and placement of the bullet, I copy it, and place a guide to vertically align the next bullets. I then paste and position the remaining bullets (14.36).

[T I P]

The best way to work with recurring objects in Flash is to create a symbol. I don't want to get into an explanation of symbols here, because I am only concerned with text in this book. However, rather than copying the bullet, creating a symbol from the bullet (Insert → Convert to Symbol), and placing that symbol for each bullet is better. Not only do you have the power to edit a symbol and change all bullets at once, you also have an excellent tool to guarantee consistency. On every page for the site, you simply use the symbol for each bullet, and are guaranteed that the bullets throughout your site will be identical.

That's all you need for a bulleted list. And that's it for Flash text. Although this tour through solutions has not taken long, it is all you need to create dynamite text in Flash. And if you think that is a common occurrence, take a tour of Flash sites on the Web. Few sites deliver really great type. You hold the secrets now . . . go forth and spread your new knowledge, always holding the ideas of legibility and clarity above all else when you create text. Flash is fun, but it can also be a great communication medium when text is carefully planned and executed. Have fun!

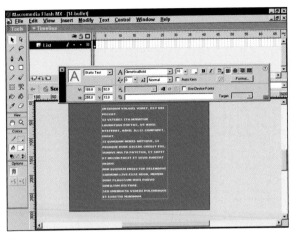

● 14.34

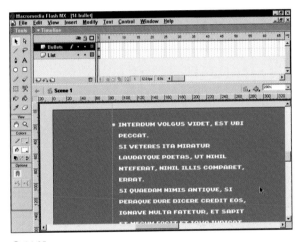

● 14.35

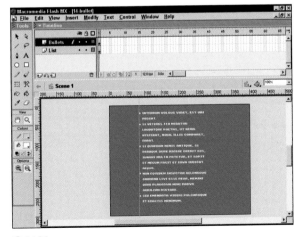

● 14.36

● 14.33

Appendix A

Where To From Here?

You have every basic tool you require to create great type with this book. However, I make no claims that I can give you everything you need to know forever about type in one book. If you're new to typography, you're probably more interested than you ever thought possible. When you're bitten by the challenge to create type as art, and as a communicating tool, you can easily become obsessed with the topic. In fact, I hope that obsession is where you are, and this section is designed to help you carry on along the learning path.

When I taught type work for print, the topic was quite different from the same topic for the Web. You cannot simply learn great kerning and justification, and expect that you have it made. In print, there is nothing you cannot control. With type for the Web, there is little you can control. Learning how type can be edited must always be tempered with how it can be presented when the subject is Web type. My learning suggestions reflect that. Separating typography principles from CSS technology and HTML restrictions is impossible. In fact, I think that learning to produce great code is more important than learning fabulous kerning skills. The amount of type on the Web that is controlled by CSS is many times that of graphic type.

Continuing CSS Learning

If you search for information on how to be a writer, no matter what other advice is given, you will always be told to write. If you want to be a writer, write. If you want to become a CSS master, use CSS. Don't wait until you know everything there is to know about CSS, just start doing it. Make a commitment that you will not create another site without using CSS to control at least your font, font color, and size for the <p> and <h> tags. From the start, try to create custom links by defining the <a> family of tags.

Those skills are relatively simple, and although you will be uncomfortable for the first little while, that feeling will pass. Create the styles in the header of your document if the idea of a separate file is just too big a jump for you. If you start with embedded font control, move as quickly as you can to creating CSS in a linked file. After you can specify your styles in a separate, linked file, the rest will come easily. From this point forward, I will assume you are creating your CSS commands with a linked file.

After you are controlling your basic type tags with CSS, add a class style. You can create a class style for captions, quotes, or any type that will break from the <p> or <h> definitions. Define the style and apply it, and you have that skill in the bag. Continue your training by combining a class style with link styles to create a menu. If you add one more control to each page you create, then before you know it, the basic CSS control will become second nature.

With basic knowledge in hand, start to apply borders or backgrounds to your styles. All of these techniques are included in Part II, "Controlling Web Type with Cascading Style Sheets (CSS)." I am simply giving you a schedule to incorporate the techniques into your work.

289

But where do you go when you have done every-thing I have given you? The first place is to search for examples of great CSS techniques. I'll warn you that not many sites out there use creative CSS styling, but there are enough to bother looking. You certainly can find many examples of sites that use CSS control for text, even if they are not using all the decorative pos-sibilities that CSS offers. Sending you surfing may seem like a frivolous way to move you ahead with CSS, but it is, by far, the best way to become familiar with what is possible in CSS.

[T I P]

You can always tell when an effect is done with CSS rather than a graphic. Right-click (PC) or ⌘+click the menu item and select Properties. If it is created with a graphic, a filename will be listed, like http://wpeck. com/type/art/images-over.gif. If the menu item is cre-ated with text, you will see only a link to a page, such as http://wpeck.com/type/personal.html.

To start your surfing, try sites like Cool Home Pages (`http://coolhomepages.com`) or NetDiver (`http://netdiver.net`). Both sites offer nearly endless collections of interesting sites, many of them controlled by CSS. Design recognition sites, like WebbieWorld (`www.webbieworld.com/`), Webby Awards (`www.webbyawards.com/`), and MIMC (`http://mimc.org`), are another terrific source for learning by seeing. While you are visiting sites, make sure you also watch what others are doing with graphic type styling.

The best thing you can do for yourself with CSS is to gain the confidence that comes with understand-ing CSS tags and acceptable properties and values for each style. You can find the latest news on CSS devel-opment, along with listings for every possible style, and the associated rules at the W3C site (`www. w3.org/Style/CSS/`). Make sure you run your pages through the CSS validator (`http:// jigsaw.w3.org/css-validator/`). Nothing can teach you correct CSS styling faster than this brutal assessment of your work.

When you have the ideas and are ready to search for the obscure knowledge that makes everything work, hit the educational sites on the Web. If you go nowhere else, make sure you visit, and bookmark,

Shirley Kaiser's Web Site Tips site (`http:// websitetips.com/css/`). Shirley has been col-lecting links for years, and includes notes on what each site offers. Little happens on the Web that Shirley does not find out about.

To stay on top of the technology, make sure you visit Eric Meyer's site often (`http://meyerweb. com`). And if you like a little opinion (under-statement) mixed in as you find out what is happen-ing in the Web development world, become a regular visitor to Zeldman's A List Apart site (`www.alistapart.com/about.html`). Keep an eye on News/Teaching sites as well, such as WebReference (`http://webreference.com`), WebMonkey (`http://webmonkey.com`), Developer.com (`http://developer.com`), and WebReview (`http://webreview.com`), to name just a few. If you're new to the development world, try regular visits to many different Web development sites until you establish which sites fit you.

Finally, I end where I started. If you want to become a CSS master, do CSS. It's easy to become so wrapped up in research that you don't actually implement all you have learned. When you start using CSS, the new things you learn will not be overwhelming. Practice paves the road to further understanding.

Learning More About Typography

Let me tell you right off the bat that you're going to have trouble finding much information about typog-raphy that is geared for the Web. Earlier in this book, I highly recommended *The Non-Designers Type Book*, by Robin Williams. Consider this mention your next shove in that direction. With the detailed type infor-mation contained in Robin's book, and the Web-related translation you have in my book, you will be well set to create impressive type. Countless books exist on typography, and your library may be the best source. Although the information will be for print design, you can use the information in this book to translate what you learn.

A few sites can take you further in your page design and type quest. The Yale Style Manual site is loaded with page design and type recommendations (`www.info.med.yale.edu/caim/manual/`)

contents.html). About.com has a decent selection of typography links (www.graphicdesign.about.com/cs/typography/).

Make sure you visit Joe Gillespie's sites, Web Page Design for Designers (http://wpdfd.com) and Mini Fonts (http://minifonts.com). You will find everything you need to know about pixel fonts on these sites, but also a wealth of information about the subject of typography. And it's all geared to the Web. Eyewire (www.eyewire.com/magazine/columns/), a company that sells both images and type to professional designers, also features articles on typography by experts such as Robin Williams.

Magazines and other printed material present rich creative ways to present text. Yes, print and Web are different, but you have the knowledge from this book to translate what you see on a page to the screen. Most of the best typography experts in the world are working in print. Major magazines and other advertising is where they ply their trade. Don't miss those constant sources of education.

[WARNING]

You can see bad examples of typography in print work as well, however. If something seems to be off according to what I have told you here, or you see in information from a type expert like Robin Williams, don't assume that just because it is in a glossy magazine that the designer didn't make an error. Great typography is not as common as it used to be. Take that situation as an opportunity for you. It's a skill that will become more and more valuable as the true experts from the print heydays of a few decades ago retire.

Visiting great sites to see what other designers are doing is also a good idea. Refer to the previous section on CSS type to find the addresses for page collection and recognition sites.

Although you can, and should, keep researching, as with CSS, the best thing you can do to advance your typography skills is to do it. Always watch for an opportunity to kern your characters just a little to balance the look. Watch your page balance carefully, and use typography tricks to equalize. Just do it! That's the only way you can reach the point where it becomes part of how you work, rather than something you do.

Learning More About Flash Type

If finding pure typography information for the Web is hard, finding good information about type in Flash is even tougher. On the plus side, it is a simple subject, and I'm confident that you have what you need for techniques from this book. If you take that knowledge, and surf through the sites recommended in the previous CSS section, you should be able to create any basic text effect you find.

If you want to learn the splashy effects, and how to make your Flash move, a simple search on any Web search engine will return more great links than you can handle. It always amazes me that you can find such a wealth of information about the pop and sizzle of the Web, and so little about the basics. Such is the Web, perhaps. But you have the benefit of the basics in this book to add to the effects. If you make a word fly across the page, you can relax in the knowledge that your visitors will see the word, not the gap between two characters.

Which Software Does What?

Web design software programs can be a confusing topic. There are overlaps in what programs can do, and techniques that you can only do in a specific type of program. It's hard to tell from reading reviews, especially reviews from software manufacturers that claim their software will stop just short of guaranteeing you will lead a happy life just for this one purchase.

Popular software programs do offer unique capabilities. That's how they become, and remain, popular. I've added this short section of the book to help you cut through the software jungle. Once you understand what to expect from a program, you are in a better decision to make wise purchasing decisions for your work.

Software for the Web Overview

I have been working with graphic programs since 1989, which is darn near pioneer days. I've worked with most graphics programs out there, although I have little experience with 3D programs. Those I will ignore. I have also worked with many software programs, like Adobe PageMaker and InDesign, and Quark XPress, but as they have no real application for Web creation, I will also ignore that type of program.

[**WARNING**]

The programs I mentioned for print work promise that you can create Web pages. Don't listen! These are print programs, and I believe the only useful pages they can produce for Web use are PDF files.

I have my favorite programs, which for the purpose of this article I will reveal. But first you must promise you will not use my selections as "the best." My situation, history, and profession is likely radically different from yours. This discussion of software programs is here to help you make the best decisions for *you*.

I use Photoshop, CorelDRAW, and Dreamweaver for the majority of my work. I also turn to Fireworks quite often. I was a print designer for nearly ten years before I moved to the Web, and was already skilled with graphic software. Photoshop is an expensive program with a long learning curve. It is essential for print designers, so when I came to the Web, I knew the program inside and out, plus, most importantly, owned it. CorelDRAW is the same. In fact, many of the best designers who came directly to design through the Web do not even use a program of this type (illustration program) in their design. They are expensive, have a long learning curve, and truly have limited application for the Web, even with the current version enhancements. Like Photoshop, I had extensive experience with CorelDRAW, and I owned it.

Dreamweaver is the one program I use on a regular basis that has been chosen on its merits alone. I'm pretty sure I have used every editor along the way. Dreamweaver, at the time I chose it (version 2), had the best combination of intuitive workflow and good code production. I've now written two books about this program, plus have added years of day-to-day experience, so I doubt any other program can catch

the cost of a top-end illustration program for Web design is tough. If you do intend to add print work to your skills, you cannot get by without an illustration program.

Illustration programs make short work of geometric shapes and text. You can also add many effects to your graphic objects, though some of the methods can be cumbersome. In my mind, illustration programs are best for line-type drawings. As soon as I want to work softly, with shadows or filters, I turn to a raster program. Often, I do the basic design in an illustration program to take advantage of the easy, object-based workflow, and then export the base to a raster program to add depth and texture.

[T I P]

Don't forget about Macromedia Fireworks if you're struggling with which direction to go for graphics programs. Fireworks does offer most of the benefits of the top illustration programs for Web graphics, and has one of the best image exporting features in the world. However, it is designed for Web use only. See the previous section for a description of Fireworks.

CorelDRAW

I've been a raving fan of CorelDRAW (http://corel.com) for years, and don't think it gets the respect it deserves in the professional design world. Some of that lack of respect comes from some very real problems with early versions on the Mac (the print industry has a high Mac user base), and overcoming that reputation is difficult. I can't recommend CorelDRAW for Mac users, as I have never known one who uses it. My words are strictly for PC users for this reason.

The illustration capabilities in CorelDRAW are unlimited, though when it comes to illustration, little difference exists among any of the top programs. My love for CorelDRAW comes mainly with text handling, which in the context of this book, is important. All illustration programs have a long learning curve. For CorelDRAW, I can point you to a comprehensive set of basic tutorials in my column, as well as several articles that feature CorelDRAW tutorials (http://productiongraphics.com).

CorelDRAW has one benefit that no other program can offer if you have no graphic software:

PhotoPaint. PhotoPaint is bundled with CorelDRAW, and similar to Photoshop. If you can find a version 8-10 copy of this program, it is usually inexpensive, and will do what you need. An outdated copy of Corel Graphics Suite is one of my favorite recommendations for someone who has lots of graphic need with very little budget. It does not have the automated export capability that Fireworks or Photoshop offer, but you can export graphics. My site, http://wpeck.com, is one of the few sites that I completed fully in CorelDRAW.

You not only get CorelDRAW and PhotoPaint, but also CorelTrace (a bitmap-to-vector conversion program), CorelCapture (a screen shot program), and CorelRave (a Flash-like program for movies). That's a lot of graphic capability for one price, especially if you can find a non-current version for your start. If you become very interested in working with a raster program, you will probably eventually want to move to Photoshop. If you try movies in Rave, and love it, Flash will be on your wish list. However, CorelDRAW can serve any illustration program needs very well. I always sound like a paid representative when talking about CorelDRAW, but the truth is that I work more closely with Adobe and Macromedia than Corel. Corel just has a unique position as an illustration program (I think it is the easiest to use, plus it blows the competition away for text manipulation) and offers so much in one package when you need to build your graphics capability from scratch.

Adobe Illustrator

Illustrator is probably the best-known illustration program in the industry, certainly for print production (www.adobe.com). It is a fine program. The native AI format is accepted by any commercial print outlet, and is probably the easiest program to use if you will be sharing files with print professionals.

The addition of the Save for Web feature in Illustrator and slice by slice optimizing does add some attractive convenience for Web work. Many sites do not demand raster-type effects, and having powerful export tools at hand when you have completed a design in Illustrator is handy. If you're a Photoshop owner who wants to add an illustration program, you should look seriously at Illustrator. The two programs talk to each other very well in later versions.

As with any illustration program, however, you should consider it as a second-level priority for Web design. Unless the Web one day moves to vector graphic display across all browsers, illustration programs will not be top priority for Web design.

Macromedia Freehand

Freehand has almost a cult following in the print industry (`http://macromedia.com`). Although Illustrator is the best known, Freehand users are adamant that it is the only illustration program for them. I'm not sure exactly what drives the loyalty, as Freehand, Illustrator, and CorelDRAW are so similar in capability. Macromedia includes Freehand as part of the MX Studio, a package containing Dreamweaver, Fireworks, Flash, and Freehand.

The marketing behind the packaging suggests that you can just flip from one program to another while creating sites. I don't recommend that type of integration, because you should maintain control of each step of the process. However, if you're a Dreamweaver or Fireworks user, and don't have Photoshop, you should look to Freehand. You shouldn't discount how easy it is to share between related components.

Visual HTML Editors

Dreamweaver, GoLive, FrontPage — these are all editors that allow you to develop your pages while seeing an approximation of the final page appearance. A few years ago, debates raged about whether a visual editor was a good idea, or the worst thing to happen to the Web. Hand coding proponents claimed you could not produce good code unless you typed in every tag. Visual editor supporters claimed that you could not create a decent page when you were worrying about typing accurately.

Luckily, the debate has died down. There are still people who hand code HTML pages, but the professional standard has stretched to include, sometimes demand, visual editor skills for creating Web pages. Does that mean the visual editing people were right all along? Not exactly. Visual editors produced a lot of very strange code in the early days. When the

honeymoon was over with how easily a visual editor could create a page, designers realized that you still needed HTML skills to perfect your pages. No longer was it a choice between learning a visual editor *or* HTML code. You must understand how to use the editor *and* be comfortable with HTML. Visual editors also produce much better code today.

You'll rarely hear that a professional should not use a visual editor. But which should you choose? I suggest that you download each editor, and try it for a while. What works for me might be awkward for you. I've heard debates raging over whether Dreamweaver or GoLive were better programs, and the points made by each side are the same. Each side claims his or her editor is easier to use.

Don't go by manufacturer, either. I've heard people say they were going with GoLive because they were familiar with Adobe products, and vice versa. I am a Dreamweaver user, but I fell in love with that Macromedia product when almost every other program I used was Adobe. I came to Fireworks after I chose Dreamweaver.

Microsoft FrontPage (`www.microsoft.com`) is another option. I've seen excellent code produced by a FrontPage designer, though I think you do have to be more aware of HTML code to accomplish great code than with other editors. It's a little more work, but also a much less costly program than either Dreamweaver or GoLive.

[**WARNING**]

Be careful with some of the extra features that are available in FrontPage. Many of the effects are easy to implement, but require a host that can support special FrontPage features.

Software is expensive. Perhaps you need a break until you can build your graphics program collection. Netscape Composer is a visual editor that is included with the free Netscape browser (`http://netscape.com`). I moved from hand coding to Composer many, many years ago. Dollar for dollar, it is the best value in the Web design software world.

Chapter 6 HTML Code and Style Sheet

You stepped through creating several CSS menus in Chapter 6, "CSS Menus." I've included the HTML code for the completed menus so you can confirm how the CSS control fits into the page layout. It's often easier to understand CSS type control when you can see the entire style sheet at one time, so I've also included the complete CSS style sheet.

CSS Style Sheet for Menu Sample Page in Chapter 6

```
body {
   margin: 0;
   padding: 0;
}

p {
   font-size: 11px;
   font-family: Verdana, Arial,
    Helvetica, sans-serif;
   line-height: 150%;
}

h1 {
   font-size: 120%;
   font-family: Arial, Helvetica,
    sans-serif;
   color: #336699;
}

a:link {
   color: #336699;
```

```
}

a:visited {
   color: #660033;
}

a:hover {
   color: #000000;
}

.mainmenu {
   font-family: Verdana, Arial,
    Helvetica, sans-serif;
   font-size: 11px;
   color: #000066;
   padding-right: 20px;
   padding-top: 2px;
   border-top-width: 1px;
   border-top-style: dotted;
   border-top-color: #666666;
}

.mainmenu a:link {
   color: #336699;
   text-decoration: none;
}

.mainmenu a:visited {
   color: #999999;
   text-decoration: none;
}

.mainmenu a:hover {
   color: #336699;
```

```
      background-color: #CCCCCC;
}


.toprightmenu {
    font-family: Verdana, Arial,
     Helvetica, sans-serif;
    font-size: 11px;
    color: #999999;
    text-align: right;
    text-decoration: none;
    border: 1px solid #CCCCCC;
    height: 18px;
    width: 100px;
    padding: 1px 5px 1px 1px;
    margin-bottom: -5px;
    margin-right: 20px;
    margin-top: 10px;
}


.toprightmenu a:link {
    color: #999999;
    text-decoration: none;
}


.toprightmenu a:visited {
    color: #6699CC;
    text-decoration: none;
}


.toprightmenu a:hover {
    color: #336699;
}


.leftmenu {
    border-right-width: 1px;
    border-right-style: dotted;
    border-right-color: #666666;
}


.leftmenu a:link {
    color: #336699;
    text-decoration: none;
    font-family: Verdana, Arial,
     Helvetica, sans-serif;
    font-size: 11px;
    line-height: 130%;
}


.leftmenu a:visited {
    color: #6699CC;
```

```
    text-decoration: none;
}


.leftmenu a:hover {
    color: #333333;
    background-color: #CCCCCC;
}
```

HTML Code for Sample Menu in Chapter 6

```html
<!DOCTYPE HTML PUBLIC "-//W3C//DTD
    HTML 4.01 Transitional//EN">
<html>
<head>
<title>CSS Menu Test Page</title>
<meta http-equiv="Content-Type"
    content="text/html; charset=iso-
    8859-1">
<link href="typetestwork.css"
    rel="stylesheet" type="text/css">
</head>

<table width="100%" border="0"
    cellspacing="0" cellpadding="0">
  <tr>
    <td width="325"
    valign="top"><img
    src="art/images/images/images/log
    o.gif"
width="324" height="115"></td>
    <td align="right" valign="top">
    <p class="toprightmenu"><a
    href="about.html">about
    us</a></p>
    <p class="toprightmenu"><a
    href="employ.html">employment</a>
    </p>
    <p class="toprightmenu"><a
    href="contact.html">contact</a></
    p></td>
</tr>
<tr>
    <td colspan="2" align="right"
    valign="top" class="mainmenu">
    <a href="today.html">today</a>
    | <a href="month.html">this
    month</a>
```

```
   |  <a
href="comment.html">commentary</a
>
   |  <a
href="archives.html">archives</a>
   |  <a href="staff.html">staff</a>
  </td>
</tr>
<tr>
    <td colspan="2"
valign="top"><table width="100%"
border="0
  cellspacing="0"
cellpadding="20">
<tr>
    <td width="200" valign="top"
class="leftmenu">
<table width="100%" border="0"
    cellpadding="0" cellspacing="0">
<tr valign="top">
    <td colspan="2"><a
href="library.html"><strong>LIBRA
RY</strong></a></td>
</tr>
<tr valign="top">
    <td><img src="art/spacer.gif"
width="15" height="1"></td>
    <td><a
href="library_tips.html">Tips and
Tricks</a><br>
    <a
href="library_faq.html">FAQs</a><
br>
    <a
href="library_release.html">Relea
se Notes</a><br>
    <a
href="library_serviceref.html">Se
rvice Guide</a><br>
    <a
href="library_refdocs.html">Suppo
rt</a></td>
</tr>
<tr valign="top">
    <td colspan="2"><strong><a
href="download.html">DOWNLOADS</a
>
    </strong></td>
</tr>
<tr valign="top">
```

```
    <td> </td>
    <td><a
href="down_patches.html">Patches<
/a><br>
    <a
href="down_documentation.html">Do
cumentation</a></td>
</tr>
<tr valign="top">
    <td colspan="2"><a
href="interactive.html"><strong>
    INTERACTIVE </strong></a></td>
</tr>
<tr valign="top">
    <td> </td>
    <td><a
href="inter_forum.html">Forums</a
><br>
    <a
href="inter_chat.html">Chat</a><b
r>
    <a
href="inter_understand.html">Unde
rstand Horizon</a></td>
</tr>
<tr valign="top">
    <td colspan="2"><a
href="usergroup.html"><strong>
    USERS </strong></a></td>
</tr>
<tr valign="top">
    <td> </td>
    <td><a
href="user_networkprof.html">Netw
orking</a><br>
    <a
href="user_meet.html">Meetings</a
><br>
    <a
href="user_international.html">In
ternational</a><br>
    <a
href="user_workgroup.html">Workin
g Groups</a></td>
</tr>
<tr valign="top">
    <td colspan="2"><a
href="training.html"><strong>
    TRAINING</strong></a></td>
</tr>
```

```
<tr valign="top">
   <td> </td>
   <td><a
href="train_sched.html">Schedules
</a><br>
   <a
href="train_agendas.html">Agendas
</a><br>
   <a
href="train_regforms.html">Regist
ration Forms</a><br>
   <a
href="train_guides.html">Training
Guides</a></td>
</tr>
<tr valign="top">
   <td colspan="2"><strong><a
href="contact.html">CONTACT</a>
   </strong></td>
</tr>
</table>
   <p> </p></td>
   <td valign="top"> <h1>Nothing
Could be Finer</h1>
   <p><img
src="art/images/lake1.jpg"
width="200" height="116"
 hspace="10" border="1"
align="right">
```

```
   <td> CONTENT TEXT OMITTED
</tr>
<tr>
   <td> </td>
   <td><p><a
href="index.html">home</a> | <a
href="month.html">
   this month</a>
   | <a
href="comment.html">commentary</a
>
   | <a
href="archives.html">archives</a>
   | <a href="staff.html">staff</a>
   | <a href="about.html">about
us</a>
   | <a
href="employ.html">employment</a>
   | <a
href="contact.html">contact</a></
p></td>
</tr>
</table></td>
</tr>
</table>
</body>
</html>
```

Index